D0839009

CANNIBAL TALK

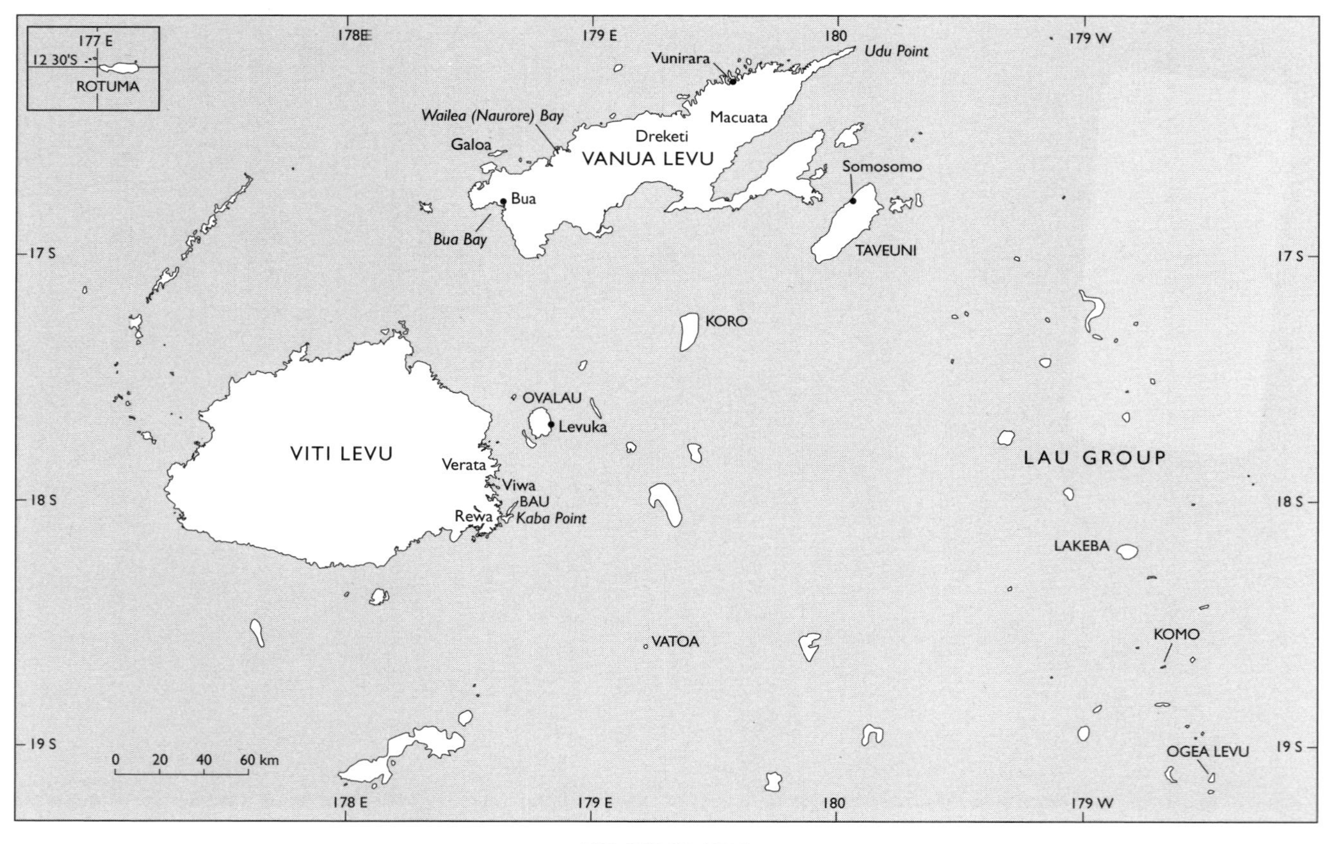

THE FIJI ISLANDS

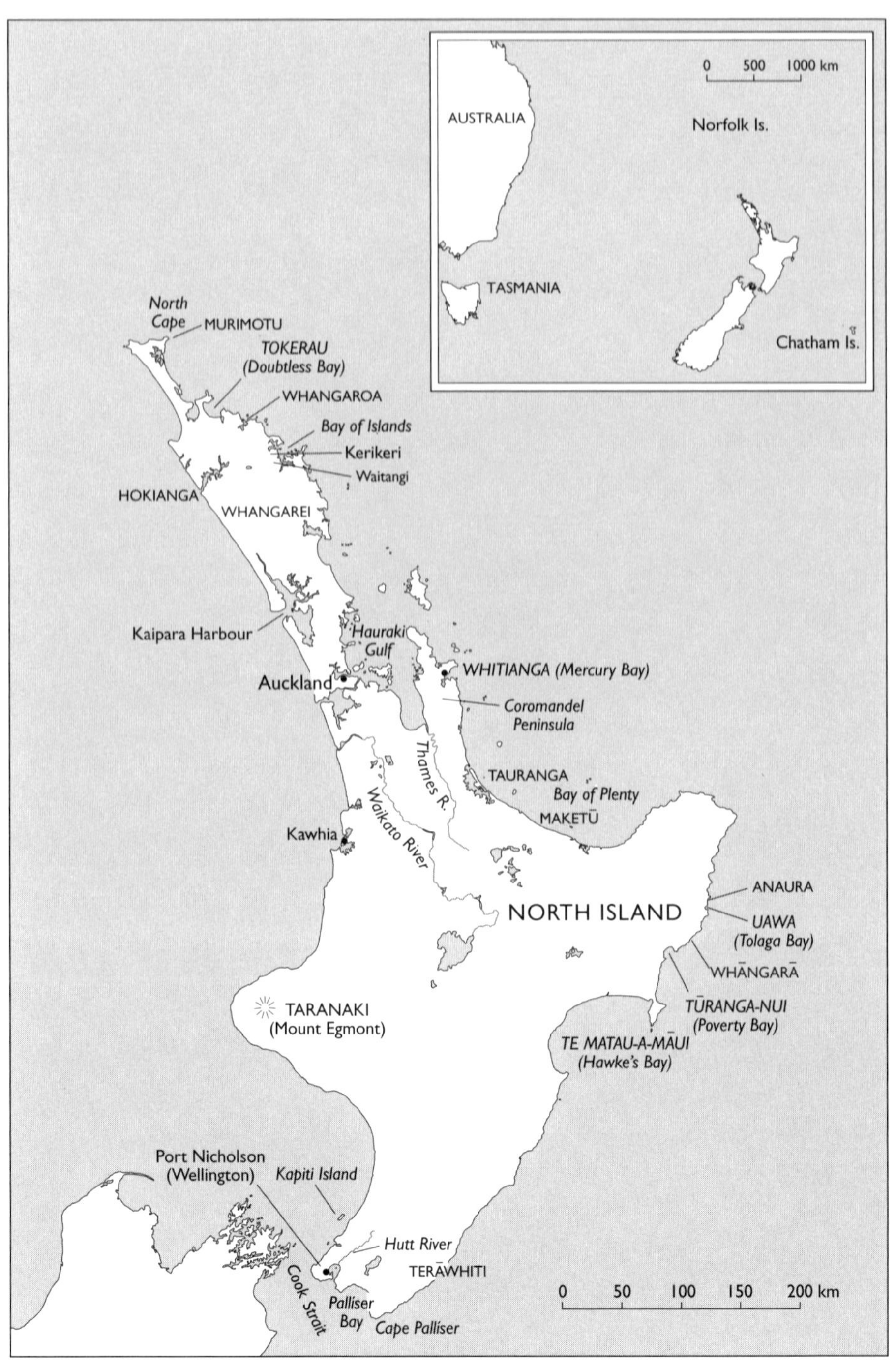

0 500 1000 km
AUSTRALIA
Norfolk Is.
TASMANIA
Chatham Is.
North Cape
MURIMOTU
TOKERAU
(Doubtless Bay)
WHANGAROA
Bay of Islands
Kerikeri
Waitangi
HOKIANGA
WHANGAREI
Kaipara Harbour
Hauraki Gulf
Auckland
WHITIANGA (Mercury Bay)
Coromandel Peninsula
Thames R.
TAURANGA
Bay of Plenty
MAKETŪ
Waikato River
Kawhia
NORTH ISLAND
ANAURA
UAWA
(Tolaga Bay)
WHĀNGARĀ
TŪRANGA-NUI
(Poverty Bay)
TE MATAU-A-MĀUI
(Hawke's Bay)
TARANAKI
(Mount Egmont)
Port Nicholson
(Wellington)
Kapiti Island
Hutt River
TERĀWHITI
Cook Strait
Palliser Bay
Cape Palliser
0 50 100 150 200 km

NEW ZEALAND: NORTH ISLAND

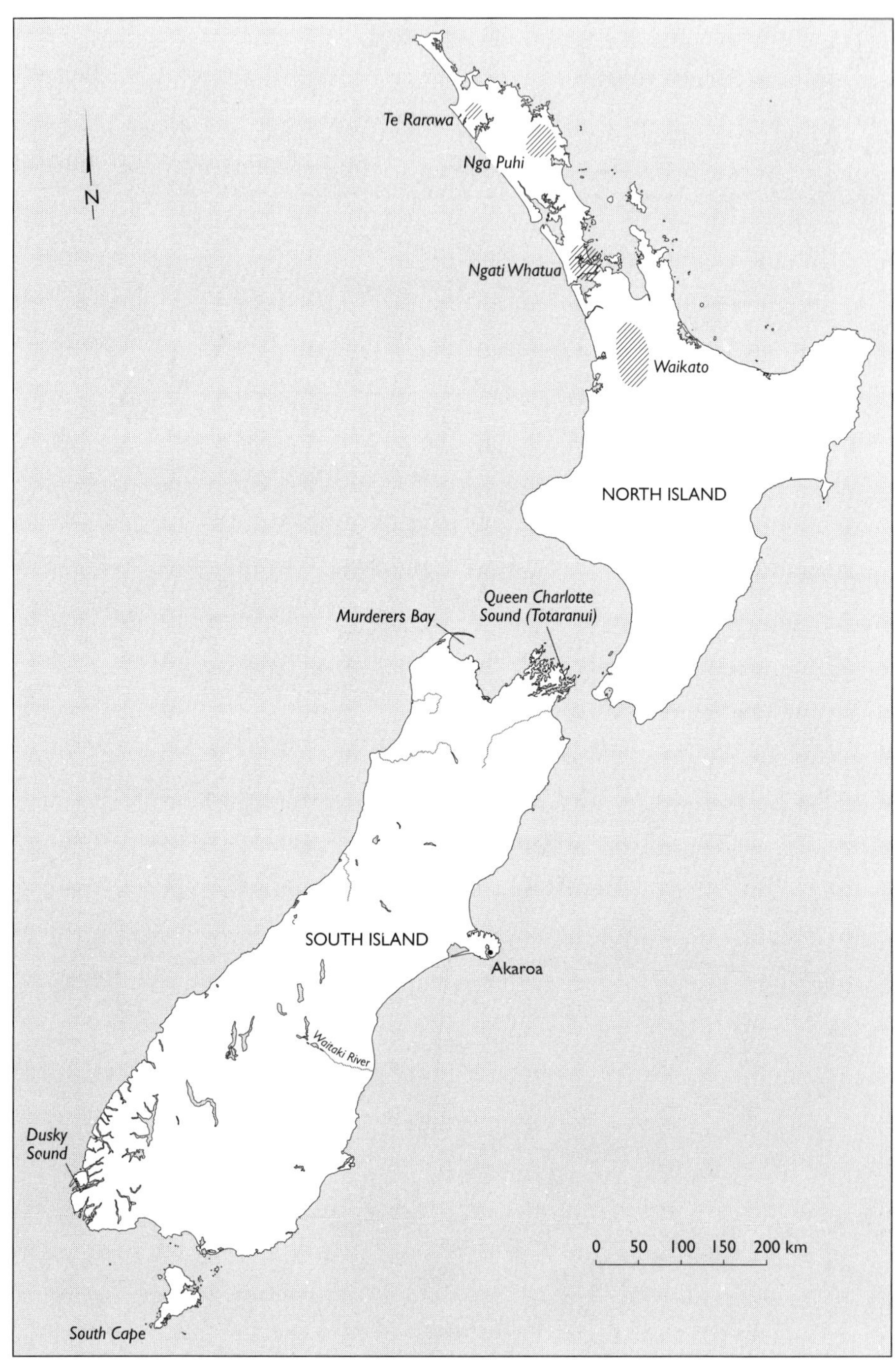
N
Te Rarawa
Nga Puhi
Ngati Whatua
Waikato
NORTH ISLAND
Queen Charlotte
Sound (Totaranui)
Murderers Bay
SOUTH ISLAND
Akaroa
Waitaki River
Dusky
Sound
South Cape
0 50 100 150 200 km

NEW ZEALAND

Gananath
Obeyesekere

CANNIBAL TALK

The Man-Eating Myth and Human Sacrifice in the South Seas

University of California Press

Berkeley Los Angeles London

5/24/06
ww
$21.95

University of California Press
Berkeley and Los Angeles, California

University of California Press, Ltd.
London, England

© 2005 by The Regents of the University of California

Library of Congress Cataloging-in-Publication Data

Obeyesekere, Gananath.
Cannibal talk : the man-eating myth and human sacrifice in the South Seas / Gananath Obeyesekere.
p. cm.
Includes bibliographical references and index.
ISBN 0–520–24307–2 (cloth : alk. paper)—
ISBN 0–520–24308–0 (pbk. : alk. paper)
1. Cannibalism. I. Title.
GN409.023 2005
394'.9—dc22 2004018117

Manufactured in the United States of America

13 12 11 10 09 08 07 06 05
10 9 8 7 6 5 4 3 2 1

The paper used in this publication meets the minimum requirements of ANSI/NISO Z39.48–1992 (R 1997) (*Permanence of Paper*).

For Ashley de Vos,
friend and master builder

Hark, villains! I will grind your bones to dust,
And with your blood and it I'll make a paste;
And of the paste a coffin I will rear,
And make two pasties of your shameful heads;
And bid that strumpet, your unhallow'd dam,
Like to the earth, swallow her own increase.
This is the feast that I have bid her to,
And this the banquet she shall surfeit on;
For worse than Philomel you us'd my daughter,
And worse than Progne I will be reveng'd:
And now prepare your throats. *[He cuts their throats]*
Lavinia, come.
Receive the blood: and when that they are dead,
Let me go grind their bones to powder small,
And with this hateful liquor temper it;
And in that paste let their vile heads be bak'd.
Come, come, be every one officious
To make this banquet: which I wish may prove
More stern and bloody than the Centaurs' feast.
So, now bring them in, for I will play the cook,
And see them ready 'gainst their mother comes.

WIILLIAM SHAKESPEARE, *Titus Andronicus*

CONTENTS

ILLUSTRATIONS

ABBREVIATIONS

BW	*Between Worlds: Early Exchanges Between Maori and Europeans, 1773–1815*
C	*Cannibals: The Discovery and Representation of the Cannibal from Columbus to Jules Verne*
CCL	*Cannibalism and the Common Law*
CJ	*Cannibal Jack: The True Autobiography of a White Man in the South Seas*
Cook B 1	*The Voyage of the Endeavour, 1768–1771*
Cook B 2	*The Voyage of the Resolution and Adventure, 1772–1775*
Cook B 3a	*The Voyage of the Resolution and Discovery, 1776–1780*, pt. 1
Cook B 3b	*The Voyage of the Resolution and Discovery, 1776–1780*, pt. 2
Cook B 4	*The Life of Captain James Cook*
Cook D 1	*A Voyage to the Pacific Ocean undertaken by the command of his majesty, for making discoveries in the Northern Hemisphere*, vol. 1
Cook D 2	*A Voyage to the Pacific Ocean undertaken by the*

	command of his majesty, for making discoveries in the Northern Hemisphere, vol. 2
Cook D 3	*A Voyage to the Pacific Ocean undertaken by the command of his majesty, for making discoveries in the Northern Hemisphere*, vol. 3
DN	"The Defence of Nga-Motu, 1832"
EE	*Early Eye Witness Accounts of Maori Life*
HR 1	*Historical Records of New Zealand*, vol. 1
HR 2	*Historical Records of New Zealand*, vol. 2
JPS	*Journal of the Polynesian Society*
JV	*Journal of Voyages to Various Parts of the World Written by Geo Bayly*
LJS	*Letters and Journals of Samuel Marsden*
LPE	*Narrative and Successful Result of a Voyage in the South Seas*
M	*Mardi: And a Voyage Thither*
MW	*Maori Wars of the Nineteenth Century*
NLA	National Library of Australia
OWD	*The Old Whaling Days*
PD	*Peter Dillon of Vanikoro: Chevalier of the South Seas*
SL	*Sea Life Sixty Years Ago*
T	*Taua: 'Musket Wars,' 'Land Wars,' or Tikanga*
VC	*The Village of Cannibals*
WC	*Wrecked among the Cannibals in the Fijis*
WF	*Wrecked on the Feejees*
WG	*Wreck of the Glide*
WL	*The Journal of William Lockerby*

PREFACE

Cannibal Talk is almost entirely based on previously written articles and papers delivered at various universities during the period 1989–2003 amidst other writing commitments.[1] My first foray into cannibalism was during my tenure as a fellow at the National Humanities Center in 1989–90 while working on my book *The Apotheosis of Captain Cook* (Princeton University Press, 1992). That was a wonderful year in my intellectual career, and I must thank the center's staff, especially those working in the library, for making my stay so successful. My first lecture on cannibalism was delivered there, and I am grateful to the president of the center, Bob Connor, for his insightful comments and to Henry Louis Gates who urged me to publish the text of my lecture in *Critical Inquiry* under the title "'British Cannibals': Contemplation of an Event in the Life and Resurrection of James Cook, Explorer" in the volume *Identities* (Chicago University Press, 1992), edited by Gates and by Anthony Kwame Appiah. That paper has been revised and expanded into chapters 2 and 3 in the present volume. Chapter 2 benefited from the assistance of my favorite folklore guru, Alan Dundes, who helped track down an obscure reference to Thackeray visiting the great cannibal Napoleon Bonaparte in St. Helena.

"British Cannibals" set the stamp for my future research on cannibal talk. Although this book may be considered a continuation of my earlier work, *The Apotheosis of Captain Cook: European Mythmaking in the Pacific*, it should also be seen against the backdrop of my recent book, *Imagining Karma: Ethical Trans-*

formation in Amerindian, Buddhist and Greek Rebirth (University of California Press, 2002). *Imagining Karma* made a case for a revisionist nomological approach to comparative religion and ethnography and argued against the naive relativism entrenched in the human sciences today. I tried to write simply, but *Imagining Karma* remains a "heavy" book to read owing to its length and sometimes complicated theorizing. *Cannibal Talk* provided me a kind of "relief" from the arduous work of its predecessor. Hence, the present volume is light in touch, and I have indulged in it my partiality for puns, sarcasm, and sometimes vulgar humor, although I hope that my lapses into levity will not undermine the seriousness of my scholarly quest.

Other stylistic quirks remain. I use the term *consubstantial community* to designate a commensal community eating of a consecrated substance, based on the literal meaning of "consubstantial" as "having the same substance or essential nature." Theologians and historians of religion may not forgive me for this, but I could not find a better term. I use the word *taboo* in the dictionary sense of something forbidden, for example, the incest taboo; but *tapu* or *tabu* refers respectively to the Maori and Fijian sense of "sacred power." The word *dialogical* does not refer to Mikhail Bakhtin's dialogism but to social life, including ethnographic inquiry, which rests on dialogue and discursive actions. Many of the texts I quote have peculiar orthographies, therefore I use *sic* only sparingly.

I do not subscribe to a single ideology or philosophy of writing social science; however, I am sympathetic to poststructuralist thought in general. But then I am selectively sympathetic to prestructuralist thought also and, indeed, to other forms of thought that simply do not fall into these convenient categories. The deconstructive strategy employed in this work suits the topic of cannibal talk because for me "method" or "against method" is not a conscious presupposition or a priori thing in itself but one geared to the particular problem being investigated. Thus the methodological strategy in *Imagining Karma* is different from that of *Cannibal Talk* though there are areas of overlap owing to my sympathy for "genealogical" inquiry and the comparison of cultural forms exhibiting "family resemblances."

This work would not have been possible but for the help of foundations and friends. I am grateful to the Harry Frank Guggenheim Foundation, which gave me a grant for a research assistant to collect data on cannibalism in Polynesia and Melanesia during the calendar year 1991, and to Sasanka Perera, who carried out the research. My next foray into cannibalism was in the Essex Symposium in July 1995 at the University of Essex where I read a paper entitled "Fergus Clunie and Fijian Cannibalism: European and Native Cannibal Talk in the Nineteenth and

Twentieth Centuries." I am deeply indebted to Peter Hulme, who invited me to this conference. His work on cannibalism has been formative in orienting my subsequent inquiries. The revised version of the Essex Symposium paper appeared in *Cannibalism and the Colonial World* (Cambridge University Press, 1998) with the title "Cannibal Feasts in Nineteenth-Century Fiji: Seamen's Yarns and the Ethnographic Imagination" and reappears here expanded in chapter 6.

I acknowledge the help from the following colleagues for research on that paper: John Koza, the Steven Phillips Librarian of the Peabody Essex Museum at the time who sent me photocopies of the relevant portions of Endicott's logs and the original cover page of Endicott's narrative; and Albert Schutz of the Department of Linguistics, University of Hawai'i, who helped straighten out the partially garbled Fijian terms in the narratives that I used. Others who helped me in the past and present research on cannibal talk are Susan Bean, Joan Dayan, Jeanette Mageo, Julie Taylor, Tom Johnston O'Neill, Geoff White, David Hanlon, Ernestine McHugh, Alan Mann, and Martin Thomas. Illness prevented me from revisiting the Peabody Essex Museum during the last few months, and I am especially grateful to Kathy Flynn, the reference librarian at the museum, for locating material from William Endicott's fellow cannibal sightseer Henry Fowler and sending me copies of whatever could be photocopied without damaging the originals. I regret not being able to read all of the Fowler material; I am aware that this might have affected my interpretation. As always I offer many thanks to my editor, Reed Malcolm, and his colleagues at the University of California Press for their many kindnesses: Colette de Donato, Kalicia Pivirotto, Kate Warne; and Alex Giardino, my very able manuscript editor.

Chapter 5 of this volume was first presented in a symposium organized by my friends Jeanette Hoorn and Barbara Creed on "Captivity Narratives and the Body" during September 24–26, 1997 in Townsville, sponsored by the University of Melbourne and the James Cook University. I was not happy with that paper, and when the symposium papers were collected for publication, I withdrew it and substituted another "Narratives of the Self: Chevalier Peter Dillon's Fijian Cannibal Adventures," which appears in shortened form as chapter 7 of *Cannibal Talk*. After many revisions the original Townsville paper reappears in chapter 5 as "The Later Fate of Heads: Cannibalism, Decapitation, and Capitalism." I am deeply grateful for my Australian colleagues who participated in that seminar and especially for their generosity in inscribing in my honor the book that subsequently appeared as *Body Trade: Captivity, Cannibalism and Colonialism in the Pacific* (Routledge, 2001). I tackled the research for the paper on Peter Dillon during my tenure at the National Library of Australia as a Harold White Fellow in 1997. I must express my deep appreciation of the library staff who generously gave of their time and cooperation, especially Graeme Powell who has continued to help me track down references in obscure journals and archives located there. After my stint at the National Library I spent some time at the University of Melbourne as a Macgeorge Fellow; this permitted me to deliver lectures at several universities in Australia including the University of Melbourne and the University of Sydney on "cannibal talk."

Chapter 8, "On Quartering and Cannibalism and the Discourses of Savagism," was delivered in various guises in several universities, including an especially exciting one in the summer of 2002 at the University of Amsterdam. I am grateful to Peter van der Veer and his colleagues for inviting me there. Most recently I delivered this lecture in the anthropology departments at Princeton and Yale and in its present form (though not with the title) as the Huxley Memorial Lecture of the Royal Anthropological Institute delivered at a meeting of the Association of Social Anthropologists in Manchester on July 15, 2003. It was a singular honor to receive the Huxley medal given each year to a person who has made a significant contribution to anthropology, broadly defined. I wish to thank the institute and Hilary Callan, who helped organize the meeting and made a difficult assignment a thoroughly pleasant one. The only chapter (aside from chapter 1 and the conclusion) that was not a part of a previous lecture or paper is chapter 4, "Savage Indignation: Cannibalism and the Parodic," the centerpiece of which is a Maori narrative recorded by colonial historians and taken by several scholars until very recently as a literally true account of Maori anthropophagy but reconstructed by me as a parodic one. The original draft of this book contained a lengthy chapter, "Tupinamba Exotica: A Concluding Visit to Brazil," but I decided to delete it for various reasons, including that of space, the difficulty in getting to know a large ethnographic area in a short time, and the resistance I encountered among Brazilian scholars who, like many lay folk and scholars in New Zealand and Fiji, remain passionately committed to the empirical reality of conspicuous anthropophagy. I hope that this book will eventually result in the unfreezing of such deeply held convictions. A long introductory chapter was pared down to its present size. Instead of dealing with the history of the European definition of the cannibal, I briefly interrogated several writers whose work has influenced my own "deconstructive-restorative" orientation.

It is difficult to list the many scholars who have indirectly influenced my thinking in *Cannibal Talk*. Yet, I must mention the "subaltern studies group" founded by that creative thinker Ranajit Guha. Although I am not a member of that august circle (or any other circle) I have benefited much from its work. Several distinguished postcolonial theorists are among my friends, and while I have not hesitated to use their insights, I must sheepishly confess that their language sometimes leaves me mystified. Jeremy Coote at the Pitt-Rivers Museum in Oxford help me locate fake Maori bone flutes, but my genealogical inquiry into such things as cannibal flutes and forks must await further research. As I write this I remember those friends from my past who have influenced my present: Melford E. Spiro, whose criticisms of cultural relativism have influenced mine own; and Mick Taussig's creative work on *Shamanism, Colonialism, and the Wild Man*. This reminds me that my friends at Columbia University have been always helpful to me, especially Nick Dirks and Val Daniel. Given my nostalgic mood I cannot but mention the man with whom I did my youthful field work in Sri Lanka, Stanley Tambiah at Harvard, as well as H. L. Seneviratne and Richard Gombrich, both constant and supportive friends.

I am indebted to several friends and colleagues in New Zealand, especially Anne Salmond for her hospitality during my visit there. I do not always agree with Salmond's positions on Maori cannibalism, but her pioneer work has enriched mine considerably. My old friend Kitsiri Malalgoda, now in Auckland, harbored a temporary refugee in his apartment and introduced me to lively New Zealand colleagues during my visit there. More recently Kerry Howe read the chapters dealing with the Maori material and helped me construct the maps. Ian Barber, whose work on Maori cannibalism from an archaeologist's viewpoint is very congenial to my own even though I do not always agree with him, offered his perspective as well. These two scholars saved me from committing mistakes in Maori ethnography, orthography, and history. Michael Reilly directed me to his work on John White, which helped me to eliminate several Maori myths from White's collection from my text! Marivee McMath and Amiria Henare helped me to locate sources and persons. I express my gratitude to Lisa Humphrey, who generously volunteered to read the two chapters on Fiji, and to Julie Fisher, who drew the map. This and the maps of New Zealand are meant as guides for the general reader but not for the specialist. I have much benefited from the work of contemporary archaeologists and anthropologists of Polynesia who have done extensive comparative work on the Polynesian cultures—kinship, the development of chiefdoms and political organization, and religious concepts—but not, I regret to say, on human sacrifice. If I do not mine their rich information here it is because my primary focus is Europe's representation of the "cannibal" in Polynesia as with my book,

The Apotheosis of Captain Cook. Nevertheless, much more than in that earlier work I also try imaginatively to reconstruct what "cannibalism" might have meant to Polynesian peoples prior to colonialism. I am sure many errors of fact and interpretation remain because my control of the ethno-historical data must remain faulty. Yet I hope that scholars of Polynesian studies would, even when they disagree with me, find my theoretical and interpretive strategies useful for their own research on the past of these societies.

In Princeton, I benefited from my colleagues and students during the many seminars I delivered there. My thanks to the department staff Mo Lin and Gabriela Drinovan, who with their computer skills helped me to tidy up a clumsily organized manuscript; Carol Zanca was as always a steadfast friend. The Princeton department remains for me a warm and congenial place even in my retirement, thanks to my colleagues there and my old friends Hilly Geertz, Larry Rosen, Jim Boon, and Abdellah Hammoudi.

Paul Lyons and George Marcus read the manuscript for the University of California Press; their comments are greatly appreciated. Paul noted that I had missed the excellent book by Geoffrey Sanborn, *The Sign of the Cannibal: Melville and the Making of a Postcolonial Reader* (Duke University Press, 1998). The postcolonial reader will benefit from reading Sanborn's book alongside my own. Unlike many literary critics I do not explicitly use cannibalism as a metaphor or stand-in for something else, for example, capitalism, though I do establish different sorts of connections between capitalism and anthropophagy. Nevertheless, I hope the reader will recognize that both cannibalism and the "dialogical misunderstandings" that flow from it ought to be seen as a parable for our own disturbing times.

Writing can become an obsession. I must thank my wife Ranjini, who was not only an unofficial editor of this manuscript but also one responsible for drawing the reluctant me away from my desk and out into the company of others—children, friends, and relatives—and to the life of the theater and the arts without which writing itself might have remained a "cold pastoral." Finally, this book is dedicated to Ashley de Vos, who created the meditative spaces in my aerie in Kandy from where I derive sustenance for my green thoughts as I contemplate the great river winding its way below and the unending ranges of mountains that keep on unendingly changing with the changing clouds and the sky.

Kandy, Sri Lanka
February 2004

ONE · Anthropology and the Man-Eating Myth

> *Aegisthus:* He [Atreus] seated each man apart and served up to my father a feast of his own children's flesh. Their heads and hands and feet were hacked into pieces and thrown into a boiling stew, from which he, in ignorance, ate his fill.
>
> AESCHYLUS, *Oresteia*

As the title of this book, *Cannibal Talk*, implies, I deal with the discourses of cannibalism and the behaviors and practices associated with such talk ("discursive practices") in the interaction between natives and Europeans following the "discovery" of Polynesia by Captain James Cook in the voyage of the *Endeavour*, 1768–72. The "South Seas" of my title is also the product of the European romantic imagination rather than an ethnographic or oceanographic category. In exploring the theme of cannibal talk I am deeply indebted to William Arens's pioneering work, *The Man-Eating Myth: Anthropology and Anthropophagy*. Writing many years later and with more data and theory under my belt, it is natural that I should sometimes move away from his work.

Arens's thesis is well known. To put it briefly, he argues that the idea of savage cannibalism has little basis in empirical reality. It is for the most part an imputation to the Other, the Savage, or the Alien that he is engaged in a tabooed practice of man-eating. This in turn is a colonial projection providing a justification for colonialism, proselytism, conquest, and sometimes for the very extermination of native peoples. The discourse that Arens highlights is familiar to us now as "Orientalism," though in the course of this work I will make a case for using "savagism" instead. Arens nowhere denies that anthropophagy might occur under conditions of starvation and he does not entirely discount forms of "ritual anthropophagy," but the overwhelming evidence suggests that the attribution of man-eating to non-Western peoples in general and to "primitives" and "savages" in particular is a Western obsession. This attitude toward native peoples has had a long run in Western thought particularly after the opening up of the New World as the etymology of the word "cannibalism" itself suggests, namely, Carib, the first land of "cannibals" discovered by Columbus. Perhaps the part of the argument that raised the ire of anthropologists is Arens's conviction that cannibalism, insofar as it is derived from Western discourse, is also part of the anthropological identity; hence the provocative subtitle of his book. Although I share Arens's view that cannibalism must be seen as a European projection of the Other, I also believe that anthropophagy existed in several human societies, for the most part as kind of sacrament associated with human sacrifice.

Arens's work brought a storm of protest, largely by anthropologists. The reviews of Arens's work have been re-reviewed by both Arens and Peter Hulme.[1] The more extreme reactions seem to vindicate Arens's idea of the relationship between the affirmation of savage cannibalism and the anthropological identity. The strongest "accusation" is that the denial of cannibalism amounts to a denial of the Holocaust, a point made by one of our distinguished anthropologists, Marshall Sahlins, and followed by others.[2] Neither Arens nor I would dispute that the overwhelming evidence clearly indicates that the Holocaust did occur and its denial is therefore irrational. Yet, like Arens, I find this accusation astonishing: the kind of evidence available for the Holocaust is surely lacking in cannibalism. Further, the analogy contains hidden implications: the Holocaust entailed the killing of millions of Jews and Gypsies and others precisely because they had been designated as the Other or the Alien and thus as objects fit for extermination. For Arens, as well as for me, cannibalism is also a discourse on the Other. And although the imputation of cannibalism did not lead to the level of genocide of the Holocaust or the later killing fields in different parts of the world, it belongs to the general class of terms that isolate the Other as an alien, an object for "Indian hating" and even for extermination. In both cases a great deal of "justification" and many "reasons for" were formulated for practicing violence. One might even say that the doctrines of the Holocaust *and* that of cannibalism exhibit in their differing ways not only the shadow side of Western civilization but also the shadow side of the modern, postmodern, and global world in which we live today.

INTERROGATING LESTRINGANT: THE HISTORICAL REALITY OF CANNIBALISM

Among Arens's strongest critics is the French historian Frank Lestringant, who, in my view, has written one of the finest books on the subject, entitled *Cannibals: The*

Discovery and Representation of the Cannibal from Columbus to Jules Verne. Unfortunately, Lestringant not only resurrects the solecism of the Holocaust but also attacks Arens as more "a sensation-hungry journalist than an *exact historian*," whatever that last phrase might mean.[3] He adds that even "responsible" scholars like Anthony Padgen have apparently fallen into the same trap, "spreading the denial of the cannibal through five continents" (*C*, 6). This statement I assume is not to be taken literally, given the fact that Padgen's important work deals with the manner in which Europe brought to bear its philosophical and popular values, including its preoccupation with cannibalism, to define the human status of the Indians of Mexico and South America.[4] Cannibal denial, says Lestringant, "under cover of idealism and intellectual high-mindedness, actually leads back to the misrepresentation of the Other" (*C*, 7). Proof that the cannibals really did exist is found in the well-known work of prehistoric archaeologists and also in "several learned refutations" of Arens's work (*C*, 191, n. 18). Hence the question posed by him: "What has the cannibal to say to us now? Did such a person ever really exist?" (*C*, 6).

Lestringant's laudable goal is to resurrect the later cannibals who "with their proud and cruel eloquence" continue to speak to us, and these voices are best heard in the "historical period between Columbus's discoveries and the death of Montaigne a century later." Because their voices "have sunk, sometimes to the point of inaudibility," it is the task of the historian to retrieve them "from beneath the stratagems, excuses, and prim attenuations of the learned, on the one hand, and, on the other, the sensational exaggerations beloved of the public at large" (*C*, 7). But Lestringant has another equally important theme exemplified in the subtitle of his work—the historical (mis)representation of the cannibal in European thought. Therefore interrogating Lestringant permits us to unravel a major dilemma of serious scholars who would affirm the ethnographic and historical reality of anthropophagy alongside its admittedly undeniable unreality.

Lestringant has an excellent discussion of how Columbus "translated the insulting names which the Arawaks had bestowed on their cannibalistic neighbors [the Caribs] in terms of the existing 'scientific' worldview" (*C*, 16). This pertains to one-eyed and dog-faced peoples eating human flesh and drinking blood, found in the writings of Pliny and taken up by Columbus and Vespucci (*C*, 22). The earliest woodcut of the cannibal scene has Brazilians with dog-faces chopping human quarters on a butcher's block, a "phantasmagorical conflation" made through the connection *canis-caniba*, a movement from Arawak to Latin. Accounts of cannibals in the Lesser Antilles (the home of the Island Caribs) depict them fattening young boys bred from prisoners of childbearing age to eat them later (*C*, 19). It seems that with Columbus's first epistle narrating the voyage of 1492 there is a important change in the nature of the cannibal, who "take[s] them [the hapless Taino Indians] as small children and castrate[s] them, as we do to capons or pigs which we want to fatten and make tender for food," thus focusing on the "horror of anthropophagy" that is "stripped of its ritual aspect and reduced to a mere matter of nutrition" (*C*, 23).

The domestication mytheme takes another turn among the Caribs according to the famous humanist scholar Peter Martyr (Pietro Martire d'Anghiera). Here women were not slaughtered because they were needed for breeding stock, reminding us, however vaguely, of their role in Plato's utopia. They are cared for by their conquerors to "bear young as we do hens, sheep, cows and other such beasts, and keep the older women as slaves for their use" (*C*, 24). Wonderful illustrations from around 1554 from Basel depict a whole human being roasted on a spit and another in which a person is being butchered (*C*, 25). Though Jean de Léry, an early observer of the Brazilian scene, protested against the representation of Brazilian cooking on open spits, he was ignored by virtually everyone. This in itself should make us pause to ponder the reasonableness of other representations of Brazilian anthropophagy. Thus the Austrian missionary Benedictine Philoponus rehashed the earlier fantasy as reality using the material collected, collated, and published in several volumes by Theodore de Bry and his family as the *Great Voyages* (1590–1634): "Hurdles laden with roasting children, women being quartered on butcher's slabs or pickled, men roasting on spits" (*C*, 26). As Léry neatly puts it, "the license to lie" is endemic among travelers to distant lands because "they cannot be contradicted" even though, he adds, some of the things people witness in other lands may be truly fantastic.[5] Similarly, Hans Staden's editor and family friend, Professor Dryander, wrote in 1557 that "land travelers with their boundless falsehoods and reports of vain and imagined things have so wrought that honest and worthy people returning from foreign countries are now hardly believed."[6] Our own problems of interpretation are compounded when we attempt to disentangle the indigenously fantastic with the invented fantastic of those given a license to lie; this is especially evident in the subject matter of this book. (See figures 1, 2, and 3.)

It seems to me that Lestringant falls into a popular trap: he brilliantly discusses the appropriation of the cannibal in terms of Europe's own preexisting values and prejudgments stemming from its past, as far back as the ancient Greeks. Yet a troubling question remains: How does one distinguish the *real* cannibal from these

FIGURE 1
Tupinamba quartering captive and boiling intestines and head. From Theodor de Bry, *America* (Frankfurt, 1590). Courtesy of the Rare Books Division, The New York Public Library, Astor, Lenox, and Tilden Foundations.

confused fusions of multiple horizons? Or to put it in his own words, how can Lestringant separate the "degrading of the image of the Other" found in the historical record from the *real* image he hopes to recover from this very same record? Lestringant tentatively attempts to do so from the Tupinamba, those cannibals made famous by Montaigne.[7] Although these fascinating cannibals are outside the scope of this work, it is worth briefly considering Lestringant's discussion of their cannibalism as represented by the French Jesuit André Thevet.

Thevet collected a mass of material, but he lived in the vicinity of the Tupinamba only for about ten weeks in 1556.[8] Like Jean de Léry and Montaigne after him, he stressed the nobility of the captive, his incorporation into the life of the enemy community and his being provided with a wife, often the daughter of the captor, who might even bear him children. He was given freedom of movement up to the eve of his slaughter, when he was put in irons, "a custom probably borrowed

FIGURE 2
Distribution of head and intestines among Tupinamba women and children. From Theodor de Bry, *America* (Frankfurt, 1590). Courtesy of the Rare Books Division, The New York Public Library, Astor, Lenox, and Tilden Foundations.

from the Europeans." He might live in the enemy village for years but would not escape because the idea of ransom is humiliating (though the connection between escape and ransom is not clear). Unlike Hans Staden, both Thevet and Léry emphasize the ritualistic and sacrificial nature of the killing of the victim, sometimes translating this as a kind of baptism. Thevet and other French writers agree on the noble defiance of the victim before an assembly of ten or twelve thousand "who will soon be feasting on his flesh, divided into infinitesimal portions"—though how this apportionment is translated into practice seems a mystery (*C*, 60). As with Léry, women receive the entrails of the victim, whose head is stuck on a pole. Thevet's later work, *Cosmographie Universelle* of 1575, adds a piece of priestly misogynist projection: in addition to eating the viscera, the women also eat the victim's "shameful parts" (*C*, 61). These vulgar acts are committed by old

FIGURE 3
Tupinamba grilling of quarters for women with sagging breasts, menfolk, and children. From Theodor de Bry, *America* (Frankfurt, 1590). Courtesy of the Rare Books Division, The New York Public Library, Astor, Lenox, and Tilden Foundations.

women with "hanging breasts" based on the model of the witches of European origin, as Lestringant rightfully recognizes. It is a theme handled with acumen by Bernadette Bucher.[9]

According to Lestringant, Thevet leaves all avenues of explanation open, whether as vengeance, Eucharist, or baptism. But is this a virtue? Or is Thevet's text a mélange of conflicting data that permits others—Lestringant and Brazilian ethnographers—to pick and chose and furnish whatever explanation of Tupinamba cannibalism seems feasible? Thevet's highly elaborated narrative with its particularity of detail "give[s] the ethnographic tableau a vivid impression of truth" (*C*, 66). Whether a virtue or a fault, Lestringant's final comments on Thevet leave me somewhat uneasy. He calls Thevet a mythmaker; instead of providing "a linear narrative, [there is] a collection of loosely collected data. The result is that the cannibal sacrifice is hugely inflated, into a liturgy lasting three or even five days. Is this the 'cannibal tragedy' of the Indians, as it really took place—over nicely graded five acts? Or is it the fortuitous outcome of a sum total of unsorted evidence? To that question, Thevet's method, which rejects nothing and leaves no stone unturned, provides no answer" (*C*, 67). But one must ask: What was the reality of Tupinamba and Brazilian cannibalism that Thevet, and following him the modern scholar Lestringant, strives to understand?

Ironically, Lestringant seems skeptical of Thevet where for me he seems strongest, that is, when he comes close to recognizing Tupinamba anthropophagy as a sacrifice, liturgical in character. Thevet's Jesuit background perhaps helped in this regard, and Lestringant may be mistaken in assuming that the ceremonial associated with the sacrificial victim is basically Thevet's invention. Owing to the distortion that arises from Thevet's attempt to fuse the horizon of Tupinamba anthropophagy with the horizon of his European historical and cultural experience and prejudices, he simply cannot provide us with even a reasonable guess as to what Tupinamba sacrifice might have looked like. And neither can Lestringant extricate us from this dilemma. Although Lestringant is at his critical best when he unscrambles the genealogy of Thevet's thought, he does not even pose the question whether the disturbing and disruptive colonial presence of the French and the Portuguese might have affected Tupinamba anthropophagy and ethnography.

Thus Thevet's voluminous work presents serious problems of validation. He was essentially a "cosmographer," and though a talented one, he, like others of his class, "pandered to public taste" and grossly oversimplified the ethnographic reality.[10] He assiduously collected ethnographic material from old Norman residents in Brazil, particularly the *dragomen* or interpreters, some of whom had gone native (*C*, 46). Thevet further tells us that twenty years after he wrote his *Cosmographie Universelle* (1557) he returned to this material in a draft manuscript, *Histoire de deus voyages aux Indes Australes et Occidantales* (1587–88), in which, according to Lestringant, the "narrative becomes yet more entangled." Lestringant adds that in this later work he was at least freed from "the 'slaves' whose task consisted not just of endless copying, but also of selecting from a hyperabundance of documentation, embellishing it with borrowings from the best authors and putting the huge mass of material into some kind of order" (*C*, 65). Thus it appears that in addition to getting secondhand information from settlers, the task of collating this material was left to an army of assistants and at least one ghostwriter, who apparently was a competent Hellenist. In the last manuscript Thevet collated hearsay information about tribes like the Tapuia who disdained the flesh of prisoners but instead "ate their dead relatives to spare the indignity of rotting in the earth" (*C*, 66). This could either refer to a distorted view of mortuary anthropophagy or, more likely, the theme of necrophagia that emerges almost everywhere in Western discourses of cannibalism.

THE "CANNIBAL SCENE": THE EMERGENCE OF MODERN CANNIBALISM

Lestringant and other scholars have provided the history of the idea of the cannibal in Europe's imagination beginning with the Greeks of Homer. But the modern cannibal, Lestringant rightly says, emerged into the European consciousness with the voyages of Columbus and the opening up of the New World to Europeans. It is certainly the case that the new cannibal had some older features, such as that of the wild man of the medieval European imagination, the fantastic cannibals found in Prester John and Sir John Mandeville, and those wonderful cannibals with dog heads and tails (*homo cadautus*) that in turn were part of a larger medieval image of the fantastic.[11] But with Columbus and the voyages of discovery, it was possible to pin the cannibal to the wall, as it were, or to empirically demonstrate the existence of the wild man in the wild tribes of the Caribbean and the Americas.

The confrontation of the cannibal with Europe, says Peter Hulme, appears in the "earliest modern account of cannibalism," that of Dr. Diego Alvarez Chanca, who sailed with Columbus on his second voyage in November 1493. Columbus ordered a "light caravel" to explore the coast to look for a harbor. The captain of that expedition then entered a native house, and the occupants fled at their arrival, leaving the household items intact. "[The captain] took two parrots, very large and very different from all those seen before. He found much cotton, spun and ready for spinning, and articles of food; and he brought away a little of everything; especially he brought away four or five bones of the arms and legs of men. When we saw this, we suspected that the islands were those of Caribe, which are inhabited by people who eat human flesh."[12]

Here is one of the earliest descriptions of the "cannibal scene": a few bones lying around, and then removed by one of the ship's officers, as mementos perhaps. Chanca was not even present at the scene, yet he writes with authority, a feature of much of the writing on cannibalism and savagism in general. Secondhand information is given an authoritative thrust through the employment of the "we" in the text. As Hulme points out, the cannibal evidence can "only refer to a collective view promulgated principally by Columbus himself as source of authority and as main conduit of information and opinion between first voyage and second."[13] Chanca's description is, one might say, the "elementary form" of the cannibal scene in which the existence of a few bones is sufficient to indicate the existence of cannibalism. This scene then can be elaborated in various ways in its later development. Thus Peter Martyr, who did not even get to the Caribbean, "pluralised the location, gave the houses kitchens, added pieces of human flesh broached on a spit ready for roasting and, for good measure, threw in the head of a young boy hanging from the beam and still soaked in blood."[14] This description becomes further elaborated and magnified in later engravings and neatly described in an account of 1892 celebrating the Columbus quarter-centenary.

> In the kitchens were found skulls in use as bowls or vases. . . . The Spaniards entered apartments which were veritable human butcher-shops. Heads and limbs of men and women were hung up on the walls or suspended from the rafters, in some instances dripping with blood. . . . In a pot some pieces of a human limb were boiling, so that with these several evidences it was manifest that cannibalism was not an incidental fact, but a common usage, well established and approved in the life of the islanders.[15]

The "cannibal feast" that I will discuss in this book is the culminating appendage to the cannibal scene as it germinates in the European imagination and resurges in the descriptions of the Tupinamba and virtually in every place in which Europe maps the world with savagism. The societies depicted are not only those of the "primitive" world but also include villages and tribal groups in the "civilized" world outside Europe. The cannibal feast also has a hoary ancestry in European thought from the time of the Greeks. Marina Warner has depicted its genealogy; it is therefore not surprising to find that mytheme imposed on the multiple forms of anthropophagy associated with human sacrifices in other cultures.[16]

Although we have isolated cannibalism in this work, it cannot be divorced from what Roy Harvey Pearce in a pioneering study labels a discourse of "savagism and civilization."[17] Pearce, anticipating the work of Edward Said, deals with the ways in which the American Indian was defined by the settlers, especially the Puritans, as savages in opposition to the civilized values of rationality, progress, and the knowledge of the true religion they possessed. The discourse on savagism deals with those who do not have these values and live in a state of nature, close to the very animals they hunted. Pearce argues that savagism has a positive and a negative component, as one might add was the case with Orientalism. The positive emphasizes the nobility of a creature living in a state of nature uncorrupted by the trappings of civilization. The negative states that in the Puritan consciousness Amerindians were children of Satan, and Satanism was "at the core of savage life."[18] Or they were those who, though belonging to a common humanity as the children of Adam, have somehow fallen from that high state during their passage from Northern Asia, or they had been removed from the knowledge of god for some other reason. Sometimes both negative and positive features define the projective image of the Amerindians; sometimes one or the other predominates, though for the most part they were defined in negative terms.

According to the prevailing biblical knowledge, seventeenth-century settlers "had to assume that the Indian's nature was absolutely one and the same with their [own] nature; the integrative orthodoxy of their society demanded such an absolute."[19] Therefore the settler's duty is to bring the savage within the orbit of civilized values. When that fails, extermination is justified, or, to use a nice phrase from a later writer, a "regeneration through violence."[20] It is not difficult to see that the term "savagism" has a wider application, and I shall use this term much in the manner of "Orientalism" to designate the ways in which people living in small-scale societies have been viewed by both the popular and the scholarly imagination.

The medieval travel literature that peopled the vaguely known world of Asia with strange monsters and wild men is now well known to us, if not fully understood.[21] But strange monsters are neither simplistic projections of the Other nor an exclusive preserve of the European mythopoeic imagination. Other peoples also had monsters that lived in mythic times and current places, and they flourish in our dream lives and fantasies. Rarely, however, did these monsters represent unknown *people* living in distant places. Rather, in those same small-scale societies it was more common to represent the Other as the sorcerer or the witch, not just the outsider or alien but the alienated part of one's own being.

Margaret Hodgen has demonstrated that after the voyages of discovery, the human monsters and wild men of the Middle Ages were being foisted on the savage, so that monstrosity became an integral component of savagism. "In the first book on America, published in English in 1511 (or even earlier in a Dutch edition), the Indians were described as 'lyke bestes without any resonablenes. . . . And they ete also on[e] a nother. The man etethe his wyf his chylderne . . . they hange also the bodyes or persons fleeshe in the smoke as men do with us swynes fleshe.'"[22] Hodgen also documents for other cultures, as Pearce does for the Amerindian, a strong strand of writing in the post-sixteenth century that identifies the savage as a being apart, not fully human. Ultimately, this strand must break or strain the medieval Christian notion of the great chain of being, wherein all humans were descended from Adam and Eve and every other being and thing was rigidly and hierarchically ordained.

In the newer spirit, John Wesley spoke of American Indians as possessing no religion, laws, or conceptions of civil society and as murderers of fathers, mothers, and children. Asians and even savage Europeans were not exempt. "What say you to thousands of Laplanders, Samoiedes, and Greenlanders, all who live in the high northern latitudes? Are they as civilized as sheep or oxen? Add to these the myriad of human savages that are freezing among the snows of Siberia. . . . To compare them with horses or any of our domestic animals would be doing them too much honour."[23] Wesley argued that according to the doctrines of original sin, Africans and other non-Western peoples were corrupt and degenerate. Wesleyans were of course important in the proselytizing work of the South Seas, and it is hard to believe that Wesley's crude views of Africans and others expressed below were not operative elsewhere:

> Your nicer Hottentots think meet,
> With guts and tripe to check their feet,
> With down-cast eyes on Totta's legs
> The love-sick youth most humbly begs,
> She would not from his sight remove,
> At once his breakfast and his love.[24]

The opening up of the world through the voyages of discovery forced Europeans into actual confrontation with strange beings, and to a realization that the world they had peopled with monsters did not match with reality. People in these strange lands, though they were physically the same, now took over the *persona* of the monsters of the mythopoeic imagination. They wore hideous "monstrous" masks, practiced face and bodily decorations and mutilations, and above all, possessed strange rituals and ceremonial practices like "war dances." The monster could easily take on the form of the Savage, and he is now opposed, in a manner rare in the medieval imagination, to the Civilized. Along with this comes the recognition, at least with Enlightenment thinkers, that the Civilized must also once have been a Savage, reflecting a persistent theme of the historical universality of anthropophagy.

The development of a sense of reality in respect to other cultures then becomes a somewhat complicated matter. In the first place, the older imagination, rooted in fantasy life, is not easily shaken. Such creatures existed in the Shakespearean imagination: in Ariel, in Caliban, and in the anthropophagi and beings whose heads grew beneath their shoulders. They existed also in the worldview of Columbus and others sketched above. When Columbus traveled into the New World of the Caribbean, he reported, "I have so far found no human monstrosities, as many expected."[25] Yet he went on to note exceptions: man eaters and men whose tails we have already noticed; Amazonian women, and the hairless. The Spaniards in 1560 saw giant men in Patagonia, the land of the *patagones* or "big feet," another recurrent fantasy.[26] Although subsequent travelers produced more reasonable accounts, the earlier perceptions continued to affect later travelers' visions of these people. Thus Byron, the English circumnavigator, wrote to Lord Egmont in 1765 of a people whose size made their own grenadiers appear like dwarfs. And he added that "[they] came the nearest to Giants of any People I believe in the World."[27] It was Wallis and Carteret who a few years later had to finally disabuse the British reading public regarding Patagonian giants.[28] Nevertheless, it is somewhat surprising to find the strange *homo cadautus* reappear in the "scientific" literature of the mid-nineteenth century: "For presently a Negro tribe with tails has become known in Abyssinia, whose cranial capacity has not yet been investigated. But owing to their animal-like voice, small size [etc.] they resemble apes so closely that only language, type of teeth and form of foot differentiate them from apes."[29] It is in this morass of delusion that scholars have, heroically as well as comically, searched for the true cannibal.

The incorporation of the savage into the model of the monster has more general implications and is not simply a matter of physical perceptions of travelers, navigators, and early explorers living under conditions of strain. Psychologically more salient is the identification of the fantasy of monsters with the nature of savages. This implied the fusion of the psychic reality of monstrosity with the physical reality of savagism. There were of course gradations in this identity. In Cook's time, as Bernard Smith has shown from the paintings made by the ships' artists, the Polynesians, especially the Tahitians, were "soft savages," those possessed of some nobility, whereas the Fuegans and Australians were "hard savages"—wild men, muscular, with stubbly beards.[30] The Maori were in between since they were defined primarily in terms of their anthropophagous propensities. Even soft savages not only possessed monstrous psychic and cultural features, such as tattooing and human sacrifices, but also worshiped monstrous gods and "fetishes."

My interest here is in the monsters of the imagination being projected onto the psychic or cultural life of the savage, even where the savage is recognized to be physically similar to the civilized. With the voyages of discovery the gradually developing reality-sense meant that monsters could only be given a metaphoric extension into savage psyche and culture; they did not exist in the real world. Nevertheless, monsters and wild men continue to exist in fantasy, and in our time as the idea of interplanetary travel becomes part of the new mythopoeic imagination, they get transformed and then transferred onto other planets in science-fiction and television adventures.

The impossibility of finding monsters in the actual world as it expanded before the European consciousness had one notable exception. The anthropophagi of the medieval world were converted into the cannibal. The term "cannibal" replaced the term "anthropophagi" and became a sign of savagism. As far as the original Island Caribs were concerned, they were wiped off the face of the earth by intruding diseases and intrusive killings.[31] The killing of monsters was after all a part of the fantasy and of the heroic myths of Western culture throughout its history.

If the monsters of the medieval imagination were symbolically or metaphorically represented in the new wild man, the savage of the voyages of discovery, so also was the cannibal, initially in the Americas and then much later in the South Seas. Hence the scientific curiosity about cannibalism in Cook's voyages, but behind that scientific curiosity lie a whole literature and public knowledge of both savagism and cannibalism, and a continuation of the earlier idea of wondrous and hybrid beings of exotic worlds. All this, combined with English fantasies and traditions of cannibalism, affected not only the representation of the Other, as I will demonstrate in this work, but also the style and quality of the writing. Medieval writings on monsters were often pure fabrications, even when the authors claimed to be eyewitnesses; one must surely expect the license to lie to occur in the new situation too but under the imprimatur of truth.

CANNIBALISM: AN ORIENTATION TO THE OBJECT OF INQUIRY

Let me start with Peter Hulme's suggestion that we make a distinction between cannibalism, which is essentially a fantasy that the Other is going to eat us, and anthropophagy, which is the actual consumption of human flesh.[32] I will adopt this distinction even though it often gets blurred for the good reason that reporters have confounded the two things. Further, in the history of Europe prior to Columbus, the term "anthropophagy" and its derivatives belonged to the same logical class as cannibalism. Anthropophagi were cannibals with the difference noted earlier: the latter were associated with actual living beings, savages. In my developing discussion in this book, the distinction gets further blurred because I show that in the context of colonial violence the two phenomena may occasionally fuse together to produce a label-defying hybridism. Nevertheless, I believe the distinction between cannibalism and anthropophagy is a useful heuristic one that I shall sometimes use and sometimes blur.

I unabashedly join those who deny "cannibalism," but I also have no problem with affirming "forms of anthropophagy." Although anthropologists might not want to make the distinction between cannibalism and anthropophagy, few would disagree that the myths and stories of cannibalism far outnumber the practice of anthropophagy. This poses a further problem: If the dread of the cannibal Other is omnipresent as *fantasy*, how is it that the ethnographers and historians have been ready to believe in humans eating other humans as an *actuality* of the empirical record? Are the fantasy and the reality independent of each other, or are they inextricably related in the complex ways I shall elucidate in this book? Cannibalism is like sorcery in this regard: the imputation of sorcery to others is common cross-culturally but the practice of sorcery is rare. And witchcraft is entirely based on accusations and on peoples' *belief* in its reality. There are no real witches in the world, even if people believe there are real witches in the world. But anthropophagy is more complicated: for example, people can be motivated to eat human flesh if they are starving, though if the taboo is strong, some may prefer to die. A good example of the latter comes from those notorious cannibals, the Aztecs, who, under conditions of dire food scarcity and physical emaciation during the siege of Mexico "did not eat that of their own people, for, if they had done so, they would not have died of starvation."[33] The best evidence for anthropophagy during starvation comes not from the so-called savage peoples but from the civilized: in shipwreck and frontier anthropophagy, as I demonstrate in chapter 2. I can also accept what is sometimes called "ritual anthropophagy" or "ritual cannibalism," though I retranslate this phenomenon as one associated with a widely dispersed and variable institution shared by both savagism and civilization, namely, human sacrifice. Here also the actual consumption of the sacrificial victim need not take place; symbolic substitution is common even in Polynesia, thereby showing a great deal of "symbolic remove" from actual anthropophagy. Archaeologists record for the American Southwest and elsewhere cases of mass consumption of enemies. From my perspective there is no need to "prove" or "disprove" the existence of anthropophagy in human culture; wanting to "prove" anthropophagy is not a problem *in* anthropology but a problem *for* anthropologists. What is difficult to prove from the archaeological record is the context or motivation for the consumption of humans, a theory or interpretation, if you will, that will help us explain or understand the data, outside of the obvious fact of the existence of anthropophagy.[34]

I do not have problems with the Dahmers of the world either. Anthropophagy can exist as pathology, as much as familial incest does. And although it is much rarer than the latter, both proliferate in fantasy. Finally, let me point out that, except for protein-deprivation fanatics, it is only in the rare case that a reporter would claim that eating human flesh is the normal or normative diet of human savages, though several observers have stated that it is the most desirable one. If eating human flesh were normal *and* desirable for those human communities such as the famed Tupinamba and their Margaia enemies, who consumed, it is said, large numbers of captives, then they will surely realize that this practice will eventually deplete their own communities. It is not indiscriminate anthropophagy but procreation that will ensure the continuity of a human community. And that ethnographic fantasy known as "endo-cannibalism" is a normative impossibility because, if carried to its logical conclusion, it would result in the depopulation of one's own group. I find it hard to believe that human beings cannot recognize this obvious fact.

It is one of the great insights of both Freud and Levi-Strauss that the incest taboo precipitates the creation of kinship networks and the beginnings of a distinctively human mode of living. So is the taboo on cannibalism, although to a lesser degree. The cannibalism taboo preserves the integrity and continuity of the human community; the exception is where there exists a "form of anthropophagy" that does not entail the actual killing of a member of one's group. In this form bones and dried organs and sometimes the flesh of dead relatives are ground and consumed as part of the mourning complex. As "mortuary anthropophagy," the consumption of human remains has been reported for several societies, especially in Melanesia and Brazil. In my view it is a mistake to label this "endo-cannibalism," and I do not deal with it in this book.[35]

Like incest, killing and eating of human beings is under the governance of taboo, and like incest, rape, and other kinds of prohibited actions (like sodomy and infanticide for some cultures), it is subject to violation. What then are the conditions in which the violation of the taboo takes place? Any violation is by definition an act of violence; therefore let me move from the past to the present where ethnic, communal, internecine, and genocidal violence have become an intrinsic feature of our global situation. It has happened in Rwanda, in Liberia, in the Congo and other parts of Africa, and in Asian killing fields, including Sri Lanka, where I was born, raised, and made aware. In the throes of violent passion people everywhere, mostly males, can commit the kinds of violence found in cannibal texts everywhere. Recently in Gujarat, in the context of Hindu-Muslim riots, crowds not only indulged in disemboweling and dismembering but also tore up pregnant women, killed infants, raped women, and practiced acts of gruesome violence that had their parallel in riots in other places, notably during the period of the partition of India. The passions unleashed during communal violence today are qualitatively not all that different from cannibal violence, imputed or real, of yesteryear. And therefore it is not surprising to find similar violence in Europe's past in the context of interreligious strife, as I describe in chapter 8. Violent verbal expressions about eating the Other, his liver or whatnot, is a way of expressing one's anger of a hated person, and it becomes a horrifying reality in situations of ethnic and religious riots. These situations also permit the proliferation of rumor and fantasy such that it is not always possible to figure out whether cannibalism actually occurred or was invented in situations conducive to the invention of such acts. As Georges Bataille says, human sacrifice itself is a rule-governed transgression of the taboo on killing, especially heinous, I would add, being the killing of a member of one's own group. Hence, "The transgression does not deny the taboo but transcends it and completes it."[36] What we have in violent ethnic conflict and religious rage is a double transgression: culturally prescribed or rule-governed acts of transgression are suspended, and ungovernable dread takes over with ungovernable transgressions.

What have the preceding comments to do with the claimed cannibalism or for that matter with anthropophagy by human beings as a normative custom? Although I can assume that eating the Other in an act of rage can occur, it is another thing to assume that such acts become customary or normative. One can make the opposite case: these acts provoke *out-rage* in us because they entail the very violation of a cherished value, the taboo against such acts. No one can say, on the basis of their occurrence in communal rage, that incest and cannibalism, dismembering and disembowelment, castration and decapitation, and rape are normative or culturally justifiable acts. Similarly, it would be foolish for us to make the inference that because a few Europeans ate human flesh in contexts of religious violence on St. Bartholomew's day and other religious festivals, Europeans were "cannibals." So with the Maori and others that I discuss: rage may produce a cannibal reaction but the cannibal reaction is not proof that such people were "cannibals."

THE SAVAGE CANNIBAL AND THE DIVINIZED CIVILIZER: THE SUN MYTH IN MELVILLE'S *MARDI*

The *theme* of cannibalism as the dread of the man-eating Other is found in most, if not all, human cultures, although it constitutes an obsessive preoccupation in Europe to this very day, witness the proliferation of novels and films on cannibalism and its sibling, vampirism. It is therefore inevitable that cannibalism gets grafted onto savagism and stands in an oppositional dialectical relationship with civilization. In this book I deal with Polynesia, broadly defined, the *place* where the European projective field finds its home. This links with my previous book, *The Apotheosis of Captain Cook: European Mythmaking in the Pacific*, where I explore the well-known myth that when Captain Cook arrived in Hawai'i he was treated by the natives as their great god Lono arriving in person during their annual festival of the Makihiki. I point out that this myth was not constructed in Hawai'i but in London and represents a specific case of a larger theme of the long run of the European as a civilizer to natives, a kind of Prospero figure of the imagination. This should not surprise us because after all the "civilizer" is the projective image that Europe presented to the native, both in terms of its civilized secular values and its Christian religion. In opposition to the cannibal, the European civilizer is represented as a godlike figure or a "superior being." Neither figure is a product of the native imagination but rather attributed to the native by European colonialism.

I would like to deal with two themes pertaining to Civilization that I failed to interlink in my earlier work on Cook, not only of the white explorer as a god to savages but also that he appears from some stellar or solar constellation. In my second edition of *The Apotheosis of Captain Cook* I discussed the widespread dispersal of the planetary myth-model in the European literature of exploration and conquest but failed to trace its complex genealogy. In that book I referred to John Rickman, the first officer to write an account of the third voyage, conversing with a chief of Ni'ihau regarding their own cosmic travels. "Pointing to the sun, [the chief] seemed to suppose that we should visit that luminary in our course, and that the thunder and lightning of our guns, and that which came from the heavens were both derived from the same source."[37] I showed that there was good reason for refusing to accept this statement at face value. Rickman got the time, place, and context all wrong because his log clearly, and quite rightly, states he was in Kaua'i, one of the Hawaiian Islands, on March 1, and far from being treated as beings from the sun, the ships' crew was subject to "every mark of uncivility and buffoonery," a fact also confirmed by James King.[38] In thinking about this problem, I became convinced that the planetary myth too was a structure of the long run in European thought, and though a later and less prolific invention and intervention, it stood after the voyages of discovery, in opposition to the cannibal in European representations of the Other. Let me begin my argument with something that I had missed, namely, that Rickman's utterance was probably a continuation of a shipboard tradition of the European as a visitor from the sun.

The discourse on planetary travel seemed to have been fully established during Vancouver's voyage (1791–95) when he visited the tiny Chatham Island off the eastern coast of New Zealand: "On our first landing their surprize and exclamations can hardly be imagined; they pointed to the sun, and then to us, as if to ask, whether we had come from thence."[39] Because these were Moriori, who were really Maori living in Chatham Island for a long time, one must assume that this was also a circulating discourse that, in this case, had spread to the Moriori from New Zealand voyagers, native or European or both.[40] I now can supplement my earlier interpretation of Rickman's statement: Rickman's cosmic conversation with chiefs is simply a continuation of the prior discourse on the planetary descent of European navigators. We know that this type of "conversation" had been going on in Hawai'i for quite some time even during the third voyage because Ledyard makes a similar but much more plausible observation around January 25 regarding the Hawaiian perception of the astronomical obsessions of the officers.[41] One must also recognize that colonial discourse is a two-way process such that on occasion natives, who had their own planetary myths, might take over these European versions in the context of colonial domination and then incorporate them as part of their own, producing a back-and-forth movement of circulating mythemes. Nevertheless, the genealogy and main locus of such myths lay, as with the apotheosis myth, in the power plays of colonization and conquest. Its antecedent genealogy has been exhaustively discussed by William Hamlin in his essay "Attributions of Divinity in Renaissance Ethnography and Romance."[42] Suffice it here to say that, like many other circulating mythemes, this also had its creative genesis in the voyages of discovery and was originally attributed to the Aztec perception of Cortés as the "child of the sun" and indeed the sun itself, who can "make the circuit of the earth in the short space of a day and a night."[43] The evidence from Rickman, Ledyard, and Vancouver suggests that such myths were alive up to the late eighteenth century. They were available to Herman Melville to interlink with the apotheosis theme and spoof in his novel *Mardi*, showing us that, unlike naive ethnographers and historians, the creative writer was not fooled by what Hamlin calls myths of "imagined apotheoses."[44]

Melville's *Mardi* is a huge, sprawling, and uneven (sometimes boring) book, but it contains priceless pieces of satire that spoof both Europeans and Polynesians, of which I can only give the reader a brief glimpse.[45] The protagonist is not named in the book; let me for convenience call him "M." It deals with the adventures of M and his two companions, a Scandinavian named Jarl and a Polynesian named Samoa. The setting is the South Seas, a vast archipelago extending forever and ever. Here our trio confronts the villainous priest Aleema and his sons, who are taking a dainty and beautiful white woman named Yillah to be sacrificed to one of their gods in Tedardee, a distant land. When M talks to her in English she seems to have a hazy recollection of a possible past as a white woman; in general he talks to her in "Polynesian." The three friends kill Aleema and rescue the maiden, but Aleema's spirit haunts them while his sons pursue them across the imagined Polynesian archipelago. M deceives Yillah by telling her fanciful stories of his being once her companion when she was living in her homeland as a small child and adds that he is a "demigod" and now wants to be her guardian. Through Yillah, Melville has a special take on European captivity narratives, which I will not deal with it here except to state that M falls in love with Yillah and feels bad about the romantic lies he had invented about him and her, but "love sometimes induced me to prop my failing divinity."[46] M is a figure present everywhere in the Pacific, inventing what I will later call "narratives of the self."

Ultimately, they sight land, "some new constellation in the sea." Many canoes come up, but people flee because they had "little or no intercourse with whites and most probably knew not how to account for our appearance among them" (*M*, 144). Therefore M sends Jarl and Samoa to "conciliate the natives." The strategy works and a "tumultuous crowd" bursts into view with Jarl "mounted upon the shoulders of two brawny natives" (*M*, 145). The natives also, expectably, "adore" Yillah and "stretched forth their arms in reverence . . . [and the] adoration of the maiden was extended to myself." Samoa, his interpreter, tells him that the king of the island is away attending a festival, but "the islanders regarded me as a superior being. They had inquired of him whether I was not a white Taji, a sort of half-and-half deity" (*M*, 146). Then, spurred by Samoa, M makes a public proclamation of his divinity: "It was [however] best to be wary. For although among some barbarians the first strangers landing upon their shores are frequently hailed as divine—and in more than one wild land have been actually styled gods, as a familiar designation—yet this has not exempted the celestial visitants from peril when too much presuming upon the reception extended to them. In sudden tumults they have been slain outright, and while full faith in their divinity had in no wise abated. The sad fate of an eminent navigator is a well known illustration of this unaccountable waywardness" (*M*, 147). It seems to me that much of this spoofery, including the tropes of "adoration" and "superior being," parody the language of Cook's journals.

We are now told that the island where M has landed is Mardi. Its ruler is Media, and Melville uses three other Mardian characters to laugh at American (and European) society and to a lesser extent at Polynesia. The characters are all introduced in a chapter called "A Gentlemen from the Sun," which is of course our demigod hero's new place of birth. When he first sees the resplendent array of native chiefs, M erroneously thinks that they must all be kings. Gradually, his sense of his own divinity is deflated. To prop it up, M addresses the assembled worthies, thus: "Men of Mardi, I am come from the sun. When this morning it rose and touched the wave, I pushed my shallop from its golden beach and hither sailed before its level rays. I am Taji." M steps back to see the effect of his speech while the chiefs converse among themselves. He then "returned to the charge" and, in order to impress them further, adds: "The gentle Yillah was a seraph from the sun; Samoa I had picked off a reef in my route from that orb; and as for the Skyeman [Jarl], why, as his name imported, he came from above. In a word we were all strolling divinities" (*M*, 148).

The spoofing continues when one of the "kings," an old man, addresses M: "Is this indeed Taji? He, who according to tradition, was to return to us after five thousand moons. But that period is yet unexpired. What brings't thou hither, then, Taji, before thy time" (*M*, 148)? He adds that Taji was a troublesome and petty demigod when he lived in Mardi prior to his apotheosis. This probably is a reference to the legends of the returning god attributed to both Cortés and Cook.

M meanwhile tries to figure out how he is held by Media, the king, "and his more intelligent subjects," only to find that the latter "was in no way overawed" by M's solar and divine credentials and treats him as a "mere mortal" and "one of the abject generation of mushrooms," and, anticipating some currently fashionable terminology, a mere "subaltern divinity" (*M*, 153–54). But why mushrooms? The reason is simple: the nation of Mardi is full of divinities of different sorts and types that mushroom everywhere and that include normal humans. Gradually M begins to realize that being a demigod is no great shakes because "the very multitude of them confounded distinction" (*M*, 156). Thus, "in several instances the people of the land addressed the supreme god, Oro, in the very same terms employed in the political adoration of their sublunary rulers" (*M*, 155). Not only did King Media treat M's divinity with indifference, but he also exhibited "an unaffected indifference to my amazing voyage from the sun, his indifference to the sun itself and all the wonderful circumstances that must have attended my departure" (*M,* 156). And Melville tells us with devastating irony that Captain Cook was adored in much the same way: "The celebrated navigator referred to in a preceding chapter was hailed as one of their demigods returned to earth after a wide tour of the universe. And they worshiped him as such, though incessantly he was interrogating them as to who under the sun his worshipers were, how their ancestors came on the island, and whether they would have the kindness to provide his followers with plenty of pork during his stay" (*M,* 154).

Even though M realizes that his pretensions of a solar divinity have been badly deflated in Mardi and he acknowledges a measure of self-awareness, he persists in affirming his invented prejudices in the other places he visits. For example, when M is on the island of Pimminee he wants to impress on the natives his solar ancestry and later descent into Mardi. But "they manifested not the slightest surprise, one of them incidentally observing however, that the eclipses there must be a sad bore to endure" (*M,* 337). Later, on this same island, he meets an old lady and her daughters named A, I, and O, who wear terribly large farthingales. Because he finds it difficult to talk to all three "polysyllables" as a collectivity, he discreetly centers his remarks on O. "Thinking she might be curious concerning the sun, he made some remote allusion to that luminary as the place of his nativity. Upon which O inquired where that country was of which mention was made." Taji responds, "Some distance from here, in the air above, the sun that gives light to Pimminee and Mardi at large." "She replied that if that were the case, she had never beheld it, for such was the construction of her farthingale that her head could not be thrown back without impairing its set. Wherefore she had always refrained from astronomical investigations" (*M,* 338).

Mardi was written in 1849. In much of Euro-American thinking the Cook mythology was still very powerful until about the 1830s, and Cook, ethnographers tell us, continued to be worshipped by Hawaiians in his relics, even though many of the latter were now traveling all over the world on American ships and momentous changes had taken place in their society. The "evidence" for this later development in the Cook mythology is partly based on an uncritical acceptance of shipboard narratives by captains who made brief visits to Hawai'i but, apparently, could nevertheless give expression to Hawaiian voices. This kind of evidence is spoofed in a marvelous chapter that I am sure some art historians might also, perhaps, enjoy because it deals with curatorial obsessions, such as collecting artifacts and old manuscripts; it also lampoons the conventional art appreciation of objects encased in museums. The old man in charge of this collection is called "Oh Oh" because every time he looks at an object in his collection he goes into ecstasies. Melville has a hilarious thumbnail description of Oh Oh, but I shall only refer to Oh Oh's collection of "ancient and curious manuscripts preserved in a vault," among which is a collection of "books of voyages." The latter contained titles such as "A Sojourn among the Anthropophagi, by One Whose Hand Was Eaten Off at Tiffin among the Savages." The one I like best is: "Three Hours in Viveza, Containing a Full and Impartial Account of That Whole Country, by a Subject of King Bello" (*M*, 320). Much of the evidence for native cannibalism and for imagined apotheoses is based on the kinds of visits lampooned by Melville.[47] This is not so, however, with the missionaries to the Pacific who were long-term visitors; but even more than transients they were profoundly influenced by their own European prejudgments regarding savagism and cannibalism, which I show in this work are linked in complicated ways to their Evangelical quest and the task of living in an alien culture among people hostile, at least initially, to that very mission.

TWO · "British Cannibals"

Dialogical Misunderstandings in the South Seas

The date is February 15, 1779, the day after the death of Captain James Cook in Kealakekua Bay on the island of Hawai'i, the place where I ended my previous narrative of the sad end of that redoubtable sea captain who, it is said, was a divinity for Hawaiians.[1] There is tension in the Hawaiian air: one group with their piles of stones, another with their loaded guns, not an unusual phenomenon in those historical conjunctures and power relations, then and now and everywhere where people unequally armed meet each other in awesome confrontation. Here in Hawai'i, the ship's officers want genuinely to defuse the tension, but they are not willing to leave for home and England until they get the bones of "our dear Captain," for a decent burial at sea. Lieutenant King, who loved Cook dearly, was in control of the situation. In a parley with the Hawaiians, King demanded the body of the captain and told them to expect "our vengeance in the case of a refusal" (*Cook D 3*, 62). This included the destruction of the town. To comply with this threat, Koah, a chief whom King intensely disliked as a man guilty of "fraud and treachery," came on board. King told Koah that he would "declare war against them, unless it [the body] was instantly restored" (*Cook D 3*, 63). That night two frightened priests, one of whom was the "taboo man" that accompanied Cook wherever he went, came up, and after loud lamentations about the loss of Lono-Cook, mentioned that they had brought with them whatever remained of him. "He then presented us with a small bundle wrapped up in cloth, which he brought under his arm; and it is impossible to describe the horror which seized us, on finding in it, a piece of human flesh, about nine or ten pounds weight. This, he said, was all that remained of the body" (*Cook D 3*, 68). The rest of Cook, they said, was cooked in the Hawaiian fashion and distributed among the king and the chiefs, a mode by which Cook was appropriated into the Hawaiian aristocracy.

It was in the course of this conversation between King and the priests that the latter came out with the phrase, "When the *Orono* [Lono] would come again?" (*Cook D 3*, 69). Lono is one of the great Hawaiian gods, and we now know that Hawaiians addressed Cook in this fashion. According to myths constructed in London and other cities in Europe and America, this is a reference to the god Lono, now manifest as Cook, who has the perverse habit (normally associated with some of us South Asians believing in reincarnation) of eternally returning after he is dead and gone.

Now let me examine the full account of the event by Lieutenant King. Naturally the ship's officers were appalled at the sight of the grisly object, but they soon overcame this because as the first modern ethnographers they were imbued with a keen scientific curiosity. They could easily change into their white coats, for let it not be forgotten they were representatives of the Royal Society. King reports, "This [meeting] afforded an opportunity of informing ourselves, whether they were cannibals; and we did not neglect it. We first tried, by many indirect questions, put to each of them apart, to learn in what manner the rest of the bodies had been disposed of; and finding them very constant in one story, that, after the flesh had been cut off, it was all burnt; we at last put the direct question, Whether they had not eat some of it?" This is was a perfectly reasonable inference on King's part because those who cut and burn flesh must surely eat it. Yet, "They immediately shewed as much horror at the idea, as any European would have done; and asked, very naturally, if that was custom amongst us?" (*Cook D 3*, 69).[2]

What was going on in this dialogue between the anxious Hawaiians and the ethnographers? To clarify this further let me get back to the first brief visit of Captain Cook to Kaua'i the previous year. On January 22, 1778, Cook himself asked similar questions of the Hawaiians. A native was carrying "a very small parcel," and since he was anxious to conceal it, Cook insisted it be opened (*Cook D 2*, 208). He saw concealed therein "a thin bit of flesh, about two inches long," and naturally he surmised "it might be human flesh, and that these people might, perhaps, eat their enemies," a legitimate ethnographic inference, I might add, since Cook says "that this was the practice of some of the natives of the South Sea islands." The questions put to the Hawaiian confirmed the hypothesis that the "flesh was a part of a man." After conversing with another Hawaiian, Cook concluded that "it was their custom to eat those killed in battle" (*Cook D 2*, 209).

When he tried to further verify his hypothesis of Hawaiian cannibalism a week later from a visitor to the ship's gun room he got a different reply. For Cook, however, this reply was proof of their cannibalism:

> These visiters *[sic]* furnished us with an opportunity of agitating again, this day, the curious inquiry, whether they were cannibals. . . . One of the islanders, who wanted to get in at the gun-room port, was refused; and, at the same time, asked, whether, if he should come in, we could kill and eat him? accompanying this question with signs so expressive, that there could be no doubt about his meaning. This gave a proper opening to retort the question as to this practice; and a person behind the other, in the canoe, who paid great attention to what was passing, immediately answered, that if we were killed on shore, they would certainly eat us. He spoke with so little emotion, that it appeared plainly to be his meaning, that they would not destroy us for that purpose; but that their eating us would be the consequence of our being at enmity with them. I have availed myself of Mr. Anderson's collections for the decision of this matter; and am sorry to say, that I cannot see the least reason to hesitate in pronouncing it to be certain, that the horrid banquet of human flesh, is as much relished here, amidst plenty, as it is in New Zealand. (*Cook D 2*, 214–15)

Something curious was going on here—from the very first visit: Cook thought that the Hawaiians were cannibals; and the Hawaiians thought that it was the British who were out to eat them!

It is clear that the British inquiry was a legitimate ethnographic hypothesis based on the practice of cannibalism in New Zealand among Maori and elsewhere. But what about the Hawaiians? How did *their* hypothesis emerge—if one dare call this savage fear of British cannibalism a hypothesis? A partial answer at least comes from King's journal of the next year (1779). Here a curious event occurred, noted by King: "It was ridiculous enough to see them [the Hawaiians] stroking the sides, and patting the bellies, of the sailors (who were certainly much improved in the sleekness of their looks . . .) and telling them, partly by signs, and partly by words, that it was time for them to go" (*Cook D 3*, 26). King adds, "If our enormous consumption of hogs and vegetables be considered, it need not be wondered, that they should wish to see us take our leave" (*Cook D 3*, 26). Leave to which place? Brittanee. Thus the home of Lono-Cook, known to some anthropologists and historians as Kahiki, the land from where gods like Lono are said to emerge, was peculiarly designated by the Hawaiians as "Brittanee."[3] What kind of place was this Brittanee though? Let King respond again: "They imagined we came from some country where provisions had failed; and that our visit to them was merely for the purpose of filling our bellies. Indeed the meagre appearance of some of our crew, the hearty appetites with which we sat down to their fresh provisions, and our great anxiety to purchase, and carry them off, as much as we were able, led them, naturally enough, to such a conclusion" (*Cook D 3*, 26).

The Hawaiians' hypothesis was based on the "pragmatics of common sense" and empirical inference that characterizes the everyday thought of most peoples.[4] Here was a ragged, filthy, half-starved bunch of people arriving on their island, gorging themselves on food and asking questions about cannibalism. Since Hawaiians did not know that the British inquiry was a scientific hypothesis, they must be forgiven for making the practical inference that these hungry people asking questions about cannibalism were cannibals themselves and might actually eat the Hawaiians. If Lieutenant King could ask what seemed to the Hawaiians an absurd question—whether they ate their enemies slain in battle—it is not unreasonable for the Hawaiians to have made a similar inference: that since the British had slaughtered so many of their citizens and kinfolk during their brief visit to these islands, it was they who ate their slain enemies. This inference is never explicitly made and does not appear in the journals, but I think we must at least recognize the Hawaiian fear that the British were cannibals. The terrible events prior to, and after, Cook's death, were well suited to that mythic reality. Those tragic events resulted in the death of at least six Hawaiian chiefs and dozens of ordinary citizens, not to mention the burning of residences and a temple. Previous to that there were constant floggings for theft and the killing of at least one Hawaiian. And to add to all this, on the death of Cook, some irate sailors chopped off the heads of two natives and displayed them on deck, not an unusual male activity among both savages and civilized, as I shall demonstrate in later chapters. These grizzly objects inspired terror in a Hawaiian who had the temerity to visit the ship during this tense time. One officer noted that "the two heads were thrown overboard in his sight, lest he should suppose us cannibals" (*Cook B 3b*, 563, n. 1). It now seems that the dread of cannibalism was a more obsessive one for the British than for the Hawaiians.

It is not only in Hawai'i that the queries on cannibalism produced a variety of responses from native peoples. On another South Sea island, Mangaia, in March 1777, the Tahitian Mai, acting as interpreter, asked the Mangaia people, perhaps inadvertently, "if they ate human flesh" and "they answered in the negative, with a mixture of indignation and abhorrence."[5] With one important difference, though:

while the British believed that the cannibalism they imputed to the savage was real, the imputation of the savage that the British were cannibals must surely be a fantasy because the British knew that they (the British) were not cannibals!

Why this British preoccupation with cannibalism? One reason, it seems to me, is clear: cannibalism is what the English reading public relished. It was their definition of the savage. Thus in the many places Cook visited one of the eager questions the officers asked was about cannibalism, and the replies for the most part seemed to have convinced them of its near universal prevalence. One month after their visit to Mangaia, Cook came across a number of people in a small Polynesian atoll, Aitutaki, cooking what seemed to be human flesh in an earth oven. Anderson says that the Tahitian Mai once again "could assign no other reason for this, than they meant to roast and eat us as is practic'd by the inhabitants of New Zeeland."[6] In this instance also the fantasy of the Polynesian Mai nicely matched the fantasy of the Europeans. Once again, apparently, the outraged citizens protested and responded with the now expectable retort: "whether it [cannibalism] was the custom with us" (*Cook B, 3a*, 85). In fact the human flesh turned out to be a hog that the protein-starved sailors happily consumed. This event brings back a Proustian memory: in my childhood, caretakers told me that it had been told to them by others who no doubt heard it from yet others, that human flesh tastes a bit like pork, linking the ethnographer as a young child with Others who linked pork and human flesh, sometimes calling the latter the "long pig," as did some Polynesians and those who lived in the film version of H. G. Wells's mythic island of Dr. Moreau. I am in good company here because Juvenal, following Greek fashion, also thought that "the taste of human flesh is . . . like that of pork," which Horkheimer and Adorno seem to imply is a dirty and yet delectable substance for ancient Greeks, and I would say for others also.[7]

My last comment provides a hint that perhaps these dialogues have tapped an anxiety on the part of both the British, the interpreter Mai, and the indigenous inhabitants—an anxiety that the Other is going "to roast and eat us." I call this fantasy of cannibalism a psychic structure of long duration, shared by both British and Hawaiians as well as most human beings. Not all Polynesians were anthropophagous; the Hawaiians did not eat the flesh of the human beings they sacrificed. But, I think, those who sacrifice humans might well carry with them an unconscious wish to partake of that substance, for remember that often enough when an *animal* is sacrificed one does eat its flesh. In this situation questions regarding cannibalism can only provoke a terrible anxiety that taps the latent wish and in turn resurrects a childhood dread that the stranger asking these not-so-innocent questions is in fact the cannibal.

But what about the British who journeyed in Cook's voyages? Surely these upright people cannot be accused of so vile a fantasy? My answer is that, like the hapless anthropologist, the British were also socialized in their nurseries with grim tales of witches, ghosts, ogres, and bogeymen that ate human flesh. Thus we find in the nineteenth century, a short, white Frenchman transformed into a black man-eating giant who erupted into the English landscape and thence into nurseries to join the other monsters nurtured therein. Children's books had pictures of "Nappy" with a cat-o'-nine tails, and nurses threatened children with this un-Santa-like monster descending the chimney:

Baby, baby, naughty baby,
Hush, you squalling thing, I say;
Hush your squalling, or it maybe
Bonaparte may pass this way.

Baby, baby, he's a giant,
Tall and black as Rouen steeple;
And he dines and sups, rely on't,
Every day on naughty people.[8]

And Thackeray on his way to England from India visited this same monster in St. Helena and there he was told that "he eats three sheep every day and all the little children he can lay his hands on."[9] These Napoleonic myths are simply continuing reinventions of the most popular mythemes in European nurseries, that of the child-eating ogre coming from Greek foundation myths such as that of Cronus swallowing his own children, into early and late nursery rhymes and tales and then projected into the savages of the new-found-lands of Western exploration.[10]

Let me now come back to Hawai'i. Underlying the detached ethnographic hypothesis of cannibalism by British officers was the British public demand for such information; underlying both the hypothesis and the demand is the childhood fantasy. Similarly, the Hawaiian view of British cannibalism was a rational inference based on British cannibalistic queries and on their physical appearance of food deprivation. Underlying both inferences is also a Hawaiian cannibalistic fantasy. These fantasies were reinforced by events: the fact of British terror, the fact of Hawaiian human sacrifice. The event gets locked into the fantasy as the fantasy gets locked into the event. All these spiral into a variety of crises that lead both British and Hawaiians to look at each other through "paranoid lenses" in times of tense interethnic relations.[11]

CANNIBALISM: SCIENCE AND THE FANTASTIC

Sir Joseph Banks, who was in Captain Cook's first voyage, was primarily interested in flora and fauna spurred by the work of the famous Linnaeus, such that the ship *Endeavour* was in effect a floating lab. Soon Banks became an ethnographer and like everyone on board also became interested in the history and practice of savage anthropophagy. After he became president of the Royal Society he gave the following advice to Vancouver, once one of Cook's young officers, now engaged in the futile errand of discovering the elusive Northwest Passage and perhaps to find new lands yet undiscovered (except by those who had discovered them and settled down there in the first place). "And if you find the abominable custom of eating human flesh, which they are said to practice . . . [you must be] present at some of their horrid repasts in order to bear witness to the existence of a practice all but incredible to the inhabitants of civilized countries, and discover, if you can, the original motives for a custom for which it seems impossible to suggest any probable cause."[12]

Although this "abominable custom" did not prevail in Hawai'i in spite of European fantasies to the contrary, wasn't there enough evidence that forms of anthropophagy did exist among the people of Fiji, the New Hebrides, Marquesas, and New Zealand? It is best to start with the Maori, who were the most notorious cannibals of them all and lived in what was sometimes called "the land of cannibals," and focus on their cannibal talk and practices with the British and also the other way round. Let me begin with the second voyage of Cook, between 1772 and 1775, the voyage of the *Resolution* and the *Adventure*. During this voyage Cook visited New Zealand twice, the first to Dusky Sound very briefly on March 25, 1773, and a second, more extensive visit in October. The two ships lost contact with each other, and Cook decided to cast anchor in Ship Cove on November 3, to repair his sails and rest his crew. I am interested in an important event that occurred a few weeks later. In his journal entry for November 23, Cook notes that "some of the officers went on shore to amuse themselves among the natives" and to engage in buying curiosities when they beheld an impressive sight: a heart of a youth recently killed was impaled on a forked stick and fixed on the front of the largest canoe (*Cook B 2*, 292). The officers also saw the head and bowels of this unfortunate youth and third Lieutenant Pickersgill bought the head in exchange for two iron nails. Apparently the natives of this area had gone up to Admiralty Bay and fought a battle there, and this boy's head was from that battle. However, according to Reinhold Forster, the distinguished German philosopher and natural scientist on board, this was no ordinary tribal war but one of the first trade wars in that nation and provoked by the British presence:

> I am afraid we are the innocent causes of this war. For having bought up all the curiosities and green stones, the natives in the Sound were possessed off, and having us constantly ask for more and offering various things, which tempted their desires; they went I believe in quest of them among their neighbors, who they knew had a great many left, and killed several of them in order to possess themselves of those things, which are so much coveted by the Europeans. I am rather tired to dwell longer on this subject, which fills my soul with feelings of compassion and horror.[13]

When Cook came on board later, he noted, "I was informed of the above circumstances and found the quarterdeck crowded with the Natives. I now saw the mangled head or rather the remains of it for the under jaw, lip etc., were wanting, the scul was broke on his left side just above the temple, the face had all the appearance of a youth about fourteen or fifteen, a piece of the flesh had been broiled and eat by one of the Natives in the presince of most of the officers" (*Cook B 2*, 293).

What really had happened was as follows: when Pickersgill brought the head on board, the ship's officers wanted to produce empirical proof of cannibalism among the Maori. This Lt. Clerke put into effect: "I ask'd him if he'd eat a piece there directly to which he very chearfully gave his assent. I then cut a piece of carry'd [it] to the fire by his desire and gave it a little broil upon the Grid Iron then deliver'd it to him—he not only eat it but devour'd it most ravenously, and suck'd his fingers ½ a dozen times over in raptures: the Captain was at this time absent" (*Cook B 2*, 293, n. 2).

When Cook returned, he did something very scientific and very peculiar when he replicated this experimental proof of cannibalism before the ship's crew and the quarterdeck crowded with natives.

> The sight of the head and the relation of the circumstances just mentioned struck me with horor and filled my mind with indignation against these Canibals, but when I considered that any resentment I could shew would avail but little and being desireous of being an eye wittness to a fact which many people had their doubts about, I concealed my indignation and ordered a piece of the flesh to be broiled and brought on the quarter deck where one of these Canibals eat it with a seeming good relish before the whole ships Company which had such effect on some of them as to cause them to vomit. (*Cook B 2*, 293)

Poor Hitihiti, the Tahitian who acted as interpreter on this voyage, not only reviled the Maori but also one of the officers who cut the flesh in order to perform this experiment. For Cook the experiment was a success: "That the New Zealanders are Canibals can now no longer be doubted, the account I gave of it in my former Voyage was partly founded on circumstances and was, as I afterwards found, discredited by many people" (*Cook B 2*, 294).

Let us for a moment reflect on this incident and ask ourselves the problem posed by Anne Salmond, the distinguished ethnographer of the Maori who says that "Clerke's impromptu barbecue mocked both experiments and cannibals, while in their finger licking responses, Maori were mocking both Hitihiti and the Europeans."[14] I think her interpretation of the Maori response is correct but not her interpretation of the experiment as a spoof. It is true that Clerke was given to practical jokes sometimes of a sadistic sort, but humor did not necessarily negate the idea that Clerke was engaged in an experiment, even if one understands that these experiments were not our modern ones. Moreover Cook, whom one could hardly accuse of having a sense of humor, took the whole episode as proof of Maori cannibalism and so did most of the experimental gentlemen on board. As did the young George Forster, son of Reinhold Forster, who also vindicated the importance of eyewitnessing: "And now as we have with our own eyes seen the inhabitants devouring human flesh, all controversy on that point must be at an end."[15]

Meanwhile a different kind of proof of Maori cannibalism awaited the crew of the *Adventure*. The *Resolution* and *Adventure* parted company end of October 1773; on November 9, 1773, Tobias Furneaux, the commander of the latter ship, took refuge in Tolaga Bay and seven days later he was back at sea. At Ship Cove Furneaux found a bottle with Cook's instructions for a rendezvous. He therefore wanted to reestablish contact with Cook at Totaranui, named by Cook as Queen Charlotte Sound (though Cook had already gone there for the second time and left for England despairing of regaining contact with the *Adventure*). On December 17, Furneaux sent out the cutter under master's mate John Rowe for a final load of greens from Grass Cove (Wharehunga Bay). But the boat did not return. He therefore sent Lieutenant Burney, brother of the famous Fanny, in search of them the next day. Burney suspected that some unfortunate accident had occurred rather than hostile action from the Maori because "I had not the least suspicion of their having receivd any injury from the Natives, our boats having been frequently higher up and worse provided" (*Cook B 2*, 749). Burney and his crew landed in Grass Cove and eventually came upon what seemed indubitable evidence that Rowe and his company had been killed and eaten by the Maori.

> We went ashore & Searchd the Canoe where we found one of the Rullock ports of the Cutter & some Shoes one of which was known to belong to Mr Woodhouse, one of our Midshipmen, who went with Mr Rowe—one of the people at the same time brought me a piece of meat, which he took to be some of the Salt Meat belonging to the Cutter's Crew—on examining this & smelling to it I found it was fresh meat—Mr Fannin, (the Master) who was with me, supos'd it was Dog's flesh & I was of the same opinion, for I still doubted their being Cannibals: but we were Soon convinced by most horrid & undeniable proofs—a great many baskets (about 20) laying on the beach tied up, we cut them open, some were full of roasted flesh & some of fern root which serves them for bread—on further search we found more shoes & a hand which we immediately knew to have belong'd to Tho Hill one of our Forecastlemen, it being marked T.H. which he had got done at Otaheite [Tahiti] with a tattow instrument. (*Cook B* 2, 750)

One of the body parts recovered was the head of Captain Furneaux's servant, who is almost always referred to as "the Captain's servant," "the Captain's man," or "the Black Man," or "Negro." Two hands were also found, that of Rowe himself and of Thomas Hill. These body parts along with the head and "with more of the remains were tied in a Hammock and thrown overboard with ballast and Shot sufficient to sink it" (*Cook B* 2, 752). The remains of the rest in their twenty baskets were left behind for the cannibals to consume. What was especially interesting is that Burney's presence provoked the natives to assemble on the hill nearby "making all signs of joy imaginable" (*Cook B* 2, 744).

The evidence for anthropophagy was compelling. William Bayly, the astronomer, who was not in Burney's search, adds further details: "Our people went on and found the Intrails of 4 or 5 men together with the Hearts and Lungs and 3 Heads roasted, one of which appeared to be the Capt's Black serv'ts by its make" (*HR* 2, 218).[16] I suspect that at least the reference to three heads is perhaps the result of fast-developing cannibal talk on a terrifying event because Burney is explicit that only one head was found. It is also unlikely that Burney would bring back the head of the black man for burial at sea, leaving the European heads for the cannibals. Bayly's version is further transformed in the telling and retelling on deck and on shore, as is evident from John Marra, a seaman in the sister ship, the *Resolution*, writing in 1775. "They had not advanced far from the water side, before they beheld the most horrible sight that ever was seen by any European; the heads, hearts, livers and lights [lungs] of three or four of their people broiling on the fire, and their bowels lying at a distance of about six yards from the fire, with several of their hands and limbs, in a mangled condition, some broiled, and some raw, but no other parts of their bodies, which gave cause to suspect that the cannibals had feasted and eaten all the rest."[17] The few facts discovered by Burney and probably exaggerated in Bayly are now reincorporated by Marra into a graphic elaboration of the "cannibal scene."[18]

Let me analyze these preceding events in some detail. It is indeed the case that cannibalism is for the British something that defines the savage, an atavistic tendency that even middling civilization cannot overcome. Before Banks made the statement quoted earlier, Reinhold Forster interpreted this practice sympathetically in relation to the process of societal evolution. But midshipman Elliott put it, as most did, bluntly in a more judgmental fashion: "They [Maori] are desperate, fearless, ferocious Cannibals, the Men generaly about six feet high, with Limbs and sinews like an Ox, dark copper coloured faces, fine white teeth, and eyes that strike fire, when angry, and I declare that I have seen a couple of them, in giving us the War Song on the Quarter deck, work themselves into a frenzy, foaming at the mouth, and perfectly shaking the whole Quarter deck with their feet."[19]

Perhaps the sole skeptic on board at this time was the astronomer Wales, who expressed doubts about the validity of the evidence that Elliott advances. "Before going to leave this land of Canibals, as it is now generally thought to be, it may be expected that I should record what bloody Massacres I have been a witness of; how many human Carcasses I have seen roasted and eaten; or at least relate such Facts as have fallen with the Compass of my Observation tending to confirm the Opinion, now almost universally believed, that the New Zeelanders *[sic]* are guilty of this most detestable Practice. Truth, notwithstanding, obliges me to declare, however unpopular it may be, that I have not seen the least signs of any such custom being amongst them, either in Dusky Bay or Charlotte Sound; although the latter place is that where the only Instance of it was *seen* in the Endeavour's Voyage. I know it is urged as a proof positive against them, that in the representation of their War-Exercise, which they are fond of shewing us, they confessed the Fact."[20] And sure enough Wales's description of this mimetic enactment was so vivid it shouldn't surprise us if it sent tap roots into childhood horror stories among Englishmen like Elliott: "They first began by shewing us how they handled their Weapons, how they defyed the Enemy to Battle, how they killed him; they then proceeded to cut of *[sic]* his head, legs and arms; they afterwards took out his Bowels and threw them away, and lastly shewed us . . . by signs which every one will allow are easily misunderstood."[21] The mimetic representation of cannibalism might well mean that Maori did eat their enemies; on the other hand, Wales asked whether "it not as likely that after the Engagement they refreshed themselves with some other Victuals which they might have with them?" (*Cook B 2*, 790). He then went on to recount the story of a sailor who claimed to have seen a Maori being killed and probably dressed for consumption. Unfortunately for this eyewitness, Wales comments wryly, "it was afterwards certainly known that the man was not only un-roasted, but even alive and well" (*Cook B 2*, 791).

Wales's comments were made in June 1773. Then following a visit to Tahiti and the Tongan Islands, the *Resolution* returned to Queen Charlotte Sound in late November, where the scientific experiment on the Maori head was performed. This completely changed Wales, and he became firmly "convinced beyond the possibility of a doubt that the New Zeelanders are Cannibals" (*Cook B 2*, 818). Though he was not physically present when Pickersgill brought his head, Wales noted that the officers were there to buy curiosities and then added, "One of the Natives with great gayety struck his spear into one lobe of the Lungs, and holding it close to the Mouth of one of the Officers made signs for him to eat it."[22]

This seems a rather bizarre thing to do because the Maori did make a difference between the raw and the cooked in respect of all flesh. Perhaps if it can be shown that the Maori in fact thought that the British were cannibals, much of the preceding Maori cannibal talk and their discursive practices might make sense. Although I have no proof for the period of Cook's travels, there is certainly some interesting evidence twenty-seven years after Cook's last visit (1777), when a young Maori aristocrat named Teina visited Port Jackson in 1803. While returning via Norfolk Island in 1805, he thought that the salted beef on board was human flesh; at Norfolk Island the sailors showed him oxen and sheep to disabuse Teina that the British were cannibals. On a later occasion when Teina and his friend Maki were on board the same ship, a Danish sailor reported that their parents were afraid for their sons because they thought the sailors were cannibals.[23] This kind of unreal cannibal talk surely would have occurred much earlier on both sides of the divide.

Let me go back to the bizarre quality of the British scientific curiosity: twice a piece of flesh from a Maori head was cut up and roasted by British officers and then given to a Maori to eat. The latter then consumed it with great relish (or so it seemed) as many assembled Maori and British crew witnessed the event. Thus, on another level, we, who think we are outside of it all, sense that both the British and the Maori are *fascinated* by the same event: the Maori by the British inquiry about their practice of cannibalism, the British by their fantasy, and both bound by the belief in each other's cannibalism. The Maori eating cannibal steaks with seeming relish and with seeming fun now begin to make sense: it was based on the fear-knowledge that the British were cannibals and hence *expected* the Maori to eat what was offered to them. It therefore seems that a common humanity binds both British and Maori, and that is what I want to tentatively explore now, for it must be remembered that what gives us all a common humanity is not only our somewhat rare noble nature but also more generally a shared dark side of our being.

SHIPWRECK CANNIBALISM: EUROPEAN ANTHROPOPHAGY

In probing deeper into the dark bond of cannibalism that united the ship's crew and the Savage as part of their common human nature, one notices an even deeper affinity. It seems that the traditions and practices of man-eating were not the exclusive preserve of the Savage, and the intuitions of the Polynesians seemed correct when they asked the British if they were cannibals. The civilized British sailors also had their tradition of anthropophagy. These British traditions and practices are thoroughly documented in Brian Simpson's *Cannibalism and the Common Law.*[24] Though Simpson's study mostly deals with cases that occurred in the mid- and late nineteenth century, he does record several remarkable prior instances. He shows that the traditions of anthropophagy were well established by the seventeenth century and seem to have been associated with the expansion of trade and conquest consequent on the European voyages of discovery. The context of cannibalism is also clear: it is almost always associated with survival after a shipwreck.

The earliest recorded case of cannibalism on the high seas, says Simpson, is found in a medical text, Nicholaus Tulpius's *Observationem medicarum*, published in Amsterdam in 1641, about an incident that occurred somewhere between 1629 and 1640. According to this account, seven Englishmen set out from the Caribbean island of St. Kitts and were driven out to sea and adrift for seventeen days. Lots were cast as to who should be the victim and who the executioner. A victim was chosen and by his own consent killed: "his blood drunk and his body divided and eaten." The survivors were tried but their judge pardoned them, since their crime was "washed away" by the acceptable legal logic of "inevitable necessity" (*CCL*, 123). On December 21, 1710, the *Nottingham Galley* was shipwrecked and eleven survivors barely managed to exist on a raft, most of them starved, frostbitten, and covered with smelly ulcers. Toward the end of December, the ship's carpenter died, "a Fat Man, and naturally of dull, heavy, Phlegmatic Constitution and Disposition, aged about 44," a good subject for consumption. He was eaten after the head, hands, skin, bowels and feet were cast into the sea; parts of the body were dried for later use. According to the captain's testimony, "It was no sin, since God was pleased to take him out of the World, and that we had not laid violent hands upon him" (*CCL*, 115). Far from being stigmatized, the ship's captain ended up being the British consul at Ostend.

In 1737, the slaver *Mary* foundered off the Canaries. An Irishman, Simon McCone, an American from Rhode Island, four other Englishmen, and two Portuguese escaped in the ship's boat after abandoning the slaves and its crew of fifteen. The Portuguese was eaten first and then six others were shot and killed; the "two survivors reached Barbados . . . and appear to have made no secret of how they survived" (*CCL*, 123). In 1759 the journal *Gentlemen's Magazine* reported the case of the *Dolphin*, where cannibalism was not due to shipwreck but simply because of famine on board. Here also lots were cast and the first victim was Anthony Galatea, a Spanish gentleman who was shot, and then eaten after his head was cast overboard. This didn't last very long and they were about to cast lots again when the captain recollected that he owned a pair of breeches lined with leather. They had begun to eat this not-so-delectable substance when they were rescued (*CCL*, 123–24). Six years later there was the case of the *Peggy*, where the crew, after eating the cat, tobacco, candles, and leather, decided to cast lots. The lot fell to a black slave, who was shot; his body was rationed to last for nine whole days (*CCL*, 124–25). Similarly, in 1766 the *Tiger* was shipwrecked and now even without the benefit of lots the black youth on board was killed and eaten and the remains smoked, though how this latter operation was performed isn't clear (*CCL*, 125).

In the nineteenth century the cases multiply, and I shall refer only to two cases and should caution the reader that these now began to be re-presented in broadsheets and ballad literature. In 1826 the ship *Francis* was wrecked and left derelict; though two vessels spoke to her none came to her help. John Wilson died on February 21, and he was quartered and hung up for food, the normal way of cutting up dead animals. When another died, his liver and heart were eaten. When the cook died, Ann Saunders, "his betrothed and a passenger cut his throat and claimed prior property rights in his blood" (*CCL*, 126). Not to be outdone, the captain's wife, "having eaten the brains of an unfortunate apprentice who had survived no fewer that three previous shipwrecks, opined 'it was the [most] delicious thing she had ever tasted'" (*CCL*, 127). And though one can sympathize with the lady's biological demands, it is also the case that this and many more examples listed by Simpson suggest that some of the references to the deliciousness of human flesh attributed by Cook's crew to Maori are refractions from cases known to seamen and refashioned as stories and ballads. The significance of the re-presentation of events in ballad form comes from one of the most famous shipwrecks, that of the brig *George* that sailed from Quebec to Scotland:

At length we drank the female's blood,
To quench our raging thirst.
Her wretched husband was compel'd
Her precious blood to taste.
And for the whole ship's company,
The same did not long last.
Her body then they did dissect,
Most dreadful for to view,
And serv'd it out in pieces
Amongst the whole ship's crew.
Eleven days more we did survive
Upon this horrid food,
With nothing to supply our wants
Save human flesh and blood. (*CCL*, 117)

One cannot treat the ballad literature at face value because they are based on stories told and retold in ships and ports, but it at least expresses the popular views of "shipwreck anthropophagy." And it is such ballads that led to Byron's marvelous parody of this custom in his *Don Juan*.

Then lots were made, and mark'd, and mix'd, and handed
In silent horror, and their distribution
Lull'd even the savage hunger which demanded,
Like the Promethean vulture, this pollution;
None in particular had sought or plann'd it,
'Twas nature gnaw'd them to this resolution,
By which none were permitted to be neuter –
And the lot fell on Juan's luckless tutor.

He but requested to be bled to death:
The surgeon had his instruments, and bled
Pedrillo, and so gently ebbed his breath,
You hardly could perceive when he was dead.
He died as born, a Catholic in faith,

Like most in the belief in which they're bred,
And first a little crucifix he kiss'd,
And then held out his jugular and wrist.

The surgeon, as there was no other fee,
Had his first choice of morsels for his pains;
But being the thirstiest at the moment, he
Preferr'd a draught from the fast-flowing veins:
Part was divided, part thrown into the sea,
And such things as the entrails and the brains
Regaled two sharks, who follow'd o'er the billow—
The sailors ate the rest of poor Pedrillo.

A potentially delectable fat man was saved luckily because of a close encounter with a well-known contamination.

The next they thought upon the master's mate,
As fattest; but he saved himself, because,
Besides being much averse from such a fate,
There were some other reasons: the first was,
He had been rather indisposed of late;
And that which chiefly proved his saving clause,
Was a small present made to him at Cadiz,
By general subscription of the ladies.[25]

Simpson argues that anthropophagy during shipwreck was so much taken for granted in England that often ordinary, innocuous survivors had to *deny* that it had taken place. Public attitudes in seaport towns were, for the most part, in sympathy with the cannibals. Though the law required such cases to be reported, there was not a single case of conviction for anthropophagy until the famous case of the *Mignonette* in 1884 (discussed at length by Simpson). On the *Mignonette* the three survivors ate the youth, Richard Parker, since he was closest to dying and also had the least family responsibilities, not being a married man. What might seem surprising to us today is that the brother of the boy, and indeed the mother herself, did not express outrage; the former explicitly sided with Captain Dudley and the other survivors. The survivors could calmly talk about the killing and subsequent anthropophagy in a matter-of-fact manner, and the executioner kept the penknife that was used to kill the youth as a memento. When the survivors were formally sentenced to prison (only to be pardoned soon after), they expressed resentment and shock at being victims of legal harassment.

In view of the convention-bound nature of British cannibalism, I find it difficult to accept Simpson's argument that anthropophagy was entirely based on hunger during shipwreck and related conditions. The preoccupation with cannibalism existed in British fantasy and in the traditions of European myth; gnawing hunger was a factor in the origin of the tradition of British anthropophagy and a precondition for its continuity and existence. Yet it must be remembered that conditions of starvation (at sea or elsewhere) did not invariably produce anthropophagy. This is true of England and anywhere: there are cultural and psychological conditions that will inhibit it, especially so when it entails an act of deliberate killing. One might be willing to die rather than kill a fellow human to eat him. These inhibitions might well extend to other tabooed foods, like a Brahmin's repugnance to beef (symbolically analogous to cannibalism). It is the legitimacy of shipboard anthropophagy, and its convention-bound nature, that fostered and perpetuated it. Thus people who were shipwrecked could, occasionally even in good conscience, eat their shipmates, since it was a perfectly acceptable, legitimate, normal, and even normative procedure.

Nevertheless, the absence of a *proclamation* of guilt does not mean its absence as a reality. Thus, keeping the knife as a memento might indicate an unsaid expression of guilt and repentance, because guilt is an emotion not easily subject to direct verbalization. Some do suffer qualms of guilt, as did both Owen Chase and more specifically Captain Pollard in the famous case of anthropophagy on the Nantucket whaler *Essex*, the ship wrecked by a whale (and immortalized in *Moby Dick*). In Joseph Conrad's novelette, there is Falk, the sea captain, who over the years suffered the torment of conscience for having had to eat the flesh of the ship's carpenter, whom he had shot in something like self-defense—but not quite.[26] Both the fictional Falk and the real-life survivors of the *Essex* felt the compulsion to confess, and, for Pollard as for Falk, also psychic anguish and a need to "tell his tale," itself a mode of coming to terms with guilt by weaving the terrible event into the fabric of a narrative.[27]

The conventions of British cannibalism, insofar as it entailed killing, seem to be both explicit and implicit. The explicit conventions are very clear: first there was to be a drawing of lots, especially to determine the victim. Second, the blood of the victim must be drunk to assuage one's thirst, a vampirism mytheme easily foisted on others. Indeed in several instances the victim was killed before he died, since only a live victim had enough of the precious fluid left. Two implicit conventions are equally and especially significant. There was a tacit complicity that wherever feasible the alien or the Other would be the victim, and lots were manipulated accordingly. Hence it was often the Spaniard, the Portuguese, the Slave, the Black—and then the more problematic case of the boy or unmarried youth or female. The strict employment of the lottery applied only to one's own comrades.

These prejudices appear in ghastly fashion in the case of the *Essex*. When it was wrecked, the survivors were put into three boats. The second boat was in the command of second mate Matthew Joy, a nineteen-year-old inexperienced outsider and seriously ill; indeed all the persons in his boat were non-Nantucketers, four of the six being blacks. With poor leadership, Joy's team was in potential trouble because "the Nantucketers did their best to take care of their own."[28] No wonder the blacks on all the boats, already discriminated against in terms of food, went fast. As Chase notes, three of the blacks on Joy's boat died and were eaten by those in his boat and the captain's between January 25 and 28, 1820. "The bodies of these men constituted their only food while it lasted."[29] And Joy's fourth black simply went "missing." The only other member, Englishman Thomas Chapple, opted (with two others from other boats) to remain on a desolate island. Joy died of his illness. It is hard to believe that the decimation of blacks was accidental, and it is easy to believe that "[o]nly Nantucketers had emerged from Pollard's and Chase's whaleboats [the two remaining ones] alive."[30]

Another important implicit convention is the rejection of human extremities, which were buried at sea as a substitute for the person eaten. This especially applied to the head, perhaps related to the dread of seeing the eye of the victim; or because a body without extremities ceases to be that of a corpse but becomes a carcass, and hence edible. In addition to the cases recounted earlier, there are many cases of this implicit convention from the nineteenth century. Thus, the ballad literature on the *Essex* disaster mentions that lots were cast, a man was selected, and they "cut off the head" as a preliminary to eating the corpse (*CCL*, 126). In 1872, the *Theka* had four survivors, a Dutchman, two Norwegians, and one Swede. "[T]he Dutchman was stabbed by Johansson and consumed, and true to tradition, the account records that 'previously Kristian Jakobsen and Alexander Johansson had cut the head off the body with a knife and an axe because it was so dreadful to look at, and the former had also cut off the hands which were thrown into the sea'" (*CCL*, 263). In 1878 the American press reported the case of a black sailor, George Seaman *[sic]*, whose head was cut off, wrapped in canvas, and thrown overboard.

"Barrett then butchered the corpse and salted some flesh; this was broiled and fried Barrett claiming that it tasted 'as good as any beefsteak he ever ate'" (*CCL*, 139).

The comment attributed to Barrett brings us to an important aspect of the mythology surrounding cannibalism: this is the widespread idea among seamen that human flesh tastes good. It is a delicacy, and at least one American cannibal, Alfred Packer, reportedly became a pathological connoisseur, finding "the breasts of the men the sweetest meat he had ever tasted" (*CCL*, 154). This mythology, of course, has gone into the popular cartoon literature in the West, and especially well known are the ones in which the anthropologist or missionary is the somewhat ludicrous victim of a "cannibal feast." When Packer was convicted, headlines such as the following appeared suggesting the inevitable mythologizing of eating human flesh: "The Fiend Who Became Very Corpulent upon a Diet of Human Steaks," "A Cannibal Who Gnaws on the Choice Cuts of His Fellow-Man" (*CCL*, 156). These and other kinds of cannibal myths kept circulating in ships and in the more diffuse popular-ballad literature.

The initial choice of the Alien or the Other for consumption is based on racial prejudice as well as notions of comradeship that were equivalent to sibling-ship in respect of one's own fellows. But it is likely that unconscious motivations, triggered in the context of terrifying hunger, were also operative. In popular thought the black man, the Spaniard, and the Portuguese were highly sexed, libidinous creatures. They represented sexuality and life power; by consuming their flesh one could introject these powers and thus ensure strength and survival value.[31]

Our discussion of British shipwreck anthropophagy helps us understand the manner in which the British *represented* Maori cannibalism in their discursive actions. First let me consider Cook's anthropology of savage anthropophagy. It seems that the experiment where the flesh from the decapitated head of a Maori youth was cut into steaks and broiled comes from the discourse of *British* cannibalism. It is interesting that the "experiment" had to be repeated when, of course, replication was scarcely necessary. Further, the language game imputed to the savage in fact comes from British cannibalism. The language by which cannibalism of the Other is described appears and reappears in European discourses pertaining to the Maori and other peoples: it is a "the horrid banquet of human flesh" or "midnight repasts"; New Zealanders are supposed to kill their enemies and "feast and gorge themselves on the spot." Their consumption of smaller pieces of human flesh is referred to as a "dainty bit," "steak," and so on.[32] New Zealand scholars and ethnographers working in remote (and not so remote) regions would continue this language game right down to our own times. As Michel de Certeau insightfully points out, from the time of Jean de Léry in the mid-sixteenth century in Brazil, cannibalism becomes "an obsessive topic whose study has always been central and which establishes the status of future ethnology."[33]

The label "cannibalism" at this period is a British discourse about the practice of anthropophagy, rather than a description about its practice. It is what I call cannibal talk and is initiated by British ethnological inquiry and stimulated in turn by the demands of their reading public. It tells us more about the British preoccupation with cannibalism than about Maori anthropophagy. Cannibal talk or discourse has to be understood in terms of a pervasive fantasy resulting from European socialization of that period and, more narrowly, from a subculture of sailors with a tradition of the practice of anthropophagy that in turn gets locked into the primordial fantasy and then, cumulatively, produces shipboard narratives and ballad literature on the subject. These in turn give direction, even form, to the British discourse with Hawaiians and Maori. It affects their practice of ethnological science such that the experimental proofs of Maori cannibalism are as much science as they are fantasy. And might not this event tell us something about the practice of some of our sciences since Cook's time? Together the discourses, practices, and fantasies that I have outlined constitute a *British* (and beyond that a *European*) "cannibalistic complex" that must be differentiated from what I think is the traditional sacrificial anthropophagy of Polynesian peoples.

SHIPBOARD COLLECTIONS AND THE EMERGENCE OF THE WORLD SYSTEM IN POLYNESIA

The next shipboard practice that I want to consider is that of collections. Pickersgill, we noted, purchased the young Maori's hand, and this curiosity was later deposited in the collection of Dr. John Hunter (1728–93), a famous anatomist. Banks and other scientists collected heads and bones of the "victims" of cannibalism. They are as much part of scientific collections as they are "trophies" for the officers and curios for everyone. Soon the horizon of the native began to fuse with that of the European, at least in respect of curious heads. Thus Reinhold Forster mentions Hitihiti, having learned the arts of collecting curiosities from the sailors and starting his own collection in the Marquesas, took his native Tahitian friends to see "the head of the New Zealand boy, which Mr. Pickersgill had preserved in spirits."[34] When Pickersgill returned to England, he "had made the ladies sick by showing them, preserved in spirits" this same head (*Cook B 4*, 444). Like Pickersgill's pickled pate, "trophies" of all sorts were eventually mounted in museums and anthropology departments. For example the head of the "Irish felon" Alexander Pearce, who escaped from the penal colony at Macquarie harbor on the west coast of Tasmania and then ate his fellow escapee Thomas Cox, found its way into the collection of Dr. Samuel George Morton, an American phrenologist. It later went into the University of Pennsylvania Museum, which contained an array of Morton's racial heads (for scientific measurement of course) from all over the world (*CCL,* 149). In the third voyage, when Cook and his crew went north in search of the elusive Northwest Passage, a brisk trade in heads, skulls, and bones had already started under the influence, this time, of Russian demand. Ellis reports for the Nootka on March 30, 1778: "There was one article of trade which some of these people exposed to sale today that we never saw before in any country: this was several human skulls and dried hands."[35] And Bayly: "We bought three or four Human hands which they brought to sell, they appeared to have been lately cut off as the flesh was not reduced to an horny substance but raw—they made signs that they were good eating, and seemed to sell them us for that purpose or at least all of us understood them in that light. They likewise brought on board two or three Human Skuls and offered them for sale—our Surgeon [Ellis] bought one of them" (*Cook B 3a,* 297, n. 1).

And soon there began the expectable pantomime on both sides, with the British seamen expressing their fantasies and the Nootka comically parodying them: "Some of our seamen made signs of eating the flesh, which signs they readily made too, probably because they saw us do it; and from this circumstance they were pronounced to be cannibals, though it is not unlikely but that we were too hasty in forming our conjectures."[36] Ellis was right: these people were *not* cannibals, only supplying extremities to satisfy European demand, even if it meant freshly plucked curious objects from neighboring tribes. Eleven days later Ellis goes on to say that "several skulls and hands were purchased to-day as curiosities, but skins of every kind were become scarce."[37]

This is not surprising because the trade in native extremities and other curiosities had commenced in the very first voyage of the *Endeavour,* as Banks's journal note in January 1770 indicates: "The people brought us several Bones of men the flesh of which they had eat, which are now become a kind of article of trade among our people who constantly ask for and purchase them for whatever trifles they have."[38] Banks himself was keen to see some dried heads, trophies of enemies killed, and an old man brought, four days before the earlier incident, "the heads of 4 people which were preservd with the flesh and hair on and kept I suppose as trophies . . . the brains were however taken out as we had been told, maybe they are a delicacy here."[39] This spurred Banks to get one for his own collection and actually threatened a man (possibly the same person) with his gun to give him the skull of a youth in exchange "for a pair of old Drawers of very white linen."[40] Some objects bartered during this first visit to New Zealand were pretty ghastly, as this one from William Monkhouse, the ship's surgeon, vindicates: "He [a Maori] brought out a child which was in a dried state, and from the position of its extremities looked as if it had been taken out of the Womb. It had undergone considerable mutilation. All that we could learn of its history was that it was the Child of his wife, that it was born alive and that it died soon afterwards—if I misunderstood him not this was his account. He readily bartered it for a trifle" (*Cook B 1*, 584–85). It is not surprising, then, that during the second voyage, as Reinhold Forster neatly notes, everyone on board ship was "mad after curiosities."[41]

CANNIBAL DOGS AND ENGLISHMEN

The fantastic nature of the scientific experiment on board the *Resolution* came from the fact that science is unconsciously conjoined with the European cannibalistic complex that in turn gave a surreal twist to the experiment. This is not to deny that true scientific activity was part of the goals of these voyages. Joseph Banks, in the first voyage, was genuinely interested in ethnography, in the descriptions of flora and fauna, and in what was known as "botanizing," such that the *Endeavour* was a floating lab containing invaluable collections and artifacts of various sorts to illustrate the life-ways of people hitherto unknown to the West. Not all "experimental gentlemen," or "botanical gentlemen" as they were also called, were scientists or natural philosophers such as Banks, Daniel Solander, Reinhold Forster, or Anders Sparmann. However, though not scientists many officers could and did adopt a detached stance when occasion demanded. This comes out clearly in respect of some rather unique dishes as far as the European palate was concerned. Thus Sydney Parkinson with a touch of irony notes for April 1769, "We have invented a new dish which is as much disliked by the natives, as any of theirs is by us. Here [in Tahiti] is a species of rats, of which there are great numbers in this island; we caught some of them, and had them fried; most of the gentlemen in the bell-tent ate of them, and commended them much; and some of the inferior officers ate them in a *[sic]* morning for breakfast."[42] Molyneux had a better appreciation of rats as food: "[Besides] shooting of rats is not only a pleasant but a profitable amusement as they are also good eating and it is Easy to Kill 1000 in a day as the ground swarms and the Inhabitants never disturb them. I have laid in the woods several nights and among other particulars I observ'd the rats play'd about me as indifferent as about a Tree; in eating rats we quite outdid the Indians who Obhor *[sic]* them as food" (*Cook B 1*, 559). This culinary taste must have developed further to embrace a non-Polynesian species of rat during the third voyage on the *Discovery* en route to the Northwest Coast on March 7, 1778: "This day gentlemen in the gun-room dined on a fricassee of rats, which they accounted a venison feast, and it was a high treat to the sailors, whenever they could be lucky enough to catch a number sufficient to make a meal."[43]

Thus humor, even of a self-deprecatory kind or an understated English humor, was also part of the discursive style of the experimental gentlemen. It did not, however, extend to a vastly different kind of food indulged in the South Seas, the eating of head lice by "children and inferior persons."[44] The "inferior persons" must in part refer to Maori women, as Reinhold Forster indicates in his journal entry of June 9, 1773: "They are very uncleanly, cracking the very large lice, which they abound with, between their teeth."[45] Yet we know from journal entries that virtually all the biscuits and bread on board were infested with vermin which were eaten by both inferior and superior persons, though not necessarily with relish. As Banks says, "I have sometimes had 20 at a time in my mouth, every one of which tasted as hot as mustard."[46] Banks qualifies this view in an entry two months later with its nice concluding irony: "Our *bread* indeed is but indifferent, occasiond by the quantity of Vermin that are in it, I have seen hundreds nay thousands shaken out of a single bisket. We in the Cabbin have however an easy remedy for this by baking it in an oven, not too hot, which makes them all walk off, but this cannot be allowd to the private people who must find the taste of these animals very disagreeable, as they every one taste as strong as mustard or rather spirits of hartshorn. They are of 5 kinds, 3 *Tenebrios*, 1 *Ptinus* and the *Phalangium cancroids*; this last is however scarce in the common bread but was vastly plentyfull in white Deal bisket as long as we had any left."[47] Perhaps it is expecting too much for the officers to see the connection between *us* eating vermin and *they* eating lice, but this case, as with cannibalism, illustrates the many blind spots in their discourses in respect of the other culture. This is surely true of the natives also, as it is also true in lesser degree of contemporary ethnography in our own dialogical misunderstandings with informants and they with us. But that such barriers can be broken down is also evident in the next dietary practice I want to describe.

Let me start with a facetious cannibal joke made by Banks, our gentleman philosopher, naturalist, and botanist in 1769 during first contact with the Maori: "I suppose they live intirely upon fish dogs and Enemies."[48] Fish, dogs, and enemies, one might say, unified and divided the Maori and the British. Fish is the flesh that binds both: both eat this as a protein staple. Eating dog meat and one's enemies is of course the practice of the Other. Maori, like other Polynesian, Melanesian, and South Sea folk, ate dog meat; Maori also wore dog skins. While the British concern with Maori canine carnivorousness was in no way comparable to their interest in Maori cannibalism, the practice was carefully noted in the journals, largely to edify and shock the British reading public. But beyond that, eating of dog meat produced a kind of inner affinity between the ships' crew and the natives, not with the Maori, who were too much tainted with cannibalism for the British to relate to easily, but with the Tahitians living in their earthly paradise.

On June 20, 1769, on Cook's first visit in the *Endeavour*, several chiefs came to visit the tents bringing provisions of all sorts including a very fat dog. Banks says that they had recently learned that dog meat was for Tahitians "more delicate food than Pork, now therefore was our oportunity *[sic]* of trying the experiment," that is, to figure whether this was so and then describe it in their journals.[49] Thus three empiricists—Cook, Banks, and Parkinson—all have detailed descriptions of the dressing and cooking of this particular animal. Here is Banks:

> He [Tupaia] killd him by stopping his breath, holding his hands fast over his mouth and nose, an operation which took up to above a quarter of an hour; he then proceeded to dress him much in the same manner as we do a pig, singing him over the fire which was lighted to roast him and scraping him clean with a shell. He then opend him with the same instrument and taking out his entrails pluck etc. sent them to the sea where they were most carefully washd, and put into Cocoa nut shells with what blood he had found in him. The stones were now laid and the dog well coverd with leaves laid upon them. In about two hours he was dressd and in another quarter of an hour compleately eat. A most excellent dish he made for us who were not much prejudiced against any species of food; I cannot however promise that an European dog would eat as well, as these scarce in their lives touch animal food

being, according to Banks, vegetarian in their habits.[50] Cook thought that "it was the opinion of everyone who taisted of it that they Never eat sweeter meat, we therefore resolved for the future not to despise Dogs flesh" (*Cook B 1*, 103). Parkinson, however, ate only "a little of it; it had the taste of coarse beef, and a strong disagreeable smell; but Captain Cook, Mr. Banks, and Dr. Solander, commended it highly, saying it was the sweetest meat they had ever tasted; but the rest of our crew could not be prevailed on to ate any of it."[51] However, soon afterward they could be persuaded to eat the aforementioned rats. This should not surprise us because it is likely that for many Europeans eating dog, even though of the veggie variety was perhaps more heinous than cannibalism, since dogs were pets and enemies were not. But rats?

However, Parkinson's taste in dog as food underwent a sea change (if I may be permitted that metaphor). After their departure from the Tahitian islands in August 1769 they had a fairly hostile reception in Hiti-roa (Rurutu) on August 15; then Cook took a westerly route into some moderately squally and chill weather. On August 27 Parkinson notes, "On [this] same day we killed a dog, and dressed him, which we brought from Yoolee-Etea [Ulietea or Raiatea]; he was excessively fat, although he had eaten nothing while he had been on board."[52] Neither Cook nor Banks mentions this episode. It is therefore possible that some of the minor gentlemen consumed the animal, perhaps owing to the lack of fresh meat. Though originally vegetarian, this Tahitian dog had become strangely fat on board even though it was abstemious, not having eaten any leftover meat substance eaten by the crew, thus in fact being effectively vegetarian in the crew's imaginings. On March 4, on their way home from the second visit to New Zealand, Parkinson notes again, "[B]eing one of the inferior officers birth day, it was celebrated by a peculiar kind of festival; a dog was killed that had been bred on board; the hind quarters were roasted; and a pye was made of the fore quarters, into the crust of which they put the fat; and of the viscera they made a haggis."[53] It is unlikely that this particular animal was vegetarian; this meant that an important taboo had been broken as a dog raised on board ship was consumed by officers. Perhaps it was not as bad as eating a dog who was truly a pet and a companion.

Soon the *Endeavour* sailed back home, and I presume the gentlemen reverted back to their normal English diets. But the problem of dog's meat resurfaced in the next voyage when, after leaving New Zealand on June 10, 1773, Reinhold Forster notes, "We had taken from the Cape a black Dog with us; it had been killed two days ago and the Gentlemen in the Gunroom had feasted upon it the day before; we had this day at dinner a Leg roasted with Garlick, and I found it very well tasted and very much like mutton."[54] And on the very next day: "We had this dinner another Joint of our Dog in a pye, and it was in every respect as good as mutton."[55]

This event soon provoked the two Forsters to formulate a general connection between cannibalism and canine nature. "The New Zealanders," Reinhold Forster tells us, "eat as true Cannibals their own Species and likewise their Dogs; with the remnants of the feast their live Dogs are fed, and this creates an habitual Instinct, which is propogated into the very Pups. The Cape-Dogs never get Dogmeat, and are therefore not used to it, and abhor it: this Aversion is confirmed and at last inherits to the very young ones. The Cannibal-Dog having one Day licked off the blood of a cut in a finger of the Captain's servant fell greedily upon the finger and began to bite in good earnest the finger."[56] Thus the earlier theme recurs; the Cape dog was hardly vegetarian, but it did not eat its own species and hence eating it is still okay, this time by the superior officers. But New Zealand cannibal dogs are still taboo. Hence George Forster mentions that their Cape bitch had ten puppies and one died and it was eaten by a New Zealand dog "with a ravenous appetite." Thus New Zealand dogs, like their human counterparts, are cannibals because from their earliest days they eat from their master's meals "fish, their own species, and perhaps human flesh," whereas "European dogs are never fed on the meat of their own species, but rather seem to abhor it."[57] These inferences are made from scrupulous observation of canine behavior.

At this time both canine and human cannibalism are linked at least in the consciousness of several gentlemen on board. But not entirely because it is also difficult to maintain the distinction; dogs are after all dogs whether Tahitian, Maori, or English. Hence, when the officers ate the Cape dog, Reinhold Forster grandiosely pontificates on his new taste and goes on to suggest, with an undertone of almost Swiftian irony, that the generality of Europeans too should follow his example:

> It is really a pity, that in Europe there are such terrible prejudices among mankind, as to think cats, dogs, horse and other Animals (we are not used to eat by custom) to be unclean and an Object of Abomination. I do not doubt, but education, custom and the remainder of Judaism have much contributed to prejudices against this food. Many a poor Man cannot keep a Cow, a Sheep, Goat or Pig; but there is hardly a Cottage without a Dog and a Cat: their numerous brood is commonly drowned, because we do not know what to do with: but were it general to eat these domestic Animals who afford both a wholesome and palatable food, many a poor Man could now and then feast upon flesh, which he but too often must abstain from, because it is not in his power to procure it for his family by his earnings. Providence seems to have this and many other Animal destined for a food to mankind, because we see they have so many young ones at a time, and they would absolutely become a nuisance was it not for the cruel custom to drown the poor creatures when they are scarce born. We complain therefore often too unjustly against

> the scarcity of food, when there are many suicidanea, which prejudice caused us to neglect and detest. Many a Lady and Gentleman fond of their Lap-Dogs and favourite Cats will be displeased with this doctrine, but true Philosophy and common sense seems to be on my side and self interest and prejudice on theirs.[58]

I believe that in spite of a distinction made between cannibal and noncannibal dogs, the contact with the Maori and other Polynesian people resulted in the broadening of the British consciousness, for eventually the ships' crew, including the Forsters, might well have consumed the despised New Zealand dog irrespective of its cannibal propensities. Or dare we say because of those very propensities? On September 8, 1773, Reinhold notes, "We had all our decks crowded with Hogs, Dogs and Cocks. We had when we came off from Huaheine 209 Hogs on board, about 30 Dogs and more [than] 50 Cocks, but very few Greens and Vegetables."[59] The final breakthrough occurred when on March 30, 1774, Cook became violently sick with the "Billious colick" and his life was in danger. "When I began to recover, a favourite dog belonging to Mr. Forster fell a Sacrifice to my tender Stomack; we had no other fresh meat whatever on board and I could eat of this flesh as well as broth made of it, when I could taste nothing else, thus I made nourishment and strength from food which would have made most people in Europe sick, so true is it that necessity is govern'd by no law" (*Cook B 2*, 333–34). The nice distinctions made earlier could hardly arise in this case as genuine dog, and the philosopher's favorite, was cut up as much needed protein for the sick Cook.

There was no way, however, that Forster's concern for the poor of Europe would have the slightest effect on European taste, but it clearly did on the taste of the ships' crew. Dog flesh broke one of the barriers that separated the Savage from the Civilized. The ships had dogs as pets, as hunters, and as consumers of leftovers. The last sentence in Forster's satirical statement, however, emphasized the obvious fact that dogs were pets for the British for the most part and full of symbolic and psychic import. As pets, dogs (and not just lap dogs) were "man's best friend," and in the case of lap dogs, objects of love, and even surrogate kinsfolk or substitutes for children. Thus it would seem that, in the European cultural context, the consumption of dog meat is a horrendous act, exhibiting a symbolic affinity with cannibalism. The ship's officers were tantalized by Savage anthropophagy; it triggered a latent wish but, since it was impossible to consume human flesh, they (unconsciously) chose dog meat. The latent rationale for this act was the commonly accepted idea that it was permitted to eat human flesh in times of shipwreck, but this equation also refused to surface anywhere in the ship discourses on savage or canine anthropophagy. The ship's officers cutting up the flesh from the severed head of a Maori youth and defining it as "steak" and the two Forsters discoursing elaborately on cannibal dogs are not simply a part of an innocuous scientific experiment or detached observation by the experimental gentlemen, but one that seems to tap a latent desire (wish).

Given our preceding analysis, it should not surprise us if during Cook's third voyage there were no qualms whatsoever in eating dog meat. Loads of dogs were purchased as a potent protein source and stacked live or salted on board the *Resolution* and *Discovery*. Yet because an important European taboo has been violated, one must ask whether the floodgates of desire will be breached when powerful taboos are broken, such as eating dog or eating humans. The possibility certainly exists, in which case new rules of appropriate behavior have to be invented, or one must revert back to more normal times and normal rule-governed behavior that restores the earlier taboo. Thus Cook and his crew reverted to normal British dietary practice when they returned home, and those Maori who, we will later see, engaged in sporadic acts of conspicuous anthropophagy during early European contact could as easily give up these practices after the Treaty of Waitangi in 1840.

Let me conclude this chapter with a little vignette of cannibal humor. If the Tahitian dogs were isolated from the charge of cannibalism, and the necessity of eating the New Zealand variety was shunned in the earlier voyages, not so in the last voyage, as this reminiscence from Alexander Home, master's mate in the *Discovery*, indicates:

> When we were in New Zealand, Neddy Rhio, one of my messmates had got hold of a New Zealand dog, as savage a devil as the savages from whom he got it, and this same he intended to bring home to present to the Marchioness of Townsend, his patroness. But one day, when Neddy was on shore on duty, a court-martial was held on the dog, and it was agreed *nem.con.* that, as the dog was of cannibal origin, and was completely a cannibal itself, having bit every one of us, and shewn every inclination to eat us alive if he could, that he should be doomed to death, and eat in his turn, *we being short of fresh provisions at the time.* The sentence was immediately executed, the dog cooked, dressed, and eat, for *we could have eat a horse behind the saddle, we were all so confoundedly hungry;* but, considering that Neddy had a best right to a share, we put past his portion in a wooded bowl, and by way of having some sport, we cut a hole in the dog's skin, and as Neddy came up the side, I popped his own dog skin over his head with the tail hanging down behind, and the paws

> before. He looked grin [painfully] horrid, told us *we were all as set of d—d cannibals, as bad as the New Zealanders we were amongst,* and dived down below quite in the sulks. I had locked up his share, and went down after him to see if hunger would overcome his delicacy, and sure enough, after growling and grumbling and swearing a reasonable time, he looks at me very woefully and says, "D—n you, did you not even leave me a share?" "That I did," says I, "Neddy, my boy, and here it is for you." So poor Rhio munched up his dog, cursing all the while as heartily as we were laughing at him. Ah! those were the glorious days . . ."[60]

This nostalgic episode brings out the issues that I have already discussed in relation to savages, dogs, and cannibals. Anne Salmond rightly points out that the trial of animals was well known in Europe, as Robert Darnton indicates in his work on the great cat massacre in Paris in the 1730s.[61] But while in Europe this might indicate subaltern protest against felt oppression, the Rhio episode was one which gentlemen officers, not those in the lower depths, enacted. Salmond argues that the young officers were offended because Cook did not punish the Maori Chief Kahura who many felt was guilty of the massacre at Grass Cove. On the contrary Cook admired Kahura's bravura and got the ship's artist John Webber to paint him. There is little evidence of a call for vengeance among the officers, though Maori enemies of Kahura, it was reported, were anxious to have him punished.[62] Moreover, unlike in the French case, the discourse is about cannibal dogs and cannibal Maori. For us today it is difficult to ignore the insensitivity of the cannibal humor in this particular case. The model for this enactment is *not* so much animal trials in Europe but Europe's tradition of shipwreck cannibalism with its hankering for fresh meat. The following example, once again from Byron's *Don Juan,* might indicate this (with a slight emendation and with some permissible facetiousness):

> What could they do? and hunger's rage grew wild
> So [Rhio's] spaniel, in spite of his entreating,
> Was kill'd, and portioned out for present eating.[63]

CANNIBAL TALK: A WEAPON OF THE WEAK

The Maori and other Polynesian discourses on cannibalism are not only a defense against the European; they are also a counterattack, an employment of one form of terror against another. It was Reinhold Forster, of the second voyage, who astutely noted the double uses of the cannibal talk by the people of Tanna, in the New Hebrides: "The natives were very jealous to let their habitations, wives and children be seen, and always desired us not [to] go on, and in order to frighten us, they told if we went on, we should be killed and eaten."[64] And even more frighteningly: "The natives of Tanna gave us more than once to understand, that if we penetrated far into the country against their will, and without their permission, they would kill us, cut our bodies up, and eat them: when we purposely affected to misunderstand this last part of their story, and interpreted it, as if they were going to give us something good to eat, they convinced us by signs which could not be misinterpreted, that they would tear with their teeth the flesh from our arms and legs."[65] But the uses of cannibal terror had other implications. For example, Maori cannibal discourse as a weapon of the weak meant that it could be put to new uses in a changed political and economic context. Cannibalism kept the settlers away for more than forty years from the time of the Cook's first voyage. Only missionaries, who were for the most part welcome, really constituted a stable community in the early years of the nineteenth century, but even the establishment of the missions was deferred owing to Maori cannibalism.[66]

Let us now consider Cook's first voyage and the initial dialogical misunderstanding of cannibalism. It seems that there is a battle going on here with cannibalism as a weapon. The British view of Polynesian cannibalism, as the various accounts indicate, is an *imagined* form, based on a reality that no one seemed to grasp. It is also a performance that emerges out of the British discourse; the Maori are at great pains to prove that not only are they cannibals, but also they are truly horrible ones. The Maori man miming this practice by eating "the flesh of his own arm with his teeth" is simply not true as an illustration of Maori anthropophagy. It is a reaction to the British inquiry that elicited information through similar performative actions. So is the bone-chewing act. And the more deadly one already mentioned where a Maori thrust one lobe of a lung "and holding it close to the Mouth of one of the Officers made signs for him to eat it." It is the kind of pantomime that some people might use to scare children, and like many such stories and pantomimes, adults seem to find them funny and sometimes not so funny.

It seems obvious that the Maori had to cope with the British queries on cannibalism in a variety of ways, soon conventionalized. Cook of course always had the help of Tahitian interpreters, Tupaia, Hitihiti (Oididee), and Mai (Omai), who managed to converse (imperfectly) with the Maori, and then even more imperfectly translate this into basic Tahitian that Cook (and several other gentlemen) imperfectly knew. But others simply used the language of gestures that, as Dutton shows, was also highly convention bound and elaborate.[67] An early use of gestural language is described beautifully in Captain Wallis's account of first British contact with the Tahitians in 1767.

> They seemed all very peaceable for some time, and we made signs to them, to bring of Hogs, Fowls, and fruit and showed them coarse cloth knives, sheers beeds ribons etc., and made them understand that we was willing to barter with them, the method we took to make them understand what we wanted was this, some of the men grunted and cryd like a hogg then pointed to the shore—other crowd like cocks to make them understand that we wanted fowls, this the natives of the country understood and grunted and crowd the same as our people, and pointed to the shore and made signs that they would bring off some—we then made signs for them to go into their canoes and to bring us off what things we wanted—they observed what we meant and some went in their canoes.[68]

This kind of gesture language was the sole means of communication during first contact or with peoples whose language European voyagers did not understand. Thus Reinhold Forster once again on the deadly nature of the language of mime and sign: "They were very eager to undeceive us, and showed, by signs how they killed a man, cut his limbs asunder, and separated the flesh from the bones. Lastly they bit their own arms, to express more clearly how they eat human flesh."[69] But this response of the people of Tanna was surely not initiated by them; it is a reaction to the British inquiry on cannibalism. The British must express exactly as the natives did, that is, "bit their own arms . . . etc.," since they did not know the native language at all. This is of course what the Maori in Queen Charlotte Sound also did. It is clear that the native reaction is a pantomimic response to the British language of gestures as the latter were engaged in the impossible task of asking questions about native cannibalism through mimesis.

How would Polynesian people respond to this gesture language regarding cannibalism? One reaction is obvious: strange, enigmatic, white people biting their own bodies and performing other imitative actions could be truly terrifying, activating fears of cannibalistic monsters in childhood socialization. Another reaction, particularly once they became more familiar with the European, is the opposite, the ludicrous. Sometimes the ship's account does not help clear up the issue. Let me get back once again to the experiment with cannibal steaks during Cook's second voyage. By this time the Maori had developed a variety of responses to British queries on cannibalism, but this was an extremely complex one. Remember that Maori do not eat broiled human steaks, and the setting of the ship's quarterdeck would have flouted all conventions of Maori sacrificial anthropophagy. They simply performed another pantomime and joined in the spirit of the game initiated by the British with good humor. What we do not know was the intention behind the Maori action in eating the steak with such obvious relish, but even here the licking of fingers, and so on, is, I think, a Maori imitation of the British expression of relish as they inquired by signs and sounds about the native's relish for human flesh. Once the Polynesians were aware of the British obsession with cannibalism, they were surely going to feed it, if I might use that expression, either to scare the British or laugh at them, or both. Consider the following native scare story noted by Forster. "There circulates on board a Story made up I believe on purpose, that the Natives told, that a ship arrived on the Northern Isle in a great Storm, and was there broke to pieces. The Men in her were safed on shore, and had an Engagement with the Natives, but not being able to keep up a Fire, the Natives came up and killed and devoured them all."[70] This scare story feeds the British fantasy, so that Forster noted that the sailors aboard the *Resolution* believed that this story portrayed the fate of the crew of the *Adventure* with whom they had lost contact. Forster adds, "The Natives are by no means constant in their story, so that there is little to be depended upon this Tale."[71]

The native populations that did not practice any form of anthropophagy had similar standardized reactions to the British imputation of cannibalism. First, there is an outraged denial; second, a feigned playful or eager admission. For Cook and his crew the admission of cannibalism naturally proved its existence because, then and now, admission, like eyewitnessing, is an indicator of truth. Yet one must ask why did Hawaiians on occasion emphatically admit to a practice they did not practice? It seems clear that here also the false admission of cannibalism must be related to the emergent discourse. Cook's cannibalistic queries provoked the Polynesian counterdiscourse, namely, that the British would be scared if they believed that they—the Hawaiians—were in fact dreaded cannibals. Then the final response: the alien visitor asking dreadful questions by biting their own bodies and performing other strange gestures and sounds were indeed cannibals themselves. All these reactions result in a fallback to fantasy life and its ontogenesis in early childhood of scare stories of man-eating monsters. This is true of the British sailors also; they too had traditions of something that approached sacrificial anthropophagy—of a divine figure sacrificed for the well-being of the world whose blood and body is consumed (symbolically or literally) in a highly charged ritual setting, and alongside a lot of stories of cannibalism circulating in both nurseries and ships. It should be remembered, however, that in terms of conventional anthropological method, such as the evidence garnered in the *Human Relations Area Files,* various Polynesian groups and primitives in general are listed as having practiced "cannibalism" traditionally. By the same methodological token, European nations too should be included, a point well taken by Arens.[72]

Polynesian cannibalism, then, is constructed out of an extremely complex dialogue between Europeans and Polynesians, a dialogue that makes sense in relation to the history of contact, unequal power relations, and the cultural values, fantasies, and the common dark humanity they both share. The discourse on cannibalism once initiated affects a variety of cultural practices in which it is embedded. It affects, for example, the early British practice of ethnological science and the Maori practice of sacrificial anthropophagy. A discourse is not a matter of speech alone; it is embedded in a historical and cultural context and is expressed often in the frame of a scenario or cultural performance. It is about practice; the practice of science, the practice of cannibalism. Insofar as discourse evolves it begins to affect the practice. Since I've already discussed the effect of this discourse on the practice of their science by the ship's "experimental gentlemen," let me now ask a much more controversial question: How did the evolving discourse on cannibalism affect the Maori practice of cannibalism?

THREE · Concerning Violence

A Backward Journey into Maori Anthropophagy

The change in Maori practice is probably the most controversial part of my argument. I present my thesis hesitantly because no one seems to have a clear knowledge of precontact or "traditional" Maori anthropophagy. In fact this phrasing might be a misnomer because New Zealand consisted of a multiplicity of Maori communities, such that, forms of anthropophagy, wherever they existed, would have shown local variations. Conventional ethnography simply constructs an ideal type of Maori cannibalism from a variety of statements—interviews with older men, myths, missionary and magistrate accounts, and even that of eyewitnesses. These sources of information are treated as reality, rather than a discourse on cannibalism. We know those who wrote about cannibalism in the nineteenth century were even less sophisticated and self-critical than the experimental gentlemen on Cook's ships. Thus any attempt to construct Maori anthropology-cannibalism in this fashion is extremely dubious, since the practice might itself have been affected by the evolving discourse. For example, the mere fact that the Maori stopped their practice without any fanfare is proof of the capacity of practice to change. In which case one is justified in moving backward to make the case that Maori anthropophagy, when it did occur, could be understood in the context of the changes brought through European contact. Therefore, let me present my own viewpoint somewhat baldly.

I start with the proposition that not one person in any of Cook's voyages or of the French ones understood anything about Maori human sacrifice, outside the knowledge that Maori were "cannibals." The latter word is derived from Western language games that orient the lines of inquiry into indiscriminate anthropophagy. The only reasonable evidence of Maori anthropophagy during the earliest contacts was from Maori consumption of white sailors, itself a new practice. The first clear example of this practice is from the incident at Grass Cove, but it might have occurred in the Marion massacre that I discuss later. If so, Marion and his officers, and then soon afterward a number of the crew, were killed in an ambush and eaten, though we do not know in what manner. There was considerable provocation for this by French thieving of important cultural artifacts and by their humiliating imprisonment of an important chief. But Marion himself was a considerate and naively trusting person and his being eaten must be seen in the context of Maori-European power relations.

Because there is no reliable account in early texts about precontact anthropophagy among the Maori or among any other Polynesian group some ethnographers and historians rely on myths and traditional "histories." But by this token virtually every human society becomes anthropophagous. My own assumption is that Maori forms of anthropophagy must be seen in the larger context of human sacrifice common to Polynesian society and many other parts of the world. Strictly speaking Polynesians did not practice anthropophagy. It is human sacrifice that is the key institution. In some places like Hawai'i human sacrifice did not entail anthropophagy; but it did elsewhere. Some Maori groups perhaps did eat human flesh consecrated at the site of the sacrifice. By contrast *pronounced* anthropophagy or conspicuous anthropophagy in Polynesia commenced with their killing and eating the European. The European discourse on cannibalism produced in very complicated ways, the Maori practice of anthropophagy followed by a retroactive "indigenous" Maori view, found also among some present-day Fijians, of the claim that they were in fact terrifying cannibals traditionally. Hence, during the early and mid-nineteenth century both the British and Maori seem to take for granted Maori cannibalism. There is plenty of evidence for this, including eyewitness accounts. However, many such accounts make the claim that anthropophagy existed, for the most part, independent of human sacrifice. Furthermore, after about 1820 it is the natives, not the British, who are being eaten. This change must also be seen in its historical context. I demonstrate in chapter 5 that the British presence not only escalated tribal wars, but the availability of guns in combination with new political alliances to capture the European trade escalated that killing to a degree unprecedented in traditional Maori warfare. The sheer availability of corpses of enemies contributed further toward a more general, nonritualized anthropophagy. Thus my conclusion: as a consequence of historic events both Maori and British cannibalism moved from a highly charged symbolic arena of religious sacrifice to shedding some of these symbolic attributes and making a translation of sacrifice and any fantasy associated with it, into anthropophagy—or is it cannibalism?

The preceding chapter suggests very strongly that the discourse on cannibalism conducted by British officers represented Maori cannibalism in terms of British values, fantasies, and myth models. Our anthropological knowledge of Maori anthropophagy thus eludes us from the very start. There is no doubt that the Maori did engage in a form (or forms) of anthropophagy, not because they admitted it, but because there was *evidence* of anthropophagy in the empirical accounts of the British. We know again from Hawai'i and elsewhere that the natives' admission of cannibalism, or its very opposite as denial, was proof of savage anthropophagy for the European outsider. Yet in the Maori case, there is the seemingly indubitable evidence of a native eating the cannibal steaks obligingly supplied by the British. Then the grisly evidence in Grass Cove and those horrible baskets, twenty in all, that surely must have awaited the Maori "cannibal feast." I suggest that the evidence is in fact indubitable, however slanted the British *representation* of Maori cannibalism. There is no denying that Mr. Rowe and his comrades were slain, their flesh placed in baskets, and some parts of their anatomies scattered around. But this event in Grass Cove can only partially illuminate Maori anthropophagy because prior to the coming of the Europeans (the Dutch, French, and British) Maori could not possibly have consumed Europeans. Thus the change in Maori anthropophagous habits and proclivities must be incorporated into our knowledge of Maori cannibalism. It is unlikely that the Maori simply fitted the British into their preexistent cultural forms and treated them as if they were traditional tribal enemies, because the British were *not* their traditional enemies.[1]

Some New Zealand scholars believe that Maori treated Cook as a kind of god or goblin. But there are two problems with this hypothesis. First, there are Maori myths which affirm a different mythic origin for Europeans. Thus the very first myth recorded by the well-known antiquarian John White says that both European and Maori came from two related culture heroes: "From Taka-roa-te-ihu-pu came the Maori people, and from Taka-roa-hau-papa came the Europeans. This is what our ancient men said when they saw the first Europeans."[2] I am not suggesting that White produced an authentic traditional myth, only that such accounts were floating in the late nineteenth century, and it is hard to privilege one over the other.

The coming of the European is a new and traumatic event in their history. British ethnographic inquiries produced a *new* discourse on cannibalism, totally unexpected by the Maori. Insofar as this discourse occurred in a historical context of power, domination, and terror, it must be located therein. It is futile to deal with either cannibalism or anthropophagy outside this context as if it was an unchanging Maori tradition. Instead we must place the events in Grass Cove and on the deck of the *Resolution* as a historical product that can best be understood in terms of preceding relations between Maori and Europeans. It must be remembered that the Maori discourse emerged from the British inquiries into cannibalism, and since Maori did not write about these events as they occurred, their discourse is hidden in the British texts and has to be unraveled by us.

"Concerning Violence" is the title of the marvelous chapter in Frantz Fanon's *The Wretched of the Earth*. Fanon was mostly interested in African colonialism and its horrors rather than those of Polynesian and Pacific peoples that were no less horrifying. Fanon's general point is clear though: one cannot understand the plight of the natives without a grasp of colonial violence and the various forms of passive and active resistance on their part. I want to sketch here the beginnings of violence in the very first European incursions into Polynesia focusing on the Maori.

The first contact between Europeans and Maori was when the Dutch navigator Abel Tasman commanding two ships, the *Heemskerck* and its consort the *Zeehaen* sighted the coast of New Zealand on December 13, 1642. On the seventeenth he anchored off Cape Farewell and saw smoke from native fires but had no contact with them until the next day when he sailed into Golden Bay in northern South Island. Two canoes came as close as a "stone shot" and the natives in the boat called out to the crew in a "rough hollow voice" (*HR* 2, 21). They also played some kind of musical instrument ("like a Moorish trumpet") and Tasman responded by asking one of the sailors to play some of their own Dutch tunes. The next morning another boat manned by *thirteen* Maori approached the ship close enough for Tasman to give a rough description of the boat and its people. Meanwhile, the officers of the *Zeehaen* came on board the mother ship for council, and it was decided "to go as near the shore as we could, since there was a good anchoring-ground here, and these people apparently sought our friendship" (*HR* 2, 22). Soon after this decision was made seven or more boats came up and paddled behind the *Zeehaen* while the other with (unluckily) thirteen able bodied men came very close to the *Heemskerck*. The crew held up white linen as they did before, but the Maori did not move.

The captain of the *Zeehaen* now put out a boat manned with the quartermaster and six sailors, the first Europeans to experience the famed bravado of the Maori (who at this time seemed unaware of the divinity of the Europeans).

> Just as the cock-boat of the "Zeehaen" had put off from board again, those in the prow before us, between the two ships, began to paddle so furiously towards it, that, when they were about half-way, slightly nearer to our ship, they struck the "Zeehaen's" cock-boat so violently alongside with the stem of their prow that it gave a violent lurch, upon which the foremost man in this prow of villains, with a long blunt pike, thrust the quartermaster, Cornelius Joppen, in the neck several times with so much force that the poor man fell overboard. Upon this the other Natives, with short thick clubs, which we at first mistook for heavy blunt parangs, and with their paddles, fell upon the men in the cock-boat, and overcame them by main force, in which fray three of our men were killed and a fourth got mortally wounded through the heavy blows. The quartermaster and two sailors swam to our ship, whence we sent our pinnace to pick them up, which they got into alive. After this outrageous and detestable crime the murderers sent the cock-boat adrift, *having taken one of the dead bodies into their prow and thrown another into the sea.* (*HR* 2, 22–23; my italics)

Tasman retaliated with gunfire and hit one person who held a "small white flag" in his hand, but he did not do any serious damage. He wisely left New Zealand alone, but only after naming the place of assault "Murderer's Bay." We do not know whether the poor Dutchman was eaten, though that was the conventional presumption of later times. Yet, these notorious cannibals inexplicably threw away one of the corpses into the sea—a wasteful action that later writers seem to have ignored. My own guess is that the Maori very sensibly carried the corpse to verify the nature of the alien people who had landed in their proximity.

One hundred and twenty-seven years after Tasman's visit, Cook came to New Zealand in his ship the *Endeavour*. It is not likely that the Maori had forgotten the earlier event, but it might have been mythologized. It was on Sunday, October 8, 1769, that Cook sighted land and established contact with the natives the following day. This initial contact at Poverty Bay was dramatic, sudden, and deadly. Cook went ashore with Joseph Banks and David Solander, but the natives there retreated.

> [W]e went as far as their hutts which lay about 2 or 3 hundred yards from the waterside leaving four boys to take care of the yawl, which had no sooner left than four men came out of the woods on the other side the river and would

certainly have cut her off, had not the people in the pinnace discover'd them and called to her to drop down the stream which they did being closely pursued by the Indians; the Coxswain of the pinnace who had the charge of the Boats, seeing this fire'd two musquets over their heads, the first made them stop and look round them, but the 2^{d} they took no notice of upon which a third was fired and killed one of them upon the spot just as he was going to dart his spear at the boat; at this the other three stood motionless for a minute or two, seemingly quite surprised wondering no doubt what it was that had thus killed their commorade: but as soon as they recover'd themselves they made off dragging the dead body a little way and then left it. (*Cook B 1*, 168–69)

A number of natives now assembled on one side of the river and Cook and his officers on the other, the former according to John Gore, with their faces "distorted," weapons brandished and "lolling out their tongues and turned up the whites of their eyes accompanied by a strong hoarse song" (*Cook B 1*, 169, n2). This was no doubt a "war dance" that thereafter typified the Maori warrior. Hence a musket was fired over their heads and this quieted them. The marines were then brought in. They landed "to intimidate them and support us if necessary" marching with the Union Jack, which incorporated the crosses of St. George the monster-slayer and St. Andrew, in front of them.[3] Meanwhile, Tupaia the Tahitian priest and interpreter told the Maori in Tahitian that the crew wanted provisions and water and they would be given iron in exchange. Cook was surprised that Tupaia understood Maori "perfectly"; Banks thought he "could tolerably well understand them and they him."[4] Tupaia warned Cook that "they were not our friends." Cook tried to give them presents but the natives made "several attempts to snatch them out of our hands." One fellow snatched the hanger [sword] from Mr. Green, the astronomer and wouldn't give it back. He waved it exultantly over his head and "this incourage'd the rest to be more insolent" (*Cook B 1*, 169). Let Banks speak of this incident:

[I]t now appeard nescessary for our safeties that so daring an act should be instantly punishd, . . . this I pronouncd aloud as my opinion, the Captain and the rest Joind me on which I fird my musquet which was loaded with small shot, leveling it between his shoulders who was not 15 yards from me. On the shot striking him he ceasd his cry but instead of quitting his prize continued to wave it over his head retreating as gently as before; the surgeon who was nearer him, seeing this fird a ball at him at which he dropd. Two more who were near him returnd instantly, one seizd his weapon of Green talk [nephrite],

> the other attempted to recover the hanger which the surgeon had scarce time to prevent. The main body of them were now upon a rock a little way in the river. They took the water returning towards us, on which the other three, for we were only 5 in number, fird on them. They then retird and swam again across the river. On their landing we saw that 3 were wounded, one seemingly a good deal hurt: we may hope however that neither of them were killd as one of the musquets only was loaded with ball, which I think I saw strike the water without taking effect.[5]

But Tupaia, the fellow Polynesian of the Maori, had better luck. "Tupias gun which was the last that was fird I clearly saw strike two men low down upon their legs, who probably would be so lame as to walk with difficulty when they landed."[6]

Now Cook decided that these people were hopeless and went upstream in search of fresh water and also to try "to surprise some natives and to take them on board and by good treatment and presents endeavour to gain their friendship" (*Cook B 1*, 179). But "this generous Christian like plan," says Molyneux, also didn't work (*Cook B 1*, 170, n4). The following afternoon, Tuesday, October 10, 1769, Cook's journal entry reads how he and some of the crew rowed round the head of the bay but could not find a landing place. Noticing two native canoes, Cook urged Tupaia to ask them to come alongside. Instead they tried to get away:

> [U]pon which I order'd a Musquet to be fire'd over their heads thinking that this would either make them surrender or jump over board, but here I was mistaken for they immediately took to their arms of whatever they had in the boat and began to attack us, this obliged us to fire upon them and unfortunately either two or three were killed, and one wounded, and three jumped over board, these last we took up and brought on board, where they were clothed and treated with all imaginable kindness and to the surprise of every body became at once as cheerful and as merry as if they had been with their own friends; they were all three young, the eldest not above 20 years of age and youngest about 10 or 12. (*Cook B 1*, 170–71)

It is likely that Cook did want to "capture some of the canoeists, transport them to the *Endeavour* and there treat them kindly in an attempt to gain their friendship" because the kidnapping of natives was established convention in voyages of discovery, sometimes as hostages and sometimes as informants, a rather neat way of learning the language and culture of the alien (*Cook B 1*, 170).[7] Besides ordinary people were being kidnapped (press-ganged) to serve on ships in England. Hence kidnapping of natives and members of the European underclass could be seen as a continuing tradition during and before the European Enlightenment. In this instance both Banks and Cook felt enormously guilty at this wanton murder, perhaps because of the age of the murdered boys, as no such emotions were expressed in earlier and later violence.[8] It is however not surprising that Cook could not understand that sudden terror followed by unimagined kindness to frightened youngsters could indeed result in the youth becoming "cheerful and merry," or to put it differently, placating the dreaded aggressor.

Cook left Poverty Bay on October 11 and headed southward. The next day there was friendly intercourse and exchanges with the natives.

> About this time two Canoes came off to the ship one of which was prevaild upon to come along side to take in the three people we had on board all night who now seem'd glad of the oppertunity to get a shore; as the people in the Canoe were a little shy at first *it was observed that one arguement those on board made us on to intice the others along side was in telling them that we did not eat men, from which it should seem that these people have such a Custom among them.* (*Cook B 1*, 174; my italics)

This account perhaps could be trusted because Tupaia could make himself understood by the Maori (though not as well by the British).

This is the first discourse with the Maori on cannibalism and the first instance of the dialogical misunderstandings that I have reviewed in the previous chapter. I shall skip much of what went on for the next two months as Cook began to map the coastline and both Maori and Englishmen began to get used to each other's presence. The only violent event that occurred was when the American on board, Lieutenant Gore, shot a Maori dead for taking a piece of cloth without proper barter. Cook was very critical of Gore's conduct, though he himself on a later date shot a native in the knee with small shot for "insolence," an event not mentioned in Cook's own journal but recorded by Lieutenant Clerke who had little sympathy for natives (*Cook B 1*, 235, n. 3). By the time the ships left New Zealand, the toll of dead and badly wounded was nine natives, including some chiefly persons invested with sacred power, or *tapu*.

On January 13, 1770, the ship was in Queen Charlotte Sound for four days; here Cook found his first proof of Maori cannibalism that must, I think, be seen in the context of the preceding violence. It was unlikely that Tupaia was present because communication in this instance was in the language of signs.

> Soon after we landed we met with two or three of the Natives who not long before must have been regailing themselves upon human flesh, for I got from one of them the bone of the fore arm of a Man or a Woman which was quite fresh and the flesh had been but lately pick'd off which they told us they had eat, they gave us to understand that but a few days ago they had taken Kill'd and eat a Boats crew of their enemies or strangers, for I believe that they look upon all strangers as enemies. . . . There was not one of us that had the least doubt but what this people were Canabals but the finding this Bone with part of the sinews fresh upon it was a stronger proof than any we had yet met with, and in order to be fully satisfied of the truth of what they had told us, we told one of them that it was not the bone of a man but that of a Dog, but he with great fervency took hold of his fore-arm and told us again that it was that bone and to convence us that they had eat the flesh he took hold of his own arm with his teeth and made shew of eating. . . . Mr. Banks got from one of them a bone of the fore arm much in the same state as the one before mentioned and to shew us that they had eat the flesh they bit a[nd] naw'd the bone and draw'd it thro' their mouth and this in such a manner as plainly shew'd that the flesh to them was a dainty bit. (*Cook B 1*, 236–37)

If we recognize that Maori cannibal talk and mime cannot be taken at face value, then one might hypothesize that the newly plucked bones of enemies were both to terrify as well as for sale to the British, which Pickersgill also seems to confirm.[9]

Soon after this first voyage by Cook, the Maori were visited by two French expeditions, not engaged in scientific work like Cook's but more concerned with opening new and profitable trade resources in the South Pacific, already made famous in 1768 by Bougainville's vision of Tahiti, the "New Cythera." The first was by Jean-François-Marie de Surville who in the *Saint Jean Baptiste* left Pondichery in June 1769 and after trading in Malacca and other places in Southeast Asia first sighted New Zealand on December 12. I refer the reader to McNab's documentation of this voyage, but for present purposes I will mention the reemergence of Maori cannibalism as noted by L'Horne, one of the ship's journalists. L'Horne mentions that the chief of the village near where the ship was anchored took them to their fortified village ("citadel") and there demonstrated to the French the manner in which they kill their enemies and consume them.

> He gave us to understand that when there were but a few enemies left on the battlefield they cut them in pieces and divide the pieces among themselves, to eat them. There was no mistaking the meaning of his signs. The chief we have in our power [as a prisoner] . . . made us understand by signs that they seized their enemies by the tuft of the hair on the top of the head, gave them a blow with their spatula near the temple, and after having killed them they dismembered them, opened their bellies with a cross-like incision, drew out the intestines, cut the trunk and members in pieces, and distributed these pieces among themselves to be eaten. I cannot say if they ate this horrible food raw or if they cook it. (*HR 2*, 329)

Monneron gives an almost identical account but from a native kidnapped and kept on board (*HR 2*, 283); both suggest that the Maori were fully aware after Cook's visit of the European dread of body dismemberment such that everyone in this area was trained to repeat the very discourse that appalled Cook and to reenact their famed "war dance," the *haka,* in parodic form. These discourses continued in the next, and crucially important, French expedition by Marion du Fresne in 1772, a year before Cook's wonderful cannibal experiment on board the *Resolution.*

Marion du Fresne was a wealthy man who set out to take back to Tahiti a man named "Mayon" originally brought to Paris by Bougainville for exhibition because Frenchmen were already thoroughly familiar with exhibits of natives and native exhibits from the Americas. Mayon was later transported to the Isle of France but, like several others from the South Seas, he died away from home. Marion however continued the work of exploration in his two ships, the *Mascarin* and the *Maquis de Castries.* Notes of the momentous events in New Zealand were written down by Lieutenant Roux of the *Mascarin* and Captain du Clesmeur of the *Castries.* I shall use Roux's journal for the most part because he was an active participant in the trail of events that lead to the death of the Marion and many of the crew and the French reprisal—a form of life known to the Maori as *utu*—that resulted in a massacre of the Maori.[10]

Both Roux and du Clesmeur recognized the affinity of the Maori language with the Tahitian, but it is doubtful whether they could conduct any serious interview in New Zealand with their smattering of Tahitian. Unlike Cook they had no Tahitian interpreter on board. Nevertheless, it is impressive that human beings could under difficult conditions communicate with each other as easily as they could miscommunicate. Marion's expedition took pretty much the same route as Tasman's. Marion sighted Mt. Egmont (Taranaki) on March 25, 1772, and eventually proceeded north to the Bay of Islands area for a period of three and a half months. This was the general area where Cook had been three years earlier. Roux describes the initial contacts with the Maori as friendly. At Bowling Bay (using the current designation) the usual exchanges of fish and "trifles" took place. Roux describes Maori nets and houses and on April 27 cavalierly notes that he "carried away a finely carved post from one of these houses" (*HR* 2, 365). On May 3 a cutter was sent to explore the area; meanwhile eight Maori came on board led by an old man and some others. They were given presents, which they "concealed" so as not to share with others, according to Roux who also noted that the old man was "trembling" while the others were "astonished at everything they saw" (*HR* 2, 369). Du Clesmeur however gives a different view saying that the New Zealanders displayed "little astonishment" and "the name of Tapon [*tapu*] which they gave our muskets—all persuaded us that they had seen Europeans on their coast before" (*HR* 2, 451). Of course he was right because Maori knew that "peace" meant not bringing their arms on board. The chiefs wanted to sleep on board for the night, and Roux says that "this we allowed them to do, and the remainder then all went away, amidst cries of delight" (*HR* 2, 371).

On May 4 a cutter was sent to take soundings of the Bay of Islands (at a place named Marion's Bay), and because the natives seem friendly, they decided to anchor there. Two days later Marion with some others went to explore parts of the mainland. There they unwittingly became participants in a battle, when a chief whom they had met earlier conducted an officer to the head of his army. "They advanced against their enemies at once, and in good order. These latter, who were astonished at the sight of the white men, and even more so at the two musket shots which were fired in the air, took to flight, and abandoned the field of battle to their victors, who loudly expressed their joy, and brought back the white man, whom they recognized as their liberator, to the place where we had remained to watch them. What surprised me most was the order in which they marched against their enemies" (*HR* 2, 375; *EE*, 145). Here was another case where the presence of the European affected native polity with one party using the Europeans to further their own political interests.

By May 9 and 10 both ships were permanently anchored in Port Marion and two camps were set up on land, one a hospital and the other a camp for making masts for the *Castries*. Relations with the Maori were very friendly, especially with those in a fortified village *(pā)* in the southern part of the island. On the mainland across from the bay where the ships were anchored was another village whose chief was Tacoury (Te Kauri), a handsome man of about forty "much shrewder and more daring than other chiefs." His ally was Piquiore (Pikorei), a chief of a village nearby. Tacoury was a powerful chief to whom others paid homage, yet the latter often implored the French to aid them against him. "This man often came to see us at our camp on Marion Island and on board our ships. It was easy to see that he took notice of everything he saw. His inquisitiveness and his boldness of manner made us distrustful of him at first, but M. Marion always believed in him. It will be seen by what follows that this man was trying to know everything he could about us in order that the might carry out his designs" (*HR 2*, 381; *EE*, 149).

The friendly relations with Maori were without a doubt fostered by Marion's policy of gentleness toward them and also by keeping the crew under control, for, in relation to theft, Marion told his men "that what is regarded amongst us as theft is not so considered by them," thus showing greater insight into these matters than Cook (*HR 2*, 463). Nevertheless, the usual "thieving" continued on both sides. During the period May 20–29, there occurred two serious events. First, a black male and three female slaves (the latter owned by Marion) assigned to wash the linen on shore escaped in a small canoe. Apparently, the canoe was overloaded and the male slave killed one of the women, while another swam ashore to tell the story. Roux says that the slave would set the natives against them. It is possible that Roux was wrong because while the Maori highly regarded the officers, they "took very little notice of the men of the crews" (*HR 2*, 435). The second was an act of thieving; a native stole a cutlass from the gun room, and Marion arrested him in order to frighten him but soon set him free when his fellows begged pardon on his behalf. The French, like the English before them, also stole things though it was not described as such, as we saw from Roux's ornamental pole. Similarly, on June 6, Roux saw "a superb canoe which was aground under some trees" and thought it was abandoned (*HR 2*, 389). Under his instruction crew members brought it to the camp the next day. (Later under pressure from the Maori the canoe had to be returned.) Meanwhile, Marion was mostly engaged in his favorite hobby, fishing with a few gentlemen in a cove near Tacoury's village.

On June 7 a further incident occurred. Natives had stolen several items including a bag of biscuits and a small stand of rope yarn. The crew chased them into the forest; meanwhile others came in and carried off a musket, some great coats, and other articles. The Maori retired into the bush and made a great noise, and the officer in command dispatched twelve armed men to prevent the masts from being burned down. Since Marion was away, probably fishing near Tacoury's village, M. Croizet, the second in command, ordered a detachment of troops to "secure two natives and detain them as prisoners."

> The party secured a chief and a young man, who were taken to the camp. The chief wore a very handsome cloak, and his head was ornamented with the feathers worn in time of war. Some one took it into his head to declare that this chief was in command of the party which had committed the theft. Without making a further inquiry, the officer in command had the chief bound to a stake, and sent the young man under a strong guard to the mast-camp, where they made him understand what they had been looking for. Thereupon the young man declared himself guilty, and showed our people how the thieves had uprooted the anchor. The chief, who was kept bound up, accused Tacoury and Piquiore of this robbery. (*HR* 2, 393; *EE*, 159–61)

According to du Clesmeur one officer had set fire to a village prior to capturing the chief. The "trial" itself was a real travesty, and Marion, who heard about it the next morning (June 9), severely blamed Croizet and released the men. Soon after this du Clesmeur recorded a treaty of peace with several Maori to restore good relations through a ritual (which I will not describe here). Roux returned the cloaks of the former prisoners to the peace party. An old chief put the cloaks in a heap "after which he chanted some words, then taking up a bough, he threw it with some animal excrement on the cloaks, repeating certain words" (*HR* 2, 405). The two young men removed the cloaks.

The next day Marion asked Roux to take charge of the hospital, since the previous officer was sick. Roux noticed that the defenses were weak; he had the blunderbusses cleaned, loaded, and placed at the entrance of the tent. In the night several Maori tried to get near the camp but ran away when they were spotted. The next day Roux expressed his concerns to Marion, but Marion responded by saying that they were only out to pilfer and the best way to deal with them was to show kindness. The same afternoon the chief of the village in Marion Island came to see Roux with several attendants and with gifts of fish. Roux recorded their astonishment at the blunderbusses mounted on their carriages. The chief wanted to know their uses, and Roux explained as best he could but was suspicious of his inquisitiveness, which convinced Roux that "this man had some design." Later that afternoon Roux went to this same chief's village.

> The chief asked me various questions as to the cleaning of our guns. He has seen me kill some birds, but he did not think a man could be killed in the same way. As there are a number of dogs in this country, he made signs to me to shoot one of them that happened to be passing by. I shot at it, and killed it,

> which completely bewildered the chief. He went and examined the dead animal with the greatest care so that he could see where the dog had been hit, and then came back to examine the gun with the same minute attention. He then wanted to do what I had done, turning at another dog, and blew upon the lock of the firearm, thinking that this was the right way to discharge the gun. I did not think it necessary to show him the right way to proceed. On the contrary, I was very glad he did not know in what way we made use of our weapons. (*HR 2*, 409–11; *EE*, 175–77)

What Roux did not know was that the natives of this bay had already felt the power of Cook's guns on November 29, 1770, (*Cook B 1*, 208), and they were now rationally trying to figure out their uses. Roux himself had previously taken charge of the hospital camp where this interaction took place, and where he had installed new guns and shining blunderbusses. This was further provocation for the Maori to find out their uses. There were attempts (mostly unsuccessful) to steal them. Hence it seems reasonable for some Maori to wrest these guns and, of course, triumph over the intruders.

Roux's journal for this day also records many interesting descriptions of Maori life including the gift of the venereal from the expeditions of Cook and de Surville. The Maori in turn continued their own cannibal talk, so effective with both Cook and de Surville, vividly describing how they killed and dismembered their enemies. And then says Roux:

> From the demonstration they gave us on several occasions, there can be no doubt that they are cannibals, and that they eat their enemies. Several of our officers are of my opinion that this is the case, but what completely confirmed what I say on this subject is the fact that one of the chiefs, who well understood what I asked him, told me that after they had killed their enemies, they put them in the fire, and having cooked the corpses, ate them. Seeing that I was greatly disgusted with what he told me, my informant burst into laughter, and proceeded to reaffirm what he had just told me. (*HR 2*, 401–3; *EE*, 169)

Maori mimeses of cannibalism from Cook to de Surville to Marion constitutes a tradition of Maori cannibalism imagined by the European. The Maori began to give a version of their cannibalism to the white visitors to terrify them, and they enjoyed the terror written on their faces. From the European point of view these accounts retrospectively incorporate the early experience of Tasman and create a European tradition of Maori cannibalism that, on another level, is simply a discourse of the long run about savages in general going back to the time of Columbus.

But this argument must contend with the fact of the Maori consumption of Rowe and his comrades in Grass Cove and a year earlier the killing and possible eating of the kindly Marion and his not-so-kindly crew. The critical event occurred on June 13 (with its unlucky number) when Marion, two officers, and fifteen sailors were ambushed in Tacoury's village and killed. Later another group of sailors from the sister-ship, *Castries*, was also ambushed; the death toll was once again the unfortunate number thirteen. In Marion's case it is almost certain that his murder was *not* directly provoked by hostile action on his part, but the crew certainly was guilty of pilfering Maori artifacts. Maori warriors employed a successful strategy by isolating one group of Frenchmen from another and then attacking them. There were signs of possible disaster the previous day. At 1 A.M. Roux was told that "[n]atives were coming down the hill in great numbers" (*HR 2*, 411); he himself saw about four hundred around the vicinity of the camp hiding in the fern hoping to overpower the camp and steal "everything we had in the island" (*HR 2*, 413).

After Marion's death, Roux expressed his own feelings of "pity, horror, and revenge" as natives gathered round the camp in large numbers and "began to shout insults at us, crying out that they had killed Marion, and would serve us the same way . . . [and] they took their tomahawks, and showed us by signs how they had killed our commander" (*HR 2*, 417, 419). Tacoury himself appeared, and Roux ordered a volley to be fired at him, wounding the chief. Then followed the French version of Maori utu: Roux led a devastating retaliatory action that led to the burning of a large fortified village *(pā)*, but not Tacoury's. According to Roux's estimate at least four principal chiefs and about two hundred and fifty people died; du Clesmeur estimated five hundred deaths (indicating that gross numbers are not reliable, whether one is Maori or white). The Maori themselves continued to taunt the French from a distance; exultantly, they wore the clothes of the dead Frenchmen and especially displayed Marion's silver pistols. This naturally was the worst that any Polynesian group had thus far experienced in their encounter with Europeans; it was also one of the worst experiences suffered by any group of Europeans in the Polynesian islands.

Roux was dissatisfied with the commanders of the two ships for not going down to Tacoury's village to find out what happened to the crew because he believed that some might have been hiding and could have been saved. But instead they reinforced their fortifications, repaired their ships, and only tracked down the remains of Marion's people twenty-eight days after the event. Hence it is not surprising that "nothing could be found or, at least, very little," yet this little confirmed without the "slightest doubt," says Roux, "that the natives are cannibals." "In Tacoury's house was a man's head on the end of a stake stuck in the middle of the room. His head had been cooked, and traces of teeth-marks could be distinguished. In another house close by there was a thigh-bone which was attached to a wooden spit. The flesh had been torn off in several places by teeth, there was still a little flesh adhering to the bone, which was cooked and dried up" (*HR 2*, 439; *EE*, 203).

Except for the head trophy there was no possibility of proving anthropophagy from this account; teeth marks and other standard projective indices must be treated with some skepticism as with the thigh bone attached to the wooden spit (an unusual Maori way of cooking, unless they learned this culinary mode from the French.) It therefore should not surprise us that du Clesmeur's journal neither speaks of Maori cannibalism nor of their teeth marks on bones, just bones that seemed to have been cooked on a fire and some intestines entangled in Maori brambles. Though the evidence for anthropophagy is at best vague, I do believe it was a real possibility given the fact that a similar event did occur at Grass Cove the following year. Hence a partial answer can now be formulated for the killing of Marion and for Maori anthropophagy at this early period of contact.

I noted that the Maori were asking rational and pragmatic questions from the French about the uses of guns. But these reasons were balanced by symbolic-affective ones. This is to triumph over the powerful Europeans, humiliate them, and at the same time to identify with them and introject their power. An example from Marion's voyage will illustrate this symbolic and creative expression of the new Maori will to power: "The natives are very affectionate, but they show such ferocity in their caresses: they particularly like kissing and do it very energetically. They never tire of admiring the whiteness of our skin and when we let them press their lips against it, whether on the hands or face, they do such with an astonishing greediness" (*EE*, 169; *HR 2*, 403). On the one hand, this will to power results in an introjection of the color of the white man's skin.[11] On the other, I think a shift in Maori consciousness has occurred, itself provoked by the presence of European firepower and wealth and their questions about cannibalism. Maori were changing their techniques of embracing to introject the European himself, symbolically sucking his body to obtain his power, or *mana*.

With the death of Marion this fantasy is given a further symbolic extension in the identification with the aggressor, by wearing his clothes and brandishing his pistols and other weapons and accompanied by Maori taunting. Between the two events is the crucial act that (perhaps) did occur—eating the Frenchmen. If so, that action is, psychoanalytically viewed, the introjection of the Other of his power through identification with the aggressor. Thus the consumption of the European (at least at Grass Cove and perhaps also at Tacoury's village) resulted, on the one hand, in a revitalization of traditional Maori (sacrificial) anthropophagy and, on the other, in a shift in its practice. Conditions of mass revitalization, even if temporary, would, I think, have resulted in a greater public participation, actual or vicarious, in dividing and eating the flesh of the powerful aggressor.

Consider the event at Grass Cove a year later when ten Englishmen were killed, their flesh cooked and placed, along with fern roots (their "bread" as the ships' crew called them) in twenty or so baskets. If indeed the flesh of the Englishmen were eaten by larger numbers seeking revitalization in the face of a threat to the very existence of their society, one can in fact speak of a change in Maori anthropophagy, particularly since the traditional conventions (whatever they were) need not apply to the new aliens in their midst. In other words, I am suggesting that large-scale anthropophagy was a reaction to the European presence; it is this that set the stage for descriptions of Maori "cannibal feasts" of the later historical and anthropological imagination.

The change in orientation of Maori anthropophagy in some senses parallels the shift in the orientation of British cannibalism from a generalized fantasy coming down at least from the time of Homer and a later ritualistic act of Holy Communion symbolically far removed from fantasy, to a tradition of seafaring anthropophagy. With the opening up of the world consequent on the voyages of discovery, shipwrecks and starvation became a regular phenomenon. Thus in the culture of seafarers the medieval fantasy of cannibalism became a modern reality, such that sailors began to accept the literal idea of consuming the blood and body of a victim chosen by lots. So among the Maori: the opening up of *their* world consequent on the European voyages of discovery shifted their rituals of human sacrifice into one characterized by pronounced anthropophagy. But more than this: insofar as this change resulted in an expanded consubstantial community that, in some instances at least, permitted commoners and perhaps even women to partake of human flesh thus violating the traditional tapu on which the sacrificial anthropophagy rested, and at the same time providing a powerful motivation for those previously excluded to partake of the consubstantial meal. It was the Europeans killed in ambush who provided the initial motive and opportunity for the expansion and consequent "pejoration" of the sacrifice because the traditional rules did not apply to them, or could be suspended, ignored, or reformulated.

MAORI CANNIBALISM: AN ALTERNATIVE "EMIC" INTERPRETATION

The interpretation of Marion's death from the so-called native's point of view is that he had violated a death tapu and *therefore* he was killed (*BW*, 209). One writer formulates the apportionment of flesh that followed Marion's death in terms of the European's view of native ideas: "Tohitapu was a famous *tohunga* and warrior of the Roroa tribe. In the cannibal feast, which followed the massacre of Marion Dufresne *[sic]* and his crew in 1772, the body of the captain was apportioned to Tohitapu."[12] Anne Salmond, one of the most perceptive of New Zealand scholars, makes a similar assertion: the case of Marion was no different from the later event at Grass Cove and this would "include the practice of kai tangata, or cannibalism, in the whaangai hau rite, when the hau of aggrieved ancestors was ritually fed and the hau of enemies ritually eaten" (*BW*, 177). Unfortunately, Salmond does not give us a source for this interpretation; hence, I am not sure whether one is dealing with Maori tradition or the invention of that tradition by a skilled ethnographer (which is perfectly reasonable so long as it is clearly stated).

Ian Barber gives a more plausible conjectural interpretation of traditional Maori anthropophagy. While later accounts of conspicuous anthropophagy might be viewed with skepticism, this was not true of the Grass Cove incident, he says. "From records of the late eighteenth to the early nineteenth century, a Maori trajectory emerges from precontact times where dire consequences loomed if enemy spirits and associated tapu matters were not appeased or satisfied. If enemy bodies were eaten, however, any malign spiritual influences could be extinguished with the absorption of the mana of the consumed. In Grass Cove, the potentially rogue powers of tapu, mana, and technology associated with the new European visitors may have been of special concern, prompting the protection of a comprehensive anthropophagy."[13] I find it hard to accept this interpretation, especially because Barber is skeptical of conspicuous anthropophagy in the archaeological record. Further, to extrapolate the evidence from contact to precontact times indicates an audacious assumption that times past and times present are equivalent and a denial of social change in troubled times, even though I think that absorption of the mana of the victim of sacrifice is probably correct. In the case of consuming the European I would agree that there was continuity with the past in Maori wanting to introject the power of the European, though I would not want to dub that as "rogue powers," whatever the phrase might mean. My disagreement is that mass-scale anthropophagy in the case of Grass Cove (and perhaps in respect of Marion and his people) produced a shift from traditional sacrificial anthropophagy with what I have designated as the expansion of the consubstantial community.

It is one thing to respect the "natives' point of view" as we engage in fieldwork; it is another to appropriate that point of view and assume that an ethnographer can present the point of view of the native in his work. The idea of another "culture" is something the ethnographer has constructed. No native has been asked to comment on this version and could not possibly comment on it, not having access to the ethnographer's language and text. To complicate the matter further, no "traditional" native exists for interrogation because the past has been overlaid by later events. At best one might say that Maori, on being interrogated by white settlers on their customs, gave the expected answer or, more plausibly, simply "explained" the fate of Marion in traditional terms, after the fact, so to speak.

This kind of interpretation attempts to give Maori a voice, but it only distorts their operative history. Often enough Maori like other subaltern peoples might come to accept the colonial interpretation of their traditional past. Violation of tapu for me is simply one strand in a conjunction of events (or an accumulating "history") that led to Marion's death. That death cannot be understood in terms of a prior tradition, like that of tapu violation, but must be seen in its situational complexity. Marion's death had no "cause," as it were; it was overdetermined by a history of events, some of the more significant being: the precedent in Maori human sacrifice; the Maori will to power by possessing the white man's weapons; the desire for just retaliation, or utu, for the French stealing of artifacts; the desire for European commodities, especially iron, such that after Marion's death the Maori stripped the canoes of that precious metal; the presence of Marion in a vulnerable position; and perhaps other situational events one will never know. Although traditional concepts no doubt were part of the native explanation for the attack, they cannot explain the situational power play that occurred there. That must be attempted by us scholars and the native point of view, traditional or otherwise, is but one strand in a more complex interpretation.

Nevertheless, most ethnographers would question the mode of analysis I employ here because it ignores the power of culture (or what some misguided ethnographies designate as an "emic" approach) whereby the local concepts are used to "explain" or "understand" the ethnographic material. "Explanation" in this case entails the fallacy of trying to explain culture in terms of cultural ideas. But not "understanding": native terms or ideas could be employed in the service of hermeneutics; the lacunae in the existing texts can be filled by Maori concepts that then give plausibility to the interpretation. Even here one cannot exclude political and economic power plays in which Maori and Europeans were implicated and which eventually might even lead to a transformation of native concepts, if not their abdication. By contrast most attempts to present the natives' point of view of the killing and eating of Marion would exclusively pose the hermeneutical problem in terms of fundamental Maori concepts necessary to understand their so-called cannibalism.

The key terms are *hau*, *mana*, *tapu*, and *utu*. "In Maori ways of being, utu was a pivotal dynamic. Hau, or vitality, was needed to master the art of successful exchanges. A person of mana engaged in oratory, song, fighting, gift exchange or in spiritual contexts. . . . These were competitive arts, in which mana might be lost or diminished" (*BW*, 395). Mana was the creative and generative power of the gods and transferred to chiefs and nobles; tapu "is a state of contact with the divine by which the particular is encompassed and bound by the general, and thereby rendered intelligible," whereas its opposite, *noa*, "represents the unbounded state of separation from the divine and the human and thereby represents the particular, the idiosyncratic and the free."[14] Though these terms cannot be easily restricted to a single set of meanings, they have similarities with concepts found in other cultures, for example, wide-ranging Hindu concepts thick with meaning, such as *shakti* and *tejas*, that could be for convenience narrowly glossed as the "creative power" and "brilliance" of the gods. "According to the waananga chants . . . the cosmos began with a surge of primal power. From this, thought emerged, followed by memory, the mind-heart, knowledge, darkness and the kore (nothingness, potential forms of existence). Tapu, or cosmic power, was the source of all creation. It brought complementary forms of life together, generating new beings" (*BW*, 401). What about hau? The Maori world, like most of the rest of the world, was governed by reciprocal exchanges. "Mind and heart were not split, nor mind and matter—they had a generative relation. From them came hau, the wind of life, producing the forms of the everyday world through generative engagement. Thus all forms of life had hau, including things and people. . . . In case of people this included the hau of their ancestor gods, called up by the tohunga (priest) at their birth and bound in them. With this hau went tapu, or the presence and power of ancestral gods, and mana, ancestral efficacy." This implies that hau, tapu, and mana were also dispersed in the kin group. Thus insults or gifts to any individual affect the whole kin group, especially if directed to a chief or aristocrat known as *ariki* and *rangatira*. "In this way utu, or reciprocal exchange, required the return of hau, whether by gifts or insults. Insults diminished the rangatira's hau and had to be requited. Gifts, by embodying mana and carrying the donor's hau, created an obligation for return gifting." If not reciprocated or requited the very life source is weakened, causing death and destruction. "Utu was thus sought after in group or individual exchanges, producing constant movement in the network of cosmic relations." Thus, "cannibalism" in which the body of the enemy is eaten is also a part of the game of hau: the ancestors who are offended by enemy violation can be now appeased when they are "ritually fed and the hau of enemies ritually eaten" (*BW*, 176). Salmond puts it well: cannibal logic brings the "offender and offended together in acts of ritual eating, destroying the offender's tapu by consuming his body, the 'living face' of his or her ancestors" (*BW*, 179).

Salmond's work is in the best ethnographic style, but whether it helps us understand the changing world into which the Maori were propelled in the late eighteenth century is problematic. Further, with these concepts and a few associated ones it is possible not only to interpret every act of anthropophagy in New Zealand but also virtually every significant aspect of Polynesian life, such as warfare that also has to do with mana, tapu, hau, and utu, and all forms of religious and mystical life that is centrally connected to these ideas. For a parallel example, I know of informants who would interpret the current brutal civil war in Sri Lanka in terms of native Buddhist concepts, such a *karma*, *tanha* (greed), *samsara* (the cycle of existence), and so on, not surprising among a people who would interpret existence itself in these terms. And others (or even the same person) might employ a different set of emic terms, derived from the past history of nationalism, yet others would employ other emic viewpoints. But interpreting the ethnic conflict in such terms is to me a travesty of sociological interpretation that needs theoretical terms from the human sciences to deal with the socioeconomic and political (even global) power plays involved. We might be dissatisfied with theoretical terms and might want to invent new ones, but that is how theoretical development must need to occur. With emics it is as if a people are imprisoned in the terms that are handed down from "tradition." I am not for a moment suggesting that these terms are not important, rather that they cannot be applied uncritically to bits and pieces of ethnography that one encounters in travel texts in order to produce a coherent whole.

Moreover, I doubt that these concepts could be applied to "traditional" Maori life either, without their sophisticated grounding in social and political action. For example, mana is handed down genealogically with "greater proportions going to first born children." Yet, "since *mana* could only be validated with results, maintaining high status required repetitive demonstrations" and "could be gained or lost by individuals."[15] One needs chunks of "traditional" Maori discourse in order to see the complexity of these terms and their usages in multiple contexts. Few such discourses exist, except texts and histories collected from Maori by European antiquarians in the mid- and late nineteenth century. Even if these texts have been recorded with reasonable accuracy I doubt that one can use them in relation to present events. Thus John White's collection of Maori texts has references to cannibalism, but there are even more references to cannibalism in European texts. I can show ghastly anthropophagous practices recorded in Buddhist texts, including forcing people to eat their own flesh.[16] In as much as one cannot use such cannibal texts to demonstrate the prevalence of anthropophagy in Europe (or for that matter the prevalence of shipwreck anthropophagy) or in Buddhist societies (except as fantasy) it would not do for us to adopt a different procedure in respect of Maori mythic texts without adopting a double standard. Cultures are not static entities and one cannot apply so-called emic terms to the world of becoming, though they might apply to the socially constructed mythic world of Maori Being.

One can put the argument differently. It seems to me that the use of "emics" is an easy interpretive task but a mistaken one because it implies the inflexibility of "culture," the worlds of meaning in which we live. My adaptation of the Weberian view of culture implies that culture is mediated through consciousness, and cultural meanings must change when life changes or the world around us changes. This is not to deny the remarkable persistence of cultural ideas, for example, that of radical good and evil in Western discourse or of karma and rebirth in the Buddhist world, but even these structures of the long run are embedded in larger universes of meaning that change through history. My position implies that concepts change and traditions are not static but are being invented and reinvented, ignored, or deemed irrelevant or simply discarded and that even stable concepts of the long run might have new or additional epistemic or other contents poured into them.

In this book I show that the opening of the Maori world to European colonial power had drastic effects on their traditional worldview and that ideas of tapu and so forth were being eroded. I have sketched this context earlier in this work, and I shall do it in more detail as we note how the century progressed and one moved into the early and mid-1800s. Salmond herself recognizes this but does not deal with it theoretically. "People had died from venereal disease and shootings, and pigs, chickens, goats and rats had been introduced, as well as a variety of European plants. Women had been used in sexual barter; children had been conceived and born [to Europeans]; iron, Tahitian and European cloth and other European items had been obtained; and there had been numerous outbreaks of violence. . . .

Totara-nui people [of Queen Charlotte Sound] had to accept that there was a new kind of tangata (human being) in the landscape, whose behavior was difficult to fathom. Life in the Sound would never be the same" (*BW*, 145). In such a context of radical change could traditional concepts such as utu, mana, tapu, hau, and so forth remain intact? And can one make assertions of this sort: "Cannibalism among the Maori was not arbitrary, but a devastating act of retribution. Where there had been hara, or offences against mana, there had to be utu (or some kind of return). If the return gesture brought matters back into balance, the sequence of exchanges could terminate" (*BW*, 144).

I suggest that there is no warrant for such assertions in relation to the death of Marion (or to the events at Grass Cove); there are no texts that can substantiate them and no evidence either, though, I will admit it does sound "emically" plausible. Moreover some of these terms, if translated, could as easily apply to the French retaliatory action. Or again, "The illnesses brought by Europeans to Totara-nui were understood as spiritual attacks, caused by the strangers' ancestor gods. In the case of venereal disease, and perhaps tuberculosis and other diseases that may have been transferred, they attacked others with whom the victim had intimate relations, leading to a series of hara associated with the victors" (*BW*, 144).

There are several problems with this level of interpretation: first, it is the ethnographer who acts as the stand-in for the native and makes the interpretation; second, the native is confronted with some sudden and unprecedented disaster, but unlike us he does not exhibit any puzzlement and try out multiple interpretations as we would do. Lastly, while the preceding quotation might indicate one possible native interpretation of illness it ignores the natives' ability to grasp, however vaguely, the emerging historical threat of European settlement, conquest, and colonialism.

Now let me further criticize the use of native terms to explain or understand native cultural anthropophagy. In other Polynesian societies like Hawai'i, Tonga, and Tahiti where tapu is also strong, no massive consumption of the enemy took place. Salmond cannot explain this difference. Further, indigenous concepts are filtered through the consciousness and the perspectival approaches of the Western reporter. Therefore such terms are embedded in Western discourses of ethnography or history or antiquarianism; they are not native discourses for the most part and though the *terms* are obviously native they are filtered through the "prejudices" of the investigator. Further, a Marxist analysis might rightly point out that these terms hide the class tensions and other contradictions in the society. For example, one does not know the feelings and reactions of ordinary people who have to observe tapus and respect the mana of chiefs they had to serve and for whom sometimes they have to give their lives. From an "emic" point of view the victim of the sacrifice, whether willing or unwilling, helps the culture to perpetuate itself through its rituals. Any notion of class or other forms of conflict are hidden in the attributed discourse of the native aristocratic male. It is not surprising that those who deal with the Maori from the so-called native's point of view tend to ignore a whole class of native men and women in a subaltern status.

CANNIBALISM AND HUMAN SACRIFICE: AN ALTERNATIVE VIEW OF POLYNESIAN ANTHROPOPHAGY

Most serious scholars of the Pacific would not deny that Maori anthropophagy must be understood as human sacrifice, known in many parts of the world including Polynesia. But what scholars cannot account for is the mass consumption of the Other, beginning with the Europeans, that does not dovetail with serious cross-cultural records of human sacrifice. While the archaeological record does provide some evidence for mass consumption of human beings in the Southwest of North America for example, there is no way to figure out whether this was due to starvation, protein deficiency, or whatever. Archaeology simply confirms the fact, obvious to me, that under certain conditions (pathology, starvation, even as sacrificial victims) human beings might well consume other humans. But neither starvation, nor pathology, nor human sacrifice can help us understand the death of Marion and members of his crew and the events in Grass Cove. Perhaps one way out of this dilemma is to move out of New Zealand and deal with the empirical evidence for human sacrifice in other parts of Polynesia.

My example is from Cook's account of a human sacrifice he witnessed in Tahiti nui where Chief Tu, the friend and ally of Cook, was preparing to invade Eimeo, the neighboring island. I have described this conflict in my book on Captain Cook; suffice it here to say that Cook wanted to witness a human sacrifice during his previous visit but he now had a chance to see one with a few select officers who were on a par with native chiefs and therefore permitted in the sacrificial arena (see figure 4).[17] Cook is at his descriptive best here, and I will quote him at length to give the reader the feel of his prose.

This was in the year 1777 before Cook's fateful final visit to the Hawaiian Islands. His Tahitian friends sought Cook's assistance in the war and some were disappointed when he refused. On the morning of September 1, Towha (Tahua) sent a message to Tu that "he had killed a Man to be sacrificed to the Eatua, to

FIGURE 4
A human sacrifice in Tahiti. From James Cook, *A Voyage to the Pacific Ocean* (1784). Courtesy of the Rare Books Division, The New York Public Library, Astor, Lenox, and Tilden Foundations.

implore the assistance of the God against Eimeo. This was to be done at the great Morai at Attahourou, where on this occasion Otoo's [Tu's] presence was absolutely necessary" (*Cook B 3a*, 198–99).[18] Here was an opportunity to see this "extraordinary and Barbarous custom" and with Tu's consent Cook, accompanied by Anderson, the artist Webber, and the interpreter Mai, went to the *marae*, or Polynesian ceremonial center, where the ritual was to take place (*Cook B 3a*, 199). Cook ordered the ordinary seamen in the canoe to wait for them. There were many men near the marae but no women as they are not normally permitted in the sacrificial setting in accordance with general Polynesian practice. The sacrificial victim was laid in a canoe in front of the marae and partly on the beach with two priests and their attendants sitting by it. Cook's company was at Tu's "station" about twenty or thirty paces from the priests while most ordinary people were further away. An attendant brought a young plantain tree and placed it before Tu while another placed a small bunch of red feathers (a precious item in these parts) and touched Tu's feet with it and then retired with his companions to the smaller marae nearby and sat down facing the main spectacle. I take it that the plantain is a symbolic replacement of the victim. Another priest uttered a long invocation ("prayer") and at various points of the utterance he placed a small plantain tree on the victim that Beaglehole rightly thinks symbolically represented other potential or possible victims in order to increase the scale of the sacrifice (*Cook B 3a*, 200, n. 2). Now let Cook himself speak:

> During this prayer a man who stood by the Priest held in his hands two small bundles seemingly of Cloth, in one as we afterwards found, was the Royal Maro [*malo,* cloak] and the other, if I may be allowed the expression, was the ark of the Eatua [*atua*]. As soon as this prayer was ended the Priests at the Morais with their attendants went and sat down by those on the beach, carrying with them the two bundles. Here they renewed their prayers during which the Plantain trees were taken one by one at different times from off the Sacrifice, which was partly wraped *[sic]* up in leaves and small branches. It was laid on the beach with the feet next the Sea round which the Priests place'd themselves, some seting and others standing, and one or more of them prayed Continually, holding in their hands small tufts of red feathers. After some time the Sacrifice was striped of the leaves etc and laid in a parallel direction with the Sea shore, one of the Priests stood at the feet and pronounced a long prayer, in which he was at times joined by the others, each holding in his hand a tuft of red feathers. *In the Course of this prayer some hair was pulled off the head of the Sacrifice one of the eyes taken out and present[ed] wraped in a green leafe, to Otoo [Tu], who however did not touch it, but gave it to the Man who presented it the tuft of feathers he got from T'towha [Tahua], which with the hair and eye was carred [sic] back to the priests.* [My italics.] Soon after Otoo sent a nother piece of feathers he had given me in the Morning to keep in my pocket. During some part of this last ceremony a Kings fisher [kingfisher, a sacred symbol and the vehicle of the god Oro] made a noise in the trees, Otoo turned to me and said, "thats the Eatua [*atua*]" and seem'd to look upon it as a good omen.
>
> The Sacrifice was now carried to the foot of one of the small Morais [*marae*] before mentioned and laid down with the head towards it; the bundles of cloth were laid on the Morai and the tufts of red feathers were placed at the feet of the Sacrifice, round which the Priests placed themselves and we were now allowed to go as near as we pleased. The Chief priest made a set speech or prayer, than [then] addressed the Sacrifice (into which the Spirit of the Eatua was entered) in a nother, the subject of this Speech or rather prayer, was to implore the distruction of their Enem[i]es whom he mentioned several times by name. After this they all prayed in a kind of song in which Potattow [Poatatu, another chief] and some others joined; in the Course of this prayer a nother piece of hair was pulled of and laid on the Morai. After this the Chief Priest p[r]ayed alone holding in his hand the feather which came from T'towha; and when he had done he gave them to a nother who p[r]ayed in like manner, then

all the tufts of feathers were laid on the bundles of Cloth which ended the ceremony at this place. They now took the bundles the feathers and the Sacrifice to the great Morai, the two first were laid against the pile of Stones, and the foot of them the latter was placed round which the Priests Seated themselves and began again their prayers, while some of their attendants dug a hole at the foot of the Morai in which they burryed the Victim. As it was puting into the Grave a boy [possessed] squeaked out aloud, Omai said it was the Eatua. In the Mean time a fire was made, the Dog before mentioned produced and killed, the hair was got off by holding over the fire, the entrails taken out and thrown into the fire where they were left to consume; the hart liver kidnies etc were laid on the hot stones for a few Minutes and the blood was collected into a Cocoanut shell and afterward rubed over the dog which was held over the fire for about a Minute, then it together with the heart kidnies etc were carried and laid down before the Priests who were seting round the foot of the grave praying, and which they continued over the dog for some time, while two men beat at times on two drums very loud, and a [possessed] boy sqeaked out as before in a long shrill voice thrice, and this as we were told was to call the Eatua to eat of what they had prepared for him. (*Cook B 3a*, 201–2)[19]

The conclusion of the ritual was on the next day, but for present purposes this is not germane. It is interesting to note though that the sacrificial victim was a middle-aged man of little social standing, who had "been privatly knocked on the head with a Stone, for those who fall a sacrifice to this barbarous custom are never apprised of their fate till the Moment that puts an end to their existence." This apparently is true of most of Polynesia. Cook also mentions that human sacrifices were not uncommon because on the face of the marae were forty-nine skulls "every one of which were those of men who had been sacrificed at this place; and I have seen Sculls at many of the other great Morai, so that it is not confined to this place alone" (*Cook B 3a*, 204). Cook then speculates that this shows the prior history of cannibalism, an argument that Beaglehole, among others, seem to concur with because it "was a fairly widespread Polynesian trait in Cook's time . . . [and] the ceremonial presentation of the sacrificial victim's eye to Tu, the *arii rahi*, was a relic of this, though the time seems to have long passed since the chief actually ate it" (*Cook B 3a*, 204, n. 1). But no writer can provide us with a reason why the older practice was abandoned unless one postulates some notion of "civilizational" or ethical development in Tahiti. We also know from the classic work of Valerio Valeri that the Hawaiian sacrifice was similar to that of the Tahitians but the eye of the sacrificial victim is actually taken up by Kahōāli'i, a close relative and stand-in for the king and along with the eye of *aku* (bonito, skipjack) is actually eaten. The eye, Valeri argues, represents the human victim himself, owing to the principle of similarity and the life principle itself, something we know from Indic cultures also where a statue comes "alive" only when the eye has been laid on it.[20]

While Beaglehole's evolutionary hypothesis is possible, it is also reasonable to suppose that there were several variations in human sacrifice in this region and one form of it—such as the Maori and the Fijian—entailed the actual ritual consumption of the flesh of the victim whereas in Tahiti the eye was offered to the god but not consumed by humans. Except for the eye, the victim is not mutilated. Instead a dog is killed, disemboweled, and symbolically cooked by being held over a fire briefly. The heart, kidneys, and organs of the dog are also symbolically cooked by being placed on hot stones and then placed before the priests who then offer them to the god. This indicates I think that the dog is a close stand-in for the sacrificial victim and the offering of the dog's organs to the priests and then to the god suggests that the human sacrificial victim must be offered whole whereas the substitute dog could be mutilated and its organs removed as an offering. The taboo on eating the flesh of the victim is so strong that the flesh of the stand-in dog is also not eaten, in spite of the Tahitian partiality for dog's flesh. Cook reports that when the rituals were continued the next day a pig was killed, disemboweled, and laid before the priests and then to the god "very much as the dog was the day before" (*Cook B 3a*, 203). In Fiji and in New Zealand it seems that the organs of the sacrificial victim are ritually consumed.

Further, contrary to Cook, the existence of large number of skulls simply indicates the accumulated sacrifices over a long time and not its commonness, because even on this important occasion only one human was sacrificed while the banana trees symbolically represented others. Sometimes, "a long banana shoot, *ta'ata-o-meia-roa* [man-long-banana], was offered on ordinary occasions as a substitute for a human being," but no mass sacrifices have been recorded for Tahiti.[21] Even if one grants that in some parts of Polynesia, such as among some Maori and Fijians, select chiefs and priests ate portions of the sacrifice, following the animal sacrificial model, mass anthropophagy was not likely to have been part of the sacrificial complex until the arrival of the white voyagers along with the threats and practices of violence and the ever-increasing possibility of colonization.

Even later evidence from this region during and after the incursions of Europeans suggests that mass consumption of human beings simply did not exist, as Ian Barber convincingly demonstrates for precontact Maori.[22] R. W. Williamson, an early anthropologist summarizes this evidence: "Sacrifices to the gods, and particularly human sacrifices, were frequently associated with Polynesian warfare. Generally these were victims of battle who were subsequently offered to the gods, but sometimes the sacrifice of human victims formed part of the ceremonies preliminary to war."[23] All his examples are from colonial texts and are not always reliable, but even with this proviso mass anthropophagy was not associated with the sacrifice, at least according to Williamson.[24] As with both Maori and Fiji, in Tahiti also the key institution was human sacrifice performed on multiple occasions for propitiating the god Oro.[25] Additionally, apparently children were also sacrificed, a phenomenon known in other cultures also.

The Tongan case is extremely interesting: there is no reference to sacrificial anthropophagy in Tonga in Cook's time, but Polynesian ethnographers, including Williamson, note that it was introduced from Fiji in the early nineteenth century, though recent evidence suggests that, while Tongans did not practice human sacrifice in as grand a scale as Tahiti, it was also a key institution here.[26] But here also the discourse on the sacrifice was converted into the discourse on cannibalism. The evidence is provided by William Mariner, the clerk of an English privateer *Port au Prince*, captured and plundered by the Tongans and some of the crew killed by them. Mariner, a boy of fifteen, was naturally afraid that he would "killed and roasted" by the Tongans, and I have no doubt that this typical cannibal fear, provoked by the noncannibal Tongans miming cannibalism, colored his later accounts of Tongan cannibalism.[27] Mariner was adopted by Chief Finau and soon became his adopted son and trusted confidant for a period of four years beginning November 1806, the date of the capture of the ship. Although one cannot take the youthful Mariner at face value, I find him one of the better and more sympathetic though unsentimental observers of Polynesian culture, warfare, and social organization.

For the Tongans, according to Mariner, the prime example of cannibalism is Fiji, something that Cook also noted much earlier. Without being aware of its significance, Mariner notes the Tongan's obsessive fear of Fijian cannibalism: Fiji was the cannibal island for them also. Indeed, everything anti-Tongan is attributed to Fiji, so that Tongans believed, as Mariner did, that violent warfare was also a Fijian aberration that Tongans learned, and so was treachery. It seems to me that Fiji became a kind of projective field for the dangerous emotions of the Tongans and their justification, much like the situation with the Arawaks and the Caribs, and Cook seems to concur with this.[28] Thus a Tongan chief who lived in Fiji for some time told Mariner about an expedition from one Fijian island to another and the victorious side brought forth "two hundred human bodies, two hundred hogs, two hundred baskets of yams, and a like number of fowls" which was offered to the gods and then to the chiefs who distributed the viands to their followers." "[E]very man and woman in the island had a share of each of these articles, whether they chose to eat them or not."[29] But Mariner notes that his informant was given to exaggeration, not only of the size of Fijian islands but also of a strange reptilian monster that lived on one of them.

More interesting is Mariner's account of a few Tongans who on two occasions ate human flesh, inspired according to him, by the Fijian example.

The first occasion was a war in which Mariner himself participated against another Tongan group and during which they captured fifteen prisoners. "[S]ome of the younger chiefs who had contracted the Fijian habits, proposed to kill the prisoners" because they thought it a warlike custom and also because the garrison as a whole was without adequate food.[30] They killed some of the prisoners, but Mariner himself desisted from eating though he said "the smell of it, when cooked, was extremely delicious."[31] And a few days later Mariner who had not eaten anything for two days resisted eating a piece of liver that was given to him. More plausibly Mariner mentions that the original motivation for anthropophagy was not just learning the habit from Fiji but that there was a famine "which rendered the expedient for a time almost necessary."[32] He mentions several stories of people who were compelled to eat human flesh during this period.

The second case is much more interesting. This was also a war in which Mariner participated. Sixty enemies were killed, and the bodies "were shared out to the different gods that had houses dedicated to them within the place."[33] Mariner describes the ritual involved whereby the bodies were offered to the gods. Most were buried except for nine or ten corpses disposed of differently: two or three were hung up on a tree, a couple were burned, and three were dissected. However, "two or three were cut up to be cooked and eaten, of which about forty men partook."[34] Interestingly, Mariner insisted that "natives of these islands are not to be called cannibals on this account," because it was only done by young warriors in imitation of Fiji. When these warriors returned home, people, especially women, avoided them saying, "Away! You are a man-eater."[35]

Even if one accepts Mariner's account as factually true what we have here is a minority practice and a culturally condemned one. Mariner says he was a witness to these events, but one must qualify this statement because often enough statements by "reliable" informants are taken as "truth" even by modern ethnographers. But Mariner was not a modern ethnographer and moreover his account was dictated to Dr. John Martin who in fact wrote the two volumes. Mariner left England as a youth of fourteen and was fifteen years old when he arrived in Tonga and sixteen when he went to war and witnessed the second cannibal episode. At age fifteen he even gives advice to Chief Finau on how to conduct warfare![36] When he was interviewed by Dr. Martin he was only twenty. Though I doubt he is a deliberate liar, it is not improbable that Mariner claimed to have seen what another eyewitness claimed to have seen or heard, or that Dr. Martin, pandering to British tastes, introduced or elaborated or reinvented Mariner's accounts of cannibalism. The second account of forty younger chiefs eating the cooked corpses certainly seems an exaggeration formulated by Mariner and Martin for the edification of the British public because it is hard to believe that such a large body of people would engage in a practice condemned by the people and the king. In any case Mariner does not explain why most of the bodies were buried and the others disposed of in the most unusual manner.[37] And it is hard to believe that traditional warfare produced sixty corpses. Tongans were not cannibals; the most one can say is that a few of them learned this nasty habit from the Fijians. But how nasty the Fijians were will be explored in later chapters.

FOUR · Savage Indignation

Cannibalism and the Parodic

To be gnaw'd out of our graves, for our sculs made drinking-bowls, and our bones turned into Pipes, to delight and sport our Enemies, are Tragicall abominations, escaped in burning Burials [cremations].

SIR THOMAS BROWNE, *Urne-Burial* [1658]

PARODY AND PERFORMANCE

In several of the discourses mentioned in the previous chapters it seems that what is parody for the Maori is deadly serious for his Other, the European.[1] Sometimes the humor is shared by both sides as in the second voyage when Cook reported of his curio-hungry sailors: "It was astonishing to see with what eagerness everyone catched at every thing they saw, it even went so far as to become the ridicule of the Natives by offering pieces of sticks stones and what not to exchange, one waggish Boy took a piece of human excrement on a stick and hild *[sic]* it out to every one of our people he met with" (*Cook B 2*, 255). Surely the parody of the European passion for curiosities as a piece of shit would be shared by those on both sides of the cultural divide, temporarily blurring that very divide. In most of these situations parody also becomes a way of dealing with a troubling or incomprehensible situation, for Maori in their dealings with powerful Europeans and for Europeans in their attempts to understand the savage. Specific parodic enactments have already been documented by us, but complex performances are difficult to recover because they appear mostly in European accounts that then have to be imaginatively reconstructed.

Reinhold Forster mentions that among "the liberal and polite arts" of Tahiti were their "dramatic performances, blended with dances and songs" dealing with the "common occurrences of life."[2] In September 1773 during his second voyage Cook and company were in Huahine, one of the Tahitian islands familiar to them, and from thence to Raiatea whose Chief Rio "expressed much satisfaction at seeing me again." In typical Polynesian fashion, they exchanged names, Cook being called Rio and Rio called "Toote" (that is, Cook). In the afternoon the chief entertained Cook and his crew to a comedy, such as "usually acted in the Isles" (*Cook B 2*, 223). Cook noted that it was similar but not identical to one acted in Tahiti-nui earlier. There Cook said that his name was uttered in the course of the performance, but he could not grasp its significance. Neither does Burney, who had a slightly more detailed but an equally uncomprehending account of this farce.[3] "The only entertaining part in it was a Thift committed by a man and his accomplice, this was done in such a manner as sufficiently desplayed the Genius of the people in this art. The Thift was discovered before the thief had time to carry of his prize and a scuffle essued betweeen him his accomplice and those set to guard it and altho' they were four to two they were beat off the Stage and the others carried off their prise in triumph" (*Cook B 2*, 224). Cook was disappointed with the plays because the thieves seem to have gotten away with their ill-gotten gains in very un-British fashion. Both Forster and Cook were wrong that this farce and others dealt with everyday life because thieving was not a "common occurrence" there until the arrival of the European.

> I was very attentive to the whole of this part in expectation that it would have had a quite different end, for I had before been told that Teto, that is the thief, was to be acted and had understood that the Theift was to be punished with death or with a good Tiparrahying (beating) but I found my self misstaken in both. We are however told that this is the punishment they inflict on those who are guilty of this crime, be this as it may strangers certainly have not the Protection of this Law, them they rob with impunity at every oppertunity. (*Cook B 2*, 224)

No one seemed to realize that this play was in all likelihood a satire on the British presence that tempted Polynesians to steal. The culprits' getting away is a comic enactment that tried to handle the problems that arose from their propensity to steal from the British and the latter's punitive reaction. Beating and death were not Tahitian punishments for "theft," but both practices were common enough with Cook as far as Polynesians were concerned. The hypothesis that these impromptu farces commented on the European presence can be confirmed when we examine a similar play enacted in Huahine followed by one in Raiatea during another of Cook's visit to these islands during May–June 1774.

The context is as follows: a young attractive woman from Raiatea who had fled to Tahiti was given a passage back home in Cook's ship. The people of Huahine performed a cruel farce dramatizing this incident.

> The Piece represented a Girl as running away with us from Otaheiti [Tahiti] and which was in some degree true as a young Woman had taken a passage with us down to Ulietea [Raiatea] and happened to be now present at the Representation of her own adventures which had such an effect upon her that it was with great difficilty that our gentlemen could prevail upon her to see the play out or to refrain from tears while it was acting. The Piece concluded with the reception she was supposed to meet with from her friends at her return which was not a very favourable one. (*Cook B 2*, 413)

Reinhold Forster mentions that the farce though "rudely performed" was designed to "put the girl to shame, and drew tears from her eyes," which was good thing, he thought, because it provided an exemplary example to others.[4] Although this might be the case the immediate context suggests that she incurred this cruel and hostile reaction because she was in the dubious company of British seamen.

The theme of cohabitation with whites was expressed in a play enacted eight days later in Raiatea and noted by Wales in another uncomprehending account.

> The Concluding Piece, they called *Mydiddee Arramy.* Which I do know not how to translate better than *The Child-Coming.* The part of the Woman in Labour was performed by a large brawny Man with a great black bushy beard, which was ludicrous enough. He sat on the ground with his legs straight out, between the legs of another who sat behind him and held the *labouring man's* back hard against his own breast. A large white Cloth was spread over both which was carefully kept close down to the Ground on every side by others who kneeled round them. The farce was carried on for a considerable time with a great many wrigglings and twistings of the body, and Exclamations of *Away! Away! Away! to perea!* (which I dare not translate) untill at length, after a more violent than ordinary struggle out crawled a great lubberly fellow from under the Cloth, and ran across the place between the Audience and Actors, and the *he-Mother* stradling after, squeezing his breasts between his fingers and dabing them across the youngsters Chaps, and every now and then to heighten the relish of the entertainment mistooke and stroaked them up his backside. On the whole it was conducted with decency enough for a Male Audience, had not Mididdee dragged a great wisp of straw after him which hung by a long string from his Middle. The Women did not however retire even from this

part of the Entertainment, or even turn their faces but sat with as demure a Gravity as Judges are said to do when hearing baudy Causes. I asked some who sat around me why they also did not laugh as I did and one of them replied '*Mididdee tooatooy*,' the aptitude of which expression pleased me as much the Entertainment itself, because the latter word has exactly the same meaning and is applied in the same manner as the word *Impotent* is with us.[5]

I might add that the "demure reaction" of females to male bawdiness during ritual dramas is similar in Sri Lanka; it is the expected modest female reaction and has nothing to do with whether they enjoyed the show. "Mididdee" taking on the role of an impotent man might well be a reference to Cook himself, who Elliot says "never had connection with any of our fair ladies: I have often seen them jeer and laugh at him, calling him Old, and good for nothing [impotent]" (*Cook B 2*, 444, n. 2).[6]

Cook noted an interesting detail in this farce in a repeat performance he witnessed later on. "I had an oppertunity to see this acted another time when I observed, that the moment they got hold of the fellow, who represented the Child they f[l]atned his nose or press'd it to his face which may be a Custom a Mong */sic/* them and be the reason why they have in general flat, or what we call pug noses" (*Cook B 2*, 420).

If we reject Cook's hypothesis that Polynesian noses are the result of their child-training practices, an alternative interpretation almost forces itself on us. Polynesians do mould their children and in Hawai'i, for example, "bodily defects that could be corrected were treated in infancy, childhood, and adolescence" through systematic massaging.[7] But that Tahitians have to enact a birth of a child seems quite unlikely since such events are perfectly normal and do not require satiric representation—unless there was an abnormality involved. I think this farce relates to British sexual liaisons during their first voyage (and previous to that in Wallis's and Bouganville's) that produced babies with un-Polynesian noses. These anomalous protuberances are then made fun of and "converted" to normal Polynesian with flattening. It should be remembered that the British thought that Tahitians were close to them in physique and color (at least aristocrats), except in respect of their noses. The Tahitians might well have been aware of this prejudice because these discussions were quite open, sometimes given to tactile probing of skin and body parts. More obviously, it seems to me, that simple observation must force Tahitians to notice this physiological difference between "them and us." Either way what is being parodied is the fact of Polynesian women giving birth to children fathered by Europeans, and the babies consequently inheriting the father's nose, because, according to Tahitian notions of conception the child will resemble the father in physical appearance.[8]

Nevertheless, this farce underlies a more complicated and somewhat sad reality for Tahitians. Remember that Tahitians permitted relatively free intercourse with Europeans; hence, one might ask why they should be especially concerned about the physiology of their offspring. But they did. Practical rationality not only forced them to notice physiological changes in their offspring, but they were also compelled to confront the implications of these changes for the physical integrity of their children. The anxieties that result from this developing awareness are dealt with parodically. They are also on occasion expressed more directly as George Hamilton's rather insensitive yet revealing comments indicate while he was serving as surgeon on the H. M. S. *Pandora:* "After telling that he had enjoyed the sexual favors of a chief's wife, upon invitation of her husband, Hamilton added that the latter '. . . was a domesticated man, and passionately fond of his wife and children, but now became pensive and melancholy, dreading that the child should be Piebald; though the lady was advanced in pregnancy before we came to the island.'"[9] This funny and sad statement also implied that the Tahitians like many other native peoples believed that sexual intercourse, even after pregnancy was established, could affect fetal formation. Given the anxieties created by these social and intrauterine complications, it is not surprising that "plays have indeed generally been acted every day sence *[sic]* we have been here either to entertain us or for their own amusement" (*Cook B* 2, 227).

BATTLEFIELD CANNIBALISM: A MAORI WAR SONG

We brought away from battle
And much their land bemoaned them
Two thousand head of cattle
And the head of him who owned them
Endyfed, King of Dyfed,
His head was borne before us
His wine and beasts supplied our feasts
And his overthrow our chorus.

THOMAS LOVE PEACOCK,
"The War Song of Dinas Vawr"

A more complex instance of the European failure to understand parodic utterances comes from Percy Smith's *Maori Wars of the Nineteenth Century.* It is an eyewitness account of a Nga-Puhi war party led by two redoubtable chiefs, Atu-One (Patuone) and Te Rauparaha in 1819–20.[10] This account is different from the many "tribal histories" that Smith reports in that work. Without entering into the question of the historical validity of Smith's work, the present narrative is couched in the first person, unlike most narratives that deal with intertribal warfare. In the latter it is the viewpoint of a particular group that is expressed in the narrative. Additionally, the present narrative contains the most detailed and graphic account of "battlefield cannibalism" reported for the Maori (or perhaps for any Polynesian group) by the natives themselves.

According to Percy Smith, this history was written by a Maori who took part in the expedition. The document eventually found its way into Mr. John White's collection of manuscripts. More likely it was spoken by a Maori and written down by a white folklorist or antiquarian. Smith says that the author's name isn't given; there is also "an absence of names of places and people" (*MW*, 96). He concludes that the reason is the author's fear of the enmity of the people who suffered so terribly during the attack—a quite un-Maori-like attitude. I shall show that there are good reasons for these omissions.

The particular expedition was undertaken by a branch of the Nga-Puhi tribes located in Hokianga, diametrically west of the Bay of Islands. These people joined with some of their "ancient enemies" to make war on other tribes, an alliance that Smith does not explain. They left Hokianga in November 1819 and came back a year later in October 1820, according to Smith. Our anonymous Maori gives the following "tribal history." The Hokianga (Nga-Puhi) fought battles with the tribes of the north and then came back to their homes. Then "after a while, we again felt a desire for man's flesh, and the idea was conceived that we should go on a campaign against the tribes of the South . . . to avenge the death of some of our people who had been killed by the Southern tribes on the occasion of a journey they made to procure mats in exchange for their Maori weapons" (*MW*, 97–98). It is very clear that this Maori is making a claim that the main motive for war was the "desire for man's flesh," no doubt disconfirming views of the sacrificial nature of Maori anthropophagy and adding fuel to varieties of later biological and nutritional hypotheses. Unless of course this was simply an idiomatic way of saying "we went to fight."

Our Maori historian gives an account of the rituals prior to war and then gives a graphic description of their first battle.

> So soon as the *karakia* and other ceremonies connected therewith were over, the *taua* [war party] arose, and at once proceeded on its journey. They went by way of the West Coast, along the beach towards Maunga-nui Bluff, and

> thence on to Kaipara, the mouth of which we crossed, and went our way, via Kumeu, to Te Whau, and as far as Wai-te-mata, where Auckland now stands. There we found a *taua* of Waikato encamped at Mata-harehare (St. George's Bay, Parnell), another at Puke-kawa (Auckland Domain), another at Wai-ariki (Official Bay, Auckland). We fell on these parties by surprise, and not a single one escaped. In the places where we killed them we cooked their bodies and ate them. It was in this wise: Our *taua* did not go in one body, but separated; one *hapu* going one way, one another, so that all these parties of Waikato were surprised at the same time and on the same day; and each *hapu* cooked and ate their own victims in the place where they were killed. This was the method we adopted—always to move silently along, taking cover where possible, and then to cook and eat all we caught. (*MW*, 99–100)

Now this is clear proof, one can argue, of "battlefield cannibalism." This Maori "historian" is documenting an important ethnological fact: the Nga-Puhi, if not all Maori, surprise the enemy, kill them, and "eat all we caught" (*MW*, 100). But something in this account isn't right: the exaggeration. We have no idea how such a destructive war was waged; not a single enemy escaped; no slaves or prisoners were taken and all were cooked and eaten in the very places they were killed. Moreover any ritualism is unthinkable for we are told earlier that the true motive for warfare is really lust for human flesh.

To continue our history: our unnamed Maori historian mentions that they journeyed south toward Te Whau where six of their spies caught a woman, then killed, cooked, and ate her. Thereafter:

> When we descended to the cultivations of Waikato (at Onehunga?) a girl was seen by some of our people lying hiding near there beneath a row of reeds. So we pulled her out, stark naked as she was, and killed her. She did not attempt to ward off the blows that were aimed at her, but placed her hands in front of her as a *maro*, or waist cloth, so that her front should not be seen. I thought, "Here is a people with whom shame is greater that fear of death"—since this girl did not use her hands to defend herself from the weapons, but as a *maro*. She was of high descent (*uri-ariki)* and *kotiro ata-ahua* (a handsome girl). When she was dead, Tarau, of Waihou (Hokianga) seized her legs and thighs, and taking her feet in his hands and using her legs as walking-sticks, proceeded thus to the ovens.
>
> None of our chiefs would cook food during the expedition, nor would they go near, or sit on the leeward side of food in preparation, for fear their *tapu*

should be interfered with. The ovens in which the bodies were cooked were left covered over night until morning, so that the food might be soft and pulpy. The body of the girl referred to was brought to our camp, and cooked for a long time *(tamoe)* that it might be nicely done. (*MW*, 100–1)

The exaggeration has taken on the quality of surreal improbability. The chief gets hold of this coy girl's feet as "walking sticks" and proceeds to the ovens, when, by the same account, no chief is supposed to do this! It is at this point in my reading that I began to suspect a spoof. Maori are wonderful raconteurs by all accounts, and we are already familiar with their cannibal spoofs from Cook's journals. Further, both on and off the battlefield, they are given to humiliating or taunting the enemy. This propensity for taunting can be creatively transformed into satire through storytelling. The preceding story is not unlike Swift's deadpan mode of narrative presentation in *A Modest Proposal*. And while the Maori narrative is not the equivalent of Swift's self-conscious work of art, it also possesses Swift's "cheeky outrageousness."[11] Consider the wonderful exaggeration of our Maori historian: the naked aristocratic girl taking those cruel blows and only concerned with covering her vagina with her hands, and the bizarre, even fantastic, account of the chief using the dead woman's legs indicates that our raconteur is, to continue the same metaphor, pulling the legs of his white listener, by parodying the latter's view that Maori's use of body parts for "implements." Moreover, a "walking stick" is a part of missionary attire that might have struck the native as decidedly odd. If I am right, then the last part of the preceding account also has to be understood in similar terms: the native is giving back to his English-speaking listener cum interlocutor the very idioms by which the European has represented Maori cannibalism. Thus the bodies have to be made "soft and pulpy"; the woman's body has to be cooked for a long time "that it might be nicely done." This is not Maori discourse per se; it is a Maori parodying the British discourse on cannibalism. It is possible that there was some kind of Nga-Puhi expedition southward in 1819–20, but this account was narrated much later, after white settlers arrived and had further developed their own discourses on Maori cannibalism.

We must now attempt to reconstruct imaginatively the minimal context in which this kind of satiric discourse might have occurred. An amateur historian or ethnographer (such as John White) is interviewing a native historian. The interview focuses on Maori warfare and battlefield cannibalism. European ideas about both are already prestructured: the Maori kill their enemies because of a lust for human meat, and they engage in cannibal feasts where indiscriminate anthropophagy prevails. By this time European antiquarians in New Zealand were convinced that the bones of the enemy were used for flutes and other implements. It is most likely that the interviewer wanted explicit information on these savage practices. It would be senseless for a Maori to say "no." "No" cannot be taken for an answer because of the predefinition of Maori warfare and cannibalism. Thus one defensive strategy for the Maori narrator is to say "yes" to the expected reply but turn it on its head by a well-known narrative technique of parodic exaggeration presented with a dead-pan face. In this case part of the fun is to make the historian-ethnographer believe that this is an accurate account, while the Maori and his fellow citizens would laugh at its satiric quality through a variety of stylistic conventions pertaining to gestures, tonal nuances, and so forth. This is also one of the few ways available to "humiliate" the new settlers in their midst.

> As I sat intently watching the people of our camp, my slave came to me and said, "Some of our people have caught a man, and are preparing him for the oven." I ran off to see who it was, and to find out what the Waikato men were like. On the way I was speaking to a red-haired girl, who had just been caught out in the open. We were then just at the eastern side of Maunga-whau (Mount Eden). This girl had been caught at the stream called Te Ruareoreo. My companions remained with the girl whilst I went on to see the man of Waikato who had been killed. When I arrived they were preparing the flesh; the bones were to be put to other purposes. One of the men engaged on the bones was working on the knee-cap. I asked, "What is he doing?" I was told, "The knee-cap is for a pipe. This man was killed in revenge *(utu)*, and his leg bones will be made into flutes."
>
> As we came back, I saw the head of the red-haired girl lying in the fern by the side of the track, and, further on, we overtook one of the Waihou, Hokianga, men carrying a back-load of her flesh, which he was taking to our camp to cook for food; the arms of the girl were around his neck, whilst the body was on his back. Tahua, the son of Muriwai [(of Utakura, Hokianga), was out collecting food, and as he returned from Onehunga towards our camp at Mata-harehare (St. George's Bay) by the eastern side of Maungakiekie (One-Tree Hill) he saw in the Waikato cultivations some of the Nga-Puhi women collecting food. He called out, thinking they were Waikato women, at which they fled in fear.
>
> One of the reasons why we went on this expedition was because some Nga-Puhi people had been killed at Motu-tapu by Waikato. When Hongi-Hika heard of this he was very angry, and started down the east coast to obtain revenge, whilst our party came down the west coast from Hokianga.

[The narrator then goes on to describe an expedition of Hongi's into Waikato, which does not belong to this period at all, but occurred in 1825.] In one of the houses we saw the hands of some of the Nga-Puhi who had been killed by Waikato at Motu-tapu; they were fastened to the walls of the house, with the wrists upwards, and the fingers turned up as hooks on which to hang food baskets. The hands had been roasted in the fire till the outer skin came off. The palms were quite white inside. (*MW*, 101–3)

Once again the absurd elements give clues to the satiric nature of the narrative. The narrator asks his fellow clansman what he is doing with the knee cap. "I was told," he says, "the knee cap is for a pipe. This man was killed in revenge *(utu)*, and his leg bones will be used for a flute" (*MW*, 102). This is absurd as serious Maori discourse, because if all this is true our narrator should have known it in the first place. "I was told," is a frequently used phrase among Europeans reporting Maori customs and is therefore an exact replication of how a good ethnologist or antiquarian of the period, like Percy Smith himself or John White, will frame his discourse while interviewing natives. I suspect that this is one reason why the parodic nature of this narrative was not recognized by scholars. These satiric narratives strategically introduce an aura of plausibility so as not to give away the joke, such as the use of leg bones for flutes (which I believe was something foisted on the Maori but believed by virtually every European as true). But a knee cap for a pipe is way beyond even European fantasy. I am excluding the musical instrument referred to by Sir Thomas Browne in 1658 in the epigraph to this chapter and take the reference to mean the smoking instrument. Thus you have a judiciously ironic juxtaposition of the seemingly plausible (flutes) with the totally improbable (pipe).[12] A similar effect is created in the description of the dried hands of enemies "with the wrists upwards, and the fingers turned up as hooks on which to hang food baskets" (*MW*, 103). It is a double parody: first, it is believable to the inquirer (bones can be used in this way) but improbable to a Maori (not freshly roasted hands where only the outer skin was off and the palms "quite white inside"). Second, it parodies similar hook hangers used in missionary households for hanging clothes and umbrellas. The gruesomely fantastic reference to the "red-haired girl" could be a pun that can mean ochre-coated hair to the European inquirer, but a red-headed European for the Maori. "We were a long time at Wai-te-mata, and all the men (victims) that we killed there had been consumed; so we left and started towards Taranaki, that is, along the road to Waikato. Not having succeeded in getting canoes, we had to proceed overland, by the seashore of the west coast. We went by the mouth of the Waikato River. We had no reason for further man-killing, having satiated our revenge on those who had killed our people, nothing but the pleasure of so doing" (*MW*, 104).

At this point the Western scholar, Smith, interweaves his own comment into the "oral history" of the native. He says that the rest of the narrative deals with "the doings at Taranaki, Whanganiu-a-Tara (Port Nicholson) and Wairarapa [southern North Island]," and adds that "like most native histories" this account is also unsatisfactory since important details are omitted, such as the existence of the Ngati-Paoa tribe that was in full force in the vicinity of Taranaki or how the Nga-Puhi could have gone to Taranaki without passing Kaipara with whom they had been in constant warfare for twenty years! (*MW*, 104). But, of course, all these details are not necessary if the account is not "historical" in the first place. Indeed the inclusion of these details will be an embarrassment to the narrator, interfering with his spoof. Now that we know the genre, the foregoing paragraph is brilliant satire with its marvelous concluding comment on the European view of the cannibal.

> I will now relate our expedition to Taranaki, which was the third in which I took part. We had with us four guns. When we arrived before our enemies' *pa* our three marksmen went in front of the *taua*, and as soon as the enemy saw us they would recognize us as a *taua* and their braves would climb up into the towers *(puwhara)* so that they might be the better able to throw down stones at us. Those braves did not know of the gun, nor of its deadly effects. When they got up to the towers they would grimace and put out their tongues at us and dare us to come on to attack them. They thought that some of us would be killed by their stones. Whilst they grimaced away we used to fire at them. It was just like a pigeon falling out of a tree! When the others heard the noise, saw the smoke and the flash, and the death of their braves, they thought it must be the god Maru that accompanied us, and that it was by his power *(mana)* and the *tapu* of our *tohunga* that their braves were killed by the thunder of the god Maru. Then the whole *pa* would feel dispirited *(wiwi)* and stand without sense, so that we had only to assault the *pa* without any defence from the people. The people of the *pa* would have all the lamenting and we all the cheers *(huro)*. Those that we killed we ate; those saved we made slaves of. We used to stay in the *pas* we took in this manner to eat of "the fish of Tu," and nothing but the smell of the bodies made us draw on to another place.
>
> In this manner we passed through the Taranaki and Whanganui districts, and to Whangaehu and Manawatu and beyond that to Otaki, killing as we went. At Otaki we found a whale ashore, and much whale-bone was lying

> on the beach near Pae-kakariki. We obtained one whale there. Then we proceeded on to Porirua and Kapiti; at the former place we saw the Kotuku (white crane), and killed some of the people of that part (Ngati-Ira), but there were no *pas;* the people were found and killed in their cultivations. (As a matter of fact this tribe was not of a *pa* building people, [according to Smith]).
>
> Thus we proceeded along with the same eating of those whom we conquered, until we arrived at Te Whanganui-a-Tara (Port Nicholson). When we got there, starvation was our food. It was due to the number of slaves we took as we came along the West Coast to Te Whanganui-a-Tara (Port Nicholson), which we killed there, that we lived in that foodless place. Twenty five of my slaves were killed as food during our stay there. It was arranged that each chief should kill some of his slaves as food for all of Nga-Puhi. We remained at Te Whanganui-a-Tara until nearly all our slaves had been consumed. (*MW,* 106–7)

It is not necessary to analyze this text in any detail. There is the now expectable parody of the standard ethnological inquiry of the nineteenth century: the wonderful account of the "war dances" of the natives, and the grimacing warriors who are shot like pigeons (with four guns and by this time with endless ammunition). Naturally, all the slaves were eaten because the invaders were starving. Little did our narrator know that his, and accounts like his, would be used by later anthropologists to develop their theories of battlefield cannibalism. The actual situation among the Maori at this time was very different because, as I will demonstrate in chapter 5, slaves were a scarce commodity and not used as a food source.

The narrator continues, "When we were at Kare-kawa we saw a ship sailing out at sea, so we lit some fires on the peaks of the hills so that the ship might come towards us, but the ship took no notice of our signals. If it had come, none of the people of the ship would have been hurt *(rahua)* by us, and if they had asked us we should have replied our business there was manslaying" (*MW,* 107). The seemingly innocent reference to the white ship whose passengers of course *won't* be eaten but whose ethnographic curiosity would be more than satisfied when they are told that "[in] our business there was manslaying" is surely a sly dig both at the European inquirers and their fascination with cannibalism. Needless to say, here as elsewhere the satiric utterances were no doubt inextricably associated with speech acts and gestures that we simply cannot reconstruct.

> Whilst at Ponke we camped on the beach at Pipitea, but there were two parties of us, one of which stayed at Te Aro. A party from one of our camps went to

the West Coast to the sea of Rau-kawa (Cook Strait), and they were all killed by the people of the land, being surprised in the night. But they were the young people of our *taua* and were tired of the careful manner in which our old men acted, hence they camped apart from us. One of our chiefs went with his tribe to pursue those who had killed our people, taking with him his daughter, who was a virgin, and engaged to a man at Hokianga. That chief, his daughter and all his *hapu* were killed by the same people who killed our young fellows.

When we heard of that event he was already dead, and on hearing of the death of the others we decided to follow up and kill those people. They ate those of ours whom they had killed and then proceeded to another place, abandoning the *pa* and went to the east to Wairarapa. We crossed the Wai-o-rotu (Hutt River) by means of *mokihis* (rafts) and followed after that people for three days, and then we found them and gave battle to them. We conquered and took many slaves, with whom we returned to the place where our chief who has been speared lay, and there killed all the slaves as food for the mourners for the chief. So soon as the funeral obsequies were over the head of the dead chief was cut off and the body buried, whilst the head was preserved to be taken back to Nga-Puhi. Whilst the work of preserving the head was proceeding and before the skin had become hard through the action of the smoke, some of ours went and took some of the *nikau* (palm leaves) from the shed *(wharau)* belonging to the *tohunga* who was engaged on the preserving, to sleep on. In consequence we were afflicted with a disease, and out of our five hundred people of the *taua,* two hundred died through the accident. For this reason we removed to the mouth of the harbour on the east side. It was at that time that our great chiefs died of that disease, and their heads were preserved and the bodies burned lest the bones be taken by the enemy. Some of those who died had relatives with the *taua* and it was these who preserved the heads, but the younger brothers who died had no relatives with sufficient *mana* to cut off their heads, so their whole bodies were burnt in the fire. (*MW,* 108–10)

Note again the exaggeration that parodies the British discourse: *all* the slaves were killed to mourn the death of one chief. In these texts there are likely to be matters known only to the local speech community and cannot be recovered by us. This is true of the first part of the text quoted above. Parts however can be recovered through our historical knowledge. For example, a striking feature of this part of the story is the reference to a disease that killed two hundred people out of a total of five hundred. This item has been incorporated from an older myth known to both British and Maori where, at the end of the eighteenth century, an epidemic swept among the Maori, killing many thousands in the North Island and believed to be a consequence of eating the flesh of whites (Marion's or Furneaux's crew, according to European exegeses). All we know is that this story too has been incorporated into the present narrative.

In spite of this affliction and a loss of a major part of their force, they proceeded southward, killing more people in another unnamed group. Two entire weeks were spent in eating them. Then their slaves (who now have reappeared after their total extermination in the earlier paragraph) mention another pā all ready for the taking. On the way to this pā they came across a deserted village. One hundred of their group stayed there while the other hundred went up to the valley. This latter one hundred were surprised by the people of the pā; only ten escaped, the others were killed. But the Nga-Puhi had four guns and they quickly subjugated the pā since "every shot told" (*MW*, 112). Then follows the brilliant conclusion that starts off with a grisly "cannibal feast" and ends with a highly improbable and (to me) a funny scenario where three-hundred-and-fifty-plus enemies were neatly and symmetrically killed.

> So the people retreated and we followed until we all reached the *pa* belonging to them into which they had entered and our people with them. We then commenced killing them within the *pa* until we were tired of it, and the *pa* was full of dead bodies. Then were cooked the "fish of Tu."
>
> Three weeks we remained here feeding on the dead bodies, but could not eat them all; the rest we used only the flesh of, throwing away the bones, and put it on to stages to dry in the sun. The flesh was then gathered into baskets and oil was poured over it, the oil being rendered down from the bodies; this was done to prevent its spoiling with the damp. The bones of those eaten were put in the fire, lest the people of the country should return and collect them and bury them in their *wahi-tapus* (or sacred places). The heads of the chiefs were severed from the bodies and collected into a heap, and then some of us got other heads and flung them at the heap. The head of one great chief was placed on the summit of the heap as a special mark for other heads to be thrown at. It was an amusement indulged in by our forefathers, but in their case the heap was made of stones, at which other stones were thrown: but we used the heads instead of stones, until they were all smashed up. This was the doing of us older men, and as soon as they were well smashed up the young men took the heads and burnt them up in the fire. Those young fellows thought this a very amusing entertainment. The bones of the legs

> and arms had the ends broken off and with a piece of fern-stalk warmed in the fire melted the marrow inside, which we then sucked out or used to flavour our potatoes with. Then the bones were burnt lest they should be buried by the people of the land.
>
> After staying a week at this place we went inland to attack another *pa*, situated up the river from the one we were at. This *pa* had been spoken of to us by our prisoners, so we went and discovered it. Te Rauparaha then advised us to make peace with the people, but to do so only in appearance, so that the people might think it a binding peace (*rongo-take-take*). We then made the sham peace with the people of the *pa*, so that they might not understand our intention of taking it. It was a large *pa* and a great many people in it; they were very numerous *(pio)*, and we were few. So we sent our messengers to the *pa* to make peace, and an invitation to their warriors (three hundred and fifty *topu*, or seven hundred) to come to our feast which we had prepared for them; we were equally numerous at that time. So the three hundred and fifty once-told came to our feast, and we arranged that we should sit alternately *(kinakinaki)* when eating the food—it was Te Rauparaha who made this arrangement. When the food came for the guests, brought into the *marae* by our women [who suddenly come into the picture], and so soon as it was deposited in front of them our people were to stand up with their *maros* on only, and so soon as they stretched out their hands to the food, Te Rauparaha was to give the sign to us, when we were to strike the head of each man who sat near him. So the feast was arranged and the food cooked and brought to the *marae* by the women, and they commenced to eat; when Te Rauparaha gave the signal, directly the people were shouting and wailing whilst our weapons split open their heads—the noise was like that of a calabash being smashed. The whole of the three hundred and fifty were killed by us; not a single one escaped. We then took the *pa* and killed those within, the people being so demoralized by our actions that they had no strength or valour left. Thus we took the *pa*, killing those we thought fit and enslaving others. By the time they were aware of our attack they were dead men. (*MW*, 113–15)

I am not surprised that scholars have missed the exaggeration involved in this narrative, but it does puzzle me why the obvious contradictions and lacunae went unnoticed and unaccounted. For example, the impossibility of the consumption of the large number of corpses by a depleted force of under two hundred people; the fact that the symmetrical killing required three hundred and fifty people, which the invading force simply did not have; that the pā are all unnamed and geographically indeterminate; the sudden emergence of the women for the first time; and so on. The first conquest of an unknown village where the victors consumed "the fish of Tu" or the "first fish" (which generally refers to the first enemy chief killed in battle), and the portrayal of themselves as killers for killing's sake ("killing them . . . till we were tired of it"), the drying of dead bodies, eating the marrow with fennel stalks, and playing an ancestral game but using enemy heads instead of stones are all spoofs of white discourse. The satirist invents events that have some basis in Maori cultural reality and then wildly exaggerates them in highly improbable ways, at least to the Maori. The improbability of arranging enemies in a totally symmetrical fashion after making a "sham peace" and then splitting their heads as if they were calabashes can sound true only in a historical climate, then and now, that could believe almost anything about Maori cannibalism and the mentality that produced it. And the protagonist of this piece of action is Te Rauparaha who, as a ferocious anthropophagite of several narratives, slips nicely into this one. I think this narrative not only parodies the European discourse on cannibalism but also the indigenous informant's narrative rendering of "Maori history" to nineteenth-century scholars. I would be surprised if such forms of satire did not exist everywhere as defensive reactions in the early context of European domination and power. They occasionally occur in the field once the ethnographer has vacated it.

The trouble with irony and with satire as a narrative form is that it is always difficult for the outsider to detect in native renderings, and even more difficult to translate when detected. Not so in folk dramas that parody the European where the satire comes through in the action, or in sculpture and other types of visual representation where one can see the ironic distortions.[13] If satiric sculpture exists, it is hard not to expect it in satiric narrative that I think exists in any well-developed tradition of storytelling. True, sometimes irony is so elusive that during a difficult historical period it may not be recognizable even to the native tradition.[14]

When I first read the account of the Nga-Puhi expedition of 1819–20 in Smith's volume, Thomas Love Peacock's poem "The War Song of Dinas Vawr" echoed through the long corridors of memory, and I was back in high school reading this poem in an anthology of English poetry—perhaps one not specifically designed for gullible South Asians. My teachers thought it was a serious poem in the manner of Walter Scott. Only later, when as an undergraduate I read Peacock's work in context, did I realize that it was a spoof uttered by a character in one of his satiric novels, parodying the fatuous romanticism of novelists like Scott.[15] Of course the culture and the genre are different in the Maori and European cases. But there is a similarity in the tone of deadpan seriousness, in the stylistic exaggerations and parody of a preexisting genre. In Peacock the parody is English heroic poetry of the fantasized Scottish past; in the Maori satirist it is the parody of Maori histories given to white scholars and the white discourses that precipitated those very histories. If one reads Peacock's poem again, even without being aware of its place in the novel, one can detect the satiric intention in the flat rhyme scheme and the deliberately vulgar punning in the very first stanza.

The mountain sheep are sweeter
The valley sheep are fatter
We therefore deemed it meeter
To carry off the latter.
We made an expedition;
We met a host, and quelled it;
We forced a strong position,
And killed the men who held it. . . .

As we drove our prize at leisure,
The king marched forth to catch us:
His rage surpassed all measure,
But his people could not match us.
He fled to his hall pillars;
And ere our force we led off,
Some sacked his house and cellars,
While others cut his head off.

And so it goes on to its conclusion quoted at the beginning of this section, not unlike the Nga-Puhi war song we have just read.

Had I had been able to translate Swift's *A Modest Proposal* to a Maori of the early or mid-nineteenth century he would, I think, have thought it a text on British cannibalism, albeit of a very low sort in its advocacy of the eating of children to solve the problems of the Irish famine. But if the context were explained to him, he would have, I am sure, responded to its satiric intention. He would be familiar with similar texts from his own tradition because such satiric traditions can be rendered mutually intelligible and enjoyable contrary to naive ethnographic relativism. So is it with the "War Song of the Nga-Puhi": there is internal evidence in its exaggeration of known detail, its forays into wild improbability, and its feigned seriousness that bind the Maori narrator with forms of life that seem to transcend the cultural boundaries that we create to isolate the other as a specimen or a cultural species radically different from our own. The results of this technique of "museologism" are seen in the later genealogy of this piece of spoofery.

Edward Tregear, a notable authority on the Maori and a major source for modern anthropological writing, refers to this account with dead earnestness.[16] He quotes the whole section where a man was carrying the girl around his neck and adds: "If one can mentally picture this scene with the man striding along carrying the headless disemboweled trunk of the naked girl, enough of this horror will have been evoked."[17] Our satirist has made his point! Tregear then continues, "When the bodies could not all be eaten some of the flesh was stripped from the bones and dried in the sun, being hung on stages for that purpose. The flesh was then gathered into baskets and oil was poured over it, the oil being rendered down from the bodies; this was done to prevent it from spoiling from damp."[18] Tregear's information comes from our Maori war song with one difference though. The original account refers to a single instance; Tregear's "ethnologism" converts each specific example into a Maori custom. He then goes on to employ that part of the narrative that deals with the use of a hand for hooks.

A contemporary anthropologist, Ross Bowden, in turn uses Tregear's account to show how "what was not eaten was packed up and consumed on the way home."[19] And Vayda, another well-known anthropologist, borrows the following account from Elsdon Best, the eminent anthropologist of the Maori who wrote at the turn of the twentieth century: "According to a Maori account cited by Best, the purpose of the burning was to prevent tribesmen from collecting the bones and depositing them in the sacred places of the tribe. The same account says that the leg and arm bones were broken at one end before being eaten and that fern stalks were inserted in the bones in order to melt the marrow which was sucked and was a very good relish."[20] "Very good relish" is Best's substitution for our Maori historian's "flavour our potatoes with." "Relish" is part of the language game derived from Cook's journals and prior to that from European children's cannibal tales and constitutes part of the Western understanding of Maori anthropophagy. Vayda also quotes in its entirety, with Best as his original source, the marvelous description of how the "heads of the chiefs were severed from their bodies" and then heaped together so that stones could be thrown at the topmost one in "an ancient game . . . practiced by our ancestors."[21] This charming game bore a striking resemblance to that described by André Thevet for the Tupinamba Indians whose children played ball with a human head, which then became the source of inspiration for Theodore de Bry's engravings in 1593 in his well-known travel book, *Dritte Buch Americae* (*C*, 56–58).[22] I do not know how Genghis Khan got into the picture, but he too apparently liked to play polo with the heads of enemies. These "circulating mythemes" cannot be pinned down ethnographically, but one must assume they traveled long distances in European ships and sailors' narratives.

In his article on war Best says, "When guns were first used against them, the natives thought they were some new and powerful *atera* (demon). . . . The Taranaki natives, when attacked by the northern tribes in their first gun-bearing southern raid, imagined that the god Maru was slaying them."[23] The latter sentence is also from our satirist's account and other accounts similar to his! It is difficult to imagine that tribes living in this region were unfamiliar with guns as to demonize them. Even if they employed such an idiom it would be wrong to give it literal interpretation. It is clear that our Maori satirist has unknowingly scored a point: his spoof has been literalized as truth and gone into Maori history and anthropology.

THE OTHER SIDE OF SATIRE, OR THE BANALITY OF CANNIBALISM

The preceding observations bring us to the other side of satire. The parodied subject (the European interlocutor) takes on humorlessly and pompously the very things the satirist protests against. The Western discourse on cannibalism existed long before the discovery of Polynesia; it surfaces there from the late eighteenth century and reaches its efflorescence in early nineteenth-century missionary and scholarly thought. Maori discourse on cannibalism-anthropophagy is for the most part *hidden;* it must be gleaned from the British ones. These "hidden discourses" take many forms, ranging from the parodic to the serious. By contrast, the British discourse on Maori cannibalism is much more uniform because they have successfully insulated Maori cannibalism from related discourses found in European culture in such things as fantasies, nursery tales, and the sacrificial symbolism of the Eucharist. One of my tasks is to make the European discourse, and the practices associated with it, much more complex than appears on the surface by restoring their hidden dimensions. The parallel task, and a more difficult one, is to restore the complexity and historicity of Maori discourses and practices because the task of the British discourse is in fact to muffle Maori historicity and cultural complexity in respect of "cannibalism" and the larger cultural frame in which it is embedded, namely savagism.

My own assumptions have been clear from the very beginning of this work when I stated that "cannibalism" is a misnomer for human sacrifice. Nowhere in the context of sacrifice is there a conspicuous or a mass consumption of corpses. It is indeed possible that the symbolic consumption can be transformed in an actual consumption of the body, if not the blood, of the victim. I think this must have occurred even traditionally in some parts of New Zealand, particularly in the Bay of Islands region. In my thinking this was never divorced from ritual and was confined to a restricted "consubstantial community." Conspicuous consumption, both as discourse and embedded practice, emerged in the wake of the historical contact with the European who then constructed a European version of Maori cannibalism, including "battlefield cannibalism." This did not mean that Maori did not practice human sacrificial anthropophagy in the battlefield, and in some instances, in wrathful rage, might even have eaten the body of a specific victim. Moreover, owing to conditions I have specified in chapters 2 and 3, in those areas subject to European contact and violence, human sacrifice shed its ritualistic quality and acquired the character of conspicuous anthropophagy. But even here the Maori practice is lost in the British discourse that now speaks of indiscriminate anthropophagy resulting in a "cannibal feast" of which we have only one clear empirical example discussed in chapter 5, and that is one in which the Europeans were coparticipants. The "cannibal feast" of the savage too is a discourse that has had a long run in European thought and is based on such fantasies as witches' Sabbaths and cannibal monsters eating children.

It is the British discourse that literalizes Maori speech. We saw this in the war song of the Nga-Puhi. Because a whole text was available it was possible for me to imaginatively restore, partly at least, the integrity of the text. In other places in Percy Smith's book excerpts from similar texts are quoted, literalized, and taken out of context. Take this description of a Maori chief: "My Ngati-Whatua friends informed me that on this expedition Te Kawau [a well-known chief] had a basket of human flesh for a pillow, all the way around the island." Although he recognizes that this might be a mere "façon de parler," Smith goes on to say that "the flesh must have been raw—no cooked food could have been allowed to touch the sacred head of this fine old chief" (*MW*, 223).

These are typical humorless statements from texts that originally were surely varied in context, argumentative style, and tone. Take Edward Tregear once again, this time writing in 1936 on "War (including War Omens and Murder, Preserved Human Heads)":

> In days near our own it is recorded that the chief Te Wherowhero ordered 250 prisoners of the Taranaki people to be brought to him for slaughter. He sat on the ground and the prisoners were brought one by one to receive the blow of

> the chief's mere, a weapon till lately in the possession on his son Matu-taera, the late Maori "king." After he had killed 250 he said, "I am tired. Let the rest live," and the remainder passed into slavery. How numerous sometimes these war-captives were may be judged by the fact that when Hongi returned from his raid on the southern tribes in 1821 he brought back 2,000 prisoners to the Bay of Islands. One of the latest cannibal feasts of consequence was held at Ohariu, near Wellington, at the close of Te Rauparaha's exploits, when 150 of the Maupoko tribe went to the ovens. In the year 1836, when the Maori overcame the gentle Morioris of the Chatham Islands, not only did they keep the captives penned up like live stock waiting to be killed and eaten, but it is said that one of the leading chiefs of the invaders would order a meal of six children at once to be cooked to regale his friends.[24]

The killing of enemies in symmetrical fashion, with each person getting it with a *mere* until the worn out chief merely says, "I am tired. Let the rest live," surely echoes our war song of the Nga-Puhi and must have been part of a similar satirical text. Even if literally true, the story of Te Wherowhero is simply a charter myth that deals with the fabulous nature of his weapon. The rate at which slaves are captured and sent to the ovens in cannibal feasts is such that, if taken literally, there would be no warriors left to fight wars. Gossip and rumor ("it is said") circulating among colonists are reconstituted as Maori cannibalism. The six children cooked and eaten are the product of Western nursery tales, but they have already appeared in classic Tupinamba (Brazilian) cannibalism of the sixteenth century. Tregear produces more "evidence" that identifies the places that these events occurred; giving dates and place identifications produces what I will call the "deceptions of verisimilitude" and of descriptive realism. "I was shown a part of the beach at Waitangi Harbour (Rekohu, Chatham Islands) on which the bodies of eighty Moriori women were laid side by side each with an impaling stake driven into the abdomen. It is difficult for one not accustomed to savage warfare to note how shockingly callous and heartless this desecration of the human body made the actors in these terrible scenes."[25] Children cooked and eaten, prisoners fattened like cattle, stakes driven into the abdomen, all are derivatives of Western fairy tales and fantasies. Yet it is these writers, and others like them, whom Ross Bowden, a sophisticated contemporary anthropologist, says provide an "abundance of valuable historical and ethnographic evidence for the practice."[26]

The European exaggeration of Maori anthropophagy is not entirely their own invention for this is to oversimplify the dialogic nature of discursive relationships.

Not only did the Maori consume the flesh and blood of a sacrificial victim, but also some Bay of Islands groups consumed human meat with the pejorative downturn of sacrificial anthropophagy. They also exaggerated their anthropophagy in the context of Western contact, and especially in the trade wars of the nineteenth century—as a weapon, as satire, as a grandiose affirmation of their greatness in war and the pathetic incompetence of the enemy. The European exaggeration of Maori exaggeration is based on their literalization of complex Maori discourses. In addition they exaggerated Maori anthropophagy, based on their own fantasies, and as the following account also vindicate: "The native accounts say that over a thousand of the Ngati-Paoa people fell in the taking of Mau-inaina [in 1823], and a traveler who visited the battlefield in 1844 records that the bones of 2,000 men still lay whitening on the plain, and the ovens remain in which the flesh of the slaughtered was cooked for the horrible repasts of the victorious party" (*MW*, 190). Maori did not possess modern arithmetic, and their numbering is always rounded and decimalized in white accounts: 500, 1,000, 2,000, 3,000, are conventionalized numbers emerging from Maori-British dialogue. In the above account the "over thousand" Ngati-Paoa killed becomes, in the European narrative, two thousand bones of men—all intact for an exact count. The important thing of course is that all these were eaten in the "horrible repasts" of the victors, while fantasy can transform ordinary Maori earth ovens into cannibal ones.

Along with the settler exaggerations are the ethnological generalizations, noted earlier. Consider these stories about Hongi's partiality for human eyes. According to Best he is said to have swallowed human eyes for the first time as a young man, and White, the nineteenth-century antiquarian, reports that he ate the eyes of all the relatives of an enemy in an act of revenge. There is also Kendall who heard that Hongi swallowed the left eye of an enemy.[27] Hongi's eye-eating propensity is generalized by Percy Smith into a universal Polynesian custom: "It is related of Hongi Hika, that on killing Te Tihi he swallowed his eyes—a very ancient Polynesian custom" (*MW*, 54). I will mention this perverse partiality for human eyes in the next chapter, but, for the moment, let me assert that there is no warrant for universalizing Hongi's actions as a customary one applicable to all Polynesia. At the time that Smith wrote native peoples were easy victims of sloppy scholarship based on rumor and hearsay. It would be quite impossible to employ the same research strategy for the study of the European past of that time.

The construction of Maori cannibalism then is a continuation and development of the same language game that began with the ships' journals. These accounts in their wearisome uniformity cannot continue for long without producing the banality of Maori cannibalism: the taken-for-granted nature of their lust for human flesh, their ravenousness, and their participation in the final act—the cannibal feast. Thus for Percy Smith the Nga-Puhi waged war to satisfy their cannibalistic desires; one group suffered badly owing "to the Nga-Puhi's lust for man eating" (*MW*, 275). Smith's text, and those that follow him, set the stage for the taken-for-granted nature of cannibalism. Thus Pomare, a Nga-Puhi chief, goes on "the *usual* errand of slaughter, man-eating and slave hunting" (*MW*, 239). Another group, the Amio-Whenua on an expedition went on "killing and eating *all* they came across" (*MW*, 214). Phrases like the following assume the banality of Maori cannibalism. "After the *usual* feasting on the 'fish of Tu' " (*MW*, 267); "[T]he chiefs killed served the *usual* feast for Nga-Puhi" (*MW*, 268); "[T]he *usual* feasting etc. took place in accordance with Maori custom" (*MW*, 271); "[T]he expedition had more than one object in view, outside the *usual* one of manslaying" (*MW*, 263).[28]

This discursive style on the banality of cannibalism is continued by practically every scholar of the nineteenth century. Coming down to modern times there is a slight humor injected into the discourse but at the expense of the Maori. Elsdon Best describes their ancient ways: "[I]n days of yore when armed bands of cannibals ranged their land in search of fame and fresh meat."[29] Best again: "Slaves were as a rule well treated, though they might at any time be knocked on the head to provide a meal."[30] Better still: "Occasionally a person was slain to add *éclat* to the tattooing of a young woman of rank."[31] "They sold the girls first, as being the least valuable. These children [boys and girls] would probably be slain and eaten."[32] Best's humor resurfaces when he describes a sham fight between a Maori chief and a British officer: "Had the tourney occurred twenty years ago, and been *à l'outrance*, the white knight would have been—done brown and supped upon."[33]

And who can exempt those writing in our own times from the tradition of scholarly fantasies of Maori cannibalism? Thus Raymond Firth, one of the anthropological icons whom I knew and admired, uses these academic myths as late as his 1959 edition of *The Economics of the New Zealand Maori* when he says, "[T]here is no doubt that with most natives there was a distinct liking for human flesh. If a slave was killed by his master for any offence he was not wasted, but taken off to the ovens for culinary purposes. As a kindly thought joints might be sent around to friends and neighbours and were much appreciated."[34] And a very modern rendering of the language game by Vayda: "[T]he available evidence indicates that the old time war parties lived mainly off the land and/or off the flesh of the enemy," when of course there isn't a shred of reliable evidence for this assertion.[35] It is not surprising that this kind of language game has gone into popular literature, a notorious example being Jules Verne.[36] The popular literature not only reinforces the banality of cannibalism but also reinforces its truth for the general reading public.

It therefore seems that much of modern anthropology has inherited the same language game from earlier European discourses of the savage. Thus the most recent anthropological accounts are caught up in the expectable dilemma that, on the one hand, treats cannibalism as ritual sacrifice and, on the other, as conspicuous consumption. The dilemma is the result of the failure to historicize "cannibalism" and the habit of reifying multiple accounts of it as a "traditional" practice. Ross Bowden neatly portrays this double fact of Maori cannibalism in the battlefield. On the one hand: "The victims would be butchered on the spot and cooked in steam ovens . . . What was not eaten was packed up and consumed on the way home."[37]

And on the other: "Considerable ritual, it seems, was associated with the first victim slain (the so-called 'first fish'). Some accounts state that no part of the body was eaten but was offered up whole as a sacrifice to the deities who presided at the war party; others that only the heart was used sacrificially and the rest eaten. . . . All writers agree that the bodies of slain enemies were never used as common food in a village, and that women were rarely, if ever, permitted to eat human flesh."[38] This in not Bowden's invention; it is a legitimate inference from the kind of ethnographic "evidence" available to him.

THE BANALITY OF CANNIBALISM CONTINUED: EYEWITNESSES

Eyewitness accounts are of course the final touchstone of reality for many people, including anthropologists and historians. Eyewitnesses are especially important because most accounts that we have—including the consumption of whites—is based on indirect evidence. Peggy Sanday, in her work on cannibalism, invokes eyewitnesses to vouch for the truth of cannibalism.[39] I am not denying the importance of eyewitnesses; one has to use them. Yet, in respect of cannibalism, an eyewitness account is particularly suspect since it taps fantasy, fascination, and latent desire, which either misperceives the event, or distorts it in its representation, or simply weaves a fabric around gossip, hearsay, and preexisting tales that circulate in ships and academia. Let me now present two accounts of Polynesian cannibalism that provide "proof" of this practice.

Mr. Leigh, the first missionary to settle in New Zealand, while walking on the beach, heard of a youth killed for a cannibal feast in 1821. He wrote the following eyewitness account in the *Evangelical Magazine:*

> As I was going to this place, I passed by the bloody spot on which the head of this unhappy victim had been cut off; and, on approaching the fire, I was not a little startled at the sudden appearance of a savage-looking man, of gigantic stature, entirely naked, and armed with a large axe. I was a good deal intimidated, but mustered up as much courage as I could, and demanded to see the lad. The cook (for such was the occupation of this terrific monster) then held up the boy by his feet. He appeared to be about fourteen years of age, and was half roasted. I returned to the village, where I found a great number of natives seated in a circle, with a quantity of coomery (a sort of sweet potatoe). In this company were shown to me the body of the youth before them, waiting for the roasted mother of the child. The mother and child were both slaves, having been taken in war. However, she would have been compelled to share in the horrid feast, had I not prevailed on them to give up the body to be interred, and thus prevented them from gratifying their unnatural appetite.[40]

One tends to assume that an Evangelical missionary, the embodiment of a true Christian, cannot lie; consequently, it is easy for many to accept the truth of this statement. Let us follow the popular "prejudice" and for the moment accept this account as truth. The language game here has its roots in the discourse of eighteenth-century clergymen, including John Wesley himself, on savagism. Leigh represents the Maori as monstrous beings in a physical and psychical sense. The ritual specialist was indubitably a "cook" of human meat; he was a savage of "gigantic stature" and a "terrific monster." The victim was a lad of fourteen, even though there was no way that Leigh could identify his age since he was "half roasted" when he saw him. The account evokes the sympathy of the reader for the youth and antipathy for the cannibals. Then there was the mother of the youth who but for Leigh's intervention, would have been compelled to share in this "horrid feast." At this point we begin to suspect Leigh's account, because it is highly improbable that Maori would have permitted a woman and a slave at that, to consume human flesh, even if Maori sacrifice had in 1821 lost much of its cultural significance and meaning. If this was not a missionary account we would have been extremely suspicious of this particular eyewitness. Therefore let us assume that missionaries too have reason to lie and ask the question whether the event could indeed have taken place.

Leigh arrived in Australia in 1815 and then went to New Zealand in 1819. Owing to chronic ill health he returned to New South Wales and soon afterward returned to England. He left for New Zealand again in 1821 after contracting a marriage in England. This account was written in 1821 when he was in England but was based on his experience in New Zealand of six and a half weeks! In considering the truth of this eyewitness one must also take seriously Leigh's friend Samuel Marsden, who stated that no missionary had ever witnessed a cannibal feast; it should be remembered that white outsiders were excluded from witnessing human sacrifices.

When Leigh arrived in Hatton Garden, London, he was interviewed by three Methodist secretaries who cold-shouldered Leigh's request for a mission to Tonga and New Zealand on the grounds that "with a debt of £10,000.00 the Society could neither enlarge old nor undertake new missions."[41] But J. M. R. Owens in his history of the Wesleyan mission in New Zealand says that Leigh was so "obsessed with his plan" that he decided to seek funds from "the manufacturing districts and appeal for goods to establish a mission among the 'savage cannibals' of New Zealand."[42] The Methodist conference at Liverpool approved the scheme and Leigh was appointed missionary to New Zealand. He successfully toured the provinces for donations. It is in this context one must consider the practical usefulness of his "eyewitness" account: to make a powerful impact on the pious reader of the *Evangelical Magazine* and to justify Leigh's demand for a mission and the necessity for the public to support it. Hence his conclusion offering redemption to the Maori in spite of their cannibalism: "But notwithstanding this melancholy picture of New Zealand, I believe they are very capable of receiving religious instruction, and a knowledge of the arts in general. They are very ingenious and enterprising, and discover a surprising willingness to receive instruction." Leigh adds that things are not as hopeless as his "melancholy picture" had indicated because the chiefs were encouraging his efforts, urging him to reside among them, and God himself "is preparing them to receive the ever-blessed Gospel of peace" (*HR 1*, 574).[43]

I think Leigh's eyewitness account is a fabricated one, by which I mean that a new "fabric" has been woven of popular hearsay about Maori and of unconscious European fantasies, producing once again the banality of cannibalism. Accounts such as this must force us to reappraise the role of missionaries in the physical and spiritual isolation of alien lands. Unlike sailors, missionaries could not engage openly in sex and violence and had to be sustained in their tribulations by the fervor and intensity of their spiritual quest and the example of the Savior himself. Further, missionaries were not a single group: their attitude toward the natives varied with their educational and class backgrounds and the missionary tradition to which they belonged. Thus Wesleyans were at one time especially derogatory of Maori and other Polynesian peoples. Here is Turner, another prominent Wesleyan missionary and contemporary of Leigh, talking about the Maori after a discussion of cannibalism and the "diabolical passions" it entailed:

> Their moral character is such as might be expected from a mind so dark and polluted. I may venture to affirm there is no crime of which they are capable of which they are not guilty. Reason is completely dethroned, and the reigns of government are given up to the passions altogether, and by these they are carried to the greatest extremes. Their temporal condition is equally bad; they are filthy in the extreme, never wash themselves, but as often as they can besmear themselves with red ochre and oil, which in the hot weather makes them very offensive. Many of them literally swarm with vermin. Their huts in general are nothing better than poor people's pigstiles in England. (*HR* *1*, 630)

Both Turner and Leigh came from lower-class backgrounds and were barely educated, quite unlike the "experimental gentlemen" of Cook's voyages. On the one hand, they, and other missionaries, lived among a generally unsympathetic and sometimes hostile native population; on the other hand, they were confronted with white traders and whalers who, from the missionary viewpoint, were no better than savages. In this situation personal bickering and conflicts among the New Zealand missionaries were acute, often plastered over by surface politeness, necessary for the continuity of face-to-face relations. An extreme case was Kendall who had "sinful and unnatural intercourse with a native girl," went partially native himself, and allegedly urged the Maori to murder the missionaries and burn the house of Hall, a fellow missionary![44] Australia in the early nineteenth century was much better, being less isolated, but even here the tensions and conflicts among the missionaries, even among those of the same denomination, were acute. Thus Walter Lawry, the Cornish Methodist, spoke of Leigh during his Australian sojourn as "this weak and envious man," full of "idleness, jealousy, ignorance, selfishness and dishonorableness."[45] The arduous missionary toils Leigh supposedly underwent were suspect "and as to many of his other kinds of sufferings, such as no beds, no food etc. I believe, if ever a solitary instance of this kind occurred, it was when he was going across the country (not to preach) [but] in search after a fair object."[46] This might be personal pique, but Owens, in his account of the Methodist missions seems to concur with this negative assessment of Leigh.[47] He adds that Leigh's accounts of Maori customs have no originality but "show strong resemblance to stock missionary accounts he must have read."[48] His colleague Turner reported that after eighteen months in New Zealand, Leigh was "not able to string ten sentences together or speak to the natives on the commonest subjects."[49]

It therefore seems quite improbable that Leigh's "eyewitness" account of the Maori cannibal feast can be anything but a calculated lie. In which case, one must doubt the truth value of his frequent reports to the Evangelical journals on Maori cannibalism, such as the indiscriminate killing of men, women, and children by the Maori and their equally indiscriminate anthropophagy; the routinized nature of the latter practice; and the travails of living among cannibals and yet maintaining a stoic and steadfast vision of saving their otherwise doomed souls. Most missionaries did believe sincerely in their spiritual vocation of saving souls, and if Leigh was one of them, it did not prevent him from lying in the interests of truth. I might add that missionary reports on native cannibalism when they reach their European reading public or are incorporated into biographies, cast the missionary into the heroic role of someone living in dire danger among cannibals in much the same way that the lay public romanticizes the ethnographer living among (mostly former) cannibals or other kinds of exotic beings.[50]

Let me now consider the second eyewitness. In his discussion of Maori cannibalism A. P. Vayda, admittedly young and inexperienced at the time he wrote his account, makes the following observation: "Clarke, who spent much of his childhood around the Bay of Islands in the 1820's and the 1830's, says that he once saw a procession of over twenty female prisoners, each with a heavy basket on her back containing human flesh."[51] Rev. George Clarke is then another eyewitness who provides more evidence for Maori cannibalism. Yet reading Clarke I realized that he was born in 1823 and he was reminiscing at age seventy when his book was written about an event that took place when he was five or six years old, in or around the year 1828! Not only is the citation worthless but also the number of baskets (twenty) is an echo of Burney's discovery of the flesh of his comrades in twenty baskets, a story well known among sailors and settlers. Presumably Maori women did carry other things besides human flesh in baskets, though this account has made the two items virtually synonymous. A childhood imagination thriving on cannibalistic stories could easily have converted a fantasy into an imagined real event, as was the case with Freud's Leonardo da Vinci.[52] Yet for Vayda this is evidence that "sometimes the prisoners [in this case female] were made to serve as porters, carrying the flesh of their late comrades."[53] A careful reading of Clarke shows that the females in his account were not prisoners; the latter are mentioned in respect of another event.

> Our parents did the best they could to keep us out of the sights and sounds of Maori savagery, and though the knocking of unfortunate slaves and prisoners of war on the head, and then putting them in the oven, was an every day occurrence around us, especially at the pah opposite, I never as a child, saw an actual murder, but I have watched the war canoes on their return from fighting expeditions with loads of baked humanity and crowds of unfortunate prisoners, who were just as likely as not to be massacred on landing by any of the fierce men or fiercer women who had lost father or son, brother or husband, in the battle. One evening when a fleet of war canoes returned with a score of prisoners in each of them, I was looking across the water at a scuffle on the landing. Fortunately it was getting too dark to see plainly, but I did see the poor creatures jump out of the canoe with their thick mats thrown over their heads—which was always what a Maori did when he expected a blow from a "mere" or a tomahawk—and then there was a crowd and a rush, and yells, and the scream of a single fury rising high above all. I was sent to bed and kept out of Maori company all the next day, but managed to find out that the wife of some chief who had been killed in battle, rushed with a tomahawk upon the wretched captives and managed to kill eight or ten of them before she was stopped. She then deliberately strangled herself in a paroxysm of rage, grief, and despair, and more prisoners were sacrificed and drowned that night as "utu", or revenge. *I once saw a procession of over twenty women from the canoes pass through the settlement, each with a heavy basket on her back containing human flesh* [my italics].[54]

The anthropological imagination converts Clarke's women into "female prisoners" who carry the flesh of their late kinfolk. It is entirely possible that if we take modern ethnographic accounts of Maori cannibalism and trace their intellectual genealogy backward into the mid-nineteenth century we will end up in similar sources that have been uncritically employed in the anthropological construction of Maori cannibalism.

FIVE · The Later Fate of Heads

Cannibalism, Decapitation, and Capitalism

> [This] here harpooner I have been tellin' you of has just arrived from the south seas, where he bought up a lot of 'balmed New Zealand heads (great curios you know), and he's sold all of 'em but one, and that one he's trying to sell to-night, cause tomorrow's Sunday, and it would not do to be sellin' human heads about the streets when folks is goin' to churches. He wanted to, last Sunday, but I stopped him just as he was goin' out of the door with four heads strung on a string, for all the airth like a string of inions.
>
> HERMAN MELVILLE, *Moby Dick*

THE AESTHETICS OF CURIOUS HEADS

For the moment let me bracket "this cannibal business of selling the heads of dead idolators" that Melville's Ishmael speaks about and shift instead to the significance of that queer trade of Queequeg trying to sell his many heads even though the "market's overstocked."[1] I will do so by continuing my earlier treatise on decapitated heads with an incident recorded by Samuel Marsden, the coordinator of the Protestant missions in New Zealand on behalf of the Church Missionary Society. Marsden was a "Evangelical Anglican" well educated at Cambridge and strongly influenced by popular Wesleyanism and other Calvinist movements of the time. After he settled in Australia, he became a large landowner and a Sydney magistrate who loved to flog those other savages, the Irish convicts. Though he was also a rabid hater of the Australian *ādivāsi* (Aborigines) he developed friendships with Maori chiefs. Perhaps the contempt his Maori friends had for the Aborigines was an infection contacted from Marsden.[2]

Writing in 1831 Marsden notes, "When the chief who was with me went on board the Prince of Denmark he saw 14 heads of chiefs upon the table in the cabin," their chiefly features identifiable by elaborate tattoos (*HR 1*, 716). Marsden must surely have known that the practice of selling aboriginal skulls for phrenological purposes had already taken place in Australia.[3] Nevertheless, Maori heads had greater aesthetic and commercial value. The practice of trading their heads became so scandalous that the governor of New South Wales forbade their importation into the colony by a proclamation of 1831, unhappily long after this nefarious activity had reached its peak. The document though couched in deadly legalese is worth quoting:

> Whereas it has been represented to His Excellency the Governor, that the masters and crews of vessel trading between this Colony and New Zealand, are in the practice of purchasing and bringing from thence human heads, which are preserved in a manner peculiar to that country: And whereas there is strong reason to believe that such disgusting traffic tends greatly to increase the sacrifice of human life among savages, whose disregard of it is notorious, His Excellency is desirous of evincing his entire disapprobation of the practice above mentioned, as well as his determination to check it by all means in his power; and with this view, His Excellency has been pleased to order that the Officers of the Customs do strictly watch and report every instance which they may discover of an attempt to import into this Colony any dried or preserved human heads in future, with the names of all parties concerned in every such attempt. (*LJS*, 500)

Apart from this belated humane concern for the preservation of the lives of natives one might ask the following question: What are the implications of this extraordinary practice of shipping Maori heads to Port Jackson to be transshipped to old curiosity shops in London and other metropolitan capitals? Let me initially focus on both the exotic and aesthetic interests involved by shifting to another scene, this time to London in 1820 where Hongi Hika, the warrior chief of the Nga Puhi along with a chief of Waikato was being entertained and treated as an "object of mere curiosity" in an English drawing room.[4] "Hongi conducted himself with an air of conscious superiority and that scrupulous regard to etiquette by which he was generally distinguished, until he observed some of the ladies evidently tracing the lines upon his tattooed countenance, while a smile played upon their own, implying as he thought a feeling of pity toward himself. He instantly rose up in a state of excitement, threw himself across three chairs, and, covering his face with his hands, remained in that posture until the company retired."[5]

The aesthetics of Hongi's head was also appreciated in the *Missionary Register* for 1820. It stated that Hongi was "of manly aspect—very much resembling the

FIGURE 5
Head of Chief Hongi carved by himself, 1814. From Judith Benney, *Legacy of Guilt*. Photograph by Leo Hsu.

Bust carved by himself, of which an engraving was given in our Volume for 1816" (see figure 5).[6] When he arrived at the House of Lords on October 21, Thomas Creevey, a well-known gossip columnist, combined curiosity with an ironic use of art appreciation in his report: "I went round, and got near enough to touch his Majesty; when I found his royal face to be one of the very finest specimens of *carving* I have ever beheld. The Chamberlain's face was fair: the sunflowers on it were highly respectable; but the King's nose, which surpassed the average size, was one blaze of stars and planets. The groundwork of their faces, of which a mighty small portion remained without ornament, was evidently fair, but had been painted a deep orange colour."[7]

There seems to have been a genuine English (and European) appreciation for carved Maori heads both as aesthetic and exotic or "curious" objects. Nevertheless the European desire for body parts of savages was rooted in much broader, and deeper, concerns. Like other Maori artifacts, body parts were collected by ships' personnel, officially for museums and patrons, and also unofficially for sale in metropolitan capitals. In chapter 2 I dealt with one direction in which Maori heads move, that is, the forward trajectory of Maori heads as they join their compatriots in the primitive world, circulating in museums, laboratories, and anthropology departments. When curators put their heads together in museums in order to classify them, savage heads begin to suffer the fate of arrowheads and other classified artifacts: they become the objects of public interest and scholarly curiosity. One might even say that the very existence of a museum collection is an inducement to scholarship. I also think that heads gave a fillip for the pseudosciences of the nineteenth and early twentieth centuries in such fields as phrenology and craniology, the latter a subspecialty of physical anthropology up to as recent as the late 1950s when I was in graduate school (see figure 6).

For present purposes I am interested in a *second* trajectory of heads, another backward movement one might say, wherein I trace the fate of heads alongside the immediate history of the fragile practice known as "Maori cannibalism." I want to posit shifting forms of anthropophagy after the period of Cook's voyages when Maori are catapulted into the history of Europe and the broader history of capitalism and an emerging modernity. This history of Europe contains a discourse about Maori culture that has smothered the Maori's own history, even when that history is re-presented by historians, ethnographers, and antiquarians of the mid-nineteenth century and after. And sadly, it seems that some Maori have taken over and selectively introjected European colonial notions, in this case cannibalism, to proudly reinterpret it as a "traditional" and admirable Maori custom. This is what one might call "self-primitivization," the process that occurs during periods of unequal power relations whereby the native adopts the image projected onto him by the colonial Other, sometimes parodically and sometimes with seriousness or a combination of both.

I pointed out in chapter 2 that, irrespective of the bizarre nature of the cannibal experiment on board ship, there was undoubted evidence to confirm or to "prove" native anthropophagy because the Maori did eat the flesh of some of Lt. Furneaux's men belonging to the *Adventure*. Thus, for the moment, let me suspend my investi-

FIGURE 6
Caricature of Dr. Gall, a famous phrenologist, delivering a lecture. From Folke Henschen, *The Human Skull* (New York: Praeger, 1966). Photograph by Leo Hsu.

gation of European consumer demands and deal with Maori consuming Europeans, which is not unrelated to *their* first contact with capitalism.

The new tradition of eating the European might well have continued into the first decade of the nineteenth century, though I have serious doubts regarding some of the imputed cases of "cannibalism" because the attribution of "monstrosity" to the Other was a feature of savagism in colonial discourse and exacerbated by whalers and sea captains who provided the confirming information on Maori anthropophagy. Perhaps the earliest case is that of the *Venus*, which was seized on the Australian coast by convicts in 1807 and eventually sailed into the Bay of Islands area with eleven persons, including two women and an infant. It was presumably shipwrecked, but no reliable information was available regarding the fate of the passengers, except the European presumption that they were eaten. It is as likely they were not. The only evidence for Maori consuming the crew of the *Venus* was reported by those in the colonial schooner *Mercury* who "learned that she [the *Venus*] had been taken by the Natives, who killed and ate her crew and burnt the hull for the sake of her iron."[8] Better evidence is available for the schooner *Paramatta*, a ship that traded between Sydney and Tahiti and anchored at the Bay of Islands area in 1812 with eleven crew members. According to an account gleaned four years later, the ship was in distress and wanted provisions and water from the Maori who did supply the crew with pork, fish, and potatoes. When the Maori demanded payment, they were thrown overboard and fired at by the crew, and some were wounded by small shot. A heavy gale blew the vessel on shore, and according to this account, "the shipwrecked sailors were cut off to a man, and the fate of Marion and his companions were theirs."[9] The fact that the crew was killed did not mean that they were eaten, but the presumption is there since Maori are cannibals. Yet some form of anthropophagy might well have occurred because of the provocation and the precedent of Rowe's people (and perhaps Marion's).

A better-documented case is the capture and burning of the *Boyd* and the consumption of the crew. The *Boyd* sailed from Port Jackson to Whangaroa, north of the Bay of Islands, in 1810 with several natives of that area on board as workers. The Maori were ill-treated by the crew; especially serious was the case of a young chief who, because he was sick and unable to work, was badly flogged and subjected to indignities and then sent ashore, full of lacerations on his body. In revenge the natives of the area enticed the captain and crew on shore and killed, by some accounts, forty of them. "Captain Thompson and his unfortunate men were devoured by the murderers, who cloathing *[sic]* themselves with their apparel, launched the boats at dusk the same evening and proceeded towards the ship, which they had determined also to attack" (*HR 1*, 307). The passengers were also killed except for one female passenger and two children. There are several depositions and accounts of this event but the outlines are similar barring one detail. Some accounts accuse the erstwhile friendly chief Te Pahi of leading the attack while others say that he tried to mediate. Later investigations mostly indicated Te Pahi's total lack of complicity in this affair. Te Pahi was unpopular with some Europeans because he had been to Port Jackson and had become Marsden's friend. Many refer to him disparagingly; one as "that old rascal Tippahee who has been so much and undeservedly caressed at Port Jackson" (*HR 1*, 311, see also 293–94). Especially vociferous was Alexander Berry of the *City of Edinburgh* who went to Whangaroa and tried to get the details of what occurred and, employing the threat of violence, managed to bring the captured woman and the two children back. Apparently, he saw the remains of the burnt *Boyd* and also "the mangled fragments and fresh bones of our countrymen, with the marks even of the teeth remaining on them."[10] The latter is a key feature of the cannibal scene noted by us earlier and recorded right up to our own times in archaeological reconstructions of the past. In the letter to the governor, Berry and two other whaling captains said, "Let no man, after this, trust a New Zealander" (*HR 1*, 311).

The bad press in Sydney was all that was needed for a group of whalers in the Bay of Islands area to send "seven armed boats before daybreak to attack the island of Tippahee [Te Pahi], where, on their landing they shot every man, woman and child that came in their way; in this attack Tippahee received seven wounds, and soon afterwards died" (*HR 1*, 354). If, according to European accounts, the natives spared a European woman and two children, these attackers were much more methodical. However, in a letter to Governor Maquarie in New South Wales they sanctimoniously noted that Te Pahi was the "chief perpetrator of the horrid transaction" and added that, on their being confronted by armed natives, they "took possession of the island by force of arms" (*HR 1*, 300). Though the government in both Sydney and England wanted to arrest and punish the perpetrators of this homicidal act, nothing actually came of it. In this discourse, as in similar ones, the natives "massacre" wantonly whereas whites "kill" with just cause, as if they had borrowed Maori conceptions of utu, or "retaliation-reciprocity," and *take*, or "just cause."

This was also the case in the French retaliation for Marion's death and the case for *any* war fought Anywhere; none can be envisaged without an imagined just cause. Thus the distinction between savage and civilized once again becomes blurred. The moment one uses the technical terms *utu* and *take* the Maori theory and practice of vengeance seem unique to them. Like Maori heads one tends to put their warfare too in a glass case. Yet we know that "vengeance" and its "justification" were as common and even more highly elaborated in Euro-American civilization, then and right now, and the practice and literature of revenge is more prolific in the West than in the South Seas. Taunting however is not (unless one is speaking of the ancient Greeks). Europeans did taunt their enemies occasionally, but had they done so in New Zealand, their language game of taunting might have sounded as exotic to the Maori as the Maori terms utu and take seemed to readers of Maori culture.

I suggest that Maori anthropophagy and British killing are analogous to the situation of communal and ethnic violence. Both are precipitates of rage against felt injustice; the Maori reacted with eating their enemies, outside of the sacrificial order that had already showed signs of strain. The killing and consumption of the crew of the *Boyd* by the Maori was practically a repetition of the Marion scenario while the brutal retaliation by whalers was similar to the French reaction. The latter was the kind of action that Cook and his officers probably could not even contemplate as a possibility because the ethics and rationality of the Enlightenment held little sway in the new social worlds opened up by European whalers and settlers. The idea that Maori would eat anyone whenever circumstances were favorable led to the presumption of anthropophagy even when there was no evidence. Thus McNab simply assumes that one of Tasman's crew was eaten when there is no justification for that assumption. This also applies to the *Venus*. In the *Boyd* case, while Europeans might have been eaten, there is no saying how many or in what manner. It is Alexander Berry, one of four to investigate the event, who insisted that the passengers and crew were "killed and eat" (*HR 1*, 296). Yet in a joint statement signed by all four, there is no reference to man-eating, only to the crew who were massacred and "cut to pieces while still alive," something that they could not possibly have verified and that sounds more like the European practices such as quartering (*HR 1*, 294, 295).

There were many instances where neither whites nor enemy Maori were eaten even when opportunities were available. For example, not a single missionary was eaten in New Zealand though they were readily available for public consumption. In 1815 a whaleboat with the remnants of a starving crew fell into the hands of natives of the North Cape coast and the crew thought they would be eaten—for isn't this what Maori do? They were humiliated and robbed of their belongings but were not killed (perhaps because there was no humiliation or hurt inflicted on the Maori).[11] In 1823 an American ship, the *Cossack*, was wrecked at the head of the Hokianga River, but the natives treated the ship's crew with kindness when they got on shore. What is even more fascinating is that Chief George, one of the men supposedly instrumental in killing and eating the *Boyd* people actually helped another group of Europeans many years later (in July 1825) so much so that the passengers could say that "he was sent by a kind Providence to be our deliverer" (*HR 1*, 642). Strange cannibals, these Maori: though, perhaps, not as strange as the ways of Providence.

Given the conventional definition of the Maori as inveterate and savage cannibals it is surprising to find John Savage, a surgeon, who visited the Bay of Islands in 1805 express a view startlingly different from both Cook and the missionary magazines. He argues that Maori, though "hitherto been considered cannibals of the worst description" are "not as horrible as represented."[12] They acknowledge consuming flesh in times of great food scarcity. "[Y]et it does not appear that they have any predilection for the practice: the motive which impels them to this inhuman deed, as customary at present, is vengeance, but even this passion is not pursued without limitation. Thus, after a conquest, the victors do not devour the whole of their prisoners, but are content with shewing their power to do so, by dividing the chief of the vanquished tribe among them: he is eaten, it is true, but I do not believe that food is the inducement."[13] And then with considerable prescience: "It is probable that an European, who should act with hostility toward them, would be treated in the same way, but if cast defenseless upon their shores, I have reasons for believing he would meet with far different treatment."[14]

It is true that Savage spent only a few weeks in New Zealand, but he took with him on the long voyage home to London a young aristocratic Maori named Mohanga from whom he learned over time a considerable amount of information about the Bay of Islands area.[15] At the time Savage wrote the Maori were already defined as cannibals but the immediately known examples of their ferocity was over thirty years previously during the Marion and Rowe episodes. Writing in 1805 Savage was not burdened with the attributed cases beginning with the *Venus* two years later. Further, Savage made an important observation of the Maori he knew: they were not obsessed at this time with guns but rather with that precious metal, iron, "particularly with axes, adzes, or small hatchets," which they traded for potatoes that were therefore "preserved with great care against the arrival of a vessel."[16] This situation was to change completely: there was an increasing number of whalers arriving in the Bay of Islands area and trading in new commodities, especially timber, seal skins, artifacts and, later, flax. These trading patterns gave the tribes in the Bay of Islands area a new prominence. I emphasize "new" because Savage also noted that these tribes were not given to resplendent display characteristic of the interior tribes. The chiefs of the latter regions were carried on the shoulders of their servitors and were accompanied by retinues with great show of pomp and prowess accompanied by "hundreds, or even thousands of dauntless warriors, armed with spears and battle axes, and decorated with war-mats, feathers etc."[17] Whereas the Bay of Islands area chiefs walked barefoot without any such display. However, a new commodity changed this picture as well as the pattern of intertribal relations: guns. Guns were available for those who controlled the new trade routes. These tribes then fought among each other to seek domination over trade rights and then moved into the interior with their superior weapons to seek the increasingly scarce supply of commodities, namely slaves, flax, and artifacts, including human heads, to meet the European demand.

THE MUSKET WARS AND MAORI CONSCIOUSNESS

"Curses on thy head thou stranger from afar"
That brought hither to this land,
The strange and powerful weapons,
That felled the mighty of this land
And laid them low in death.[18]

The "musket wars" is the term used by scholars to designate the intertribal warfare that developed as a result of the introduction of guns to Maori warriors hitherto possessing only a rudimentary technology of warfare. As Angela Ballara says, "[T]he use of muskets meant that unprecedented success was often achieved in war, with greater numbers being killed in each campaign for nearly a decade after 1818," even though the numbers cited might have been exaggerated.[19] For me "musket wars" is a convenient label to refer to wars waged after the advent of the Europeans when guns began to have tremendous symbolic and practical value for Maori, as indeed for other peoples also when confronted with European power. I noted that during Marion's expedition the Maori used the word "tapu" in relation to European guns, which seem to imply that these new objects were invested with traditional Maori notions of power if not sacredness. This is not surprising. Guns were powerful phallic objects and their possession gave males a sense of personal power as it gave groups both prestige and power that then found expression in panoply and public display. Guns however have to be bought, and the buying of guns further linked Maori with the newly opening outside world and trade—especially for those tribes in control of the crucial sea ports. Trade did not make sense unless there was an emerging entrepreneur class among chiefs who could creatively exploit the new resources presented by the nascent capitalism.

The critical date in the development of the musket wars was the establishment of a New Zealand mission in 1814 and the arrival of the first three agents of the Church Missionary Society, Thomas Kendall, a school teacher; William Hall, a joiner; and John King, a shoemaker. They were all nonministers because of the society's belief that the Maori ought to be taught the practical arts of civilization before they could comprehend higher scripture. Judith Binney has nicely documented their inner and outer isolation, mutual enmities and recriminations, and unending squabbles.[20] For our purposes I want to recognize the whalers and traders who began to arrive in larger numbers at this time and for whom the Bay of Islands area chiefs would not provide provisions unless they had guns. Thus the missionaries had no choice but to act as brokers and mediate between the missions and the ships with the missionary Kendall himself becoming a key arms entrepreneur, one of the earliest in the trade that flowered in the next century. Others also emerged: I refer to a European Philip Tapsell, alias Hans Falk, alias Te Tapihana, who established his arms trade in Maketū around 1830 "to trade muskets and powder and other commodities for flax," cementing his power base by strategic marriages to three chiefly women (*T*, 258–59). He used his vessel, the *Fairy*, for both trade and for offering arms on credit to Maori chiefs (*T*, 259). On the Maori side it brought into prominence the impressive leader Hongi Hika, who protected the mission at Kerikeri and thereby consolidated the gun trade in his hands much more effectively than his rivals in the same area.

In 1818 the first significant impact of the new arms was felt, as Ballara notes:

> Muskets on one side could undoubtedly be deadly. Te Morenga's account to Marsden of how he encountered Te Waru of Tauranga in 1818 was probably factual because of its moderate claims. His taua [war party] had 35 muskets, Te Waru's people at this stage had none. Te Waru's men attacked in traditional style in a massed charge; Te Morenga's people fired one volley at close range, killing 20. . . . [T]he next day Te Waru's forces rallied and prepared to make a second attack. This was seen as it approached, so that the musket wielders had time to prepare. . . . Ultimately, according to Marsden, the dead numbered 300 or 400, and 260 prisoners were captured. (*T*, 407)

Te Morenga had a take, or good justification, for the war: fourteen years ago a "niece" of his was taken as a mistress by the captain of the *Venus* and later abandoned. She was killed and "eaten" by Te Waru's people; now, according to Te Morenga, he was going to exact utu for the injury. In this terribly destructive war the victors are supposed to have spent three days "feasting," presumably on the three to four hundred dead in the battlefield (*LJS*, 267). Everywhere in both Maori and missionary and colonial accounts the numbers are exaggerated, but the economic implications are reasonably clear: Te Morenga avenged the death of his niece in traditional manner and, at the same time, obtained slaves and virtually eliminated a competitor for the European trade. The fate of the dead heads is unknown but some of them must have found their way into the European market.

Ballara adds that those armed with muskets did not always win (*T*, 408). To me this is a truism because people with stones can on occasion overcome those with guns, if they have a good strategy, such as surprise or ambush or systematic guerilla warfare, itself a strategy invented in unequal power relations.[21]

In 1819 the missionaries informed Commissioner Bigge that the natives in this area "have acquired much skill in the use of gunpowder and firearms and obtain them and other warlike instruments from the European and other ships . . . in exchange for wood and the productions of the soil" (*HR 1*, 443). Two years later Kendall wrote, "I do not think there can be less than two thousand stands of Arms among the Natives" of this area.[22] A critical event occurred in 1819 when Hongi Hika went to England with the sole intent of getting arms. He did not get them there, but on his return to Sydney in 1821 he purchased three hundred muskets with the many gifts he had obtained in England (with the exception of the coat of mail and helmet given by King George and few other accoutrements). According to Percy Smith's information the Nga Puhi under Hongi was able to set off in September 1821 on a mission against their enemies with more than two thousand men and about a thousand muskets (*MW*, 179–80). Ballara also notes, "Because of their muskets, generalship and experience, and the fear inspired by the name by which they were become known to their enemies throughout the country, 'Nga Puhi', their success was too great by their own standards; their victories and a great number of people of rank killed set up innumerable *take* against themselves," thus upsetting the traditional balance of power in the region (*T*, 192). The numbers of men and muskets cannot be relied on, but they illustrate that both natives and missionaries gave enormous significance to the new weaponry.

All this altered the traditional relation between the tribes. Many of the wars of the nineteenth century cannot be understood except as trade wars of a sort totally new in Maori history, resulting in the expansionism of the Nga-Puhi and their allies who were fortunate to have several outstanding chiefs. The control over the seaboard by a few tribes meant that those in the interior had little access to these weapons. The latter in turn had to engage in trade with the coastal tribes, since the absence of guns could spell annihilation or at least the dread of annihilation. Best notes that the Bay of Plenty tribes such as the Tuhoe and Ngati-Tuwhoreetoa (Tuwharetoa) obtained their guns from coastal tribes. A party of Tuhoe, according to Best, once visited the Ngati Maru of Hauraki Gulf. Initially ten slaves were given in exchange for each of the guns, but the price soon came down to five slaves per gun.[23] I do not know whether slavery was a "traditional" institution or one influenced by European labor practices of the time but, irrespective of antecedent history, slave capture and trade assumed great importance and began to serve a new purpose among interior tribes. And those coastal tribes in possession of slaves could in turn sell them to white traders and labor recruiters. They were also sold for local labor for cultivating potato fields and harvesting and preparing flax. Slaves, like guns, flax, heads, and artifacts, became a valuable commodity in the expanding world system in which the Maori were beginning to be implicated. Hence accounts of this period that dealt with the large-scale eating of slaves in cannibal feasts must be viewed with extreme skepticism unless their heads served a commercial purpose in addition to the commensal one.

Best notes the massive loss of population in the northern part of the North Island during a twenty-year period up to 1840. "[Missionaries] estimated that the introduction of firearms had caused, directly or indirectly, the destruction of 80,000 natives."[24] These numbers are grossly exaggerated. According to Vayda's guesstimates at least, the total precontact Maori population was around one hundred to three hundred thousand distributed among forty tribes; about one-third of them were fighters.[25] However, there was little doubt of the depopulation of this region consequent to the introduction of the new form of warfare and new forms of disease.[26]

The escalation of wars was, then, directly or indirectly related to trade, and especially to the Maori demand for guns, also a trade product. This trade in turn led to the commodification of the Maori body: in prostitution that got started in Cook's voyages, in slavery, and in the procurement and sale of artifacts including preserved and dried heads and other extremities. The capture of slaves and specially dried heads were crucial motivations for warfare: even granting exaggerations, many accounts depict the intensity of this quest. Traditionally when a chief was killed in battle the enemy preserved his head but this traditional predilection was boosted by modern trade demand, producing through warfare an increase in the deaths of chiefs. When demand outran supply nonchiefly heads of those dying in wars were expertly carved after decapitation. Then, says the Maori historian Ranginui Walker, "chiefs resorted to tattooing slaves, killing them and selling their heads."[27] It is true that slaves could be occasionally used for this purpose though it was more profitable to sell them with their heads intact. All this meant that a new market in art forgeries began to take place in addition to tourist art that also was being created at this time for the world market.

Expeditions for procuring trade items started in Cook's time, we noted, but in the early nineteenth century they took on larger proportions and up to around 1840 the northern part of North Island was consumed by intertribal wars. Nineteenth-century narratives had to disguise the motivation for plunder for trade purposes as utu or take as Maori began to resurrect old grudges or invent new ones. These in turn skewed scholarly interpretations that emphasized the reciprocity-retaliation motive or utu, neglecting the economic imperative behind these raids. Best says that to avenge insults and wrongs "was considered to be one of the most important duties of man" and "a slight mishap might develop into a feud, and that feuds might continue for generations."[28] Maori no doubt couched their recent narratives in these traditional terms, and old motivations always coexist in situations of even drastic change. But they can be and were used to rationalize or justify the new motivations for controlling the coastal trade, for predatory expansion and land grabbing and for mobilizing new alliances among tribes for those very purposes. Once the dynamic of trade wars got started, then Maori warfare also I think took a new turn.

This of course depends on one's scholarly take on the nature of traditional warfare. Both Kerry Howe and more recently Paul D'Arcy make the point that warfare in this region was highly ritualized. "No matter how serious the issue the formalities of consultation and the 'etiquette of war' were always strictly followed."[29] Consequently, warfare did not result in many casualties, and this was true, one might add, for much of Melanesia also. Guns altered this picture in a highly qualitative fashion for though the flintlocks of the period were of poor export quality "en masse they threatened established ways. The indiscriminate hail of lead that characterized battles involving firearms was no respecter of rank or prowess; it knew no code of conduct, and feared no sanctions for breaking social norms. . . . As with any projectile weapons, the more that were used in battle the greater the chance of being struck by an unseen missile."[30] One might add a few details to complete this picture. First, the terror that guns created among those who did not have them could lead to their demoralization and ultimate defeat. Second, one expert marksman could kill a chief at a distance and the death of a chief, could be "a turning point in the battle," a not unusual phenomenon in "traditional" warfare and even today in small guerilla groups rallying round a charismatic leader.[31] This picture changed when virtually every tribe had access to guns. The universality of gun possession meant that wars fought after 1832 were effectively "musket wars."

Let me present a few cases prior to 1821 (the date of Hongi's return from England and his procurement of arms) to further illustrate the developing trade patterns. I will first use the evidence of late missionary and colonial writers followed by one of their strongest critics. Muru-paenga (Murupaenga) of Kaipara, the great chief of the coastal Ngati-Whatua strategically located on the west side of North Island lead an expedition in 1816 against the Taranaki way down the same coast. "Muru-paenga was so delighted with the country and its fertility, its stores of food, the beauty and variety of the flax growing so luxuriously in all parts, the quality of the mats or *kaitaka* cloaks . . . that he burst into song . . . still sung by the people of Taranaki" (*MW*, 62). There is a strong possibility that Maru-Paenga's praise of Taranaki flax and cloaks were not entirely aesthetically motivated. The Ngati-Whatua at this time did not have guns and needed the flax and artifacts for barter with Europeans.

A predatory expedition against Taranaki and tribes beyond was led by Tau-Kawau of the Nga-Puhi in 1816–17. Here it was clear that the Nga-Puhi had no cause, or take, for fighting Taranaki except "the desire to acquire *kaitaka*s [cloaks]" (*MW*, 68). In this war fourteen chiefs were killed and "eaten" and their heads preserved and taken back.

In 1814 Korokoro, a Nga-Puhi chief in the Bay of Islands area told Marsden that he had been engaged in lengthy voyages on the east coast and went as far as the South Cape in what were purely trading expeditions (*MW*, 71). Nonmilitary trading expeditions rarely entered into Smith's recounting of Maori war narratives.

Hongi Hika told Marsden about an expedition in 1818 (before Hongi went to England). According to this account a very large number of prisoners (that is, slaves), amounting to two thousand, were brought back to the bay and also many preserved heads of the slain. One canoe that landed in Rangihoua had as many as seventy heads. The number two thousand has to be glossed as "a large number" while seventy heads probably meant "a canoe load." In the last case it is virtually certain that the preserved heads were for sale (*LJS*, 173). That which started as collections by Cook, Banks, and other early Pacific explorers was now given a bizarre extension as Maori in the Bay of Islands area moved hesitantly into the capitalist world order.

Now let me selectively present a few cases of the new warfare, as discussed by Angela Ballara, who argues against the idea of "musket wars," though for me the evidence she carefully garners reinforces the deadly nature of the new warfare in the period 1821–32. I only want to give the reader a feel for the changes going on especially in the Bay of Islands area; Ballara's work describes the context of warfare in great detail. Consider a war planned in August 1821 by Hongi and other notable chiefs of the Bay of Islands area and the Waikato who had arrived home a month before with "a great quantity of guns, swords, powder, balls, daggers, etc." Various chiefly contingents left the Bay of Islands area early September 1821. "The missionaries thought that the whole taua numbered 2,000 and carried 1,000 muskets." The defenders at the battle of Mauinaina were sheltering behind an earthen wall, "impervious to their muskets." "At some stage Hongi himself tried to scale the palisade and got his foot stuck. He was seen by one of the defending chiefs, who feared to come close to attack Hongi, however, because he was armed with two pistols. The taua then managed to build a platform which overlooked the entrance to the pā and managed to shoot all those guarding it. They were then able to overrun the pā and take possession, killing all those who resisted, as well as women, children and three Pakeha [white] sailors who resided there. Ngati Paoa lost 300 killed of whom 100 were eaten. This modest figure derived from a primary source, contradicts the 'thousands' often said to have been killed in secondary sources. There were many captives. No doubt a large proportion of the 2,000 slaves brought back to the Bay of Islands derived from Mokoia and Mauinaina" (*T*, 219).

Another Nga Puhi war was fought in the Maungatautari District, east and west of the upper Waikato River. "[M]any of the pā in the district were abandoned without fighting from fear of Nga Puhi and the guns displayed" in two pā in that area (*T*, 240). Ballara describes yet another battle, this time in 1831 where both sides had guns. "The fighting had lasted from early morning to late afternoon, and Ngati Haua, who had borne the brunt and lost at least 60 chiefs and other men" (*T*, 246). The mass killing of chiefs would have resulted in serious cultural and physical dislocation, something totally outside traditional warfare. If such casualties occurred often in the Maori past, as Ballara claims, then her "traditional warfare" could hardly be labeled "traditional."

Here is a "blow-by-blow" description of a battle by the missionary Henry Williams and summarized by Ballara (*T*, 147–52). This was a long-distance campaign against Tauranga in 1831–32, and I use only a segment of the war waged around March 7, 1832. For sheer chaos in warfare this account is wonderful with children even picking up the shells of the guns as they were fired (*T*, 151). Fed up with the whole business the missionaries went back and forth and so did the various taua that took part in the campaign. Titore, a prominent chief, remained outside the battle area longest returning around November 27. "Williams visited him the next day; he had with him fourteen heads of 'Natewa' and three of his own people. On 30 November Williams heard that there had been two major battles, both commenced by 'Nateawa,' and that up to 200 had been killed altogether" (*T*, 152). About this and related taua, Ballara writes, "This taua to Tauranga was typical of earlier ones in many respects but significantly different in others. The style of fighting was by long-range musket volleys and 'great gun' [cannon] firing, rather than hand-to-hand fighting or one-sided barrages of firing (which occurred when only one side had significant numbers of firearms)" (*T*, 152). Unfortunately, having described these wars in detail, including the arms sales by the notorious Philip Tapsell with his three aliases and three alliances, Ballara goes on to say, "But these differences were all superficial and technological" (*T*, 152).

It is clear that I take a different stand that I will now sum up. Whether to label the new wars "musket wars" is a red herring. The larger issues have to be addressed. Wars with muskets did have dread consequences in spite of the unreliability of the numbers of dead that, like the numbers eaten and the numbers captured as slaves, have been exaggerated or are outright false. Guns articulated the Maori into the larger capitalist world order, and this articulation resulted in new strategic alliances and new forms of predatory expansion such as Te Rauparaha's, which will be discussed later. Then new techniques of warfare such as the innovative Hongi's; the readaptations of traditional fortifications (pā) to meet the new challenges; the emergence of entrepreneur chiefs, some of whom went to England and must surely have been influenced by their experiences there; the constant contact chiefs had with Australia and the white settlers and their farming and shipping practices; and the introduction of new crops like the potato with the utilization of slave labor that in turn increased the demand for arable land; the constant interchange of goods and services between Maori and whites: all had profound consequences for Maori culture and consciousness without necessarily causing a "fatal impact." Additionally, what of the public humiliation suffered by chiefs in their relation with white traders and whalers that began to erode traditional notion of chiefly mana and tapu? A particularly gross example is from 1846, during the resistance consequent to the Treaty of Waitangi when Governor Grey "boldly and treacherously seized Te Rauparaha." "Caught naked and unarmed in his house, the old chief struggled desperately until, according to one version, a sailor grabbed his testicles" to bring him under control.[32] Finally, one might even make a case that the involvement of Maori chiefs in the new trade enterprises and wars produced a shift in consciousness in some of them, a shift in mentality one might say, making them "new men" constitutive of part entrepreneurship and part "traditionalism" and sensitive to profit making in the new capital markets.[33]

BATTLEFIELD CANNIBALISM

I will now deal with the significance of the "musket wars" of the nineteenth century for the further development of that historically contingent phenomenon that I label "Maori cannibalism." Virtually all the narratives of the period deal with "battlefield cannibalism," in contrast to Maori sacrifice where, as I understand it, the body was never indiscriminately eaten. Instead, there was a high degree of ritualistic formality in dividing and eating the body. The near total preoccupation of the Maori in the nineteenth century with warfare was such that there was little evidence of the formalized types of human sacrifices noted for Hawai'i and Tahiti. Yet Best's reconstructed ethnography of the Maori past indicates that humans were sacrificed in a variety of contexts, though the details of the ritual symbolism can perhaps never be recovered.[34]

The empirical evidence of nineteenth-century battlefield cannibalism cannot, I think, be projected to the past as early ethnographers of the Maori have done. It must be seen in its own historical and socioeconomic context, as was the case with consuming Europeans or with the changed strategy of disposing dried heads. Let me shift my perspective with an illustration: we cannot say that European seafarers indulged in eating human flesh from time immemorial on the evidence of Europeans eating human flesh consequent on shipwrecks during voyages of discovery. But the idea that the savage has no history is hard to dislodge. It is true that modern anthropology has resurrected the historical dimension of ethnography in relation to traditional myths and legends, but it has yet to seriously deal with the historical forces that impinge on peoples' lives, including those forces that influence the very construction of myths and legends rather than, or in addition to, the manner in which myths help construct events. "Cannibalism" that is recorded in the nineteenth century cannot be understood aside from the historical situation of new trade relations with the West.

Consider the sheer number of chiefs killed in order to obtain their heads for trade. Surely, the preservation of the heads of enemies (and animals) is not unusual from the cross-cultural record, but not its new quantitative manifestation. This would not be feasible in traditional warfare without the new weapons of mass destruction in combination with the newly proliferating political alliances needed for capturing the European trade. Nor is it likely that the heads of Marion's and Rowe's crews were treated for eventual sale to Europeans, because for Maori the world demand did not exist at that time. Further, when there are a large number of dead chiefs, the logic of the ritual requires that they too should be eaten. But eating fourteen chiefs, for example (as in the Nga-Puhi battle of 1816–17) must produce a qualitative shift in the meaning of consuming the enemy, accelerating the logic of traditional Maori "battlefield sacrifice" where a chief is decapitated and ritually eaten. Additionally, there is a huge quantitative increase of bodies of chiefs and ordinary folk and with it problems of division and disbursement. The new situation makes the ritual procedures difficult and time consuming, if not impossible to implement fully. Ross Bowden is rightly mystified as to why these quantities of human meat cooked and eaten in the battlefield situation did not affect the ritual status of chiefs who, by their very presence in this profane environment, would lose their sacredness.[35] I think it did. If my analysis is correct, the initial, perhaps partial, secularization of sacrificial anthropophagy had already taken place in the previous century in parts of North Island, owing to the availability of the foreigner and the expansion of the consubstantial community. I suggest that one should look at the antecedent history of conquest and colonialism in order to unscramble other seemingly well-documented cases of indiscriminate man-eating.

If one assumes that traditions are created out of historical conditions as they confront the past, then it can also be argued that the creation of a new tradition, and the historical conditions that produced it, might well lead to the erosion of preexisting ones. Thus, as I see it, the eating of Europeans is not a manifestation of precontact Maori anthropophagy, but rather it is a *break* with an older symbolic order of the sacrifice where Maori chiefs or other sacrificial victims are eaten in a sacramental act. In the case of Rowe (and perhaps in some other instances also) there is the expansion of the consubstantial community consequent on the large number of corpses and the larger number of Maori "eating" them. I put "eating" in quotes because there is not a single account of the manner in which the flesh was eaten outside of the European imputation to the Maori of acts of devouring, feasting, relishing, and so forth. Battlefield cannibalism, too, was a new tradition built on the immediately prior tradition of the consumption of whites that in turn was built on previous Maori traditions of sacrifice without ever replicating them. If battlefield cannibalism led to the further expansion of the consubstantial community it would also have lead to a "pejoration" and a loosening of the regulations governing the Maori form of the older pan-Polynesian sacrificial system where who ate whom and in what manner were carefully regulated. Hence pejoration inevitably led to the erosion of chiefly tapu. It was further affected by the European definition of Maori as anthropophagous savages to be avoided and by Maori who used this image as a protective shield or an aggressive self-primitivization in the face of the unequal power relationships and the emerging colonization of their land.[36] It is also sobering to reflect that while battlefield cannibalism becomes synonymous with Maori cannibalism in the scholarly imagination, many tribes were *not* involved in the wars of the nineteenth century and therefore could not have practiced conspicuous anthropophagy. The patterns of battlefield cannibalism can be fairly well traced; with a few exceptions they were almost entirely practiced by groups in the Bay of Islands area and after 1820 most frequently with the wars waged by Hongi Hika and Te Rauparaha. There were many groups in the North Island (like the Hokianga people) who did not participate in the emerging battlefield cannibalism; these folk and those who lived in the less-populated South Island rarely appear in the Western construction of Maori anthropology and anthropophagy.

CANNIBALISM AND THE IDEA OF "DISCURSIVE SPACE"

Let me digress a moment and get back to the kind Dr. Savage and his interpretation of anthropophagous proclivities of the Maori. As I continue with his narrative I find him not altogether kind, at least not from my current twenty-first-century perspective, because Savage tells his reader that Maori-land is an excellent place for European colonization. It seems that Dr. Savage could not think otherwise because his space for relatively open, but never free, discursive reasoning has been restricted by the all-pervading ethos of imperialist and colonialist expansionism of his time. By contrast, the definition of the Maori as a cannibal has not yet congealed during his stay at the Bay of Islands. The missions hadn't physically arrived yet, the date of the last massacre was long past and the new ones hadn't yet occurred; consequently, Savage perhaps saw no visible physical evidence for Maori anthropophagy in the places he visited. Thus it is not as if Savage was telling us a truth about Maori cannibalism, but rather that he had a relatively free space to talk about what he felt was the truth. Soon after Savage's visit there were larger numbers of traders and whalers visiting New Zealand followed by the first permanent community of missionary settlers in 1814 not to mention those outside as in Fort Jackson in Australia, who considered the Maori inveterate cannibals.

In this situation it was difficult to find discursive spaces for reasoned and reasonable inquiry, as I shall show in the case of the missionary leader, Samuel Marsden. The problem that a sympathetic person like Marsden faced was not unusual even in later times. It concerns a fundamental puzzlement regarding Maori cannibalism at this historical juncture: cannibalism is supposedly sacrificial and ritualistic, yet it is not, witness the real and imputed cases of conspicuous anthropophagy. The "liberal" interpretation of Maori cannibalism of later ethnographers had to contend with this dilemma. Nevertheless, it is significant that, in spite of the prevailing definition of the Maori as cannibal, it was possible for Marsden to come up with a less-pejorative view of Maori anthropophagy irrespective of whether it was empirically valid because it must be reiterated that none of the missionaries was permitted in the sacrificial arena.

Let me start with an early statement of Marsden in December 1814 in his first visit to New Zealand.

> The New Zealanders are all cannibals. They did not appear to have any idea that this was an unnatural crime. When I expressed my abhorrence at their eating one another, they said it had always been the custom to eat their enemies. I was unable to ascertain whether they ever ate human flesh as a meal, or from choice, or in cool blood; but it strikes me to be only from mental gratification and in retaliation for some great injury. As far as I can form an opinion of this horrid custom, I am inclined to believe that the New Zealanders do not consider it any more crime to eat their enemies than civilized nations do to hang an offender, although at the same time it stamps as much public disgrace upon the surviving relatives as the public execution of a criminal in Europe reflects upon the family of the sufferer. (*LJS*, 129)

Although more sympathetic than most accounts, this is simply a digest of accepted prejudice or a recounting of what was known about Maori cannibalism among Europeans, including the axiomatic view that all New Zealanders, without exception, were cannibals. But the following account, from Marsden's second visit in 1819, is more interesting. There is detail, and we know that his informants were from the Bay of Islands area. I refer to this at length because it begins with a startling commentary on the internal trade in heads that might have arisen as a consequence of recent external trade, a fascinating indication that internal trade had also received an expected but bizarre fillip from the emergent capitalism. "If the conqueror never intends to make peace, he will dispose of the heads of those chiefs whom he kills in battle to ships or any persons who will buy them. Sometimes they are purchased by the friends of the vanquished from the conqueror and returned to their surviving relations, who hold them in the highest veneration and indulge their natural feelings by reviewing them and weeping over them" (*LJS*, 168). He then describes the manner in which the victim's head is cut off and the performance of the "accustomed religious ceremony" for figuring out through priestly utterances whether they will be successful in battle. If the priest does not give a good prognosis, then they will quit the field of battle. "The head already taken is reserved for the chief on whose account the war was undertaken as a satisfaction for the injury he had received, or some of his tribe, from the enemy." After the war is over it is cured and displayed "to show them that justice has been obtained from the offending party." The dead body of the chief is cut up into small portions and dressed and eaten by the participants; on occasion portions may be sent to friends. Marsden then goes on to say that the bones of the chief are distributed among friends "who make whistles of some of them and fish hooks of others. These they value and preserve with care as memorials of the death of their enemies." It is also customary to taste the blood of a slain enemy because this will make him "safe from the wrath of the god of him who is fallen, believing that from the moment he tastes the blood of the man he has killed the dead man becomes a part of himself and places him under the protection of the *atua*, or god, of the departed spirit" (*LJS*, 168).

Marsden's informants were chiefs from the Bay of Islands area who either spoke to him in their broken English, or he had someone like the missionary Kendall to interpret for him. He could not possibly have got complex information such as pertaining to the "first fish." He then added that eating human flesh originated in religious superstition, and there was "no instance of any man ever being killed merely to gratify the appetite; nor of any killed for the purpose of selling their heads to the Europeans and other nations. The heads which are cured and sold are those of the slain in war which are not intended to be returned to their friends" (*LJS*, 169). Yet, though an ideal typical account, this contains considerable information. It appears that in 1819 Maori of North Island were selling preserved heads of "chiefs" to Europeans, and this is seen as an extension of normal practice. The theme is taken up in the last paragraph where Marsden says that chiefs were not killed explicitly for trade purposes. This might at least be partially correct because the escalation of warfare and sale of heads as pure commodity occurred only soon afterward. The rest of the description, though thin, emphasizes the religious significance of the sacrifice: it is the head of a chief that is taken and it is part of religious ritual. The flesh is distributed to "friends" and consumed in a thanksgiving ritual to the gods. The paragraph that deals with the tasting of the blood of the enemy in order to obtain the mana (this term is not used) of the dead man's god is entirely possible, but no information is given on how it is "tasted," that is, whether it was a symbolic act. This particular ethnographic information is the basis for considerable fantastic elaboration in later accounts, based I believe on European notions of vampirism.

Soon afterward, in his continuing cannibal talk with Hongi, as to whether they eat those they kill in battle, Marsden was told that the dead chief as well as his wife might also be ceremonially killed and then eaten. I think that in spite of communication difficulties one must treat this account seriously because it is in Hongi's wars that the clearest pejoration of Maori sacrificial anthropophagy had taken place.

> When they have got possession of a chief and his wife, after the woman is killed, their bodies are placed in order before the chiefs. The areekee *[ariki]*, or high priest, then calls out to the chiefs to dress him the body of the man

> for his god. The priestess, who is also an areekee, then gives the command to the wives of the chiefs to dress the woman for her god. The bodies are then placed on the fires and roasted by the chiefs and their wives, none of the common people being allowed to touch them as they are tabooed.
>
> When the bodies are dressed, the areekees take each a piece of the flesh in a small basket, which they hang upon two sticks stuck into the ground, as food for their god, to whom they are going to offer up their prayers and to consult relative to the present contest in order that their god may partake first of the sacrifices.
>
> While these ceremonies are performing all the chiefs sit in profound silence in a circle round the dead bodies with their faces covered with their hands or mats, as they are not permitted to look on these holy mysteries during the time the areekees are praying and picking small pieces of the flesh from their sacrifices, which they eat at the same time. These consecrated bodies are only to be eaten by the areekees. When all the sacred services are completed, the areekees return the answer of their gods to their prayers and offerings. If their prayers and offerings are accepted the battle is immediately renewed, as was formerly mentioned, and all in common feed upon the after slain. (*LJS*, 174)

Something else is going on in this statement: Marsden has to reconcile the information on conspicuous anthropophagy among the Maori and bring this information into his discursive space. If the information is correct, as I think it is, then a serious change has taken place: chiefs and even chiefly women actually participate in the cutting and dressing of victims, something that is alien, according to most scholars, to "traditional" Maori sacrifice. Thus Marsden's account reflects the changes mentioned by me earlier, but it still depicts a ritualistic and sacrificial quality rather than eating for meat's sake. Finally, Marsden comes back to the earlier theme to show that Maori were not anthropophagous by nature but only by their culture, itself an argument against the many that held the reverse position. "They eat the slain, not so much as an object of food but as a mental gratification and to display publicly to the enemy their bitter revenge" (*LJS*, 174).

A few months later he again reinforces the information he derived from Hongi Hika.

> When a chief is killed in battle and his body roasted by the chief who slew him, it is consecrated by the priest and no common person is permitted to taste it. The priest takes a portion of the flesh and sets it apart for his god. He then takes a portion for himself which he eats, and also tastes the blood. The chief

> follows his example. The New Zealanders believe that the soul of a chief, when departed from the body, becomes a god and has the power of life and death. They also believe that, by eating the flesh and drinking the blood of the departed chief, his system becomes incorporated into their system, and by that means they are secured from all danger from the departed ghost of the dead chief, and his spirit will then take up its residence in their bodies as being part of its former habitation. (*LJS*, 220)

The chiefs "roasting" the flesh are possible only in the context of the emergence of changes in Maori warfare and anthropophagy. However the phrase "eating the flesh and drinking the blood" is deliberately used to make the Christian connection. "Our Saviour told the Jews: 'He that eateth my flesh and drinketh my blood dwelleth in me and I in him.' Their eating human flesh is part of their religion. The New Zealanders cutting off the heads of the chiefs, their enemies, and collecting them together, is similar to what was done to Ahab's sons when Jehu rebelled against him" (*LJS*, 220). Once again we are back to the older theme of the sacrifice as it is performed in the battlefield, which has now become the only place of sacrifice. Further, this discourse taps the fact of the large number of chiefly heads being cut and "collected together." It is as if the enormous preoccupation with the nineteenth-century wars by the Maori of the Bay of Islands area has eliminated the discursive space for Marsden and others to discuss other forms of sacrificial anthropophagy in New Zealand. The reference to Jewish custom and Christian parallels is not so much an explication of Maori cannibalism as an attempt to view it sympathetically, given Marsden's view that the Maori came from Jewish stock. Yet, Marsden's sense of Maori sacrifice as having affinities with the Jewish tradition is not free of equivocation either because it exempts his own Protestant faith from any such barbarism though he generously concedes that it is not unrelated to Christian (Protestant) prayer (*LJS*, 373).

From Marsden's accounts we see that while serious changes have occurred with chiefs directly involved in roasting and dressing the flesh and with women as coparticipants, Maori anthropophagy still remains sacrificial at least in the worldview of Hongi Hika, re-presented by Marsden. But the direct involvement of chiefs and women would surely have lead to the loss of the tapu of chiefs, already threatened by the presence of white traders who paid scant regard to chiefly tapu. Marsden cannot tell us whether there was at some point a further expansion of the consubstantial community with commoners also engaged in consuming human flesh owing to the number of corpses made available, especially of alien whites who were not part of the traditional sacrifice. In any case, it is not surprising that later scholars have transferred Marsden's model backward in time as reflecting a generalized Maori past containing a notion of sacrifice with its sacramental community alongside a notion at variance with it, that of conspicuous anthropophagy, originally stemming from Cook's descriptions and "verified" during the succeeding period when a form of conspicuous anthropophagy seems to have become a reality among warring tribes in the North Island. However, the substantive content and details of that reality cannot be described by us because there is no reliable evidence as to how chiefs consumed the flesh of the large numbers of enemies killed; in other words, we cannot know whether the so-called cannibal feasts took place. There is, however, one instance in which there is good documentation for a "cannibal feast," no longer as an exclusive Maori practice but one in which the British were coparticipants.

THE MONSTER WITHIN: CAPTAIN STEWART, TE RAUPARAHA, AND THE "NEW MAN"

He who fights monsters should be careful
lest he thereby becomes a monster himself.
And if you gaze long into the abyss, the
abyss will also gaze into you.

FRIEDRICH NIETZSCHE,
Beyond Good and Evil

The whalers were a special case because they had to confront two sources of monstrosity, the savage cannibals and the monsters of the sea, both of whom could be eliminated without qualms. But, as both Nietzsche and Melville point out, this is at the risk of becoming a monster oneself in a psychological sense. To illustrate this phenomenon of "psychic monstrosity" let me begin with Gawan Daws's remarkable summary of Melville's vision of the frightening ethos of whalers and their inner and outer isolation.

> The crewmen of the *Pequod* lived in the vile stench of boiling blubber, doused themselves in blood, hacked their way through the monstrous carcasses and cathedral-tall skeletons of whales till they were grubbing with their hands 'amongst the unspeakable foundations, ribs, and very pelvis of the world.' And at last a sailor called the "mincer," who sliced the blubber for the try-pots—"bible leaves" the thin slices were called—would attack the giant

> penis of the whale, man-tall and black, skin it, stretch the skin to dry, and cut armholes in it, a barbaric cassock to wear as he worked, 'invested in the full canonicals of his calling.' . . .
>
> The omens of apocalypse were there. At the wheel of the *Pequod* one night, Ishmael had a vision in which the working of the forward-looking, government-encouraged American whale industry turned savage before his eyes, and, having turned savage, turned mad. The try-works furnaces burned like funeral pyres. Flames licked up at the masts. The pagan harpooners fed the blubber fires and the pots with long pronged poles like so many devils, and the resting crewmen, smoke-and sweat stained, lounged and swapped stories and looked into the red heat of the fires until their eyes scorched in their heads. 'As they narrated to each other their unholy adventures, their tales of terror told in words of mirth; as their uncivilized laughter forked upwards out of them, like the flames of the furnace; as to and fro, in their front, the harpooners wildly gesticulated with their huge pronged forks and dippers; as the wind howled on, the sea leaped, and the ship groaned and dived, and yet steadfastly shot her red hell further and further into the blackness of the sea and the night, and scornfully champed the white bone in her mouth, and viciously spat round her on all sides; then the rushing Pequod, freighted with savages, and laden with fire, and burning a corpse, and plunging into the blackness of darkness, seemed the material counterpart of her monomaniac commander's soul.'[37]

Melville's Ahab, the monster killer, was someone who stared into the abyss but, lacking the belated insight of a Lear, could not make sense of the abyss that peered back into him.

For Melville the killing of the new monsters was a bizarre commentary on Europe's past. The images he conjures in *Moby Dick* parody Western chivalry: the weapons used for killing the new monsters are javelins or lances; the whale is a "demi-gorgon," evoking the adventures of Perseus, St. George, and dragon killing; the officers are "knights" with their "squires" from the lower depths or decks.[38] These thick images force us to question whether the monster-killing knights of Western myth were not, like Ahab himself, possessed by a form of psychic monstrosity. Ahab had no illusions regarding his "savage crew," yet in his deluded thinking, "their savageness even breeds a certain generous knight-errantism in them."[39] And this, thought Ahab, impels them to give chase to that white whale, Moby Dick, and then adds somewhat cynically, perhaps with the voice of Melville himself: "For even the high lifted and chivalric Crusaders of old times were not content to traverse two thousand miles of land to fight for their holy sepulcher without committing burglaries, picking pockets, and gaining other pious perquisites by the way."[40]

Melville's Nantucket was one of the centers of whaling life. Nathaniel Philbrick describes its socializing ethos well: "The first words a baby was taught included the language of the chase—'townor,' for instance, a Wampanoag word meaning that the whale has been sighted for the second time. . . . One mother approvingly recounted how her nine-year-old son attached a fork to the end of a ball of darning cotton and then proceeded to harpoon the family cat. The mother happened into the room just as the terrified pet attempted to escape."[41] In Nantucket there was also a secret society of women whose members "pledged to marry only men who had already killed a whale," a modern Quaker version of the old chivalry.[42] "Bedtime stories told of killing whales and eluding cannibals in the Pacific."[43] Whales and cannibals: the equation has its corollary in eating whale blubber, a foul substance for which veterans had a special fondness, and living and sometimes reveling in the stink of whale oil. Charles Nordhoff says that "old whalemen delight in it. The fetid smoke is incense to their nostrils. The filthy oil seems to them a glorious representative of prospective dollars and delights."[44] It is hard to believe that related ethoses did not prevail in centers of the whaling industry in Europe.

Melville describes in frightening detail the transformation of the whale into commercial products, all processed on board the ship. Whaling in New Zealand and along the Australian coast was not the exclusive preserve of American whalers; Europeans were there also, but the industry was dominated by the British. Moreover, many famed British whaling companies such as the Enderbys were originally from Nantucket.[45] But the crew was mostly convicts and ex-convicts and otherwise rough characters who not only killed monsters but also had little compunction in killing their human counterparts. Whaling combined with trading for flax and sandalwood commenced off the northern coast of New Zealand from around 1794. This meant that the Bay of Islands with its fine inlets and harbors became a place for provisioning.

But soon the strategy changed as whalers familiarized themselves with the seasonal movement of whales to the coasts of New Zealand, when in the "beginning of May, [they] skirted the western coastline of the North Island, passed between Kapiti Island and the mainland" and then moved to other places along the coast.[46] This meant that Melville's famed try-works were now established on the beach and boats went out to sea to kill whales and bring them ashore. In the early thirties whale fisheries were such a flourishing business that several whale stations were established along the coast by Sydney entrepreneurs, with the first cargo of New Zealand whale oil reaching Sydney on February 3, 1830. But whale oil, bones, and sperm were not the only products, because a new profitable New Zealand commodity, flax, soon became equally important and gathering parties went along the coast to collect it. Flax, provisions, and landing rights were dependant on the new Maori entrepreneur chiefs who demanded muskets, gunpowder, pipes, tobacco, and rum in exchange for flax, thus further escalating the musket wars.

Sydney citizens did realize, says McNab, that trade was flourishing simply because Maori tribes wanted the now-no-longer-new weapons to fight one another, but there was no resisting free-market operations. Along with the escalating intertribal warfare was the eternally recurring European ideological fantastic of the war-to-end-all wars because some thought that the "supplies of muskets and gunpowder which were pouring into New Zealand would make war such a fearful thing that the natives would hesitate to embark on it and peace would result" (*OWD*, 6). Kapiti Island, also known as Entry Island because it provided entry into Cook Strait and thence to Queen Charlotte Sound, had become the "great flax emporium of New Zealand," owing to its strategic location that commanded the increasing sea traffic.[47] The commercial importance of this place in turn led to the rise of its chief Te Rauparaha of Kawhia. He left his home tribe in 1819 and in a complex series of maneuvers led a remarkable heke, or migration, jointly with his allies, from Hokianga down the west coast and over the Taranki mountains, then to Kapiti, which his taua captured around September 1822. Te Rauparaha himself claimed that by 1830 his people had possession of about two thousand muskets.[48] This same year traders took from Kapiti "a total of 102 tons of flax, about one-eight of the total exported from New Zealand to Sydney in that year."[49] In this new game whalers and chiefs like Te Rauparaha entered into alliances to plunder those tribes who possessed stocks of the precious commodity (*OWD*, 12–13).

I have already presented in this chapter some of the atrocities committed by whalers and traders in the early nineteenth century. Reading the documents collected by McNab one has the impression of a litany of violence, humiliation, and outright homicide perpetrated on native populations. Whaling provided economic benefits to regions such as Kapiti, but the increasing presence of ships meant that Maori and other South Seas people also went on journeys in British ships, not only to the adjacent regions but also to England. The journeys of a few Maori have been recorded by Anne Salmond, but I do not see them as "explorers" as she does in the European sense of that term, or any other sense. Unequal colonial power relations meant that Maori and others were seen as inferior, and Anne Salmond's actual record of their fates is a pathetic one, because most of these native "explorers" ended up living in misery, suffering maltreatment, and even dying prematurely.[50] The fates of ordinary people were no better; sometimes they were shot at with impunity but they were also captured or bought as slaves such that "young men and women were sold in the Malayan bazaars, at prices varying from thirteen to twenty shillings" (*BW*, 365).

Let me give a few examples of violence directed against the Maori by the new whalers and dealers. In a "memorial" of 1817 to Samuel Marsden in his role as justice of the peace the Church Missionary Society noted that "[a] year or two before this [the Boyd incident] the captain of an English ship which was sailing by one of the islands fired, without any provocation, five or six large guns, loaded with grape shot, among a multitude of natives, men, women, and children, who were assembled on the beach to look at the vessel, and killed and wounded several of them." The captain himself formulated his prescient vision of shock and awe very explicitly: "When remonstrated with for this act of wanton barbarity he only said it was necessary to strike terror into the minds of these natives, and convince them of what power we possessed" (*HR 1*, 419). In 1812 "the brig Daphne was off the Island of Riematerra *[sic]* when eighteen natives came off in three canoes with fruit; they were invited on board, behaved in the most friendly and respectful manner, and delivered their cargoes of supplies, for which they received a trifling remuneration. The captain then ordered the crew to turn them out of the ship; this was done in the most barbarous manner; they were beaten with ropes to force them over the sides of the ship into the sea; they swam to their canoes, which were swamped, and fourteen of them were drowned within sight of the brig" (*BW*, 428–29). Those inured to the killing of monsters have become inured to the killing of natives. Psychic monstrosity has become prevalent among whalers and traders, especially among monomaniacal commanders all too frequent in the good old whaling days.[51] But the interaction between whalers and chiefs sometimes produced a "synchronicity" between them, a theme I shall now discuss in some detail getting back to the whaling and trading emporium of Kapiti Island with its two chiefs Te Rauparaha and Te Hiko, both new Maori men spawned by the emerging capitalist world system.[52]

In 1830 the whaling and trading vessel, the brig *Elizabeth*, under the command of Captain John Stewart, the hypocrite shadow of Melville's monomaniacal commander, arrived in Whangaroa and then went to Kapiti Island. The object of Stewart's voyage was to collect flax in exchange for muskets, but since nothing was available there, Te Rauparaha persuaded Captain Stewart to collect flax from

Akaroa (Banks Peninsula, way down on the east coast of South Island), whose chief Tamaiharanui had slain Te Hiko's father. Tamaiharanui had already been given a bad press by Captain Briggs, commander of the *Dragon*, to a Hobart Town editor as "a monster, the recapitulation of whose atrocities would fill a dozen of your numbers." Rauparaha's plan was to extract utu (in the now narrow sense of "revenge") from Tamaiharanui and at the same time barter flax for guns with Captain Stewart. Apparently, Te Rauparaha had previously tried to enlist Captain Briggs for this task, but unlike Briggs, Stewart's trading master Cowell "would have no scruples how flax or any other cargo was obtained, so long as it was got" (*OWD*, 24). The account of this nefarious alliance is put together from sworn depositions of several persons who were present during the expedition.

Apparently about 120 Kapiti Island Maori, armed with muskets, were placed in the hold of the ship "for the purpose of capturing the chief called Maitraruni [Tamaiharanui] of that District, bring him back to Entry [Kapiti] Island, when they would receive a quantity of flax in payment."[53] When the *Elizabeth* first landed there in early November 1830 Tamaiharanui was not at home but on the flax ground with the women preparing flax. Stewart brought ten muskets and two casks of gunpowder to lure the chief, and this succeeded because a few days later he and his eleven-year-old daughter peacefully boarded the *Elizabeth*.

According to the sworn testimony of seaman W. Brown before a Sydney magistrate, he along with the captain and the trading master Cowell went ashore to shoot and on their return they met a canoe with a chief in it. Cowell persuaded the chief to come on board accompanied by his eleven-year-old daughter and three or four natives. "The Chief and the little girl went down into the cabin and they were kept there" (*HR 2*, 584). This is pretty much confirmed by Pery, a native of the area and Tamaiharanui's "brother's son" who was taken prisoner but managed to escape to Sydney. The mother, who according to some accounts was already in the ship, strangled the daughter (perhaps aided by the father) fearful of what might happen to her. The Kapiti Islanders, according to ordinary seamen Brown and Swan, went ashore in their enemies' canoes along with a skiff and a whaleboat belonging to the ship (*HR 2*, 585, 587). What happened was reasonably clear: they burned the place and, says Pery "a great number of people were taken as prisoners on board the ship"(*HR 2*, 582). He also said that the chief was killed by strangulation with a cord by the people of Kapiti Island and later eaten, though there are many more versions of this event.

According to all accounts the English sailors also participated in the massacre at Banks Island. Pery says that "in the fight that took place I saw the white people of the ship take prisoners many of the Banks people and hand them over to the natives of Entry [Kapiti]" (*HR 2*, 582). Many were killed and, according to virtually all depositions, baskets containing dressed human flesh were brought on board and cooked there.[54] The captain was apparently in the boat at this time, but the next morning he went ashore with several sailors fully armed to savor the killings still going on and to witness the village still in flames (*HR 2*, 585). In his deposition J. Swan claims he saw on the shore another act of dressing the dead for later consumption (*HR 2*, 596–88).

The whole episode brought to the fore the quest for mementos and trophies. On the European side when Tamaiharanui was killed "one of the sailors brought two of his fingers on board the ship" either as a memento or possibly for later sale.[55] Governor Darling of New South Wales suggests that some on the Maori side also brought "remains of their victims" as trophies, presumably heads for sale to European sailors (*HR 2*, 593). In fact one can no longer speak of the Maori or European "side" because there were dialogical understandings on both sides that related to commercial development in this region and the development of new forms of monstrosity.

It seems that warfare cannibalism can now hardly be distinguished from "trade cannibalism" motivated more by the emergent capitalism than by the desire to extract utu or reprisal-reciprocity for an old injury. I have already noted that utu had become established as a cultural rationale for trade and barter in muskets, slaves, and heads; or, to put it differently, there was a harmony between the native institution of reprisal and the newly introduced capitalism. The British coparticipation in cannibalism gives their capitalism a fantastic quality as the flesh brought on board after the first round of violence was cooked in the ships "coppers" (cauldrons) used for processing whales. These actions on the ground and aboard ship would have violated all older ideas the Maori had about time, place, and ritual procedures. The British brought the armed Kapiti Islanders to Akaroa; they even participated in the killing; therefore it is likely that the Kapiti Islanders thought that the British ought also to participate in the act of eating the enemy. Cooking the flesh on board could only have occurred with the Captain's permission. We do not know whether some of the sailors actually ate the flesh. Cannibalism however has fully become the self-fulfilling prophecy for both "savages" and the "civilized" possessed by the monster within their separate yet interpenetrating consciousnesses or synchronicity.[56]

Some of the sworn depositions link up with the Marsden's discourse on Hongi's version of Maori anthropophagy. I see no reason why J. Swan had to invent his own complicity in the violence and invent the account of cannibalism (or is it anthropophagy?). "On the morning of the general landing, two chiefs, one of them called Rupaura [Te Rauparaha], Richardson, William Brown, George Wall, and Mr. Cowell were in the boat. We were armed with swords and pistols, and we all landed on one side of the harbour. The chiefs joined some of the natives of Entry Island. There were lying on the ground fifteen or sixteen dead bodies of men, women and children. I saw some of the Entry Island natives, and the two chiefs, cut up some of the bodies and make a fire" (*HR 2*, 587).

Chiefs cutting up bodies and preparing a fire seems too far out of character even at this late period (1830), except that one can no longer speak of Maori anthropophagy or that of the Bay of Islands area but only individual chiefly versions of it, such as Hongi's mentioned earlier and Te Rauparaha's in this case. It seems that the mad savagery of the white whaler that Melville describes has merged with the native madness of the chief. Te Rauparaha himself was the new Maori produced by the political and economic conditions of colonialism and early capitalism in this part of the world. He was also given to a "violent taste for liquor," and this might indicate some of his neglect of convention. A paradoxical figure, he was also a resistance fighter against British rule.[57] Either way if, as Ross Bowden and others say, cooking was a profane activity and chiefs were not supposed to be even in the vicinity, then a real erosion of traditional values regarding mana and tapu had taken place in the cases of both Hongi and Te Rauparaha.[58]

The depositions also provide some evidence regarding the exaggerations that take place in respect of the already perverse anthropophagy of Kapiti Island chiefs and their followers.[59] John Swan says there were twenty prisoners in the hold of the ship, and he saw the bodies of fifteen or sixteen men, women, and children lying on the ground. William Brown saw six or seven dead, but there might have been more. Soon we are in the realm of pure rumor: A. Kemmis, a merchant on board, heard a "general report" that 190 were made prisoner (*HR 2*, 583). Governor Darling in a letter to the secretary of state said that "Rauparaha and his people . . . indulged their natural ferocity to the utmost, by putting everyone to death, without distinction of sex and age, and turning their village to the ground" (*HR 2*, 593). Both ignore the complicity of the whites, who joined the fray and captured prisoners for Te Rauparaha. And rumor and hearsay can be converted to fact when some accounts say that Tamaharanui was given to a chief's wife who fattened him, decked him in nice clothes, and then when he was ready for eating, took a long iron rod and stabbed him in the jugular to drink his blood as it gushed forth, placing her mouth over the orifice. Others credit this same lady with fixing Tamaiharunui to a cross and cutting his throat, a wondrous combination of the fantasy of Roman-style executions and of European vampirism. "It was also said that while she drank a portion of the blood as it flowed from the wound, her son, Te Hiko, tore out the eyes of his victim, and swallowed them, to prevent them being fixed in the firmament of stars, as Maori believed would happen on such an event" (*OWD*, 32).

Consider this infamous episode in light of the pejoration of Maori cannibalism that now seems to have occurred with Western contact and the beginnings of trade. The nefarious alliance between the European traders and Kapiti Island Maori and their coparticipation in warfare, the capturing of slaves, trophy collections, and cannibalism are an expression of capitalistic involvement. There is nothing unusual in this development either because we know that the introduction of capitalism in modern third world nations and in the former Soviet Empire immediately creates the rise of a Mafia and an alliance of politicians, brigands, and robber barons for the control of the economy and the polity. But let me go beyond this political and economic dimension: the shift in cannibalism where the bodies of the enemies are cooked on board has produced what seems like a confirmation of the Maori cannibal feast. It then becomes easy to weave Western fantasies into this fabric, including that of vampirism, and re-represent this as an expression of Maori cannibalism.

The sequel is a sad commentary on white justice in the new colonies. The depositions were forwarded to Governor Darling. Darling consulted Mr. Moore, the crown law officer who said that Stewart could not be charged under the criminal law of England. When protests from England compelled the Sydney authorities to take action, there were so many delays in executing official orders that neither Stewart nor Cowell was available. McNab says that "the responsibility for this shocking miscarriage of justice must rest with someone in Sydney" (*OWD*, 35). But the evidence he has garnered suggests that the vague "someone" is a stand-in for influential persons in Sydney who had multiple ties with whalers and traders and no doubt shared with them the projections of monstrosity onto the native. They were only too eager to *deny*, in the psychoanalytic sense, psychic monstrosity in their own community and within their own selves. The miscarriage of justice has its parallel in a miscarriage of truth as this statement from a contemporary scholar indicates: "Captain Stewart, who single-handedly gave a boost to the notion of violent European ravages, was really no more than Te Rauparaha's taxi driver."[60]

By the middle of the nineteenth century anthropophagy of any sort ceased to exist among the Maori though the cannibal fantasy continued to burgeon in the imagination of both the natives and the settlers. The critical date for the end of anthropophagy is the beginning of history, so to speak, when New Zealand was declared a crown colony and the Treaty of Waitangi was signed by the Maori in 1840. Soon European settlements were in full force along with European judicial, military, and bureaucratic control over the island. Even though Maori rebelled against the British and killed quite a few of them, they apparently had no longer a need for eating their enemies! That they could give up man-eating with changed political conditions suggests that the Maori were not the inveterate anthropophagites they were made to be in the first place in the European consciousness.

What then happened to the powerful European fantasy of Maori cannibalism? First, the Maoris were now one's neighbor and getting to know them better showed that they no longer practiced anthropophagy. Moreover, it is not pleasant to have cannibals as neighbors and members of the same state, if not the same nation. Second, and very importantly, there [were] other groups of cannibals that the European imagination could feast on: the Marquesans and the Fijians. In this work I shall only deal with the Fijians who became truly ferocious cannibals displacing the Maori in respect of this achievement. The Fijian narratives of cannibalism became more and more graphic as they began to take the place of the Maori in the European imagination. Thus, when cannibalism virtually disappeared among the Maori, it resurged in the Marquesas and Fiji. Both places were at some time or other designated as the "cannibal islands."

The term *cannibal islands* entered into cannibal discourse for the first time in 1533 and was identified with the Leeward Islands in the Antilles, home of the notorious island Caribs, where Columbus landed in 1493; then to Dominica and soon to black Africans in 1544; then the term migrated to Brazil, which was for a long time the land of cannibals until the South Seas captured the European mind and New Zealand became the "land of cannibals" (*C*, 33–36). One can even make the case, albeit somewhat facetiously, that the decline of Maori cannibalism in the European consciousness was the "cause" of the rise of cannibalism in Fiji. And so it is to that unholy city that we shall now sail to talk of what is past and passing though not of the to-come.

SIX · Cannibal Feasts in Nineteenth-Century Fiji

Seamen's Yarns and the Ethnographic Imagination

FIJI AND THE METAPHYSICS OF SAVAGISM

Despite that fact that I am not as familiar with the political and economic situation of Fiji in the late eighteenth and early nineteenth centuries as I am with the Maori, I believe that in Fiji also there developed a form of pronounced anthropophagy that must be seen in terms of the European presence. The lure of trade, the musket wars, and the rise of powerful chiefdoms and the political confederations that resulted drew Fiji gradually into the world capitalist order. We know that pronounced anthropophagy existed in New Zealand mainly, though not exclusively, in the Bay of Islands area. Similarly pronounced anthropophagy was most evident in the areas that were influenced by the new commerce and political relations with the West, especially Bau, followed by Rewa and Somosomo and perhaps Bua and Macuata. As I deal with Fijian cannibalism I will, even schematically, consider the political developments in this region in the early nineteenth century. The interlinkage between pronounced anthropophagy and the new developments must await further research.

How then could one approach Fijian cannibalism and anthropophagy? I suggest that this could be done in a preliminary way by looking at Fiji through the metaphysics of savagism. Why "metaphysics" though? The reader will know that I borrow this term from Melville's *Confidence Man* where he speaks of the "metaphysics of Indian hating."[1] But Indian hating does not exist in isolation. As I see it, it is a general emotional reaction arising from the metaphysics of savagism and which, we noted, makes an essentialist definition of the Indian living in a state of nature, the quality of his very being. The metaphysics of savagism can be quite complicated, as Anthony Padgen shows in his discussion of Catholic and especially Jesuit theologians beginning with the discovery of the Americas. These theologians developed their metaphysics from Aristotle's concept of "natural slavery," that is, the idea that some people and groups were by nature slaves and given to serve others. Some scholar-priests defended the idea of natural slavery in respect of Amerindians, but others used Aristotle to show that the Indians, especially, the Aztecs and Incas, could develop a civilized order that would permit them eventually to become fully Christian and to live in cities, which for thinkers like Francisco de Vitoria and Bartolomé de Las Casas was the hallmark of being civilized and rational.[2] But, as Padgen points out, even the most sympathetic theologians saw the Amerindians, including the Aztecs and Incas, living under the dominion of Satan. For José de Acosta the religions of Incas and Aztecs were a result of "satanic intervention," while practices like sodomy, masturbation, bestiality, and especially cannibalism were forms of "satanic pollution."[3] And when it came to tribes such as the Caribs and those Amerindians who lived outside native cities, they were either natural slaves or a version thereof and sometimes no better than the beasts in the jungle.[4]

One could add all kinds of essentialist components to the intrinsic conception of savagism as a state of nature: positively, the nobility of the savage, his freedom from the constraints that beset European societies of the time, the early classic example being Montaigne's paper "On Cannibalism" and fully developed in European romanticism. It would not surprise us if the negative components are the more powerful ones and omnipresent in settler and ordinary missionary discourse—the lack of civil society, Satanism, or the worship of demons, the absence of civilized morality that impels savages to commit acts of brutality, even fornicating with close kin and killing them in times of need. Other components might include infanticide, familial incest, and sodomy as the more common ones, and then cannibalism. Cannibalism becomes the most powerful component of the metaphysics of savagism at every level of discourse; it did not matter whether or not the society that Europe confronted had an antecedent tradition of sacrificial anthropophagy. Hence it is not surprising that cannibalism has been found in virtually every part of the expanding world after the fifteenth century. Cannibalism, one might say, constituted a projective field for the European outsider, an arena wherein his personal conflicts and anxieties and those anxieties attendant on living in an alien community could be expressed. Thus the powerful emotional appeal of savagism: it provides a justification for Indian hating and, in its extreme forms, of Indian extermination. Therefore the metaphysics of savagism shows a strong family resemblance to Orientalism, but more than in Orientalism there is a continuing oppositional dialectic with Civilization. While the content of that dialectic might vary, its metaphysic remains as a structure of long duration. As such it antedates Orientalism, in the sense that Edward Said defines it, and similarly exerts power at the service of colonial domination. Civilization also has an intrinsic value: unlike savagery it entails the taming of nature, a gift given by God on which can be erected notions of rationality, progress, and civil society. Even when god drops out of the picture the other components remain with rationality given prominent place and associated with scientific thought. In missionary discourse in Fiji this dialectic has produced the radical and ostensive distinction between Heathenism and Christianity (or Religion) and the polarization of Fijian society in these terms, something that did not occur in New Zealand on quite that scale. The scale of imagined Fijian anthropophagy began to increase with that developing polarization.

Savagism shrinks discursive space. Thus it seems to me that even the most enlightened of thinkers in Cook's voyages, like the Forsters for example, are imprisoned within its dialectical frame, generously noting that European civilization was once savage, thus opening the movement from savagism to Civilization. But discursive space becomes narrower still when we move to the Methodist missionaries. Going back to the Maori, consider this statement by Judith Binney on the settlers (mostly artisans) who were first introduced by the Methodist missionaries:

> The Maoris were considered by the settlers to be guilty of the 'truths' declared by St Paul about the Romans: they were 'filled with all unrighteousness, fornication, wickedness, covetousness, maliciousness; full of envy, murder, debate, deceit, malignity . . . haters of God . . . proud, boasters, inventors of evil things . . . convenant-breakers, without natural affection, implacable, unmerciful.' Kendall [the first missionary] described Maori religious beliefs in terms explicitly drawn from St Paul: 'Pride and ignorance, cruelty and licentiousness are some of the principal ingredients in a New Zealanders religion.' The overt prejudices of the missionary caused him to distort the intention and significance of customs which he must have habitually observed. Any similarities in ritual or beliefs which could be drawn with Judaic-Christian worship were used to 'prove' that such corruptions of the true religion were the direct work of Satan. New Zealand represented the greatest degree of Barbarism [savagism] into which isolated man could fall.[5]

This needless to say is not much different from the Puritan attitude to the Amerindian that Pearce speaks of. Cannibal talk then is a discourse that can be grafted onto savagism, giving the settler, the missionary, and the traveler the license to lie and the license to take hearsay as truth. Even when honest motivations are involved, cannibal talk owing to its restriction of discursive space does not permit my hypothetical outsider to see native custom in its complexity. It is not surprising that he would convert, sometimes unintentionally, any form of sacrificial anthropophagy into cannibalism. Unfortunately, both in New Zealand and in Fiji the political situation did produce forms of conspicuous anthropophagy, which compounded the issue of savagism and furnished "proof" of it.

I cannot discuss in any detail the development of conspicuous anthropophagy among Fijians. Nor can I deal with the discourse of missionaries, except to illustrate the metaphysics of savagism in their cannibal talk with a few brief excerpts. Thus the Methodist missionary Thomas Williams writes, "Captives [sometimes] have been given up to boys of rank, to practice their ingenuity in torture. Some when stunned, were cast into hot ovens; and when the fierce heat brought them back to consciousness and urged them to fearful struggles to escape, the loud laughter of the spectators bore witness to their joy at the scene. Children have been hung by their feet from the mast head of a canoe, to be dashed to death, as the rolling of the vessel swung them heavily against the mast."[6] Williams also mentions the case of a chief, a "monster" who ate nine hundred people, permitting none to share his repast. This man kept a count of his victims with stone markers, a myth that has gone down into subsequent Fijian history.[7] Elsewhere in cannibal talk Fijians fatten children to eat them later; they practice vampirism and necrophagia, thus helping us to link the Fijian with similar reported cases from all over the imagined savage world. In 1847, the Reverend Walter Lawry, superintendent of the Wesleyan missions in New Zealand, visited Viwa and gave a grim account of their cannibalism from eyewitnesses and fellow missionaries. This included eating of rotting human meat as delicacies; the tender meat of children and women; accounts of impatient cannibals waiting to eat ears and noses of victims raw and then cutting up their body parts with dishes to collect blood (even licking the drops that fell on the ground); and, in one instance as in the Buddhist myth I mentioned in chapter 3, a young girl was forced to eat her own flesh.[8] For Lawry as with other missionaries, Fijians "are in a state of nature, and quite free from education and religion."[9] In combating cannibalism the missions were also combating Satan for "[w]herever Christ's Gospel is preached with purity and power, there Satan falls, whether it be in India or in Feejee."[10] It is easy to see how Indian hating can easily coexist with the metaphysics of savagism.

CANNIBALISM IN THE CANNIBAL ISLANDS

If one takes literally the accounts of cannibalism reported by sea captains, missionaries, beachcombers, and traders, then Fiji was indeed the haunt of "cannibals" by the early nineteenth century. The earliest accounts of Fijian cannibalism were from castaways, travelers, and traders engaged in the sandalwood trade. When this supply was depleted by around 1815, the search for bêche-de-mer (sea slugs) took its place. In this chapter and the next I take several well-known eyewitness accounts of anthropophagy-cannibalism and show that they are without any foundation whatever. This does not mean that other more truthful accounts do not exist, nor does it imply that Fijian anthropophagy is nonexistent. But, as in the case of the Maori, it is doubtful whether outsiders were permitted to witness human sacrifices. The situation in Fiji is further complicated by the possible development of a form of "conspicuous anthropophagy" with the coming of Europeans. This would mean that while some missionary descriptions might have had an anchorage in reality, others were fantastic imaginings based on a skimpy knowledge of human sacrifice and an inflation of numbers killed and eaten.

I shall now discuss in some detail two writers—John Jackson and William Endicott—who have descriptions of cannibal feasts that seem, on the face of it, very persuasive, so much so that one ethnographer of Fiji thinks they provide "unimpeachable testimony" of the truth of Fijian cannibalism.[11] I will, however, impeach these testimonies: for me, they are fictional narratives based on the tradition of yarning on ships and islands. I begin with a quotation from John Jackson who might have lived in Fiji around 1840–42 and who, it is said, reports "three detailed descriptions of cannibal feasts."[12] Here is one of them:

> The bodies, which were painted with vermillion and soot, were carefully handed out, and placed on the road, or rather square, between the king's house and the bure [temple]. . . . At last they hauled them up to a place that was used purposely for the dressing, cooking, and eating of human flesh. . . . The king being very impatient to begin, and not choosing to wait till it was properly prepared, told the butcher just to slice off the end of the noses, and he would roast them while he was getting the other parts ready. The butcher

> did as he was ordered, and handed the three ends of the noses to his majesty, which he grasped hold of very nimbly, and put on hot stones to warm a little, not wishing to lose any time. The first he hardly let warm through, but while he was eating it, the second got a little better done, which he demolished.[13]

The king greedily eating the noses of the victims comes, I suggest, from the kind of discourse I have called "cannibal talk." Jackson's description is more in tune with European castration fantasies, children's stories, and nursery rhymes like "Sing a Song of Sixpence" than any Fijian ethnographic reality. Virtually every authority tells us that Fijian chiefs did not touch the meat lest they lose or diminish their tapu (or, tabu). They had to be fed by others. Some apparently used crude forks, while others had more elaborately carved ones. Therefore I want to ask the following question from the Fijian chiefs who appear both here and in virtually all missionary and travelers accounts: Why did you, sirs, deign to drop your elegant table manners and, especially, discard the cannibal forks used for your cannibal feasts?[14]

In 1977 Fergus Clunie published his authoritative monograph on *Fiji Weapons and Warfare,* which contains detailed accounts of Fijian cannibalism, also based uncritically on such sources as John Jackson's.[15] More recently, in her comparative study of cannibalism, Peggy Sanday, relying entirely on the information supplied by ethnographers and historians like Clunie and Sahlins can describe, not unreasonably, Fiji as a "pure culture of the death instinct."[16] In impeaching conventional cannibal testimonies I suggest that narratives such as Jackson's are totally unsuitable as an ethnographic resource and those who invent complicated relations between kinship and marriage and cannibalism on the basis of such evidence are simply refashioning in ethnographic terms the fantastic nature of the European construction of the cannibal. I shall present my own critique of Fijian cannibalism by first examining William Endicott who claimed to have actually witnessed a Fijian cannibal feast; then to his shipmates; then to the more complex case of John Jackson.

ENDICOTT'S NARRATIVE OF A CANNIBAL FEAST

William Endicott, the third mate of the *Glide,* wrote about his experiences during the period 1829–32 in a journal published only in 1923 as *Wrecked Among Cannibals in the Fijis,* with an appendix entitled "A Cannibal Feast at the Fejee Islands by an Eye-witness," reprinted by the editor from an article by Endicott in *The Danv-*

ers Courier of August 16, 1845. It is the latter narrative that is used by ethnographers to further substantiate the accumulating evidence on Fijian cannibalism. To give the reader a feel for the narrative, I shall quote liberally from Endicott's eyewitness account of a cannibal feast in the region of Macuata, in the northeastern part of the island of Vanua Levu sometime during March 1831.

The narrative starts "on a pleasant afternoon in the month of March, 1831, our ship at anchor off the town of Bona-ra-ra [Vunirara] the crew on board employed in making sennet, yard mats, and other ship gear to fill up the chinks of time." They had worked hard in the forenoon, "boating oil to the ship, beche-le-mer */sic/*, weighing, and stowing it away in the hold."[17] They were indulging in telling tales, singing songs and reflecting on "better days gone by" (*WC*, 55–56).At this time women who came on board ship to sell fruit informed Endicott "that the men had been to a fight with the Andregette [Dreketi] tribe . . . and had killed and taken three of their enemies, and were now going to have a grand Soleb */solevu/*, or feast."

"I had heard David Whippy, a man who had long been a resident upon these Islands, tell many a long tale of the manners and customs of the natives, and especially of their cannibalism, and I had a strong desire to see the manner in which they prepared and ate human flesh" (*WC*, 56). Accordingly, Endicott asked Captain Archer's permission; Archer urged him to take care of himself. Because he was friendly with the natives, Endicott felt in no danger and eventually "landed on the beach just ahead of the savages who were coming in single file to the village;" they were sixty in number but attended by many others (*WC*, 57). "The bodies of the three dead savages were carried in front, lashed on long poles in a singular manner. They were bound with wythes by bringing the upper and lower parts of the legs together and binding them to the body, and the arms in a similar manner by bringing the elbows to rest on the knees, and their hands tied upon each side of the neck. Their backs were confined to poles which were about twelve feet long. One was lashed on each pole, with six men, three at each end, to carry it." The carriers had a limping gait and were singing a war song to the rhythm of the gait. Endicott then says that the king sent the smallest of the three bodies to a friendly neighboring tribe "from whom he had received similar tokens of friendship." This was a great day in Vunirara (Bona-ra-ra), because "more is thought of the savage who kills one man and carries him home, than of the individual who may kill a hundred and let their dead bodies fall into the hand of the enemy. Their chief glory consists not so much in killing, as in eating their enemies" (*WC*, 58).

Now we come to that section of Endicott's narrative that Clunie employs for showing how "the carcases *[sic]* of someone who had committed a particular wrong against certain members of the community was subject to further insult."[18] Endicott noticed a particular interest being taken in one of the dead savages who apparently had killed a young chief, the son of an old woman present at this scene. This woman went to her hut, got all her son's belongings, and came back. "The angona [*yaqona*, that is, *kava*] bowl was placed near the head of the dead savage; a bamboo of water was brought and laid by his side, when several young men after well rinsing their mouths, were employed in chewing and preparing a bowl of angona. After the drink was made ready this old savage after a short speech from the priest who had continued to make low guttural sounds and shake himself through the whole ceremony, took her small dish full of liquor and presenting it to the lips of the dead savage bade him drink. No sooner was this done than a general yell ran through the tribe—'Amba cula boy thu-ie,' he is a stinking dead man.[19] She then dashed the liquor in his face and broke the dish in pieces upon it" (*WC*, 59–60). Thereafter she went her way because females could not participate in preparing or eating human flesh. "The head of the savage on whom this ceremony commenced was first cut off and laid aside, then the furniture that was brought by the old woman was broken up and placed around it, and fire set to it so that the whole was entirely consumed about the head, and rendered thereby in fit state for cleansing; the hair burnt off and the flesh so singed that it was scraped perfectly white" (*WC*, 60).[20]

After this there was a dance, "customary on all such occasions," with warriors in a state of complete nudity. "They were painted in a most frightful manner, as great a diversity of painting, or marking . . . each one attempting to outdo the other in the most loathsome obscenity and savage appearance" (*WC*, 60–61). There were about one hundred dancers "who came upon the ground at one and the same time with terrific yells. Their dance was made up of the most violent and distended motion of the limbs, often prostrating themselves on the ground upon their backs, and springing again instantly to their places, without for a moment ceasing to chant their war song in a very low but distinct manner" to the accompaniment of two savages beating on the end of a hollow log (*WC*, 61). Endicott has a graphic description of the cutting up of the two bodies: the heads were removed, then the right hand and the left foot, and finally "all the limbs [were] separated from the body" (*WC*, 62). After which an oblong piece was removed "commencing about the bottom of the chest and passing downwards about eight inches, and three or four inches wide at the broadest part." This was for the king and it was laid aside. "The entrails and vitals were then taken out and cleansed for cooking.

But I shall not here particularize. The scene is too revolting. The flesh was then cut through the ribs to the spine of the back which was broken, thus the body was separated into two pieces. . . . I saw after they had cut through the ribs of the stoutest man, a savage jump upon the back, one end of which rested upon the ground, and the other was held in the hands and rested upon the knees of another savage, three times before he had succeeded in breaking it" (*WC*, 58).

> To show their excessive greediness for human flesh, and their savage thirst for blood, I need only to relate a particular circumstance which took place at the time. The head of the savage which was last taken off was thrown towards the fire, and being thrown some distance it rolled a few feet from the men who were employed around it; when it was stolen by one of the savages who carried it behind the tree where I was sitting. He took the head in his lap and after combing away the hair from the top of it with his fingers picked out the pieces of the scull which was broken by the war club and commenced eating the brains [raw]. . . . There was no part of these bodies which I did not see cleansed and put in the oven. (*WC*, 63)

Realizing that the cooking would take some time, Endicott went back to the bêche-de-mer shed on the opposite side of the village for a break and then at dawn came back to witness the tail end of the feast. He was invited by the king to sit with him and eat some of the meat. "I unwrapped it and found it to be a part of a foot taken off at the ankle and at the joints of the toes. I made an excuse of not eating it, by saying that it had been kept too long after it was killed, before it was cooked, it being about thirty-six hours" (*WC*, 66–67).

> As the light of day shown into the hut, it revealed a sight seldom witnessed by civilized man. Around the hut sat sixty or seventy cannibals, more frightful than ever if possible; their paint being rubbed together in many instances, gave their bodies such an appearance as for a moment to lead one to doubt that they were human beings. Before one savage, would lay a human head, save that part which could be released from it, the lower jaw; which would be in possession of another. The bones of these bodies were well distributed among them, showing conclusively that none had failed to get their share. I had understood by them that the oven was opened about midnight, and that they had now done their feast; what was left was to be given to the boys; the women . . . were not allowed to taste of it though they frequently got it by stealth. (*WC*, 67)

Endicott's narrative does seem like a firsthand account, especially convincing when he recounts minute details like the part of the victim reserved for the king. It is not surprising that Clunie and other anthropologists have used his, and similar accounts, for their construction of Fijian cannibalism. Some doubts surely should have arisen though. If Captain Archer cautioned Endicott when he gave him permission to witness the cannibal feast, it is odd that he did not recommend him going there with a comrade or two, or that Endicott himself did not think of it. Again the extreme "accuracy" of the description of the king's portion should have sounded too good to be true. What is true is the discourse on savagery, the idea that these cannibals are not fully human.

Now let me present Endicott's own evidence to show that he could not possibly have witnessed this particular cannibal feast. His journal *Wrecked Among Cannibals* describes his voyage to the Fijian islands in the *Glide*, commanded by Captain Archer, to procure bêche-de-mer and tortoise shells in high demand in China. The account is thin, but because it was probably based on his log Endicott has an almost obsessive interest in dates. I will present in outline the devolution of events as they took place from the very beginning of the trip to the wreck of the *Glide* and the immediate aftermath.

On May 21, 1829, Endicott joined the ship *Glide* in Salem bent on trading for sandalwood (now is short supply) and bêche-de-mer and tortoise (turtle) shells in the Fijian islands. One hundred and seventeen days after leaving home they reached the Bay of Islands, on September 17, where they replenished the ship and also hired six Maori to help procure cargo in Fiji. They left for Fiji on October 8; Endicott already knows that Fijians "are extremely fierce and savage, frequently at war with each other and are addicted to the horrid practice of eating their enemies who are killed in battle" (*WC*, 19). On October 10 they reached Turtle Island (Vatoa), the southernmost inhabited island of the Fijis and steered toward Bua on the western tip of Vanua ("Miambo Bay") with the dubious help of poor navigational charts (*WC*, 20). As a result the ship hit a rock but managed to reach Bua on October 19, 1829, where they found the brig *Quill* commanded by Joshua Kinsman who had come from Bau. With the help of Joshua Kinsman's crew they got the *Glide*'s cargo back on board by October 28 (*WC*, 20–22). The *Quill*, having collected eight hundred *picul*s (each picul a "back-load" or about 140 lbs) and tortoise shells, sailed to Manila on December 21.

The *Glide* has already started collecting bêche-de-mer, and Endicott mentions that as many as of eighty canoes, each on average carrying about ten natives, assisted in the task of collecting, then boiling the slugs in a separate hut, then drying with fire in another hut, and finally storing the dried product in yet another. Unfortunately, on January 30, 1830, the "house" for collecting bêche-de-mer was set on fire "maliciously" by natives and the ship lost sixty piculs, some trade goods, and clothes. The crew sent for the "king" of Bua who directed them to the huts formerly used by the *Quill* and which he had constructed for their use. No one therefore would destroy them. The crew started collecting the bêche-de-mer on February 2 but soon the supply diminished perhaps owing to overharvesting. The king advised them to go to another bay forty miles distant called "Aloa" (Galoa) and build new huts employing local labor. By April 9 they had collected one thousand piculs of sea slugs and 350 lbs of tortoise shells and were ready to go to Manila. But they first went to Bua because they had heard that another ship, the *Clay*, had arrived in Bua with letters for the crew. On April 15 the *Glide* sailed for Manila and there discharged the cargo, which was sold to Chinese merchants. Then in early July 1830 the ship left Manila and arrived in Maui on July 17, 1830.

Three months later, after restocking, the ship sailed south toward Fiji but had a skirmish with natives in Penrhyn's Island (Tongareva), during which the crew killed seven or eight of them. On November 17 or 18 they sighted Vatoa (Turtle) Island. On November 24 the ship anchored off Ovalau, twenty-five miles from Bau. They contracted with the king of Bau (Naulivou) who was overlord of Ovalau for building two large bêche-de-mer sheds. But because the natives were hostile they had to search for another place for the second collection. On December 16 before they could leave a violent gale struck the ship and broke her cable chains. Fortunately, they could steer the ship to safety to Somosomo in Taveuni where they bought two cable chains and three anchors from natives from the wreck of a ship, the *Fawn*. The *Glide* sailed back to Ovalau "to try to get our things [left behind earlier] from the shore" (*WC*, 33). The next day the same hostile natives killed two sailors, one of whom had shot and killed a chief (*WC*, 34). They managed to procure the badly mangled corpses (which incidentally were not eaten!) for decent burial on shore.

On December 29 the ship sailed for Bua, and when it reached Galoa the crew started building the bêche-de-mer sheds, which were completed on January 13, 1831. But on January 29 the "houses" caught fire (perhaps accidentally) with one hundred piculs of sea slugs and some trade goods. With the assistance of the king and other chiefs they started fishing once again on February 4. More skirmishes with natives in which several Fijians were killed, but the crew managed to rescue the goods and set sail once again after deliberately setting fire to the bêche-de-mer sheds (*WC*, 36). Hoping for better luck they now sailed toward "Mutt-Water"

(Macuata, north of Bua on Vanua Levu) and anchored the ship in a channel north of Macuata. Once again on February 21 they started to purchase and cure the sea slugs with the cooperation of the king and local chiefs. Endicott says that "nothing particular occurred until the 22nd March" by which time they had collected about five hundred piculs of sea slugs and three hundred lbs of tortoise shells (*WC*, 36).

The ship was hit by a strong gale on the night of March 21 and drifted seven or eight miles. The storm increased to hurricane strength the next day, and the ship "bilged and fell over on her side" but did not sink (*WC*, 38). The influential chief of Vunirara (in Macuata) persuaded the crew to leave the ship because the mountaineers would come down, plunder the ship, and kill them. The crew left the vessel in the chief's custody and managed to get on shore "with no property but our clothes" (*WC*, 39). But this too not for long; they met a party of mountaineers who stripped them of their clothes except for one single garment each. Next morning the exhausted men reached the king's town of Vunirara. The king had given orders for the crew to be housed and fed while he himself went to the ship and plundered it of its goods, including muskets and cannon but spared the salt provisions. But the crew members were treated well and given cooking vessels and clothes.

News came of another ship in Bau and the king provided Captain Archer with a boat and a crew to seek help. Accordingly Archer left for Bau on March 28. Those who stayed continued to be treated well by the king, and they all had friendly intercourse with the natives. Endicott says that the king was sovereign over the whole of Tackanova, the second largest of the Fijian group, but he was subject to the overlordship of Bau who "was the great sovereign of the whole group" (*WC*, 41). ("Tackanova" is possibly Cakaudrove on the western side of the second-largest island, Vanua Levu, both a region and a political federation tied to Vanua Levu and Taveuni. All our journalists identify "Tackanova" as the island of Vanua Levu.) They stayed here for about three months. On April 1, the king beautifully dressed and accompanied by his courtiers went a distance of fifty miles in an expedition with thirty canoes to accept tribute from mountaineers in a place located "on a beautiful plain where houses were built for the King and the chiefs and their families" (*WC*, 46). This is the same king who played such a crucial role in the cannibal narrative. The sailors were invited to the grand festivities, which lasted for about twenty days, and while there was dancing, eating, and carousing with kava there was no consumption apparently of human flesh conventionally expectable on such occasions. The second officer, a carpenter, and some crew left for Bau after Captain Archer only to learn that the brig *Niagara* was also shipwrecked. Fortunately on May 22, 1831, captain and crew boarded the *Harriet* bound for the Hawaiian Islands.

Endicott's journal is full of dates, as we have shown; even trivial events are recorded such that the journal reads like a ship's log. It is strange to find such a compulsive recorder of dates vaguely staging his cannibal narrative "in the month of March, 1831." The internal evidence of this latter narrative suggests that he, along with others, was working hard during the forenoon, loading the ship and doing other tasks. It was impossible for him to perform these tasks after March 22 when the ship was wrecked. Note what he says in his *journal* account for the period prior to March 22: "[W]e continued to fish and nothing particular happened until the 22nd March, 1831" (*WC*, 36–37). It is hard to believe that witnessing a cannibal feast was of no particular significance. After March 28, he could not have witnessed the feast because Archer wasn't around for him to get permission. This leaves us the period between March 22, the night of the shipwreck, and March 28, the day of Captain Archer's departure. But this is not likely, since there was no ship for loading bêche-de-mer (which is what he claims in his cannibal narrative), and contrary to his account, the natives were hostile (*WC*, 36); when he and the rest of the crew reached the town of the king of Macuata they were tired and exhausted. Finally, Endicott kept a log, now in the library of the Peabody Essex Museum. Nowhere in the log is there a reference to his having witnessed a cannibal feast.

But there *is* a catch: James Oliver was a sailor on the *Glide* who also mentions the cannibal feast in his book *Wreck of the Glide*, a richer and more interesting account of the experience of shipwreck.[21] In the preface Oliver says that he wrote from memory but benefited from the perusal of the manuscripts of his shipmates, E[Endicott], P[oole], and F[owler], using Endicott's log book for dates. For us the relevant part begins with chapter 2, when he sails for Vanua Levu. In this chapter and the next Oliver mentions all the events described by Endicott, but in more graphic detail, with descriptions of gathering bêche-de-mer, the native town that sprang up overnight near the workplace, and the whole process of curing and storing the bêche-de-mer (*WG*, 37).

Oliver's account of life in Fiji is continued in chapter 5 and on to chapter 11, which concludes with the grand festival described in lesser detail by Endicott, followed in chapter 12 with their journey to Bau and departure from the Fijis on the *Harriet*. However, wedged between these is chapter 4, which deals with the geography of the Fijis and an account of their hairstyles, dress, barbarous customs, wars, and religion. The description of the "customs and manners" of natives is de rigueur in travel literature and is often, as in Oliver's case, written without context. It is here that the "confirmatory" cannibal account appears.

"One afternoon, whilst the Glide, was at anchor off Bonne-Rarah [Vunirara], my attention was directed towards the shore by the loud shouts of a party of natives. *From what I afterwards learned from several of the crew* who were on shore at the time, it seems that the warriors of Bonne-Rarah . . . were now returning to the town with two slain warriors" (*WG*, 53; my italics). He then gives a synoptic version of Endicott's cannibal feast. It seems to me obvious that Oliver borrowed this account from one of his comrades, either E (Endicott) or P (Poole) or F (Fowler). Like Endicott, Oliver also does not give us any dates or any specific context for the cannibal feast. Moreover, when we look at Oliver's vivid descriptions of the events in March 1831 in his book, there is no reference whatever to a cannibal feast.

With one proviso: Oliver mentions an interesting episode that occurred on their way to Bua after the shipwreck, sore footed and tired. According to Fijian theory any shipwreck belonged to the chief of the area. Thus, in the several instances mentioned by both Endicott and Oliver, even friendly chiefs simply "plundered" the ships that were wrecked. When the *Glide* was finally wrecked, it was appropriated by a Macuata chief and later by his king. Most sea captains seem to have accepted Fijian law on this matter, Captain Archer included. Thus Oliver tells us, the contents of the wreck were the "lawful property" of the king and his chief ("Santa Beeta"), who was the first on the spot. But the "mountaineers" seemed to have flouted this law by stealing some of the cargo, including guns. Hence, "the warriors of the latter chieftain attacked the mountaineers, regained the muskets, and killing their chief brought his body to Bonne-Rarah, where it was served up at a cannibal-feast, which was celebrated on this joyful occasion. *The circumstance was kept secret from us at the time, as was said by Santa Beeta in relating it, from considerations of our feelings*" (*WG*, 95; my italics). Endicott also says in his newspaper account that those officiating at the cannibal festivities are the "King" and "Chief Sina-beatee" (*WC*, 66). It is this secondhand account that has been elaborated by Endicott into a firsthand one and put down as one of the barbarous customs of Fijians by Oliver. The time and place are right: around March 23 in the territory of Macuata. How much of Santa Beeta's own discourse was understood by the journalists is not clear, because Oliver admits that their lack of knowledge of the language and recourse to sign language meant that they could not grasp Fijian religious practices (*WG*, 55). It therefore seems to me that one has no choice but to be skeptical of Endicott and Oliver on the cannibal feast. And one must be equally skeptical of ethnographers like Marshall Sahlins who, in a very recent paper, finds Oliver's reference to this "cannibal feast" proof of the empirical reality of that elusive object of scholarly desire.[22]

For my part I do not have to rest easy with "skepticism" because another account provides almost certain disconfirmation of the cannibal feast. Oliver mentions William Cary who joined the *Glide* late as a linguist, interpreter, and assistant trading master (*WG*, 98–99). Cary was a Nantucket seaman shipwrecked near Vatoa ("Turtle Island") on April 5, 1825.[23] All the crew in his ship were killed (but not eaten) by the natives except Cary who hid in a cave and was later befriended by a local chief (*WF*, 21–23). He managed to get to Lakeba on the eastern end (Lau group) of the Fijis where he witnessed an elaborate feast but not a cannibal one (*WF*, 31–32). Later, in Lakeba he met David Whippy, the fellow Nantucketer whom he had known in his hometown. He then went to Ovalau where Whippy had now become a prominent chief (*WF*, 37). However, he decided to live in Bau, perhaps owing to the receptivity of King Naulivou and the large presence of fellow whites. There he heard about Charles Savage, the Swede, who helped to create Bau as the paramount power but who, it was said, was killed "in a battle at the town of Uylah [Wailea]" (*WF*, 39).

Cary participated in several battles against the king's enemies. In one he joined "4,000 warriors, of whom about 100 had muskets," to attack the fortified town of "Angarmy" showing in this instance the power of the new weaponry (*WF*, 39). "As soon as we drew near enough the enemy attacked us with arrows and stones. We then opened fire with the muskets, which frightened them so they made offers of peace" (*WF*, 40). They took with them five or six prisoners and some dead bodies; the latter were "carried before a priest and songs of victory sung over them after which they were divided among each tribe" (*WF*, 41). Although Cary says they were destined for a cannibal feast, he saw none of it even though by now he was a prominent citizen of Bau living with other white beachcombers, deserters, castaways, transients, and settlers.

In October 1827 the ship *Clay* was in the Fijis for collecting bêche-de-mer and sandalwood, and Cary worked for its captain, Benjamin Vandaford (*WF*, 59). This was a successful enterprise, and the ship headed for Manila but stopped in Ovalau on February 17, 1828. There Cary met his friend Whippy once again and decided to stay on in Ovalau. Then back to Bau, a not-too-difficult transition given that Bau was just south of Ovalau and under the suzerainty of Bau. There he participated in a war with another tribe, with David Whippy leading the fray "dressed like a native" (*WF*, 69). "[Whippy] got shelter behind a stump, singled out one of their chief warriors, fired and shot him through the head. As soon as their chief fell, the enemy fled for the woods and the mountains. Then we rushed forward, broke down their bamboo fence and entered the village. We killed all who had not made their escape, plundered the town and set it on fire, then marched to Navarto [to Chief Naulivou?], singing songs of victory" (*WF*, 69). If Cary's account is true, which I think it is, possessing guns is not only a matter of killing large numbers of enemies but also the now-familiar dread created among those who did not possess these weapons. Additionally muskets permitted the strategic killing of chiefs; hence, the importance of white mercenaries and settlers for Bau and other kingdoms in Fiji (and elsewhere).

When the *Clay* returned to Ovalau in July 1828, Cary joined Captain Vanderford, who after collecting his usual cargo returned to Manila once again. In Manila, Cary joined another ship, the *Quill*, for better wages; this ship came back to the island of Koro in mid-March 1829. David Whippy "and a host of natives" visited Cary there and informed him that the old king (Naulivou) was dead and his brother "Veserwanker" (that is, Tanoa, the father of the famous Cakobau) was now king (*WF*, 76). In the middle of October the *Glide* arrived badly damaged by the sunken rock (mentioned by both Endicott and Oliver). Cary joined the *Glide* for a further increase in pay, perhaps owing to his acquaintance with local chiefs and some language skills (*WF*, 79–80). The rest of the account matches almost completely with that of Endicott's journal and Oliver's book. He makes no reference whatever to a cannibal feast or even rumors thereof during his stay aboard the *Glide*.

Let me make a methodological point. Once these stories were written or told and retold on ships and beaches, they produce their own progeny, such that many more tales of maritime adventures are created on these models. Both Endicott and Oliver mention the cannibal episode; even their journal accounts of sojourn in the Fijis are similar. Further, dates of publications are misleading; it is possible that Oliver's came first and Endicott followed suit. By normal methodological standards the one account would "prove" the empirical reality of the other one, and this is how texts of this sort have been examined by historians and ethnographers. But the second account does not necessarily confirm the first; one can argue that it simply repeats the earlier one; or both accounts use material borrowed from each other or from some other common source.[24] In some instances, a later text might contradict the earlier one, such that one is tempted to see one or the other as the "true" account or one might be tempted to construct a "true" or master narrative by juxtaposing the two texts. However, even when they are not fictional narratives, the second differing account might simply indicate a person conducting a debate or argument with the first rather than producing new empirical evidence. But none of these critiques apply to Cary's narrative; he was not a member of the group that exchanged information (William Endicott, Leonard Poole, Henry Fowler, and James Oliver) and had no access to their journals or logs. Cary's journal was published only in 1887 in the *Nantucket Journal* in installments after it was found by accident a few years earlier in a fish house (though the latter event by itself does not render his account credible!). His evidence makes it virtually certain that Endicott fabricated his eyewitness account thirteen years after his visit to Fiji to meet the European demand for savage cannibalism, perhaps provoked by the emerging literature on the subject. What else but cannibalism could one expect to find in the Cannibal Islands?

FOUL PLAY: A SURREAL AFTERMATH TO ENDICOTT

The anthropologist Marshall Sahlins refuses to let us get rid of Endicott and for good reasons. He points out that it was not Endicott but his shipmate Henry Fowler who wrote the account of the cannibal feast in the *Danvers Courier* on August 26, 1845, and signed it with the letter "F."[25] There is no doubt that some confusion exists. The published version that appears as an appendix to Endicott's book has him sign as "Yours, etc, William Endicott" (*WC*, 70). Either the editor of Endicott's journal, Lawrence Walters Jenkins, the assistant director of the Peabody Essex Museum, thought that "F" was really Endicott and added Endicott's name at the end of the text! Or alternatively, he thought that Fowler had borrowed from Endicott and, with his permission or without it, had written the *Danvers Courier* account. Or, more likely, Endicott revised Fowler's text with its execrable prose!

Who wrote the true and original cannibal adventure is not all that important because most of what I say about that episode is relevant irrespective of authorship. It is interesting however to find out whether there is independent confirmation of Fowler as the true author. On July 9, 1832, Fowler wrote to his "Beloved Parents" from Oahu in Hawai'i where he recounts briefly his experience during and after the shipwreck of March 1831 and then adds, "But thanks to Providence I have got clear of those feejee *[sic]* cannibals (I may well call them so), for I have seen them cook and eat the flesh of their own brothers. They tried several times for me and once was so sure of me that they built the fire upon the beach and their spears and clubs ready for my life. But having been well armed I shot one of them which frightened all the rest."[26] The latter account is pure invention; while the crew shot several natives in Penrhyn's Island none of the other writers mention any cannibal feast; nor did the context permit such a feast being held (*WG*, 70–71; *WC*, 31). The former could simply have been invented, or perhaps Fowler misunderstood well-known native mimetic enactments of cannibalism for frightening the Other. Both these statements are devoid of context and have no relation to the very specific and elaborate cannibal feast Fowler describes in his letter to the *Danvers Courier.*

The Fowler archive in the Peabody Essex Museum is not in the best condition, but what I read adds to my confusion as surely as it adds to Sahlins's clarity. In his handwritten notes Fowler mentions that on March 22, after the shipwreck, he suffered greatly as others also did when they were stripped of their clothes. Fortunately Fowler was permitted to keep his flannel shirt, which saved him from the bitter cold.

> The Natives finding they had got all from us . . . finally left us to pursue our dreary way to the town; after traveling about three hours together, the strongest began to go ahead of the weaker ones, among the last of which was myself owing to a verry bad sore on my foot I had not been able to walk the length of the ship's deck, for two months previous to the ships reck, it had just begun to get better, but was then as big as dollar. . . . In coming ashore the bandage was torn off and the sore wounded by the stumps and bushes and set to bleeding. . . . [A]fter traveling about 12 miles in this manner and getting to be about 9 a clock PM. I intreated Mr. Wm. Endicott who had been kindly assisting me for the last hour to leave me and go on with the rest who were almost out of sight, this he was unwilling to do, but I told him it was useless to stay with me, as I could not proceed with him and he would perissh if exposed to the storm all night with no shirt on and no shelter. I finally prevailed on him to leave me. . . . I sat some time on the ground tore off a part of my shirt, and bound up my bleeding foot. . . . I proceeded in this way with great difficulty, and pain about half way up the hill when I was obliged to give up entirely. I could not go any length further, I had expended the last grain of strength I possessed and here I was without shelter from the wind and rain which now came in torrents, chilling me to the heart, I felt as if I could not be more miserable, my cup was full.

Outside of the fact that this poor writing is vastly different from Endicott's, there is another problem with this account. Oliver, Fowler's shipmate, tells us that it was not Fowler who suffered these aches and pains but another person within their group of friends! "P[oole], one of the crew, who, beside the common distress, was troubled by an exceedingly painful ulcer upon his foot, which had confined him to the forecastle for several days before the loss of the ship, found himself utterly unable to proceed further, and, notwithstanding all entreaty, placed himself on the side of a rock least exposed to the wind" (*WG*, 92). When the rest of the crew arrived safe in the king's town, Oliver expressed "much anxiety concerning our shipmate, the young P[oole]" but "at length he made his appearance in the village" (*WG*, 97).

Poole had remained in the same spot partially sheltered from the tempest and was eventually helped by "an old native woman passing that way" who "lent her aid in conducting him to the town" though, for Poole, with difficulty owing to "the ulcer in his foot, from the sand and sea-water" that was "a source of exquisite torture" (*WG*, 97–98). To complicate matters, Fowler in the letter to his "beloved parents" says he broke his arm while "launching the topmast" during the storm and then clearly implies that he was not alone but with the rest of his comrades during the long trek to Bua: "Our sufferings were very severe being oblidged */sic/* to lay on the ground till morning while the storm raged with great fury. After arriving at the village called Bunarra [Vunirara] to which we were all sent by the Indians we felt very conscious for our expecting every hour to become food for their voracious appetites." Oliver agrees with Fowler that this event of sleeping on the ground did occur though only *after Poole was left high but not dry on a lonely rock*. "Night was gathering about us with almost impenetrable darkness, and the storm, though much abated, was yet howling through a neighboring forest. We were to lie in an open plain, upon the wet ground, pillowing our heads on rocks, sheltered from the chill and dampness" (*WG*, 96). Was Oliver imagining Poole was Fowler, or was Fowler imagining he was Poole? Or did Fowler appropriate material from Poole to include in the notes which he says he wrote for Oliver's projected book? Or was some other form of surreal interborrowing taking place among folks who hardly honored, or even knew, the conventions of modern scholarship?

CANNIBALISM AND YARNING IN ENDICOTT-FOWLER

It seems to me that Endicott-Fowler (hereafter referred to as Endicott) is writing two kinds of texts. Endicott's narrative of the voyage is in the tradition of shipboard journalism, and though not a sophisticated journalist, he gives a fairly straightforward account of his experiences. The second narrative however belongs to the genre of sailors' yarns, and it does not matter whether Endicott wrote it or Fowler or both. In the South Seas these yarns deal with the purported firsthand experiences of the protagonist, generally with his adventures among the natives and witnessing that quintessential attribute of savagism, the cannibal feast.

Endicott himself sketches a plausible context for inventing this account in the beginning of his essay. After working hard in the afternoons, his comrades had time to spare and indulged themselves in "reveries and yarns" and "in a sailor's privilege of telling tales, singing songs and reflecting upon 'better days gone by'" (*WC*, 55–56). While speaking of these he also mentions a raconteur, our Nantucket friend David Whippy who, we noted earlier, could narrate "many a long tale of the manners and customs of the natives, and especially of their cannibalism" (*WC*, 56). Whippy reappears in 1840 as one of Captain Wilkes's principal informants in the famous (or infamous) United States Exploring Expedition; Wilkes was so pleased with Whippy that he later nominated him to be a U.S. consular agent. About ten years later the Englishman Captain John Elphinstone Erskine also praised Whippy as "a man of excellent character" who gave "a tone of order and true respectability to the community" both white and native, signs of which we have already glimpsed in Whippy's warrior role.[27] No wonder the accounts of Fijian cannibalism that Whippy recounted to people like Wilkes and Erskine carried the stamp of authenticity. In *Typee* Melville's protagonist might have been speaking about settlers like David Whippy and John Jackson: "Jack, who has long been accustomed to the longbow, and to spin tough yarns on a ship's forecastle, invariably officiates as showman of the island on which he has settled, and having mastered a few dozen words of the language, is supposed to know all about the people who speak it."[28] Endicott himself, in true yarnster fashion, has a wonderfully ironic and deliberately give-away line at the end of his essay: "I am about to the end of my yarn, yet I might lengthen it by knotting on other strands, but my timepiece reminds me that it is past midnight; so I shall take the liberty to belay this and turn in" (*WC*, 70). I must make one qualification: although it is true that the give-away line provides us a clue that this is a fabricated account, it is also the case that seamen's yarns can be based on actual events that are then woven into a story. But like cannibal ballads, yarns cannot be taken at face value.

The missionary James Hadfield in his introduction to John Jackson's *Cannibal Jack* mentions another yarnster, a trader named Hayes, "one of the cleverest raconteurs I have ever met. He had heaps of stories in his repertoire, chiefly of whaling expeditions and cannibal feasts he attended."[29] While Hadfield states that "no one gave credence to any statement he made," he accepts without reservation Hayes's accounts of cannibalism. Even Melville in his preface to *Typee* (1846) published the year after Endicott's cannibal tale identifies himself with this yarnster tradition: "The incidents recorded in the following pages have often served, when 'spun as a yarn', not only to relieve the weariness of many a night-watch at sea, but to excite the warmest sympathies of the author's shipmates."[30] There is a difference though: Endicott's is an unmitigated yarn; whereas the events in Melville's story could be spun as a yarn, implying that *Typee* is based on yarnster material that could be reconverted into a yarn. It seems that yarnsters like Endicott, Hayes, and the young Melville were a well-known feature of the South Seas land, sea, and beachscapes. Their lifeways have been nicely documented by Greg Dening.[31]

CANNIBAL NARRATIVES OF JOHN JACKSON, ALIAS CANNIBAL JACK

Fergus Clunie relies heavily on an account known as "Jackson's Narrative" appended to Captain Erskine's book on his first cruise to the islands of the Western Pacific. On Erskine's request John Jackson wrote this account "during his leisure hours" when he was employed as an interpreter during Erskine's second voyage to New Caledonia in 1851. Thus Jackson, unlike Endicott, was not a ship's journalist but made into one by Erskine. The talented Jackson met the situation by emulating the style of shipboard journalism.

To properly understand this work one must consider two other books that Jackson wrote for publication, the first *Jack, the Cannibal Killer*, now lost, written sometime after "Jackson's Narrative," and the second, *Cannibal Jack*, written in 1889 when he was seventy.[32] "Jackson's Narrative" does not read like a novel though it records utterly improbable adventures, whereas *Jack, the Cannibal Killer* was explicitly meant to be one. *Cannibal Jack* was labeled an "autobiography" self-consciously addressed to a European reading public. But "autobiography" like Poe's *Narrative of Arthur Gordon Pym* is itself a fictional device.[33] In "Jackson's Narrative" the author is John Jackson, which is how he introduced himself to Erskine. In *Cannibal Jack* he has clearly changed his name to William Diapea (he was also called Diaper). I shall refer to him as John Jackson or Cannibal Jack, the popular cognomen by which he was known and one he personally favored.

"Jackson's Narrative" and the lost novel, *Jack, the Cannibal Killer*, were probably thematically related. The facetious title of the latter suggests that it was a story about Jack who kills cannibals, and these must obviously be Fijian ones. "Jackson's

Narrative" also deals with Jackson's description of wars culminating in cannibal feasts. In this text he is merely a witness of these events; in *Jack, the Cannibal Killer* he must surely have been the hero who, having killed cannibals, saves damsels from the ovens (assuming that he employed the themes of "Jackson's Narrative" and *Cannibal Jack*). If "Jackson's Narrative" is not a novel, one can legitimately ask, to what genre does it belong? The clue is provided by Endicott who wrote a similar narrative that I have already identified as a yarnster invention. John Jackson's account was published in 1853 in Erskine's book; it is likely that this event stimulated his alter ego William Diapea, alias Cannibal Jack, to produce his own books, now more in the style of adventure stories than straightforward yarns.

Unlike in Endicott's case we cannot prove that the accounts of cannibalism in "Jackson's Narrative" and *Cannibal Jack* are fabrications, but one can seriously question their value as ethnography. I will demonstrate this by examining the interconnections between these two narratives and their style and content. Though the events of *Cannibal Jack* take place around 1843–47 and "Jackson's Narrative" during 1840–43, there is one incident ("the Bonaveidogo episode") occurring in both, which confounds Jackson's own periodizations.[34]

According to "Jackson's Narrative," Chief Bonaveidogo (Bonavidongo, Bonavidogo) asked the reluctant Jackson at about two in the morning to go with him to a nameless uninhabited island to gather calabashes. They were to go very furtively "lest we should be seen from the main by the Namuka natives," their enemies.[35] Soon they saw people coming from Namuka in eight or ten canoes. The company trapped their Namuka enemies and killed many of them (and later ate them in the narrative segments utilized by Sahlins and Clunie). One "fugitive" was seen swimming, following a woman who had just escaped. He was being shot at, but when Jackson pleaded with the men not to kill him they scoffed at the idea. "By this time we were up to the fugitive, when the chief, lifting his tomahawk to dispatch him in the water, I stopped the blow with my hand, and begged him to let the man get on board alive. He threw down his tomahawk, and told me to save him, and I would see the result of being merciful, saying that, instead of being grateful for his life, he would kill and eat me the first opportunity that offered."[36] In fact the "fugitive" gave some crucial information, namely, that Bonaveidogo's father Tui Mativata (Tui Macuata, chief of Macuata) was now residing at Namuka where he had fled for protection, strangely enough among the very people his son has just killed! Naturally, Bonaveidogo was pleased that Jackson saved the life of this man.

This is followed by a description of the dead being dragged uphill prior to being cooked. John Jackson tries to persuade Bonaveidogo to bury the dead. Bonaveidogo says that he himself was never a cannibal ("daukanatamala") or an adulterer ("dauyalewa"); yet "he had eaten a little piece now and then just to be in the fashion of the older chiefs," and "he took great pleasure in killing his enemies for the old and infirm chiefs to eat."[37] The cannibal feast is prefaced by a women's lewd dance for humiliating the dead, an event crucial to Clunie's conception of Fijian cannibalism. "I saw their animosity was so great, that they did not consider their enemies being killed and eaten sufficient to gratify their revenge, without deriding and degrading them, as it were, after death, which the young girls were doing in the most lewd kind of dance, touching the bodies in certain nameless parts with sticks as they were lying in a state of nudity, accompanying the action with the words of the song."[38]

The other work, *Cannibal Jack*, begins with the same "Bonaveidogo episode," and one can feel Jackson's physical presence and hear his colloquial voice speaking the winding and long sentences characteristic of his style here.

> Whilst I was enjoying myself as best I could, eating and drinking—drinking the 'yagone' in unlimited quantities and bidding fair to become quite a sot, like the rest of the whites in other parts of Fiji, the principal portion of them being located in a settlement called Levuka situated in the island of Ovalau,—I say, whilst I was doing all these things, alternated by mending muskets and amassing property, and living quite content with my three wives, one morning, or rather perhaps in the middle of the night, as it could not have been much past twelve o'clock, if any, Bonavidogo came along, rousing me up from a long sleep, telling me to buckle on my cartridge box, and which, by the by, contained sixty rounds of cartridges, shoulder my musket, and also not to forget my dirk or sheath knife, and follow him, for the enemy were astir, and 'Bakolas' were to be had just for the killing of them. I followed quite drowsily, not being more than half awake, through the effect of the beastly habit I had lately given way to, of imbibing the juice of that very lethargic root, and besides, I followed reluctantly enough, because I was not interested at all in their murderous kinds of warfare, not caring two pins which side beat, as neither party had, at present, injured me, but still I followed in silence, as all the natives maintained the strictest silence, as is their wont when on the war-path. (*CJ*, 10)

The group went down to the shore and then sailed in canoes until they sighted a small island where their enemies were collecting coconuts to make sennet from their husks. The "poor doomed creatures" had not seen the canoes that had "kept the island between us and the main as well as between their intended victims' canoes and ourselves" (*CJ*, 11). Now follows a terrific description of the battle in those same long sentences that involve the reader in the action.

> I had not left Bonavidogo, but remained with him in his canoe, and just as we reached the other side and were right in among the enemies' small canoes, I heard the crash of murder on shore, some of the people being speared and clubbed just as they descended the coco-nut trees, and some as they were in the act of ascending or preparing to do so, and others as they were rushing along towards their canoes, which the one or two which had been left in each one were now fast paddling away, were either speared or shot down with muskets! But there was one man, who had rushed through the spears, clubs, tomahawks, handybillies, and musket balls of our murdering shore party unscathed, and into the water, towards the last of the small canoes, all the rest having got clear of the melee, paddling for their bare lives towards the main. This last and hitherto lingering small canoe now being pulled away by one single paddle, following the rest, all of which were out of all danger now, and this poor fellow, who had already run such a terrible risk, was swimming after it in order to embark with his life. But Bonavidogo's large canoe was being sculled after him and fast coming up to him, but in the meantime some half a dozen muskets had been fired at him. He seemed to have a charmed life. Every shot had missed him. (*CJ*, 13)

Bonaveidogo asked Cannibal Jack to fire at him and kill the *bakola*, but he didn't. When they came close to the swimming man, Bonaveidogo tried to tomahawk him. Cannibal Jack interposed himself between Bonaveidogo and the victim and pleaded with the former to save the man's life, warding off the blows intended to the victim and telling Bonaveidogo that the man could provide valuable "news of the movements of the general enemy." Bonaveidogo responded that it is not the Fiji custom to spare enemies, to which Cannibal Jack replied that "it was the humanity fashion, asking him to place himself, in imagination, in that poor man's predicament" (*CJ*, 14). Bonaveidogo continued to be obdurate, but when Cannibal Jack swore that he would not be killed while he (Cannibal Jack) was alive, Bonaveidogo yielded. He told Jackson that the man he saved would show his gratitude by murdering his benefactor. Now the prisoner (in Friday fashion) "clung to my legs with the most frantic terror, kneeling on the deck" (*CJ*, 15). Then there follows a graphic description of Cannibal Jack saving this man from the rest of the crew, something not found in the earlier version (*CJ*, 15–16).

The upshot of all this is that Cannibal Jack had his way; the prisoner was saved; and even Bonaveidogo was pleased because the man provided information on enemy movements, as Cannibal Jack had predicted, but not, as in the previous text, on the fate of Bonaveidogo's father. There follows a description of the dead bodies being "set up in formal array" though there is no description of the lewd female dance and the cannibal feast. Jackson does say though that the bodies were taken to the temple of Dagei [Degei], "the god of war," the young girls going through "the usual degrading obscene rites with their antics over these much-abused bodies . . . [which then] were conveyed to the ovens and cooked, and then down the gullets of these determined cannibals" (*CJ*, 20).

Let me now compare the same event in the two texts to show how futile it is to treat these accounts as ethnographic verities. In "Jackson's Narrative" they sail from Udu Point down the northern coast of Vanua Levu; in *Cannibal Jack* the group starts off from the island of Ovalau, which is off the northern coast of Viti Levu, and sails down the coast. In "Jackson's Narrative" the enemies are the Namuka; in *Cannibal Jack* they are unnamed perhaps because Cannibal Jack realized both the geographical confusion in the former account and the absurdity of Bonaveidogo's father seeking refuge among the very people his son had just butchered. In *Cannibal Jack* Bonaveidogo's group go to the island to kill an unnamed enemy collecting coconut husks; in "Jackson's Narrative" they go to gather calabashes and are well armed because the island to which they are going is off Namuka, the home of their enemies. In "Jackson's Narrative" the enemy espy Bonaveidogo's group and try to ambush them but fail and are surrounded by the latter; in *Cannibal Jack* the enemy are simply trapped and killed. The saving of the prisoner is quite different in the two accounts, *Cannibal Jack* being the more exciting one. In both accounts John Jackson acts in an arrogant manner before Chief Bonaveidogo, and the latter, in very un-chiefly fashion, meekly accedes to his request.

It is time to consider another crucial piece of information, namely, John Jackson's knowledge of local languages. We do know from Hadfield and Erskine that he knew the language of Mare and other islands of New Caledonia, not surprising because this is where he lived longest. Yet "Jackson's Narrative" starts with his adventures in a Samoan island "about the beginning of 1840." As soon as he arrives he speaks fluent Samoan. It is of course possible that he had lived in Samoa before this narrative commenced but, nevertheless, such fluency must be suspect. In *Cannibal Jack* he claims to speak "the purest Fijian" but the publisher's note says that the sample of two pages of Fijian he employed in the text was "tedious and inaccurate" and had to be omitted.[39] However, he is more knowledgeable about Fiji and its language than Endicott, though the Fijian words that he uses in both texts are perhaps basic beachcomber vocabulary. If so, his rendering of complex Fijian dialogues must be suspect; therefore, we must ask the question: What is the function of language knowledge in these kinds of narratives? The answer is simple: language knowledge is also a fictional device to render the authenticity of the narrative. This is true of almost everyone writing "authentic" cannibal texts.

Suppose we accept the conventional ethnographic wisdom that Jackson's is a true account of Fijian lifeways, consider what we are up against. In "Jackson's Narrative," Jackson has several adventures before the Bonaveidogo one, including witnessing the cannibal feast cited; the Bonaveidogo episode is in turn followed by other adventures. *Cannibal Jack* commences with the Bonaveidogo episode and then with the events that followed soon after. Yet, contrary to our expectations, the succeeding events in the two accounts haven't the slightest substantive similarity with each other, again suggesting that we are not dealing with the narration of factual events but with a literary imagination.[40] Now let me deal with this fictional imagination in *Cannibal Jack* expressed in the events that immediately followed the adventure just recounted.

Following the cannibal feast and the lewd dances of the women, there were seven or eight days of sexual abstinence and men slept in different heathen temples. Cannibal Jack slept in the temple dedicated to Degei. There he describes a possessed priest "smashing old coconuts into atoms on his forehead, and reducing those very hard substances to fragments by the mere clutch of his right hand" and uttering prophecies while foaming in the mouth which Cannibal Jack confidently translates (*CJ*, 21). I doubt whether this custom is found in Fiji; it is certainly known in South and Southeast Asia, and if it is the case that Cannibal Jack had traveled to that part of the world as he claims, he might have witnessed it there (or heard about it through shipboard gossip) and grafted it to the present narrative. In any case, the upshot of these prophecies was the god demanding, among other things, the life of "my poor prisoner." This time also Cannibal Jack saved his prisoner by paying the priest four whales' teeth (the valued currency in all of Polynesia) "too good to be refused by the avaricious son of the Fiji Church!" (*CJ*, 22). This last event provokes a humorous aside on the obtuseness of the local Wesleyan missionary, the Rev. J. Hunt, which I omit.

The next section deals with the impending demise of Bonaveidogo's father, the "arch-cannibal," Tui Macuata. His wives were ready, and willing, to be strangled "to accompany him to those regions, where he would have to be waited on in the same way as he had hitherto been in this, which he was now fast leaving" (*CJ*, 25). One of the doomed women, a murdered Englishman's widow known as the "Rotama [Rotuma] beauty," cast a forlorn glance at Cannibal Jack and said that she wished to run away with him. Cannibal Jack pleaded with his friend Bonaveidogo to let him have her, but Bonaveidogo said that, while he was sympathetic to his friend's proposal, he couldn't help him because his half brother, the powerful Vasu Taukei, was a stickler for tradition.[41] Nevertheless, Cannibal Jack did manage to elope with the woman. Soon Vasu Taukei's men constituting "half a dozen niggers" ambushed them, took Cannibal Jack's belongings, stripped them both naked, and after tying them with large green vines, lashed them back to back, Cannibal Jack's head downward and the Rotuma beauty in the upright position, and hung them on a tree, in a gruesome parody of a well-known French custom, but not one solely confined to them.

There was no question that Cannibal Jack would die; if he did not die "they would revive me by feeding me on my own flesh, cooked or raw, according as their diabolical fancies struck them, and drinking my own blood!" (*CJ*, 31–32). The woman would survive because she would be returned to be sacrificed to the "manes of the old man-eater" (*CJ*, 31). There follows a description of poor Cannibal Jack's suffering as he awaits death. But this does not happen because he is rescued, in almost miraculous (and improbable) fashion, by the prisoner he had saved from Bonaveidogo's tomahawk! This rescuer is no longer a "fugitive" or "my slave" ("kaisi") of the first text: he is now explicitly called my "protege," "my faithful 'bobula' [prisoner]" and finally, inevitably, "my man Friday" (*CJ*, 36–43). Cannibal Jack now brings his new wife to his home in Natewa on the eastern side of Vanua Levu to join his other three spouses.

At several places in the story, Cannibal Jack says that he has written an autobiography of the first twenty-six years of his life in nineteen copy books and that Cannibal Jack deals with only three of them, nos. 9, 16, and 17. In fact the book is in three parts and the episode just mentioned is in the part designated as No. 9. The author says that because this copy book has much blank space he now wants to copy nos. 16 and 17 into it, so that this composite work can be made available for sale. Interestingly enough he does not tell us why he chose 16 and 17 when he could have as easily chosen 10 and 11, which would have provided narrative continuity. It seems to me that the "autobiography" in nineteen books is also a fictional device. He has to deal with the discontinuity between the sections of the text whose locale is the island of Ovalau and parts of Vanua Levu, while the rest of *Cannibal Jack* (books 16 and 17) is located in Taveuni with its well-known capital of Somosomo and on the islands of the eastern group. The book has no conventional plot of the sort found in later adventure stories; it is held together by the presence of its protagonist and by the improbable adventures and funny vignettes he sketches. From our point of view one of the most interesting of his adventures is about Litia, which starts at the end of book 16 and spills over to 17. It is here that he introduces the Pocahontas theme for the first time.

This episode starts with a "shipwreck," another feature common to adventure stories and the experiences of sailors. In this case every single native Tongan in Jack's canoe drowned or were eaten by sharks except Jack himself. I will deal with this episode later, but for now let me say that when Jack regained consciousness it was Litia who was by his side. She was a Christian and a daughter of the chief from "Komo" (on the Lau, or eastern side of Fiji). Then there follows a description of Litia's beauty. Never before has Cannibal Jack been enamored of any woman to this same degree. As a matter of fact, in books 16 and 17 none of his former loves, including the Rotuma beauty, or his children are mentioned. The heroine of this part of the book is Litia whose passion for him is single-minded. She has been betrothed to a young man but this caused in her a "violent grief (this violent paroxysm almost annihilating her)" (*CJ*, 142–43). The upshot of the first meeting is that Litia thought that Providence has sent her a husband, but she dared not bring him home directly because a shipwrecked person was considered unfortunate, generally destined for the ovens. Therefore she persuaded Cannibal Jack to sneak onto a ship that was in port so that she could welcome him as a new arrival. The ploy succeeded, and Jack was eventually incorporated into Litia's father's household. But this is not what Litia wanted: "[S]he aimed at nothing short of adoption, and absorption too, of my whole being, body and soul, into her very essence!" (*CJ*, 153). Eventually they decide to marry in Christian fashion in deference to Litia's wishes. Because there was no missionary in Komo they went to the nearby island of Ogea (Ogea Levu). They came back with the Wesleyan pastor's younger brother to form a new church in Komo, "the chief having renounced all idolatry from the moment that he had put the cloth on at the giving away of his daughter" (*CJ*, 159). The reference is to Litia's father having to put a piece of decorous calico round his middle before he could enter the church. At first it was decided to build a chapel at the site of the heathen temple, but this plan was abandoned.

The result of these events was the polarization of the native population into two groups, the Christian or the "religious party" and the "heathen" or "cannibal party." The heathen party led by the chief's brother and Litia's uncle began to pollute the chapel every evening with garbage so that the religious party had the task of cleaning the place the following morning. The heathen party meanwhile had heard that Cannibal Jack had been rescued from the sea and was therefore unwelcome here except as food. The plantations of the religious party were also vandalized and ultimately the chapel itself was burned down by armed members of the heathen party.

To defend themselves Cannibal Jack went to the chief's house and began to load muskets "when Litia came along in a terrible fright . . . she would show me a safe hiding place in the bush" because her uncle was planning to kill him (*CJ*, 165). And sure enough the uncle came up with his followers. When the chief tried to stop him, his brother knocked him down with the back of his tomahawk and stunned him.

> He then rushed to the chief's prostrate body, shifting his spear from his left to his right hand and the tomahawk to his left hand, not caring about facing me at too close quarters, as he saw that I had a musket in my hand and my finger on the trigger, it being fully cocked. He poised the spear and quivered it at me, Litia sheltering my body all the time with her own, begging at the same time in the most suppliant accents for my life; but he cursed her with one of the worst oaths in Fiji, making a most indelicate allusion to her mother . . . swearing if she did not get out of the way he would pass the spear through the pair of us. I hesitated no longer, but pulled the trigger and shot him dead. (*CJ*, 165–66)

The chief who had now recovered did a "novelistically" appropriate (even though a highly un-Christian chiefly) action: he proceeded to the heathen temple and burned it down with those inside. As the people there "began to roast inside they rushed for the one low narrow doorway, where they were most of them tomahawked, and the few who managed to get outside were shot down" while the others were burned to death (*CJ*, 166–67). Meanwhile the women of the dead heathen party retired unperceived to the bush where they all strangled themselves with the native bark cloth "effecting the voluntary sacrifices to the manes of their unfortunate husbands" (*CJ*, 168). Not only this: "The children had to be forcibly dragged out of the graves, whilst they were clamouring to be buried alive with their—forever lost to them—parents" (*CJ*, 169). To add to these calamities Litia, who was pregnant, "sickened, and all the attention, care, and embrocation, outwardly to the affected part—the stomach—and inward herb-medicines, which these people so thoroughly understand, besides the various fomentations, good diet, composing of nourishing soups of different descriptions,—I say all these things proved of no avail, for poor Litia died, and I tried to die too, but could not, and so I was obliged to endure a living death, or more properly speaking a death-like life, and which was, by the by, ten times worse, I suppose, than death itself" (*CJ*, 170).

Peter Hulme makes the point that the myth of Pocahontas represents on one level the "ideal of cultural harmony through romance."[42] Cannibal Jack incorporates the Pocahontas theme into his narrative only to give it an added twist. It is the theme of the civilizing of Fiji through its Christianization but without the mediation of either the missions or white intruders. In previous episodes Cannibal Jack was not only an unbeliever but also hostile to the missions. When he and his Tongan comrades were shipwrecked he, unlike the Christianized Tongans, did not seek the help of the deity. Something changed however when he was adrift, clinging to a piece of the wreck for who knows how long: he had a religious experience, a vision of his saintly mother and his sister Marianne "who died a most exemplary Christian." He was made to understand that he survived "partly through their prayers" (*CJ*, 136). He then mentioned the sea-change the tempest wrought: "I thought that we were all mixed in one rapturous joy, in the company of innumerable angels—black and white. The Virgin Mary, also her blessed Son, were there also, and they were all receiving me with unfeigned delight" (*CJ*, 137).

When he awoke he was with Litia in Komo which, I think, has little to do with the actual island of Komo in the central Lau of Fiji; it is completely fictionalized in his narrative. The people here could be saved because the denizens of these small islands are not fully cannibals. The black and white angels of his vision anticipate the union between the native and the white. But this is not a harmony between the "races"; it is a harmonious union between the narcissistic Jack and the lovely Litia that anticipates the Christianization of the island. The killing of the heathen party and the death of their wives clear the way for the establishment of an indigenous Christian civilization. Meanwhile, his true love Litia must die because the hero of these adventures has to move elsewhere (and Jackson must write new books about him), and Litia alive can only chain him to this island. Why at childbirth though? Cannibal Jack leaves no heirs because, I think, the truly Christianized land is for native Christians in his idealized conception. It is no accident that he does not get Mr. Calvert the missionary at Lakeba to marry them; instead a native catechist of Ogea performs the ceremony. And it is this catechist's brother who brings Christianity to Komo. In Cannibal Jack's undogmatic and catholic conception, Christianity is not the Roman Catholicism of his vision; the author knew, as everyone else did, that Wesleyanism was the most powerful of the Evangelical missions to Fiji. Finally, Jackson gives implicit recognition to a critical theme in the European discourse of savagism: the savagism of the savage expressed in such things as cannibalism and widow immolation makes it impossible for the white person to identify with it. Civilization in spite of its discontents cannot be abandoned. In Jack's novel Komo is purged of the heathen-cannibal party as a new indigenous Christian civilization is inaugurated there.

YARNING AND NARRATIVE FICTION IN JOHN JACKSON'S FIJIAN ADVENTURES

I hope it is not difficult to persuade the reader that *Cannibal Jack* is neither autobiography nor ethnography but fiction, not the kind of historical novel like Walter Scott's, but a well-written, straightforward, and thoroughly enjoyable adventure story emerging from the European contact with exotic lands. Polynesia gripped the European imagination in the late eighteenth and nineteenth centuries. The stage had already been set by Melville in *Typee*, and it is possible that John Jackson, alias Cannibal Jack, who was in his own way a learned man, had read this work.[43] Nevertheless, similar adventures by sailors and beachcombers were being produced elsewhere in the Pacific, as Greg Dening reports for the Marquesas, Melville's islands.[44] Along with work by those with experience in ships and islands were also the beginnings of adventure stories by those who had no firsthand knowledge of the South Seas, the most notable case being *The Coral Island* by the prolific and popular writer of adventure stories for boys, R. M. Ballantyne, and published in 1858. The imaginary locale for this story is an idyllic island in the South Seas where the flower of English youth thwarts both cannibalism and savagery and exemplifies in their own lives Evangelical morality and the "message of empire."[45] These kinds of narratives culminated in the proliferation of travel adventures in the late nineteenth and early twentieth centuries, many of which contained the word "cannibal" (sometimes the related term "headhunter") in the title, even when cannibalism never appeared in their contents. This was also the fate of Endicott's own journal. Endicott's manuscript was only published in 1923, forty-two years after his death, with the invented title *Wrecked Among Cannibals in the Fijis: A narrative of shipwreck and adventure in the South Seas* whereas his own honest one read: *Narrative of a Voyage to the South Seas; Shipwreck etc In the year 1829, 1830 and 1831, 2.*

What makes *Cannibal Jack* so interesting is the aura of verisimilitude it conveys.

Quite unlike *Robinson Crusoe,* there are very specific and recognizable geographical, political, and cultural details in this new writing, such that it might tempt the unwary scholar to assume that if such details are empirically correct, then the text as a whole is true. The incorporation of cultural or ethnographic information into a yarn was anticipated in the Pacific by certain personae: by beachcombers, by wanderers turned on by the lure of adventure, by unsettled settlers like David Whippy belonging neither to one culture nor the other, and sundry "outcasts of the islands." Cannibal Jack injects himself into this context and weaves a first-person narrative as his precursors did in the Marquesas; this is what Melville also does in *Typee.* The anthropological assumption is that naive sailors writing in the first person must surely be speaking the truth. But, as Salman Rushdie says, "In autobiography, as in all literature, what actually happened is less important than what the author can manage to persuade his audience to believe."[46] It is entirely plausible that Jackson, alias Cannibal Jack, lived in Fiji for at least two years, but this does not render his adventure "true." The sense of verisimilitude that Cannibal Jack conveys is because he, like a good novelist, can vividly express the sense of time, history, and place that frames his hero's improbable adventures.

Does our examination of *Cannibal Jack* as fiction mean that his earlier work "Jackson's Narrative" is the nonfictional ethnographic account it is made out to be by some anthropologists? Endicott's narrative surely should give us pause. Clunie says that "Jackson's Narrative" is far superior and more truthful than *Cannibal Jack,* even though he does use the latter as a resource for documenting Fijian warfare. Can a particular text be more truthful than another written by the same author and recounting similar events? What has happened is that while one cannot miss the fictional quality of *Cannibal Jack,* one cannot also miss the "ethnographic feel" of texts like "Jackson's Narrative" and the Endicott yarn. While Endicott produces sly comments that his is a yarn that parodies ethnographic narratives, there are only veiled hints in "Jackson's Narrative" and mostly through irony. Reread the text of the cannibal king impatient to eat not-so-fully-cooked noses and you will appreciate Jackson's comic talent, expressed in sentences like the following: "The butcher did as he was ordered, and handed the three ends of the noses to his majesty, which he grasped hold of very nimbly, and put on hot stones to warm a little, not wishing to lose any time." These textual complexities compel us to further investigate the genre of yarns that developed among beachcombers and settlers in the wake of the discovery of Polynesia.

Rev. James Hadfield commenting on *Cannibal Jack* says that he has complete confidence in the veracity of its author because there is "little or nothing in his book inconsistent with what I have learned during more than 40 years of service in the South Seas" (*CJ*, XVIII). Erskine makes the same point about "Jackson's Narrative": "[T]here is not one of the savage practices he there describes that I had not been either previously informed of by the missionaries, or of the truth of which I have not since received corroborative testimony."[47] This is true for the most part: the kind of stories that Endicott and Jackson narrate have circulated in this region for some time but that does not in itself endow them with credibility. The term "narrative" itself occasionally blurs the distinction between seamen's journals and the fictional accounts based on that genre. Thus Poe's 1837 novel is titled *The Narrative of Arthur Gordon Pym of Nantucket;* Poe could "hoax the general public" (fortunately not all of them) into believing the truth of his account, as John Jackson could gull contemporary ethnographers.[48] No wonder, because Poe employs the narrative technique of shipboard journalism and is very specific about dates and times even as he presents the "exquisite horror" of anthropophagy: "Let it suffice to say that, having in some measure appeased the raging thirst which consumed us by the blood of the victim, and having by common consent taken off the hands, feet, and head, throwing them together with the entrails, into the sea, we devoured the rest of the body, piecemeal, during the four memorable days of the seventeenth, eighteenth, nineteenth, and twentieth of the month."[49] This is followed by his later incredible, sometimes impossible, adventures in a fertile Antarctic island, "a country differing essentially from any hitherto visited by civilized men" and full of exotic landscapes and creatures![50]

Seamen's yarns are often characterized by their utterly improbable events, generally of a "marvelous or incredible kind," as the *Oxford English Dictionary* tells us. One technique in spinning a yarn is to make the fantastic seem matter of fact. In our examples yarnsters incorporate well-known ethnographic truths that then are turned inside out and woven into an episode in a story. Further, as in all oral narratives, we must imagine the setting of their telling. Walter Benjamin tells us that for the storyteller "boredom is the dream bird that hatches the egg of experience"; and Melville speaks of "beguiling the weary hours with chat and story."[51] In the telling and retelling and in their circulation on islands and ships, these stories get refashioned in multiple ways. Jackson, like Melville and Endicott, comes from this tradition of storytelling, but he is no ordinary yarnster. As a relatively educated person with an enormously creative mind, he is reconverting his yarns into two types of written narrative, first in the ethnographic mode of ships' journalism and, second, with greater experience in "scribbling," in the fictional mode of adventure stories. But in doing so Jackson is giving up yarning for novel writing because, as Walter Benjamin once again tells us, "the birthplace of the novel is the solitary individual," cut off, imaginatively or in reality, from his comrades in the deck or in the beach.[52] One person who knew Cannibal Jack refers to his "mania for scribbling," not exactly the talent of conventional yarnsters (*CJ*, XXI).

The fictional account that replaced the shipboard journals occurred at an important historical moment. The era of shipboard journalism was coming to an end; Captain Erskine's own narrative was one of the last. The islands of the Southern and the Western Pacific were already well charted by the middle of the nineteenth century, and there were settlements of white missionaries and traders everywhere. The kind of ethnographic knowledge that sea captains could bring home was no longer significant; the missionaries and settler whites knew, or ought to know, more about native customs and manners. Erskine, for example, relies very little on information that he himself collects; instead his sources, like Wilkes's before him, were the settlers, and among them were the beachcombers and yarnsters we have talked about. But all these accounts have a theme that must appeal to European readers entranced by another feature of savagism. They deal with *difference* or, as Endicott (as if echoing Poe) puts it, "sight[s] seldom witnessed by civilized man." Difference resonates almost as cliché with the savagism-civilization contrast also found in European romanticism and which, for Cannibal Jack, means "a yearning . . . for the sweets of that exhilarating, wild, natural life, so distinct from the artificial, craving, envious, selfish, and greedy life of civilization!" (*CJ*, 82).

Hence in important ways "Jackson's Narrative" anticipates the novel, *Cannibal Jack*. It is the counterpart of *Typee* in its relation to *Moby Dick*. It is a fact that Melville lived with the Typee for four weeks (not four months), but *Typee* is no more an account of his stay there than is Jackson's story an account of Fiji. In Melville's own time his publisher wanted "authentication" of his adventures among the Typee, simply because the genre of travel narratives had to be true. Melville wryly noted that he would go down to posterity as a "man who lived among the cannibals."[53] And while he had little sympathy for colonialism, or the missions, or even the "scientific" ethnography of that time, he too met the demands of his reading public by evoking in his protagonist the fear that he might be eaten by the Typee. As the story progresses, the fears are dissipated but not fully; it is supplanted by the hero's claustrophobic dread of being held or holed up on the island unable to get out. The dreaded picture of the cannibal Typee that Melville skillfully evokes resurfaces in the rather bathetic reality of their cannibal practice—seen in three skulls, including that of a white man, hanging from a rafter, and then, in more sinister fashion, a prize of victory in war, that of a "disordered members of a human skeleton, the bones still fresh with moisture, and with particles of flesh clinging to them here and there!"[54]

Jackson had much less scruple or talent than Melville, such that his seeming ethnography, "Jackson's Narrative," contains elements of high adventure that one finds in *Cannibal Jack*. In both Jack has fights with natives; he describes great battles; in both he rescues damsels in distress; both deal with the exotic life worlds demanded by an expanding reading public and seen through the free life of the peripatetic European. Nevertheless, while both narratives contain similar ingredients, the mature novel deliberately employs these themes in a much more creative way. Thus the "fugitive" rescued from Bonaveidogo's raid is converted into a "Man Friday" with a crucial role in the denouement of the narrative; the "Rotama beauty" episode in *Cannibal Jack* is a lot more interesting than his rescue of a beautifully decked virgin in "Jackson's Narrative" whom he "was quite certain was to be cooked with the [pile of] yams" on which she was seated; and to balance this stock idea of rescuing damsels in distress is the Pocahontas theme of the heroic Litia.[55]

In both cases one can show how ethnography is refurbished into story. It is a well-known ethnographic fact that when a high Fijian chief dies his wives or senior wife are strangled as a sacrificial offering and then buried with him.[56] This is put to good use by Jackson when, in the Western narrative mode, he saves the Rotuma beauty from strangulation and this in turn provides the dynamo that pushes the narrative forward. In Polynesian ethnography there are several ways in which sacrificial victims are killed, but I doubt that they would have to employ Cannibal Jack's stone anchor as "the site for immolating some yet unborn infants to the bloody gods by dashing their brains out upon it!" (*CJ*, 83). Although Cannibal Jack does not describe the procedure involved, a similar idea of "dashing of [aboriginal] infants upon the stones" was attributed to white settlers during the British conquest of New South Wales long before Cannibal Jack wrote his narrative, and it is also found in a novel of captivity written in 1793.[57] In the Litia episode, all the wives of the heathen party immolate themselves; thus the custom of wife strangulation is converted into a heathen habit of mass voluntary self-immolation. The "ethnographic" text "Jackson's Narrrative" shares the same propensity. For example, early Polynesian ethnography records the fact of human sacrifices performed at the dedication of newly built canoes, using bodies as "rollers." However, consider Jackson's whimsical chief who uses the bodies of forty people under his protection for getting his canoes "hauled across the isthmus" to the accompaniment of "the demon-like laugh of their bloodthirsty victors."[58] There is nothing inherently improbable about the corpses of sacrificial victims bound in the manner described by Jackson. That was common knowledge, but the details of what went on, including eyewitness descriptions of cannibal feasts are as suspect as Endicott's. What persuaded Polynesian ethnographers probably was Jackson's style of "data" presentation, though they miss his give-away irony. The enormously talented Jackson imitates the detached and objectivized style of shipboard journalism, the only "reliable" ethnographic resource available to scholars for early Polynesia.

The relationship between the fiction of ethnography and the ethnography in the fiction can be quite complicated, as it is with the fact of human sacrifice and the fantasy of cannibalism. Take Clunie's example of the "custom of hanging the enemy's sexual organs in the sacred trees."[59] Lieutenant Pollard visiting Bau in 1850 noted a building to house visitors; behind this was a tree in which were hung "several scraps of skin like scalps, but from another part of the body."[60] Even if Pollard's is a valid empirical observation and he is correct in coyly hinting that the "scraps of skin" were from dead men's genitals, very little ethnographic insight could be gleaned from this description. However, Clunie's primary ethnographic source is not Pollard but Jackson's vivid description of what one might call the "genital tree" of fantasy. A neat example of a similar fantasy comes from Cook's last voyage when William Anderson in February 1777 mentions that in Maori cannibalism "the Penis of the men [they kill and eat] they commonly make a musical pipe."[61]

When one reads Jackson's and Pollard's texts alongside descriptions of evisceration and dismemberment during cannibal feasts, one is reminded of the *corps morcelé*, the "fragmented body" of Jacques Lacan's mirror stage of early childhood fantasy.[62] "Certain nameless parts of the bodies were taken care of to furnish the 'akau tabu' (forbidden tree) with a new supply of fruit, which was already artificially prolific in fruit, both of the masculine and feminine gender. The akau-tabu is generally a large ironwood tree, and selected according to the situation it is found in, the most conspicuous being generally preferred."[63]

Jackson's "ethnographic information" originated on beaches and ship decks where it was possible to enact some of these seemingly real scenarios in humorous fashion. Sailors could enjoy such comically surreal accounts in their multiple re-tellings, with mimetic enactments alongside vulgar or raucous responses of an audience of comrades. And part of the fun the genital tree provoked was surely this: it boggles the mind how the action in respect of "female fruit" could be performed in reality. Peter Brooks suggests that what is transmitted from the storyteller to the listener occurs in a special space that seems very much like the space of the Freudian transference.[64] This must be the case especially when one is narrating such things as cannibalism and castration. These narrations may have some vague connection with native ethnography, but for the most part they are as much invented as Endicott's account of the old woman humiliating a corpse or Fijian girls dancing lewdly and poking at the genitals of corpses waiting to be eaten. All such stories probably receive "collaborative testimony" in the yarns, chats, reveries (and even ethnographies) about "savage practices," to use Erskine's phrases, as they operate in the space of the transmission-transference.

Sometimes the "fantastic" of these accounts anticipate the stuff of later novelists like Rider Haggard. Jackson's sacred "king eel" is a case in point. Once Jackson was conducted to a temple beside which lay a fresh water hole wherein he saw "an immense sized eel." "His body at the thickest part was as big as a stout man's thigh, and his head was enormously large and frightful, but his whole length I could not tell; they said it was two fathoms long . . . he was a "kalou" or spirit. . . . [H]e was of a great age, and that he had eaten several infants which they had given him at different times—children of prisoners taken in war."[65] There is enough of the fantastic in the real-life worlds described by ethnographers to seduce one to accept the truth of accounts that tap infantile bogie fears. Nevertheless, when such accounts went into early, and sometimes later, Polynesian ethnography, that genre itself developed what one might call the "ethnographic fantastic." Thus a critical theory for this region must entail a rewriting of the Polynesian ethnography invented in the nineteenth century and after. It requires more than a scholarly deconstruction of traditional ethnographic writing. It forces us to explore the deeper question posed by Michel de Certeau and William Arens, namely, the relation between the anthropological identity and the reality of cannibalism, at least in the period under review. But this is an issue that shows the power of savagism both among the lay public and professionals and cannot be dealt with here.

"HISTORICAL IGNORANCE": WILLIAM LOCKERBY AND THE FIRST CANNIBAL FEAST

I have already stated that the deconstruction of some accounts of cannibal feasts does not mean that others could not have taken place in reality. Therefore I feel obliged to take the reader briefly to the first eyewitness account of a Fijian cannibal feast by William Lockerby, the mate of the *Jenny,* a ship engaged in the early sandalwood trade. Lockerby was apparently a difficult man; his captain left for China leaving him stranded on May 21, 1808. He lived in Fiji until June 2, 1809, most of the time under the kind protection of the chief of Bua on the island of Vanua Levu, where much of the sandalwood trade took place. I have not been able to find the original Lockerby manuscript, nor have I been able to locate his descendants, rendering difficult any attempt to deconstruct his narrative. Instead I will let Lockerby himself give his account of the unspeakable act he witnessed during an attack on Tavea by a chief "Bulendam" (Buli Dama), from a district near Bua. Incidentally, Lockerby gives a good account of the kind of war where confederacies among small tribes were formed in opposition to other groups in order to capture the emerging trade with the Europeans.

Let me begin with the killing of a fifty-year-old wounded prisoner who with great stoicism and calm awaited his death. He was brought forward by the order of a "Callow" ("priest possessed by spirit," or *kalou*) and clubbed to death, his flesh eaten by the chiefs in a "hearty breakfast."[66] The invaders were engaged in scorched-earth policy, destroying trees and fields in the whole area and burning homes. Afterward the invaders discovered about 350 old men, women, and children, some of whom ("the younger class") tried to run away but unsuccessfully.

> I saw two men bring down at one time five. Each of them had a pole, at the ends of which were hanging two children, and between them they dragged by the feet a woman of about forty years of age, most probably the mother of those four that were suspended from the poles. When this woman reached the canoe she was not quite dead . . .. They then placed her in the canoe and gave her some fresh water: she I believe might have recovered again, but one of the infernal monsters by one blow with his club, laid her silent for ever. (*WL*, 43–44)

After this act of brutality comes the scene of carnage that "surpasses conception." There were the "shrieks and groans of the wounded and dying; the songs, the dance, and the hellish yells of the conquerors; their savage looks and gestures." In Lockerby's own canoe there were forty-two dead bodies, and the victors spent the night "cutting up and cooking the dead bodies of their prisoners." Some were cooked whole in earth ovens, but most were "cut into pieces and after being broiled in the fire" and then packed in baskets for later consumption. The head was held over the fire to singe the hair and then scraped with shells and "made up with the rest of the body" (*WL*, 44). The feet was also held up in the fire and peeled off as is the case with a pig's foot. The intestines were cleaned with water and then broiled and eaten, indicating to the reader, the "dreadful abyss of depravity these poor wretches are sunk" (*WL*, 45). Like others in cannibal narratives Lockerby was offered part of a leg, and when he indignantly refused, someone considerately "brought me a piece of a child." When Lockerby continued his protests he was shown a "woman, who had a child sucking at her breast eating some of the same," to prove to Lockerby its edibility (*WL*, 45). Unfortunately, poor Lockerby was compelled, presumably by hunger, to eat yams cooked in the cannibal pot, that favorite culinary item of later cartoonists. It seems as if Lockerby qualifies the earlier argument that the dead were cooked in earth ovens or broiled on the fire. "They put the flesh or what they want to cook into them; the pot is then placed into a hole in the ground, which is covered over with red hot stones and green leaves; afterwards they cover all with dry earth, and in a short time they are sufficiently done" (*WL*, 45). In a later event women were employed "in cutting up the bodies of their prisoners" while in a house nearby an old woman "was eating the foot of a child" (*WL*, 58–59). I find it surprising that Lockerby's flagrant discourse of Fiji savagism could be accepted as truth, as some ethnographers have, even though his account seems to be "confirmed" by fellow prisoner Thomas Smith, second officer of the *Favourite* who, unlike Lockerby, was in Fiji for nine days only.

For Smith's account one has to rely on the *Sydney Gazette* of December 11, 1808; it was also republished in Im Thurm's edition of Lockerby (*WL*, 193–97). Im Thurm says that Smith validates Lockerby though there are some minor differences. Smith omits reference to the fifty-year-old man but mentions a young boy who was killed and eaten. He mentions the massacre of women and children found in a mangrove swamp and taken to the chief's canoe, but the gruesome details of Lockerby are missing. Smith counts forty-two bodies in the chief's canoe, which agrees with Lockerby's figure. One of these was a beautiful girl whom the chief eyed, presumably for personal consummation or consumption. This event is not in Lockerby, which is not surprising. The canoes are taken to the mainland, where the bodies are dismembered and suspended in trees for cooking afterward, though the latter inference is Smith's. This reminds one of Mariner's account of bodies being hung on trees, but Mariner, unlike Smith, does not claim that these bodies were for later eating. It is now time to examine the significance of hanging bodies or body parts on trees. My interpretation is based on my Sri Lankan experience and knowledge of European quartering. It was fairly common for Sri Lankan rebels, both Tamils and Sinhalas, and also for army personnel to strategically place body parts in public places in order to humiliate the dead and to set a deterrent example to the living, as was the case with European quartering that I describe in chapter 8. Hanging of bodies and body parts served a similar function in Fiji: additionally, I think, it served to express triumph in vanquishing an enemy, in which case hanging of these objects is like hoisting a flag. We know not what motivated Pollard-Jackson-Clunie (and significant others) to imagine it as the genital tree, though such fantastic imaginings seem to echo Anderson's mentioned earlier: "the Penis of the men [they kill and eat] they commonly make a musical pipe."

To get back to Smith: like Lockerby he is offered a leg. Later he saw twenty or thirty men arrive with half-roasted human flesh in baskets, which Lockerby also mentions but not in such detail. Basically, in spite of differences, Smith seems to confirm Lockerby. In this situation what choice does the analyst have? One can believe in the truth-value of these discourses, in which case Fijian men, women, and children are truly large-scale consumers of human meat and killers of a particularly brutal sort. There is little or no ritualism associated with the practice either, and this would confirm that Fiji is truly the culture of the death instinct. The alternative would be to deconstruct these narratives, but how can one do so if the one account seems to confirm the other? It seems to me that we have no choice but to fall back to our knowledge of other cannibal narratives. My own guess is that Lockerby, who wrote about his experiences much later, simply used Smith's account from the *Sydney Gazette* easily accessible to him. But what about Smith himself? How valid is his version? He, like others I discuss here, seems to have invented much of what took place during that fateful time. As far as Lockerby or Smith is concerned, it seems to me that one has little choice but to practice the kind of "genealogical" operations I perform in this chapter and the next, and this requires enormous patience and time. Who knows whether such work will even be rewarded with useful results.

The other choice is to take the cannibal descriptions of Lockerby and Smith at face value. I find it hard to accept that in 1808–09, even though Fiji was being articulated with world capitalism, mass anthropophagy virtually without ritual or decorum was established there and that women were permitted to cut up corpses and eat of the flesh of victims. As far as Lockerby is concerned I have no doubt that he was present in Vanua Levu, but he has injected into the narrative a discourse on savagism at the appropriate moment when he is describing native wars.

What then is his motive? Even before Lockerby arrives in Fiji he notes that "the Feegee Islands are inhabited by cannibals," influenced by Cook's designation of them, I think, and shipboard rumor and yarning (*WL*, 9). He is left stranded near Bua; "[b]y this accident I was left among a race of cannibals, far from every object that was near and dear to me" with faint hopes of a vessel calling at such a "dismal corner of the Globe," thus preventing him from getting back "into civilized society" (*WL*, 19). Strangely enough for the first nine months he personally saw no evidence of anthropophagy in spite of rumors of three men being cooked and eaten (*WL*, 22, 19). The reason seems simple: "[T]hey eat no human flesh except that of the prisoners they take in battle" (*WL*, 22–23). Irrespective of whether the destruction of Tavea took place, wars are the appropriate place to graft imagined cannibal events, satisfying the narrative demand for such a description and fulfilling the desires of Lockerby's reading public.

Lockerby wrote his narrative addressed in epistle form to his "honoured father and mother" when he was in Fiji, he claims. In it Lockerby says that because his last letter to his parents was written from Boston in June 1807, he worried about not being in touch with them for two years. But in fact Lockerby's "letter" or journal concludes with his arrival in Liverpool and meeting his wife and child at home after three years and seven months and finding them in good health (*WL*, 79). Thus the evidence of the text is clear: the journal was in fact written *after* his arrival in England and "Honoured Father and Mother" is simply a way of dedicating the manuscript to his parents. Lockerby claims that he had books and writing material in Fiji but how could this be because he was left behind, literally high and dry, by his captain without any warning whatever. Moreover it seems that it is not just to his mom and dad that the narrative is addressed but to a larger reading public when, for example, he says that "it is impossible to convey to the mind of the reader an adequate idea of this scene of human misery" (*WL*, 44). Thus Lockerby's account, far from being something written in Fiji, was written in tranquility long after and addressed to a reading public. As for Thomas Smith from whom, I have said, Lockerby derives his account, we have little information and we have no idea why he had to invent the cannibal feast. In this case and in many other narratives the ethnographer has no choice but to plead "historical ignorance," because much of what we write as ethnographers, however entangled in theory and bristling with hypotheses and abstruse terminology, must in effect remain unknown.[67]

RE-VIEW: THE LATE ARRIVAL OF CONSPICUOUS ANTHROPOPHAGY IN FIJI

My hypothesis underlying Fijian anthropophagy is that both colonialism and the European intrusion had consequences similar to what happened in New Zealand, though I cannot document them adequately. A similar stance was taken by early colonial historians like Basil Thomson who, writing in 1908, says, "Whereas in times past cannibalism was confined to the ceremonial sacrifices in celebration of victory, the launching of a chief's canoe or the lowering of its mast, it increased alarmingly about the end of the eighteenth century—that is a few years before the arrival of the Europeans."[68] There is little evidence for the last assumption. As a colonial historian Thomson simply exonerates Europe and refuses to recognize that the beginnings of conspicuous anthropophagy from a sacrificial base occurred in this region after the arrival of Europeans. The rise of Bau and the emergence of new native confederations that were designed to capture the new trade in turn brought Fiji within the orbit of the world capitalist order. More persuasive to me is Chief Verani of Viwa, newly converted to Wesleyanism, conveying to the missionary Lawry in 1847, "All the old people, and especially his father, used to tell him, that these bloody wars, and this eating of one another, upon the present enlarged scale, sprang up in their days, and did not much obtain to such an extent in the generation before them. All testimony speaks to this effect throughout Feejee."[69]

SEVEN · Narratives of the Self

Chevalier Peter Dillon's Fijian Cannibal Adventures

PETER DILLON IN DAVIDSON'S BIOGRAPHY

Historical ignorance compels us to leave aside Lockerby and Thomas Smith and move on to Peter Dillon who on September 6, 1813, presented an eyewitness description of a cannibal feast that has not been surpassed in its detail before or since. Dillon was a well-known sea captain, trader, and self-designated explorer living in Sydney. Virtually every writer on Fiji mentions with approbation his account as truly authentic, and I considered it so too when I first read about it in J. W. Davidson's well-known biography of Dillon.[1] It required several months of hard work at the National Library of Australia examining Davidson's original notes and archival sources to deconstruct Dillon's narrative and present a reconstructed or restorative understanding of his text. Dillon himself was the author of a two-volume work on his search in Vonikoro on the Santa Cruz Islands for the remains of La Pérouse's two ships, *L'Astrolabe* and *La Boussole,* which were lost in the South Pacific in 1788.[2] The first chapter of this two-volume work gives his eyewitness description of the preparation, cooking, and consumption of European and native enemies at a Fijian cannibal feast, which, fortunately for him and us, excluded Dillon himself.[3] The title of Dillon's work informs us that he is not only concerned with the French wreck but also with the manners, customs, religion, and the "cannibal practices of the South Sea Islanders," self-consciously based on the journalistic example of "the immortal Cook."[4]

Let me introduce the reader to the events leading up to the cannibal feast presented in chapter 3 of Davidson's biography of Dillon, *The Path to "Dillon's Rock."* We are in the period of the decline of the once-profitable sandalwood trade that in a few years virtually depleted the forests of Hawai'i and Fiji in order to aromatize temples, homes, and bodies in China and India. In 1813 Captain James Robson of the *Hunter*, based in Calcutta, asked Peter Dillon to join his ship as third officer in the quest for sandalwood because Dillon was already familiar with Fiji, having been in Vanua Levu in 1809 for four months with Robson himself and perhaps also at other times.

Robson could not get enough sandalwood in Wailea village in 1809; two years later he returned to Fiji and entered into an alliance with Vonasa, the chief of Wailea at Naurore (Wailea) Bay on the northwest coast of Vanua Levu. Robson, Dillon claims, once helped the Fijian chief to fight his neighbors who had then been "cut up, baked, and eaten in his presence" (*LPE*, 29). Robson returned in January 1813 from Norfolk Island on his ship the *Hunter* and entered the Fijian Islands along the little-known southeastern coast of Viti Levu, where the ship ran aground and lost her false keel. It did manage to get into Naurore Bay on February 19 and anchored in a creek near Wailea village. Robson's friend Vonasa informed him that there was little hope of collecting sandalwood because the people that Robson had helped to fight last time had revolted and joined with Dreketi, a village further east. The enemy would strike again if Vonasa's forces were to be deployed in gathering sandalwood; the chief urged Robson to help him once more to fight his enemies. Robson initially declined but, because the precious commodity was coming in too slowly for Robson's comfort and purse, he finally agreed, on the condition that he would be supplied with a cargo of sandalwood two months after the anticipated victory.

If Robson helped forge an alliance with the chief of Wailea, another group of European beachcombers and deserters had already helped the local chiefs of the tiny island of Bau to become a powerful kingdom, strategically located as it was off the coast of Viti Levu for capturing the emergent European and American trade. Among these outcasts was the Swedish man, Charles Savage, briefly mentioned in the preceding chapter, one of the oldest European of residents in Fiji, having lived there since the time of the wreck of the brig *Eliza* in 1808. With his knowledge of European warfare, Savage became a terror to savage Others. Assisted by fellow beachcombers and outcasts he served Naulivou, the chief of Bau, and helped him to conquer Verata, a powerful neighbor. Savage was rewarded with chiefly titles and given two high-ranking women as wives. These Europeans also worked for sandalwood traders, including Robson, in order to obtain supplies of European goods and alcohol.

Meanwhile the *Hunter* was joined by the cutter *Elizabeth*, also belonging to Robson. The *Hunter*, under first mate Norman's command, stayed in Naurore Bay to collect the Wailea sandalwood. Because sandalwood was slow in coming, Robson decided to gather bêche-de-mer, which was in great demand in China and plentiful on the reefs at Kaba Point, a few miles south of Bau on the Viti Levu coast. To ensure success the *Elizabeth* dropped the European and Fijian workers ashore under the command of Dillon while Robson left for trading elsewhere. Kaba was separated from Bau by a short strip of water, and the workers were under the protection of Naulivou of Bau. According to Davidson (though Dillon himself does not make this point) Dillon cultivated the friendship of the chiefs of Bau during his three-month stay in Kaba and had close relations with Chief Naulivou and his brother. This stint ended when Robson returned in the *Elizabeth* in late August with some Europeans and about two hundred Fijians from Bau in two canoes and anchored in Naurore Bay (*PD*, 32).

At the Wailea end where the *Hunter* was anchored things were going badly, and there was only 150 tons of sandalwood, one-third of the expected cargo. Robson would not accept the chiefs' reasonable explanation that the forests were already depleted. He was furious and felt betrayed by his friends whom, says Davidson, quoting Dillon, he "helped to glut with the flesh of their enemies" during the earlier visit (*PD*, 33). But shortly afterward they were told of the plentiful availability of sandalwood in Macuata, forty miles east. Robson, with Dillon, set out in the *Elizabeth* accompanied by several Wailean canoes to procure the wood but apparently only three boat loads were available.[5] About that time Charles Savage arrived from Bau with a message from Mr. Norman, the *Hunter*'s first officer, that there was a Wailean conspiracy to seize the cutter. Robson therefore detained one Wailean in the canoe and sent seven or eight others, some of high rank, to the *Hunter* with a note saying they should be held as hostages. A couple of days later when the *Elizabeth* was returning to Naurore Bay she encountered several Wailean canoes with armed warriors. These were attacked on Robson's orders; ten canoes were sunk and one native Fijian killed. That same evening first officer Norman of the *Hunter* set fire to a part of Wailea and killed several people.

Trading with Waileans for sandalwood was over, but it was not possible to sail out of Naurore Bay because both vessels had run aground. To repair them amidst hostile Waileans would be difficult. Therefore, following the advice of their Bau allies, they thought it best to destroy the rest of the enemy canoes. To put this into effect on that fateful day of September 6, 1813, three officers—Norman, Cox, and Dillon from the *Hunter*—along with the beachcombers and native Bau warriors landed in three boats at Black Rock, carefully keeping their boats and canoes in deep water to prevent them from grounding. The assembled party found that the Wailean canoes could not be sunk because they were in shallow waters owing to the low tide. The party then broke into groups of three or four with Norman and Dillon in one group. This group then moved down a level path and climbed a hill, where they were confronted by the Waileans. Norman then led his men to a hamlet, where they were challenged once again. Some of the Europeans fired their muskets, killing one native and then burning more than fifty houses to the ground.

They now heard enemy drums, which, the Bauans told them, indicated that other members of the landing party had been killed. Dillon and Norman's group came down the hill where thousands of Waileans and their allies were gathering around the area between them and their boats. They came upon the body of Terence Dunn, an Irishman living in Wailea, with his brains beaten out by a native club. Frightened, John Graham, living in Bau, ran into the bush, where he was also killed. Then Norman himself was struck by a spear which "entered his back and passed out of his breast" (*PD*, 34). Dillon killed the killer only to find another European named Parker dead. Dillon concluded that their best chance now lay in climbing a rock, known today as Dillon's Rock, "on the seaward flank of Korolevu, a great flat-topped hill which dominates Naurore Bay . . . a commanding position readily defensible by a few men."[6] Besides Dillon only five managed to get to the top of the hill, these being Charles Savage; Martin Buchert (a Prussian living in Bau with his Fijian wife); Luis, the Chinese man (also from Bau); and William Wilson and Thomas Dafny from the *Hunter*. They were safe here; arrows were deflected by the wind, and spears and slingshots could not reach them.

Dillon, now in command, ordered that shots should be reserved for those enemies who dared to climb the Rock. Several Fijians who attempted to do so were killed; meanwhile down below preparations were being made for a cannibal feast. While this preparation was going on Dillon kept hoping that the Bau chiefs and Robson's crew would come to their rescue, even though he could see from his vantage point the former leaving for Bau in their canoes. Savage was planning to make a run for it, but Dillon threatened to shoot the first deserter.

Meanwhile Dillon initiated discussions with the Fijians, reminding them that eight Waileans were still held prisoner in the *Hunter* but would be released if his group was permitted to go free. Eventually a priest came up and Dillon got Dafny, who was wounded, to take a message to the ship. According to Davidson's rendering of Dillon the letter stated that four hostages should be released; the others only when the men were safely aboard. Because Dafny went through unharmed, Savage also left thinking he could make it because he knew the Fijians and their language. Luis, the Chinese man, who felt he could trust a chief whom he personally knew, stole away without Dillon's knowledge. Neither was successful. Says Davidson, "Charles Savage was seized by the legs, and held in that state by six men, with his head placed in a well of fresh water until he was suffocated; whilst at the same instant a powerful savage got behind the Chinaman, and with his huge club knocked the upper part of his skull to pieces" (*PD*, 37; *LPE*, 18). They too were cut up and cooked in ovens (*PD*, 38; *LPE*, 18). Meanwhile Dillon and his two comrades on the Rock had virtually given up hope; they would rather shoot themselves than be tortured and killed in this gruesome manner (*LPE*, 20).

Davidson describes the situation of Dillon and his two companions thus: "By now the afternoon was well advanced, a time at which the offshore wind usually falls away. The sun, sinking behind the shadowed mountains of Yaqaga and Naivaka, illuminates a motionless landscape. This was the scene in which the three men on the hill-top awaited their fate against the background of exultant shouts from the Fijians feasting on human flesh below them" (*PD*, 38). Worse, for some inexplicable reason, Captain Robson, flouting Dillon's request, released all eight of the Wailea prisoners. Accompanied by the same priest who had been there earlier they now came up to the Rock. They had obtained presents from Robson; they also claimed that they had instructions to Dillon to hand over their arms before being escorted to the boat. Dillon refused to part with his musket. Instead he pressed it to the priest's head and let him know that "I would shoot him dead if he attempted to run away, or if any of his countrymen offered to molest me or my companions. I then directed him to proceed before me to my boat, threatening him with instant death in case of non-compliance" (*PD*, 39; *LPE*, 22). The ruse worked, and Dillon and his two companions safely arrived on board.

THE DECEPTIONS OF VERISIMILITUDE AND THE INVENTION OF THE SELF

What seduced me to accept the truth of Dillon's own narrative was its stunning verisimilitude. Yet on reflection I came to believe that a strict description of fast-developing events can exist only in a few limited ways and, though it appeals to our sense of reality, perfect verisimilitude is only possible in invented genres or fiction. In ethnography, for example, it is the rare observer who can with reasonable accuracy describe performances he or she has witnessed because such activities are always complex and one must be especially lucky to get a visually undisturbed vantage point. Hence any semblance of verisimilitude in ethnography comes not from witnessing an event but from more formal settings where one sits with a specialist and gets idealized accounts of ritual procedures. Perfect verisimilitude with regard to a ritual for example is an ethnographic deception because actions on the ground rarely fit such idealized accounts.

I will examine parts of Dillon's text to illuminate his self-valorization as he represents his adventures in the first person; I refer the reader to my earlier paper for a more detailed analysis.[7] Dillon is in the forefront of the battle and his "We" and "I" are everywhere in the text. Gradually the "We" becomes "I" as the narrative develops and Dillon starts constructing a heroic role for himself and posterity. He tries (futilely) to imitate the immortal Cook's journalistic style, but unhappily he has very little to say about "native customs and manners" in the places he visited. They have been better described by earlier navigators and in more detail. In Vanikoro itself he was too preoccupied with hunting and gathering pieces of the French wrecks to pay much attention to that country's ethnography. He pads the second volume of his journal with an eighty-page summary of Mariner's narratives of Tonga, and his first chapter deals with his cannibal adventures of 1813 even though they are only indirectly related to his theme. Yet that first chapter is the most vivid, well-written, and absorbing part of his book. No wonder Davidson and I joined the ranks of the many readers who fell for it.

Let me give a few examples of the manner in which Dillon further develops his heroized self in his continuing narrative. "On landing, the Europeans began to disperse into straggling parties of two, three, and four in a group. I begged of Mr. Norman, our commander, to cause them to keep close together in an attack from the islanders; but no attention was paid to my remonstrance" (*LPE,* 9). Clearly if Norman followed Dillon's advice many lives would have been saved. There is a graphic description of Norman's death when a native "threw a lance at Mr. Norman, which entered his back and passed out of his breast" (*LPE,* 11). Dillon heroically shoots the killer. Expectably, as Dillon takes over the leadership, the "I" becomes more pronounced: "I fired at this native"; "I dashed along with all the speed that was possible"; "I came across the dead body of William Parker . . . with his musket by him, which I took up and retreated with," but later "I was obliged to throw Parker's musket away, as also a pistol which I had in my belt" (*LPE,* 11–12). "In a moment after this I reached the foot of a small steep rock that stood on the plain. Finding it impossible to get to the boat through the crowds of natives that intercepted the pathway, I called out to my companions (some of whom were on my right), 'take the hill! take the hill!'" (*LPE*, 12). Dillon is now the intrepid leader who takes over command as the narrative moves forward.

Let me focus on the cooking scene, which Davidson quotes in full:

> Fires were prepared and ovens heated for the reception of the bodies of our ill-fated companions, who, as well as the Bow [Bau] chiefs and their slaughtered men, were brought to the fires in the following manner. Two of the Vilear [Wailea] party placed a stick or limb of a tree on their shoulders, over which were thrown the body of their victims, with their legs hanging downwards on one side, and their heads on the other. They were thus carried in triumph to the ovens prepared to receive them. Here they were placed in a sitting posture while the savages sung and danced with joy over their prizes, and fired several musket-balls through each of the corpses, all the muskets of the slain having fallen into their hands. No sooner was this ceremony over than the priests began to cut up and dissect those unfortunate men in our presence. Their flesh was immediately placed in the ovens to be baked and prepared as a repast for the victors. (*PD*, 36; *LPE*, 14–15)

Once again the description is deceptive; it is quite unlikely that Dillon holed up in his rock would have seen these activities in all their detail. They were simply invented to show the savage cannibalism desired by his reading public, especially that of savages singing and dancing with joy over their prizes, firing musket balls through each of the corpses and the priests cutting up and dissecting these unfortunate people within sight of the Europeans on the hill. Dillon is an eyewitness to this wondrous savagery. When the "savage" Savage decides to leave with the poor Chinese man, look what happened: "Charles Savage was seized by the legs, and held in that state by six men, with his head placed in a well of fresh water until he was suffocated; whilst at the same instant a powerful savage got behind the Chinaman, and with his huge club knocked the upper part of his skull to pieces" (*LPE*, 18). Verisimilitude deceived Davidson even more than in the cooking scene, for how could Dillon have seen all this with such complete clarity amidst the bustle and confusion of the fight and from his vantage point on the hill?

This fictionalization of a truth is continued as the narration proceeds.

> We, the three defenders of the hill, were attacked on all sides by the cannibals, whom our muskets however kept in great dread, though the chiefs stimulated their men to ascend and bring us down, promising to confer the greatest hon-

ours on the man who should kill me, and frequently inquired of their people if they were afraid of three white men, when they had killed several that day. Thus encouraged they pressed close on us. Having four muskets between the three of us, two always remained loaded; for Wilson being a bad shot, we kept him loading the muskets, while Martin Bushart [Buchert] and I fired them off. Bushart had been a rifleman in his own country, and was an excellent marksman. He shot twenty-seven of the cannibals with twenty-eight discharges, only missing once. (*LPE*, 18–19)

Dillon, however, was no cold killer: "I also killed and wounded a few of them in self-defence" (*LPE*, 19).

The narrative continues with its combination of the probable and the improbable.

The human bodies being now prepared, they were withdrawn from the ovens, and shared out to the different tribes, who devoured them greedily. They frequently invited me to come down and be killed before it was dark, that they might have no trouble in dissecting and baking me in the night. I was bespoken joint by joint by the different chiefs, who exultingly brandished their weapons in the air, and boasted of the number of white men they had killed that day.

In reply to all this I informed them, that if I was killed, their countrymen confined on board our vessel will get killed also, but that if I was saved they would be saved. The ruthless savages replied, "Captain Robson may kill and eat our countrymen if he please; we will kill and eat you. When it is dark you cannot see to shoot at us, and you will have no more powder."

Myself and companions, seeing no hope of mercy on earth, turned our eyes towards heaven, and implored the Almighty Ruler of all things to have compassion on our wretched souls. We had now not the most distant hope of ever escaping from the savages, and expected to be devoured as our companions were but a few minutes before. The only thing which prevented our surrendering quietly was the dread of being taken alive and put to the torture.

These people sometimes, but not very often, torture their prisoners in the following manner. They skin the soles of the feet and then torment their victims with firebrands, so as to make them jump about in that wretched state. At other times they cut off the prisoner's eye-lids and turn his face to the sun, at which he is obliged to look with his bare eyes: this is said to be a dreadful punishment. From the fingers of others they pull off the nails. By all accounts, however, these punishments are very rare, and only inflicted on persons who have given the greatest provocation; such as we had done this day, by shooting so many men in our own defence.

> Having no more than sixteen or seventeen cartridges left, we determined, as soon as it was dark, to place the muzzles of our muskets to our hearts with the butts on the ground and discharge them into our breasts, thus to avoid the danger of falling alive into the hands of these cannibal monsters. (*LPE*, 19–21)

We know the rest from Davidson's narrative. In it Captain Robson gets even worse press than first officer Norman. Why did he not keep four hostages as Dillon suggested? Why did he release all eight, and is it true that he had suggested to the chiefs that Dillon and his comrades give up their arms and trust the chiefs? "I expostulated with Captain Robson on his extraordinary conduct, in causing so many human beings to be unnecessarily sacrificed. He made use of some absurd apologies, and inquired if we were the only persons who had escaped: I replied, yes; but that if the natives could have made proper use of the muskets which fell into their hands on that occasion, we must all have been killed" (*LPE*, 24).

In Davidson's description he stands tall, this man Dillon—all of "six feet four in height, heavily built, with a mop of red hair" (*PD*, 17). Davidson is caught up in a not atypical biographer's dilemma. Dillon is a good character for a biography, but biographers find it hard to escape admiring the creature they create. Consider the title of Davidson's book: *Peter Dillon of Vanikoro, Chevalier of the South Seas*. Sure Dillon was knighted by the French for his discovery of the fate of La Pérouse's two vessels but he was not knighted as "Chevalier of the South Seas." That is Davidson's creation. But Chevalier is very French; how does one convert that into an English title? "Peter Dillon of Vanikoro" reminds us of the English aristocratic tradition, even though Peter Dillon neither discovered Vanikoro nor settled there for any length of time.[8] The actual French artifacts he collected were meager though they did come from La Pérouse's ships. It is as if Davidson is creating what Dillon himself wanted to do, to identify with those Dillons who had aristocratic connections. The rock from which Dillon conducted his heroic defense is also mythologized in the later history of Fiji. It is a shifting site impossible to locate from Dillon's description, but Davidson located it, and later historians and cartographers finally gave their imprimatur to the new site in 1970.[9]

Although Dillon was "physically impressive," Davidson was mostly impressed by "his qualities of mind and spirit that principally distinguished him from the common run. He possessed both great courage and the instinct of command, was calm and effective in times of danger. He possessed intelligence and imagination that enabled him to gain a ready understanding of indigenous society. Above all, he possessed the capacity to appreciate pre-literate people in their own terms, unencumbered by a sense of cultural superiority. He judged them as individuals, not as types produced by a 'savage' culture."[10] Admittedly, Dillon was a complex person, and he occasionally spoke with sympathy about Maoris and Tahitians. As an older man he wanted to write a history of Fiji which he never did (and I think was incapable of doing). Again in his later years he championed the cause of natives and was strongly critical of missionary appropriation of native lands in Polynesia, though he himself had elaborate plans for colonizing New Zealand.[11] Nevertheless, one wonders how Davidson could read Dillon's account of the Fijians and still write about him as someone who understood native peoples.

THE CONTEMPORARY ACCOUNTS: THE *SYDNEY GAZETTE* AND DILLON'S DEPOSITION

Davidson's narration of Dillon's Fijian adventure is based on the various versions that Dillon himself gave during different times in his life. Instead of treating them as different stories, Davidson, following the conventions of his time, constructed a single coherent narrative, eliminating information that seemed flagrantly contradictory. For the fight with the Waileans and the retreat to Dillon's Rock Davidson relied almost entirely on Dillon's La Pérouse narrative of 1829. Yet this does not quite match with two contemporary accounts based on information supplied by Dillon himself. The first was published on October 23, 1813, in the *Sydney Gazette*, the day after Dillon landed in Sydney following his Fijian adventures. The second is his sworn deposition before a Sydney justice of the peace on November 6 of the same year.[12] While the two contemporary accounts contain in outline much of the Davidson-Dillon narrative sketched above, neither contain any reference whatever to natives engaged in a cannibal feast! Let me now explore this extraordinary finding in some detail.

The *Sydney Gazette* explicitly claims to have reported Dillon's own version. It agrees with the La Pérouse one depicting the sailors and their allies surrounded by upward of eight thousand hostile natives. In this deadly situation the newspaper simply says that "the people in the vessels unconscious of their danger, were separated into straggling parties."[13] There is no question of Norman, the first officer, acting foolishly and flouting Dillon's wise instructions. Norman comes out as a despicable character in both versions, but only the La Pérouse version says that he burned a chief's house. In that account Dillon is focusing on Norman's ineptitude and his own circumspect and wise instructions. Had he been the leader none of this would have occurred! In the *Sydney Gazette* version Norman does not die in quite the graphic manner of the La Pérouse story. Instead "six of the Europeans, among whom were Mr. Norman, M'Cave, and Graham, confounded at the charge, threw down their muskets, and ran towards the boats but were intercepted, and massacred with spears and clubs."[14] Dillon and nine others made for a summit of a hill near the sea beyond the reach of spears and stones. The rest agrees with the La Pérouse version except for some important details. The *Sydney Gazette* says that the priest came to see Dillon, and that "the business of his mission was to promise them security, provided they would release the eight natives who were prisoners in the vessels. *Gladly consenting to this proposition, one of the Europeans accompanied the priest . . . down to the boats; he went on board, and the eight natives were released accordingly.*"[15] By contrast, in the La Pérouse version Dillon asks Captain Robson to keep four of the natives as hostages; hence it is no wonder Robson appears there as a villain who released all eight hostages. Robson might well have been a scoundrel, but the *Sydney Gazette* clearly indicates that he merely followed Dillon's own instructions. And Dillon arrogantly "expostulating" with his commander also does not appear in this contemporary account.

According to the *Sydney Gazette*, two *Europeans*, contrary to Dillon's orders, decided to go down; they were treated reasonably well; the natives urged Dillon also to come down, and when he did not, Dillon had the mortification of seeing these two "perish beneath the weight of innumerable weapons."[16] It is of course entirely possible that one of the Europeans was Charles Savage, but it is not likely that the Chinese man was called "European" by Dillon. The priest then came back with the eight prisoners and urged Dillon and his comrades to come down with the assurance that they would not be killed. But Dillon refused. Instead he put a gun against the priest's back, and they arrived safely on board the ship.

The names of Dillon's two companions who defended the hill are missing in the newspaper account. Nowhere is there any mention of preparing European bodies for a cannibal feast or of the feast itself. Instead, here is what happened the day after Dillon reached the ship: "Next morning, the 7th, a party went on shore with a considerable property, to offer ransom for the bodies of their late ill-fated companions—but, alas! not one could be produced; and the wretched cannibals replied to the request, that they had been devoured the night before."[17]

Two weeks later Dillon made his sworn statement. This contains a great deal more information on the activities of the ships' crew in collecting sandalwood and bêche-de-mer but the rest of it follows the *Sydney Gazette* account. The deposition repeats the event of priestly intervention. Here also there is no indication whatsoever that Dillon urged Captain Robson to keep some of the prisoners as hostages.

One can, I think, make a reasonable inference: Dillon believed that if the hostages were freed he and his comrades would be sent home unharmed. But something soon fouled this expectation: the Chinese man and Charles Savage (as in the La Pérouse version but not the two Europeans of the *Sydney Gazette*) decided to go down on the urging of several native chiefs. The natives "suffered" them "to Walk unmolested, entreating Deponent and the two others to go down also, and finding Deponent would not consent they killed those two who were down."[18] Whether Dillon did the right thing or not one can never know; but Dillon's refusal to come down changed the equation and the two Europeans (or Savage and the Chinese man) were killed. The changed situation obviously did not permit Dillon to come down peaceably. Instead Dillon made the bold move to put a gun against the priest's back. The two contemporary accounts therefore exonerate Robson from acting irresponsibly. Robson was probably dead when Dillon published his later account in 1829 and there was little likelihood of contradiction. Finally, the deposition says that Dillon lead the party to recover the bodies but was told, as does the *Sydney Gazette*, that "the Bodies had been eaten on the Evening before."[19] Neither account even vaguely hints that Dillon witnessed the dressing of bodies and the consequent cannibal feast.

BODIES AND BONES

If the *Sydney Gazette* and the deposition do not mention the cannibal feast, do we know when the latter entered Dillon's narrative repertoire? This is a difficult question to answer but I can at least provide some insights into Dillon's inventive talents. Let me go back to the two earliest versions and their common agreement that after Dillon's escape either he (in the deposition account) or a party from the ship (in the *Sydney Gazette* account) tried to get the bodies of their dead comrades. Something anomalous stared at me: there was no way that Dillon could get hold of the *bodies* of his comrades, if one were to trust Dillon's La Pérouse version, because the bodies of *all* his comrades and the Bau chiefs had been dressed and cooked in full view of him (*LPE*, 14). If so, he should have known that only the bones and not the bodies were available for barter the next day.

The *Sydney Gazette* article was reprinted in the *Calcutta Gazette* on February 6 when Dillon was in Calcutta in 1817. It was reprinted again on Thursday May 8, 1828, when Dillon, now the famous discoverer of the French wrecks, entered that city again. Both accounts are faithful to the *Sydney Gazette* in affirming that it was their comrades' *bodies* that the Europeans sought the day after the adventure on the Rock. The second *Calcutta Gazette* article, however, has an addendum by the editor identifying William Wilson and Martin Buchert as the two companions on the Rock and goes on to say that Dillon deposited Buchert and the lascar in Tikopia because, if they were left in Fiji, they too would eventually have been "sacrificed." This version, including the editor's addendum, is reprinted as an appendix to Dillon's two-volume work but with one important change: "Next morning, the 7th, a party went on shore with a considerable property to offer a ransom for the *bones* of their late ill-fated companions."[20] Dillon has found out, as Obeyesekere did, that it was not possible to have the bodies recovered and astutely substituted "bones" in the addendum to the *Calcutta Gazette* reprint over which he had complete authorial control, thereby bringing it in line with the La Pérouse account.[21] The La Pérouse thus says that Dillon was anxious to purchase the *bones* of a friend (Mr. Cox) and that the natives reply that "they had *neither the flesh nor bones* to spare, as they had all been devoured the night before. One of the savages held up the two thigh-bones of Mr. Norman (as he informed us), and inquired what I would give for them. I offered an axe. He exultingly laughed, and flourished the bones about, saying he would not sell them; they would make excellent sail-needles to repair his canoe sails" (*LPE*, 27; my italics). Many aspects of Fijian savagism are brought together in the fabric that Dillon finally weaves into his book: Fijian cannibalism, their exultant brandishing of bones, and their prospective conversion of bones into tools. It is impossible to figure out how the natives could have identified Norman from his thighbones.

THE CHARACTER OF INVENTION AND THE INVENTION OF CHARACTER

I now refer to Davidson's interesting diagnosis of Dillon's character, though he does not fully appreciate its significance. "The dangers he saw [from the ship's surgeon, Tytler] was not chimerical; but, because he was a romantic, they assumed unreal proportions in his mind. He saw himself as the successor of Magellan and Mendana, of Drake and Dampier and Cook—and of lesser men as Bligh" (*PD*, 138). "Romantic" is hardly the word to describe him, but that dangers assumed unreal proportions in his mind is right on target. To express it differently, Dillon harbored delusions of grandeur in his identity with the great navigators of history. This self-delusion finds a parallel in his personal life. In a letter to Lieutenant Governor George Arthur, he wrote, "I am the son of the late Peter Dillon Esquire, of Meath Ireland, Nephew of the late Sir William Dillon of the same place, and related in the next degree of affinity to the Countess Bertrand" (*PD*, 149).

Little of this is true. He was born in Martinique in 1788, a son of an Irish immigrant named Peter Dillon, originally from County Meath. Owing to political troubles in Martinique he was taken home to Ireland around 1791 and later entered the Royal Navy and even claimed to have "had the honour to serve at the battle of Trafalgar" (*PD*, 13). His childhood could not have been pretty, if one infers that a man given to outbursts of violence, who later in life was a sadistic wife-beater and whipped his servant mercilessly, could possibly have had a pleasant childhood.[22] His early life, Davidson says, is full of obscurities. Davidson surmises that Dillon entered the navy as a servant of an officer or a petty officer and perhaps had to leave it around age sixteen or seventeen owing to Dillon's propensity to violence. Be that as it may, he seemed to have gone to Calcutta afterward and worked in ships that traversed Asian ports. No one knows when and why he came to the Pacific; his writing and letters do not reveal much either. "As an older man, when he devoted much of his time to writing, he was obsessed with gentility, so that the humble capacities in which he was obliged to seek work as a youth probably became matters that he deemed it needless, or even undesirable, to record" (*PD*, 14).

Contrary to Davidson, the letter to Governor Arthur suggests a much earlier "obsession with gentility." There he claimed connections with aristocratic Dillons, such as Comte Arthur Dillon, the seventh Viscount Dillon, and with Arthur Dillon's elder brother who served in 1786 as governor of Tobago (and who was subsequently guillotined). Arthur Dillon's second wife was Marie Joseph de Girardin, cousin of the woman who later became Empress Josephine. The daughter of that union married Henri-Gratien Bertrand, companion to Napoleon in his last days in St. Helena (*PD*, 13–14). In my opinion the fact that Dillon named his second son Joseph Napoleon was overdetermined by these imagined Napoleonic kinship connections and his idealization of great figures, in this case combining the names of the Emperor and Empress.[23]

Davidson records many events in Dillon's life whose significance he does not fully appreciate. In May 1837 he was a witness at a trial in which he Frenchified his name into "Chevalier de Dillon." "At this time," says Davidson, "he seems to have been stressing his French connections, and he may himself have been using 'De Dillon'. Throughout his later life he was very sensitive to the dignity of names and titles: Don Pedro Dillon, Count Dillon, the Chevalier Pierre Dillon, Chevalier Sir Peter Dillon, all appear at one time or another. . . . [I]t is also clear that he was disappointed at not receiving a British knighthood for the discovery of the fate of La Pérouse " (*PD*, 266). Davidson noted, "The title chevalier had become so much a part of him that he could not forebear reference to it even when signing his name" as C. P. Dillon, the "C" standing for chevalier (*PD*, 289). He claimed he was the French consul for the South Seas when he was not, though he tried very hard to get that position.[24] In January 1838 he was in Levuka (Ovalau, Fiji), where he signed a memorandum in his imagined capacity as French consul "and sealed it with a rough seal." The well-known French navigator Dumont d'Urville, who saw this document, sarcastically commented, "Je souris en lisant cette pièce de l'invention du Capitaine Dillon, et des titres qu'elle confère et à son possesseur et à son donateur" ["I'm smiling as I read this document, invented by Captain Dillon, and the titles that it confers upon both its possessor and its bestower"] (*PD*, 277).

Three years later, in a letter to the Duke of Bedford soliciting recognition (probably a knighthood), he inflates his own doings: "At the risk of my own life I undertook to make peace [between natives and missionaries in New Zealand] and establish a mission there."[25] Even minor actions reveal his wish to construct himself as a person of significance. In 1842, toward his life's end, he anonymously edited a book, *Conquest of Siberia and the History of the Transactions, Wars, Commerce, etc, etc, carried on between Russia and China from the Earliest Period*, which was, the title further indicated, "Translated from the Russian of G. F. Muller . . . and of Peter Simon Pallas." Dillon did not know Russian, and Davidson says this book's content was "actually taken from the English of William Coxe and anonymously edited by Dillon" (*PD*, 311). But the next year a new edition appeared with Dillon's name squarely in front: *Conquest of Siberia, by the Chevalier Dillon, and the History*. . . . One could put the matter thus: Dillon was trying to forget his past and his own personal and social inadequacies and, by identifying with the great navigators of history and especially his immortal Cook, he was trying to invent himself by constructing a grandiose and imagined self wherever he could. The title "Chevalier" granted by the French was surely something he deserved: thereby his delusions of grandeur could at last merge with reality but could hardly help resolve some of his fantasized imaginings, grandiose self-constructions, and delusions as he went on covering up his past as a someone born in obscurity, a violent man, a wife-beater. His obsession with gentility, I think, has deeper psychic roots in the infantile dilemma of the fantasized foundling who is in psychic reality the child-prince found among the bullrushes.[26]

FANTASY AND PSYCHIC REALITY IN SELF-INVENTION

It is time to move away from Dillon's narcissistic self-centeredness, his authoritarianism, his vulnerability to real and imagined slights, and his grandiose self-imaginings and return to his representation of the cannibal feast, the first on-the-spot description of an important event—though an imagined one constructed from what he has heard or known of such repasts.

Initially I had no methodological choice but to treat Dillon's deposition and the *Sydney Gazette* accounts as true in order to demonstrate the falsity of the truth claim of the cannibal feast in the later La Pérouse account. Having accomplished that task, it is now necessary to get out of that methodological tangle for even those earlier statements are after all self-representations, and there is nothing to say that the Dillon who invented the one did not invent the other. Dillon was a nominal Roman Catholic; I doubt he would be terribly concerned about swearing to an untruth in his deposition.

Let me begin with the frontispiece of his book, entitled "Massacre at the Fejee Islands in September 1833 *[sic]*: Dreadful situation of Captain Dillon and the other Survivors" (see figure 7).[27] In this piece of self-aggrandizement, we see a tall Dillon in his uniform, gun in hand, standing on the Rock that now bears his name with one person on his left, much smaller, and another, probably Buchert, the Prussian marksman, kneeling down and firing at the savages below. Further away on Dillon's left is the ship, the *Hunter* no doubt, while before him and Buchert are the hordes of savages whose physiques and gesticulations imitate (rather poorly) Webber's paradigm piece of savage violence toward a noble European, "The Death of Captain Cook." One comrade is lying dead; the other is about to be killed while in the distance a human body is cooked in an open fire (instead of the earth oven mentioned in the text).

This adventure is true, according to the La Pérouse account, but that truth cannot be accepted uncritically. One can cast some doubts on the details: Buchert killing twenty-seven natives with twenty-eight shots is highly improbable given the kind of muskets available at that time, as is the claim that one could count enemies being killed during the difficult situation in which Dillon and his men found themselves. It is unlikely that Buchert retained his early marksman's skills, if he ever had them, during his fifteen-year stay in Fiji and Tikopia, where he had practically gone native. Equally dubious are the versions of Dillon taking a priest hostage and going past the savage multitude without being killed by a musket or spear. And how does one know the truth of the multiple fates of Charles Savage and Luis, the Chinese man, except that they were killed by the Fijians? No one knows what had happened to the other survivors by the time Dillon wrote his La Pérouse narrative fifteen years later. I shall deal with the enigmatic Buchert later, but consider Dafny (who went unmolested to the ship to procure the release of the

FIGURE 7
Peter Dillon and the defenders of the rock. From Peter Dillon, *Narrative and Successful Result of a Voyage in the South Seas* (London, 1829). Courtesy of the Rare Books Division, The New York Public Library, Astor, Lenox, and Tilden Foundations.

Fijian hostages). He must have been a sight for sore Fijian eyes according to Dillon's description of his bodily state immediately before ascending the Rock: "He was wounded in several parts of the body, and he had four arrows stuck in his back: the point of the spear had pierced his shoulder, having entered from behind and came out in the fore part under the collar bone" (*LPE*, 13). Wilson, the second defender of the Rock, simply disappeared from the La Pérouse scene. And Buchert? He could hardly speak English according to Dillon; he did not even speak Tikopian even though he lived there for thirteen years (*LPE*, 156–57). There is little doubt that a "massacre" of Europeans did take place that year, and it is in Dillon's character to act with courage and impetuosity. But Dillon's self-constructed role in all his narratives is open to suspicion.

I now want to address a deeper and possibly unresolvable question: Though the Fijian cannibal feast was an imagined one, did Dillon imagine it as an imagined one? Do imagined self-constructions *remain* imagined? Dillon's case compels me to explore this theme, albeit tentatively, by getting back to the letter he wrote to the Duke of Bedford in 1841 where he mentions his Fijian experience: "I miraculously escaped, after seeing several of my shipmates murdered, cut up, baked and devoured. On this occasion I saved my life, to be useful to the friends of humanity and science."[28] Science and humanity aside, Dillon might well have come to believe the truth of his own story at this late stage of his life.

Let me start with a simple proposition: the prototypic condition where fantasy and reality meet is childhood. It is here that the boundary between the two is blurred. But diverging from the classic Freudian, which argues that as the child grows older the reality principle supervenes and fantasy is pushed into the lower depths of the unconscious, I take the position that the boundary between reality and fantasy is being constantly blurred even through old age and unto to the point of death. To rephrase the issue in Todorov's terms, the fantastic permeates multiple sites and in some instances fantasy is converted into reality through those complex processes that I have identified as "the work of culture."[29] In Freud's own time the Protestant work ethic was such that the role of fantasy in everyday life was poorly recognized. Yet even here one could act out one's sexual fantasies, for example, in special arenas such as brothels and bordellos. There was another realm where ordinary settlers, colonizers, and seamen could act out their fantasies, on ships and islands, where their imaginations are peopled with noble or ignoble savages and, in terms of our present argument, with cannibals.

I am interested in the permeation of fantasy in our everyday lives as we think of ourselves, as we recount or recollect our past or begin to give it meaning and significance through narrative. Few can escape this "fantasizing in everyday life," not as "the psychopathology of everyday life" that Freud spoke of, but as everyday normal creativity (which is what Freud probably meant anyway). As I recount what happened to me when I did this or that, visited such-and-such a place or met so-and-so, I often embellish my account with splashes of invention, wittingly or unwittingly. Memory often helps by being selective in precisely this sense: the eliding or censoring of past occurrences and the harmless invention of events that never occurred gets woven into one's story. Our lives are continual self-inventions of this sort. Once we begin to narrate our favorite experiences we might even begin to believe in them ourselves, until some occasion or other forces us to recognize the invented nature of our narratives of the self.

This everyday self-invention can easily merge with "pathology," the extreme case being that of paranoid and other psychotic fantasies. But between the ordinary self-inventions of most of us and the extreme psychotic forms are those shadowed areas where individuals begin to invent and construct their selves under the governance of fantasy. We are familiar with them in fiction. Consider John le

Carré's *The Tailor of Panama* where Harry Pendel has a shop, "PENDEL AND BRAITHWAITE, Panama and Saville Row Since 1932," patronized by the Panamanian elite. Pendel is heir to this dignified family business. His life revolves around this identity and not even his wife knows that he learned tailoring in an English prison until he is forced by a British agent to confront his invented life as a falsehood. But that life was not fiction to Pendel and for everyone who knew him. His invented identity is part of his being, inseparable from it, and Pendel's forced recognition of its empirical falsity produces the disastrous consequences that follow and eventually engulf him in his own death. Pendel is not a Dr. Jekyll and Mr. Hyde character leading two lives; he *is* his invented persona, even though he knows that it is an invented one. He is not a confidence trickster either. The confidence trickster knows that his assumed identity is a false one; he sheds it when it is expedient; his play with a double identity is intrinsic to his persona. But even here the assumed identity sometimes becomes the dominant one, as with Thomas Mann's brilliant rogue Felix Krull, a trickster who revels in his invented identity, though the self-consciousness of his past which, as with any confidence trickster, is necessary for his self-reveling.

In other instances, such as that of Martin Guerre, the assumed identity might become more real that the other persona.[30] At the O. J. Simpson trial, Detective Fuhrman, we are told, had invented himself as someone who had encountered adventures in Vietnam even though "the closest he got to a ground war there was aboard a ship in the South China Sea."[31] I have known others who have invented Vietnam War experiences. One can weave into the phantasmagoria of war a new segment of the self because there is hardly any way of others knowing whether one's self-construction is a "fabrication." That Freudian touchstone of "reality-testing" can have no sway over areas that are in fact governed by the very absence of familiar life-forms or the "reality principle." And war is one of those arenas where genuine heroism can be enacted and also genuinely or disingenuously invented.

I am acquainted with this condition in Sri Lanka during a period which Sri Lankans themselves label as the "time of dread" (*bhiṣana kālaya*). I will not theorize its ethos here, except to say that the period produced not so much a "culture of fear" but the very erosion of what one can reasonably call "culture" when multiple and shifting forms of terror, intimidation, and dread began to take hold over the spaces in which human beings have constructed their reality-norms. Dreadful happenings, unbelievable in normal life, seem to happen every day. In such a situation one does not know whether stories one hears are true or false or compounded of both. The ethoses of dread permit individuals not only to act out their fantasies and even create fleeting life-forms out of them, but they also permit persons to invent stories about themselves and others that can pass muster as real. Fabrication thrives in "times of dread." There are plenty of invented stories of disappearances and horror stories of such things as vampirism and cannibalism, even cannibal dances by paramilitary forces dressed in black, based on the dread actualities of that Sri Lankan time. Invented stories sound true in the ethoses of that period because the fantastic as horror has also become real, fusing the real of everyday life with childhood's "real."

The "time of dread" was roughly 1985–89 when ethnic Sinhala youths took over vast areas of the country and practiced enormous atrocities. They were only eliminated by equally dreadful state terror. Trigger-happy rebels disfigured corpses and did not permit families to hold normal funerals. In a familiar scenario, military and paramilitary forces, trigger-happy through fear, shot innocent people at check points and also at points where checks did not obtain. Such forms of coexisting terror resulted in the deaths of thousands of noncombatants as social, political, and personal grudges began to be paid off. This period produced males who became addicted to torture and killing, which tapped their own unconscious fantasies, permitting them to act these out in the shifting ethoses of dread.

This youth rebellion had its precursor in 1971; here also dispossessed youth from rural areas controlled vast parts of the nation for about a month until they were quelled by massive government force, though not on the level of brutality unleashed during the dreaded second revolt. I was teaching in the University of Sri Lanka at Peradeniya at that time. In June 1971 I interviewed several students and activists on the run. One person I interviewed was an older man wanted by the police who came to see me in various guises, now dressed in this garb, now in that, now as an Anglican priest, now as a beggar. I was fascinated by his life as he gave me graphic accounts of his adventures. Those at home were nothing in comparison to his adventures in the British army during the Second World War in Burma: graphic, vivid, full of detail, verisimilitude. A white female diplomat was so seduced by his stories that she slept with the hero and protected him from the police. I was also seduced as I later was by tall Dillon's tale. I fancied I could write a brilliant biography of a revolutionary not knowing at that time that real-life heroes have to be invented.

One day, as my friend was talking to me about his Burmese adventures, I was suddenly jolted from my own fantasy. My god, I thought, this is plain invention of truth. There were no Burma days. His adventures were just another of his many guises. It was not too difficult for me to verify that my friend joined the youth movement late and his work in blowing up bridges and his life in training camps were at best only peripherally true. He had lived in London for a long time and might even have been in Burma (though this was not clear), but his adventures there were mostly invented. My informant-cum-friend and I were both caught up in a double fantasy. Both of us were bound, me by my youthful academic fantasy of writing a biography of a "true revolutionary" and he by fantastic self-constructions in two ethoses, that of the Burma war and the youth rebellion, arenas or spaces especially well-situated for inventions of the self. Many of his friends, me included, could believe his stories because such stories seemed appropriate to the "time of dread" in which we were living. I am convinced that my friend, like the tailor of Panama and Detective Furman, came to believe (for most of the time) in his own fantastic self-inventions.

And so, I think, was it with Peter Dillon. Born a "foundling" he wanted to be a prince; he achieved this when he was knighted by the French, but that could not assuage his insatiable thirst for recognition. To be recognized he had to constantly invent himself. Dillon would have been pleased with the lordly title of Davidson's book. Yet, let us be fair by Dillon. Not all his self-inventions were fictions; I am sure he fought natives in Fiji, perhaps bravely, and no doubt killed many, though perhaps not in the heroic manner he recounts in his several narratives. Nevertheless, he can be credited with the first-published (imagined) eyewitness account of savage cannibalism as Cook was the first eyewitness of Polynesian human sacrifice. But Dillon was no Cook; a minor figure, he had to perforce invent his role as explorer-cum-ethnographer and simultaneously invent himself as hero, following the route of the great navigators of his imagined history. Let us now see how that history repeats itself as Dillon begins to repeat his history to other listeners and, I think, begins to believe in his own fiction of the Fijian adventure and the cannibal feast.

THE CONTEXT OF NARRATIVE INVENTION: THE GEORGE BAYLY VERSION

Dillon's cannibal adventures also appear in the literary record in two versions written by George Bayly. The first is an unpublished work, entitled *Journal of Voyages,* written in 1831 in a straightforward journalistic style; the second, a book based on the first but published in 1885, colored by Bayly's sentimental reminiscences of "sea-life sixty years ago," which is its title.[32] The latter has a vividness and immediacy lacking in the former; it is as if one can see through Bayly's reporting Dillon recounting his adventures before an audience of shipmates.[33]

> Though naturally very excitable, and, when anything occurred to displease him, tyrannical in the extreme, he would frequently unbend, and would then entertain his brother-officers with such graphic accounts of his adventures during voyages among the southern and eastern seas as made him *pro tem*, a very agreeable companion. From these he would sometimes diverge to tales of the "ould counthry," and all unused to the melting mood, I have seen the big tear steal down his cheek as, in low murmuring tones, he would sing "Savourneen Deelish," and other plaintive songs of his native land. (*SL*, 9–10)

Again: "[H]e had been spinning a long yarn about some adventure in those fairy lands, and he had an eager and attentive listener in myself" (*SL*, 83–84). One might say that Bayly is reinventing Dillon, but insofar as Bayly's invention is based on Dillon's own storytelling on board ship, one might reasonably argue that Dillon's invention of himself is re-presented by Bayly. We do not know whether Bayly had read Dillon's book when he wrote his first account in 1831: the two versions do not always tally, suggesting strongly that *Journal of Voyages* contains an earlier version of the Fijian adventure than that found in Dillon's *La Perouse's Expedition*. The former anticipated the full-blown description of the cannibal feast in Dillon's own book. However, it is Bayly's "second narrative" that casts Dillon in the role of yarnster regaling his comrades with a feast of cannibal stories.

Let me begin Bayly's second narrative with the description of Captain Robson's sense of betrayal by his Fijian friends for not bringing his full quota of sandalwood and his determination to use force to obtain it: "Having been informed that a considerable quantity of sandal-wood was lying concealed in the native huts opposite the ship and having bargained with the Europeans on shore to side with the ship's crew, the captain sent a well-armed party on shore, under the command of Mr. Peter Dillon, with instructions to demand delivery of the sandal-wood" (*SL*, 11–12). This narrative eliminates Mr. Norman, the first mate of the other accounts; Dillon is put in command and then he was joined by unnamed Europeans on shore. This does not fit with Bayly's first narrative, which says that Dillon "was an Officer on board the ship Hunter" and also mentions the (unnamed) second mate as the one responsible for burning native huts (*JV*, 35).

The Fijian response was to summon their men for war by sounding their conches. "A fight ensued, in which many of the poor creatures were shot, and the remainder, with the women and children, fled to the woods, whither Dillon did not deem it prudent to follow them." The raiding party took whatever sandalwood they could find, set fire to village huts, and loaded on board their booty together with eight natives they had captured. "Under the impression that they would find another store of sandalwood at the neighboring village called Vilear [Wailea], on the following morning the officers asked permission of the captain to proceed there and get possession of it" fired by the success of the previous day (*SL*, 12). Then:

> Suspecting that the natives were lying in ambush at no great distance, Dillon ordered his men to keep together, with the intention of retreating at once to the boats; but he had a lawless set to deal with in many of the men who had joined him. Deaf alike to his commands and warnings, and enraged at not finding any plunder, they separated into small parties, in order to set fire to the whole village at once, thus losing their only chance of getting back to the boats. Dillon only succeeded in retaining five to stand by him—Martin Buchert (a Prussian), two Englishmen, and a Chinamen, all of whom had been living with the natives, and William Wilson, a lad belonging to the ship. Each had a musket and pistols.
>
> Whilst Dillon was giving orders to these men as to what they should do in case of a sudden attack, the rest of them straggled about among the huts and commenced their work of destruction. Several huts were on fire, and with pirate-like recklessness the sailors were exulting in the fast-spreading desolation, as the towering flames rose up from the crackling bamboo huts, when suddenly, far above the shouts of the seamen and the noise of the blazing village, burst forth the war-cry of the savages and the boom of their war-conches, as with hideous yells they rushed from the woods where they had lain concealed. (*SL*, 13–14)

The raiders put up a good fight but were killed as they tried to reload their muskets. "The savages then celebrated their victory by a fiendish dance over the prostrate corpses, while the air was rent by their horrid imprecations" (*SL*, 14). The bare information of the first narrative is vividly elaborated in the second. However, both narratives say that the number of natives who confronted the group were about one thousand, not the "several thousands" of the La Pérouse version or the eight thousand or more of the *Sydney Gazette*.

To get back to the narrative: Dillon and his five men escaped the fate of their comrades as they climbed to a "steep eminence." While on the hill

> the natives came rushing on, with the intention of serving them as they had served their late companions. Dillon allowed them to come within musket-

> range, when he and Buchert fired, and dropped the two foremost of them; then, handing their muskets behind, received the two loaded ones instead. Meanwhile, the two Englishmen fired and killed two more; then received the two reloaded muskets. They took good aim, and every shot told. In this manner they kept the natives in check until they succeeded in taking up a position on the top of the rocky knoll. During this extraordinary retreat, Buchert killed twenty-seven men with twenty-eight shots, only wounding once, and this with the old Brown Bess; there were no rifles among them. Dillon and the other two also killed a great number. (*SL*, 15)

Buchert killing twenty-seven with twenty-eight shots is also found in Bayly's first narrative, and one can assume this narrative element was invented by Dillon for the first time when he was on board the trip with Bayly, sailing from Tikopia to Calcutta.

The natives had by now surrounded the hill to cut them off and then "collected a quantity of wood, with which they made a number of large fires over the smouldering embers of their ruined village, and dragging along some of the bodies of the unfortunate seamen, cut them into pieces, and, with furious yells of triumph and demonaical *[sic]* dances and gestures, scorched and devoured them within sight and hearing of the unhappy remnant of the expedition" (*SL*, 16). Once again the inevitable savagism that is more detailed than the first narrative, which says that the natives began to "make a feast of Captain D's shipmates before his eyes" (*JV*, 37). I have already noted that in the La Pérouse account Dillon has the victims placed in traditional earth ovens; yet the frontispiece painting of the adventures on the Rock depicts a victim being cooked in an open fire, more in keeping with the two Bayly narratives, strongly suggesting that this was the version Dillon had in mind when he authorized the painting. "Stimulated by their cannibal feast, they made the air resound with their war-shouts, uttering the most frantic expressions of hatred and revenge. The chiefs boasted of how many men they had killed, and called out to Dillon, 'Aromai no, Peter! Come down, come down, and bring your men! If you don't come down now, we shall kill you and eat you as soon as it is dark; for then we'll rush up, and you won't see us.'" But the savages had to contend with a "master mind." Dillon hurled back insults at them with his "powerful lungs," telling them that the captain would probably kill the hostages (*SL*, 16). The natives did not seem to care: let the captain kill the prisoners, they will kill Peter and his comrades. Thereafter the natives went through the "pantomime of cutting them up and roasting them" (*SL*, 17). Both narratives refer to an interesting event missing in the La Pérouse story. "After they had remained some time on the hill Martin Buchert spied a man creeping up behind a hedge, he laid a musket on Captain D's shoulder and shot him in the act of throwing his spear which however wounded William Wilson one of their party severely" (*JV*, 37). Quite appropriately it is Wilson who was sent with the priest in Bayly's first and second narratives, whereas it is William Dafny with native barbs sticking all over him who performs this task in Dillon's surreal La Pérouse version.

The two Englishmen (whose names are not mentioned) decided they could stand it no longer and risked going down because they had lived on friendly terms with the chief. "The natives never stirred till the sailors reached the foot of the hill, when a number of them suddenly sprang up, and in an instant despatched them with their clubs. They then cut up their bodies, and scorched the still quivering flesh in the fire" (*SL*, 18). There were only four left. The Chinese man grew desperate, "Maski, mi go down" because he recognized a principal chief, his patron, down below. Dillon tried to dissuade him by warning him of the fate of the two Englishmen, but heedlessly the Chinese man left while the natives urged Peter Dillon to come down. "Aromai no Peter!" "Come down now, Peter; we will not hurt you." But Peter was too smart to trust them. Meanwhile the Chinese man was led to a pool of water and "one of the natives stooped down, seized the poor little fellow by the ankles, and tilted him over with his head in the water. The two held him in this position, amusing themselves with his convulsive struggles until life was extinct, when they cast him aside like a dead dog."

When Dillon was wondering whether it would not be better "to fight their way through the mass of natives rather than endure such agonizing suspense" he saw a priest approach. "They leveled their muskets at him; but he threw open his tappa [dress] to show that he was unarmed, shouting at the same time that he would take them past the natives and down to the shore" (*SL*, 19). They allowed him to come near. He wanted Dillon to send word to the captain to give him a box of tools and cutlery and release the prisoners on board. He would guarantee that Dillon and his friends would come to no harm. Dillon, however, was smart. "Inspired by a ray of hope," he tore a leaf from a notebook in his pocket and told the captain to give the priest whatever he wanted but "on no account release the prisoners until he and his two surviving comrades had been rescued" (*SL*, 20). To his great disappointment, shortly afterward he saw that *all* the prisoners come down from the ship's side.

> They now almost gave themselves up for lost; but Dillon instructed his two followers how to proceed in the event of the priest coming back to them.

> Having secured his prize, he came directly up the hill, and said he was ready to take them to the water-side. Dillon gave the preconcerted signal, and instantly one of the priest's arms was pinioned in his own iron grasp, whilst the other was seized by the almost equally powerful grip of Martin Buchert; at the same moment, the lad Wilson brought a musket to bear on his back. Dillon assured him that if the natives attempted to molest them in the least, Wilson would immediately shoot him. (*SL*, 20–21)

This ploy succeeded; the priest told his people that if they threw spears, the whites ("pakehas") would shoot him, which would cause the sea to rise "and swallow up the island" (*SL*, 21).

Although the second narrative is couched in Bayly's words Dillon's presence is unmistakable. At one point Bayly lets Dillon himself speak: "Dillon, when relating the story in after years, used to remark with grim humour, 'Auch! an' it's not iv'ry one that's had the j'ints of him bespoke for supper by the haythin [heathen] cannibals'" (*SL*, 17). Dillon belongs to a yarnster tradition of seafarers when he relates stories on board ship before an audience of mates, putting himself forward as hero in improbable adventures. This the second narrative captures well. Mr. Norman, the first officer and "our commander" of the La Pérouse story, is ignored in the second narrative. He is simply the second officer of the first narrative who wantonly killed natives, ignoring Dillon's advice. Norman's dramatic death obviously cannot occur in this story as Dillon is in command from beginning to end and has no part in the lawless acts of the Europeans who were deaf to his commands. As in the La Pérouse version, he stands firm on the Rock with five others. In the La Pérouse version Savage, the Swede, decides to take a risk because he knows the Fijian language; he is unnamed in the Bayly version but was probably one of the two "Englishmen" who decided to risk it because they knew a chief "under whose protection they have been living," a singular mistake for Savage to make (in this account and elsewhere) because his patrons happened to be the Bau chiefs, the very ones who were fighting the Waileans and were being consumed by them down below! (*SL*, 17).

Because the *Sydney Gazette* also refers to two *Europeans* who went out and were killed one must once again assume that this part of the story is Dillon's and not Bayly's invention. In the La Pérouse version Dafny is hurt; hence, one reason to send him to the ship with the priest and instructions to Robson. In the Bayly versions, Dillon fishes out his notebook and cunningly writes a letter to Captain

Robson, which he has the priest deliver. But Wilson the seaman who was one of the three on the Rock takes over Dafny's wound. Further, in Bayly, Luis the Chinese man does not scoot off unseen by Dillon; he goes to seek the protection of a principal chief only to be shoved into a pond and suffocated, a fate that overtook Charles Savage in the La Pérouse version. This man did not even have the dubious honor of being eaten by the Fijians in Bayly: instead "they cast him aside like a dead dog" (even though Fijians had no real aversion for dog meat) (*SL*, 19). When the priest came to the Rock, Dillon of Bayly's second narrative did not put the gun against his neck as he did in the La Pérouse. Instead he pinioned one arm of the priest in his own iron grip; the other arm was in the equally ferrous grip of Buchert while Wilson "brought a musket to bear on his back" (*SL*, 20). This wonderful bit of bravura is not in Bayly's first narrative, which has Buchert and Wilson walk "each side of him, while he walked with their 3 muskets leveled at him [the priest]" (*JV*, 39). The version in the second narrative is either Bayly's later invention or an alternative version narrated by Dillon and recollected by Bayly when he wrote his book.

In general one could say that Bayly's second narrative is for the most part an elaboration of his first one, which in turn was probably based on the information supplied by Dillon himself during the voyage from Valparaiso to Calcutta, perhaps after Dillon picked up Buchert in Tikopia. There is too much of Dillon here for us to say that these are Bayly's inventions. Davidson thus engages in a completely futile task when he constructs a master historical narrative of what went on during that period from Dillon's own multiple narratives. Dillon is a raconteur, but one who believes, partly or wholly, in the shifting truths of the stories of himself that he has woven.

THE INVENTION OF MARTIN BUCHERT

In December 1827 a further account of Dillon's adventures appeared in the *Asiatic Journal*, published in Calcutta.[34] Dillon was now a famous man in that city, having returned with the French relics. This journal in turn refers to an account in one of the Sydney papers (whose name is not mentioned) purportedly by Dillon himself. While this unknown Sydney newspaper apparently follows pretty much the earlier accounts that have appeared, there are some anomalies that the *Asiatic Journal* reports.[35] The major anomaly is Dillon's "omission of all mention of Martin Buchert, the Prussian sailor, who survived the massacre, and was his witness as to the story respecting Pérouse . . . circumstances irreconcilable with the above account." It adds: "There appears to us to be a strange obscurity or mystery in this affair."[36]

The "strange obscurity" or "mystery" of Martin Buchert is not difficult to resolve. Let me begin with Dillon's first interview reported in the *Sydney Gazette* in 1813 and reprinted with or without variations in many journals up to 1828. It gives a list of "several Europeans and other strangers" living in Bau and now assisting in procuring the cargo. "These persons were Charles Savage, John Graham, Michael M'Cave, Terence Dunn, Joseph Atkinson, William Williams, two Lascars, a Chinaman and an Otaheitian." It does not mention Martin Buchert who, according to Dillon's La Pérouse account, was one of these European settlers. In its conclusion the *Sydney Gazette* states that these ten people lost their lives in the affray along with the following persons from the ship: "Mr. Norman and Mr. Cox, officers, Hugh Evans, seaman, and a lascar, named Jonno, belonging to the vessel, in all fourteen persons." Let us see whether the details provided by Dillon confirm his number of fourteen dead.

During the first stage of the battle six of the Europeans, including the officers Norman and M'Cave "threw down their muskets and ran towards the boats" and were killed. "Nine others, among whom was Mr. Dillon (who reports this tragical event) collected themselves with a determination to resist as long as they were able" and climbed the summit of a hill. Only six managed to reach the top; the other three had to be left on the way as they were either dead or dying. One of the Europeans (the man Dafny according to the La Pérouse account) went to the ship with the priest, leaving five on the Rock. Soon two Europeans (Charles Savage and the Chinese man, according to the deposition and La Pérouse) went down and were killed leaving only three on the Rock. The *Sydney Gazette* adds that the number of people killed in this encounter is eleven, not fourteen. If one were to take Dillon's count of fourteen seriously, then there was no one to defend the Rock—just Peter Dillon![37] But hold it: the elusive Mr. Dillon seems to have soon realized his arithmetical inconsistencies; he therefore avoids or bypasses the number of the dead in the deposition given two weeks later. In the deposition Dillon only names one dead or dying person, a Bau resident, Terence Dunn, while the others are simply referred to indeterminately as "the remainder." Dunn's demise with unnamed others in the deposition now permits Dillon to defend the Rock with two others in the La Pérouse account.[38] Nevertheless, whether the defense of the Rock took place as Dillon describes it, it is virtually certain that Buchert was not there.

But who was Buchert? There is little doubt that Buchert was a white settler in

Fiji who fled from there and was taken to Tikopia with his wife and the lascar.[39] Dillon met them again when he went to that island in May 1826 en route to Calcutta from Valparaiso. The lascar did not recognize him until Dillon told him that he "was the captain of the cutter which brought him from the Beetee [Fiji] Islands and landed him with Martin Bushart" (*LPE*, 32). The lascar's forgetfulness was understandable because he was not a defender on the Rock. But Buchert? "Having invited him on deck, I found that he also had lost all recollection of me; until I told him of our old acquaintance, and providential escape from Vilear [Wailea]."[40] We can be certain that if Buchert was a Rock survivor he would have remembered Dillon, for such a powerful event would have been branded into memory.[41] The deposition actually clinches the issue: not only is there no reference to Martin Buchert in both the *Sydney Gazette* and the deposition but the latter clearly provides a clue to his identity. "Sayth that Deponent then proceeded to the Island of Topie [Tikopia] in Company with the Hunter, at which place a European Man and a Woman, belonging to the Feejee Islands, and a Lascar, who had long resided among those natives, were by their own request Landed."[42] Thus, it is virtually certain that Buchert was simply a passenger, who with his Fijian wife and the lascar left on the *Hunter* and were dropped off in Tikopia.

But why invent Buchert as a defender of the Rock? I think there is method to both Dillon's madness and his inventiveness. For Dillon the two volumes of La Pérouse's expedition was his magnum opus written in the tradition of the immortal Cook. This work is introduced with Dillon's adventures in Fiji in 1813 and includes his description of the cannibal feast. In order to give his text a narrative unity he has to place this imagined feast alongside his discovery of the French relics in Tikopia followed by his search and discovery of the whereabouts of the shipwrecks. But there is no substantive connection between Dillon's Fijian adventures and his motivation to search for the site of the two French wrecks, the latter being the main reason for writing the text in the first place. How can the two narratives be linked? Through Buchert, of course. If Buchert is a defender of the Rock *and* the person whom Dillon dropped off in Tikopia with his wife and the lascar *and* the person who, with the lascar, was connected to the relics that spurred Dillon in his search, then he is the figure that links the Fijian adventures with the main body of the text. He is the link that integrates the text; he must be invented as the defender of the Rock for the narrative to make sense. He was invented during the trip from Tikopia to Calcutta in the *St. Patrick* in 1826. It is Bayly's account, I think, that gives the context in which that invention took place.

CONCLUSION

I think Peter Dillon helps us to better understand both John Jackson and William Endicott. His narrative might also mean that William Lockerby and Thomas Smith are not innocently reporting eyewitness accounts of cannibal feasts. Dillon's case clearly indicates that archival research and new sources of information can open up our historical ignorance and lead the way to historical knowledge. Dillon is a persuasive story teller who invents his imagined self and in that process comes perilously close to believing his imagined self-creation. He is a trickster, one whose motive is to persuade us to believe in his invented story unlike Cannibal Jack and William Endicott, who at least permit us to penetrate their trickery through their ironic asides and other kinds of veiled stylistic devices. In presenting Dillon's seemingly real account of Fijian man-eating, I have also dissected what many have taken as a true historical event that, along with others of a similar sort, have provided fuel for the ethnographic discourse on savage anthropophagy. To show the fictional and invented nature of cannibalism entails a tremendous amount of archival research and an imaginative reconstruction of how the various parts of the narrative have been invented and put together to form a story. Unhappily there is no shortcut to this method of systematic deconstruction and restoration. This strategy could very well apply to similar cannibal narratives, yet unanalyzed. However, it should not surprise the reader if my own narrative retelling of Dillon reads like a detective story, a genre to which I am somewhat addicted. Consequently it may seem that the ethnographer, in showing the invented nature of the cannibal myth, is himself in effect inventing another, more plausible story, grounded though it is on the painstaking cultivation of "evidence." Yet it is this weaving of evidence, however opaque, into the body of an ethnographic text, that differentiates ordinary storytelling and fiction writing from ethnographic and historical narratives. And this is what I do in the next chapter that takes us to the earliest European exploration of the Western Pacific, to the Solomon Islands close to where Peter Dillon discovered the relics of the French wrecks.

EIGHT · On Quartering and Cannibalism and the Discourses of Savagism

And soon as the men had prayed and flung the barley,
first they lifted back the heads of the victims,
slit their throats, skinned them and carved away
the meat from the thighbones and wrapped up them
  in fat,
a double fold sliced clean and topped with strips of flesh.
And the old man [priest] burned these over dried split
  wood
and over the quarters poured out glistening wine
while young men at his side held five-pronged forks.
Once they had burned the bones and tasted the organs
they cut the rest into pieces, pierced them with spits,
roasted them to a turn and pulled them off the fire.
The work done, the feast was laid out, they ate well
and no man's hunger lacked a share of the banquet.[1]

HOMER, *The Iliad*

I shall leave the Greeks of Homer for the moment and begin this chapter with an aside on African cannibalism by T. H. Huxley in his popular book, *Man's Place in Nature*.[2] Stephen Jay Gould refers to Huxley as "a fierce defender of evolution and the greatest prose stylist in the history of British science," and, I might add, a man given to an unrelenting rationality, an opponent of Christian theology and the inventor of that wonderful term "agnosticism."[3] Yet, serendipitously, I found an interesting section, entitled "African Cannibalism in the Sixteenth Century," wedged between the first and second chapters of Huxley's book largely based on a late sixteenth-century description by a French explorer M. Du Chaillu of a people described as the "Anziques" inhabiting the Congo.[4] These people are apparently of "of incredible ferocity, for they eat one another, sparing neither friends nor relations."[5] They also eat their enemies captured in battle and, apparently unsatisfied with this diet, they also eat their slaves whom they "fatten, slay and devour," unless they can be sold for a good price.[6] "Their butcher's shops are filled with human flesh instead of that of oxen or sheep."[7] M. Du Chaillu saw a woman carrying a human thigh "just as we should go to market and carry thence a roast or a steak."[8] Huxley's source has a wonderful engraving of such a shop with one quarter being cut up and the others hung, just as in any European shop of the period—but for the small matter of human cadavers and a head nicely perched on a butcher's block (see figure 8). Huxley himself says, "I cannot refrain from drawing attention to it in a note, although I must confess that the subject is not strictly relevant to the matter in hand."[9] Here then is a great rationalist who is critical of this same French explorer's work on apes, yet he uncritically incorporates the latter's description of African cannibalism into his own text even though it has little to do with his interests in human evolution.

Huxley's late nineteenth-century obsession with African cannibalism is stereotypic of Europe's representation of savagism and is a good introduction to the theme of this chapter dealing with cannibalism and quartering. Let me switch continents to witness Huxley's African cannibalism refracted about the same time in the Solomon Islands during the voyage of discovery led by twenty-five-year-old Alvaro de Mendana, the nephew of the then governor of Lima. He left Callao on November 19, 1567, in two ships, the *Capitana* and the *Almiranta*.[10] Mendana, according to the English translators of these voyages, "seems to have been a man of humanity [with] sympathy with natives rare enough in those days, and of a policy and self-restraint far beyond his years."[11] Under his benign leadership the crew spent six months on these islands and their charts and descriptions were so accurate that "it was possible, 333 years after, to identify every harbour and islet and creek which they passed."[12]

Mendana's expedition not only resulted in the first major discovery of any of the islands of the Western and South Pacific but also provided us with the first detailed proof, or so it seemed, of savage cannibalism in a region that later became notorious for its association with that detestable custom. I am interested in an episode that has been dealt with from different viewpoints by several journalists on that voyage. Unfortunately for us some of the senior officers simply got dates and times all wrong and this included the very start of the voyage itself. Moreover, there was endemic conflict between a senior navigator Captain Pedro Sarmiento and the commander, the youthful Mendana, who gave much of the responsibility of the navigation to Hernan Gallego, the most experienced of the ships' pilots. The narratives were addressed to the king of Spain, which meant that events had to be doctored so as not to offend his majesty. Further, in case an official inquiry was held, these narratives could be converted into politically salient "evidence"

FIGURE 8

Butcher's shop in the Anziques. From T. H. Huxley, *Man's Place in Nature*, ed. Stephen Jay Gould (New York: Modern Library, 2001). Photograph by Leo Hsu.

owing to Sarmiento's hostility. Apparently, the only narrative that got the dates reasonably correct was that of Gomez Catoira who was not directly involved in the conflict among the ships' officers and wrote the most detailed and exhaustive account of this expedition.[13] I will rely on Catoira for the chronology of the voyage and for most of the critical events I describe here.

On February 9, 1568, Gallego led the ships to a port that they named Santa Ysabel de la Estrella in what is now the Solomon Islands. The port and the island itself was named Santa Ysabel after the patron saint of the voyage on whose day they departed from Callao.[14] Gallego says he took possession of the island in the name of his majesty, the king of Spain, and began looking for a convenient spot for building a brigantine, a small vessel used for reconnoitering in the coast and inlets. General Mendana's narrative, however, claims that it was he who named the island. Mendana established friendly contact with the chief of this area, Bilebanara (also shortened to Bile and by Catoira as Vylevanarra or Vyle), with whom he exchanged names in accordance with the custom of the whole region. While the construction of the brigantine was going on, the general dispatched Pedro Sarmiento on February 16, along with the master of the camp and a force of thirty men to explore the interior, especially the mountain ridge.[15] Sarmiento was a difficult man who was once hounded by the Inquisition (unfairly it seems) for magical practices. The group had several skirmishes with Indians, including Bilebanara's men, during which several were shot but not mortally; one Spaniard was injured. Sarmiento tried to take Bilebanara hostage but because the chief eluded his trap, he captured his father's brother instead. This capture of a relative of a friendly chief annoyed Mendana who ordered his release. However, Mendana's qualms did not apply to the capture of natives as "informants" or "interpreters" (and occasionally as "consultants"), which we noted in chapter 3 was a standard practice in virtually all voyages of discovery.[16]

On March 4 the general sent the master of the camp, Pedro de Ortega, to explore the interior, this time without Sarmiento. He took with him thirty-five soldiers, several boys and "Negroes," amounting to fifty-two personnel. The master of the camp was absent for seven or eight days during which time he later reported that he had several "skirmishes" with Indians, but, the editors of these texts tell us, "in obedience to Mendana's humane orders, they continued to fire in the air, setting fire to huts and temples in the hope of delaying the enemy."[17] Gallego describes it more bluntly: "He [de Ortega] was absent seven days on this service, and had many skirmishes with the Indians, wherein he burned many temples of the worshipers of snakes, toads and other insects."[18] Catoira's account states that not only were insects, scorpions, reptiles, and other creatures found in the temples but also hung in the houses near the hearths.[19] Another account says that their carved representations adorned the temples.[20] The reference to natives worshiping insects and their mythic representations has perhaps some basis in reality because there is a pan-Polynesian belief that "the original gods were spirits without form who were able to incarnate themselves in living beings such as lizards, geckos, sea snakes, turtles, sharks, porpoises (i.e. a kind of whale), and human beings."[21] Thus in Tonga the deity Taufa'itahi could appear as a shark, a gecko or in the body of the priest Kautae, and similarly with other deities.[22] This means that the deity might well have been represented iconically in living species and kept in temples and domestic shrines where they are "worshiped." Needless to say, the worship of these lowly creatures provided a rationale for burning native temples.

A more detailed account of the "skirmishes" is found in Mendana's second narrative.[23] It seems that Ortega followed the same route that Sarmiento took; he passed the lowland territory of their friend, the chief Bilebanara. The Spanish forces climbed the ridge of the mountain and went into the territory of an influential chief of this territory Tiarabaso (Sarmiento's Tieragaja, Catoira's Baso). Apparently, after the burning of the temples, Ortega met some of Baso's people "some fair-haired, and well-featured, amongst whom was one of fifteen years, the son of the *tauriqui* ['chief,' from the Polynesian *Te Ariki*] of Baso, who was good-looking and of a good figure; his hair was like gold, and there was no lady who has her hair so well-dressed and frizzed."[24] Baso, the chief, wanted to speak to Ortega but "it seemed to him that both he and his Indians had some evil design," because he called for his club from the person carrying it. The Indians grew increasingly restless; "therefore he [Ortega] seized the *tauriqui*, because, while he [Baso] was a prisoner, the others would not dare harm him [Ortega]."[25]

Catoira adds some interesting details. When Baso was bound and held prisoner another Indian known to them as Bilebanara's friend, and with whom one of the officers had exchanged names, came to see the village huts where the Spanish were encamped and arrogantly demanded to see Baso. The Spanish felt this was a treacherous man; they bound him also and kept him near the other prisoner. But this prisoner managed to loosen his bonds and escape into the bush, and in the night Baso himself managed to escape.[26] Then the natives attacked the Spanish and "he [Ortega] fought them everyday until they reached the land of Bile [Bilebanara, the friendly chief]."[27] The final battle "lasted from daybreak till nearly three in the afternoon."[28] Two soldiers were wounded and one died of tetanus eight days later in their camp.

It must be remembered that these expeditions were outside Mendana's control, and it was the master of the camp, one of the most influential officers in these

Spanish voyages, who led them. Here is an important passage: "The Master of the Camp gave account to the General of all he had seen. These people are mulattoes, and their hair is crisp; they go naked, their private parts being covered with prepared palm leaves. They use for food a kind of maize or roots, which they call *benaus* [taro], and cocoanuts, and plenty of fish. I believe that they are a cleanly race, and I think it is certain that they eat human flesh."[29]

We have here a predictable stereotyping of the Other based on preconceptions that the Spanish had of cannibalism elsewhere. This was not the first indication of native cannibalism however. Around February 13, soon after their arrival, their friend Bilebanara warned Mendana "plainly by signs" that another Chief Meta, his enemy, was coming with three of four others "to kill and eat us," which, obviously, proved to the Spanish that "they were cannibals."[30] The more dramatic proof of native cannibalism came around March 10 while Ortega was still fighting Baso's army. Other journalists mention it, but I shall use Catoira's vivid and detailed account.

> While the Master of the Camp was in Baso [the territory] it was understood that the workmen, who were building the brigantine, should make haste, and not lose time, the General giving every assistance. One day, whilst they were hearing Mass in the morning, some soldiers saw eight large canoes, brightly painted, and full of people, near a point which bounds this harbour towards the east. And the General ordered his men to remain quiet to see what they did, and they watched them whilst they were on their knees, hearing Mass. These canoes came towards the spot where we were, and presently we saw seven others, which came in the same manner, all the people being in their war paint, with their bows and lances of palm and ebony in their hands; and when the soldiers saw them they told the General. And they came on, the first approaching us, and the others behind them; and when they had met together, they sent two of them to the ships, and the rest came towards the land, where the arquebusiers were. And one of these would have fired upon them with the arquebuses, but the General took his from him. And the Indians called to him saying "*tauriqui.*" . . . When the General saw them coming, he withdrew apart under an awning, and made the people stand aside. And presently one of the principal of them approached, standing up, *and he held up a quarter of a man, which he brought in his canoe, and showed it, and he appeared to be explaining that it was a gift to the Master of the Camp, who had killed one of their Indians* [my italics]. . . . When the General saw it, he came out, and the Indian took some roots of *vinahus,* and held them up with a quarter of the man that he had

brought, and showing them, said in his language that they should eat them, saying "*Nalea!*" "*Nalea!*" which in their language means "to eat." And presently another Indian threw himself to the sea, and took the quarter of flesh and the *vinahus*, but he dared not come out of the water, and called out to them to come into the water for it. And the General wished the Indian to come ashore, but he, when he saw that they were coming for the quarter, returned to his canoe, and they threw it back to the sea, and he took it to the canoe again, and would not come ashore. And the General ordered a Negro to go in, but not to take what the Indian had brought until he told him to come out. And the Negro went in, carrying a knife in his hand, but the Indian was afraid of it and turned back; and the General ordered the Negro to leave the knife which he had in his hand, and go in without it. And the Indian waited for him, and held out his arm, and gave him the quarter of the man, and the Negro did not wish to take it, and the Indian threw it at him, and went away. And then the Negro took the *vinahu* and the quarter of the man, and brought it on shore, and we all saw it done. It was the right arm with all the shoulder. It seemed to be a boy, who had a small hand and a thin arm. We were all struck with a great wonder and pity, to see so much cruelty and so strange a thing, such as we had never seen or heard of; for though many people had seen them eating human flesh, yet not one had ever heard of it being offered to anybody. When the Indians saw that we were astonished at it, they came back to tell us to eat it. And some of the soldiers wished to fire upon them, but the General prevented them, saying that these people did not know good from evil. And the soldiers said that they knew it perfectly well, because they went away from their own lands to look for Indians to eat. And the General appeased them, saying: "Christian brethren, it is for this reason, that before we make war upon them we should show them that they ought not to do these deeds; until then, all the harm that we shall do to them would be upon our consciences. Presently, he ordered them to bury the quarter of the man, and directed all to stand aside, so that the Indians might see it. And after they had dug a hole, he ordered the Negro to hold up the piece in his hand, and turning to them, show it to them. And they all saw what we had done; and they said: "*teo nalea*, " that is to say, that we did not eat it. They were standing so near that they (our men) heard it. And presently we buried the piece before them all, to which all of them paid great attention. When they saw what we had done, they went away with an injured look, bending forward over their canoes. . . . And the Indians went to a small island which they call Cuia. And after a little we saw that they had made a great fire on it, and we suspected that it was for eating what remained of their gift.[31]

Let me comment briefly on these events. The gift was meant for the master of the camp who, according to the natives, had killed one of them. Prior to the Indians bringing it up none of the accounts refers to this killing. The context is left blank. I shall later fill this space in the text with my own interpretation. The accounts inform us that the two-way conversation was by signs and stock words each side knew about the other's language. The Indians are so scared to come up to the shore probably because they were afraid of the Spanish whom they perceived to be cannibals. It is reasonably clear that the whole project was to propitiate the master who had killed a native. Note that the general selected a black to go pick up the human quarter and the taro; perhaps this task was assigned to a representative of another group labeled as "cannibals," or simply because as an Alien or Other, the black was considered suited to this terrible task.

It seems that the Spanish are bringing their preconceptions to bear on the situation. Many of them claimed to have seen Indians eat human flesh, the reference being to Indians elsewhere, as the editors of the volume suggest.[32] Nevertheless, Indians have already become a generic term, and the European preconception of the Indian as cannibal is given a presentific interpretation: if Indians ate human flesh elsewhere, they must surely do here. Therefore it is no problem to graft that knowledge onto the present narrative as if it were an eyewitness reality. This has an awesome implication because, as is evident from previous discussions, the grafting of preexisting knowledge or prejudice is characteristic of cannibal knowledge and savage ethnography in general. Mendana, even though he is persuaded that these people are cannibals, has a more benign attitude: they cannot distinguish Good from Evil, therefore one should persuade them to desist from cannibalism rather than firing at them. But underlying this benign statement is a latent threat, that if they continue to do these deeds, then there is good reason to declare war on them. Mendana wanted to show the Indians that they, the Spanish, were not cannibals and this they did by enacting a miniritual of their own. This enactment is important for Mendana and for the Spanish because it is emphasized in several places in the journals.

There is no doubt whatsoever that the episode of the gift of a quarter did occur; three journalists—Gallego, Mendana, and Catoira—give us the details, and it obviously had a profound effect on them. I do not want to contest this. The only anonymous journalist on this voyage, whose racial prejudices are clear, simply multiplies the one incident and rephrases native actions in terms of a discourse on savagism and cannibalism. "The people of this island are brutish; they eat human flesh, and devour people when they catch them, in time of war, or in time of peace by treachery; and thus they presented the General on several occasions with quarters of Indians, as things greatly esteemed and valued among them."[33] None of our journalists indicate that this event was repeated, and our anonymous writer is simply universalizing that one occurrence as a normal custom of these people, very much in the ethnographic fashion that went into later times in Polynesia.

From our point of view there is no need to accept the accounts by the ships' journalists as evidence for what the Spanish called "cannibalism." It provides evidence for "Spanish cannibalism," or, to use the marvelous phrase from the European encounter with native cooking during Cook's third voyage, the dread that the Other is going "to roast and eat us." Now we are back to the familiar dialectic highlighted in chapter 2: the natives thought that the Spanish were cannibals, a belief that the Spanish also thought the natives thought; hence their complicated attempts to disabuse them. Working on the hypothesis of two-way misunderstandings let me go back to the impressive oblation of a human quarter meant for the master of the camp. Quartering a human being or animal is *not* a culturally defined act among Melanesian or Polynesian people. It is however a well-known European custom, and Mendana himself provides a beautiful (or not so beautiful) spectacle of it on June 9, about four months after the first episode of quartering. I cannot describe the whole context of occurrence; suffice it to say that during an expedition of the brigantine to the island of Santiago several Spanish seamen were killed. Here is Catoira's graphic account of Mendana's terrifying reprisal:

> And arriving at the spot where they had killed our men, the General ordered them to bring the dead Indian and the wounded one, and to cut off their heads, and to quarter them, and their (quarters) were placed (there). And the other two were hanged further on, in sight of the ships, in such a manner that the living Indians saw it, and he ordered that another should be taken to the River Gallego, which was near by, from whence the Indians issued forth every day, and that he should be hanged by the legs; and the heads of both were placed on poles. And this having been done in the sight of many Indians who were visible from thence, they returned to the ships, and brought the two living ones.
>
> On the following day the General went ashore with all the company to hear Mass; and they say that the natives had already removed the four quarters of one Indian, but had not come to the one who was hanged, nor the heads; but returning to the ships we saw that they were approaching him. The order was given to aim a piece of artillery at them in all haste, and it was leveled at the place where they were; and when the shot came among them they went flying

> off without removing [the bodies], and afterwards they dared not come near to take them; but one night they took away one head, making much wailing, for we heard it from the ships.[34]

Now let me look at this extraordinary text focusing mainly on the quartering episode by the now not-so-benign Mendana. Consider the public quartering and hanging of natives and the Spanish matter-of-fact attitude toward those actions that are conventionally attributed to savagism, namely, the cutting off of the head of someone only wounded, the hanging of the body upside down, and the wonderful spectacle of heads stuck on poles to scare the natives. All these actions did not seem to affect the Christian conscience; the officers and crew went to mass as usual the next day. We have here a Nietzschean spectacle, one that had its antecedents in European history, as I shall soon show.

What does one mean by "quartering?" Here are some of the meanings of "quarter" and "quartering" from my favorite source of arcane knowledge, the *Oxford English Dictionary:* "One of the four parts, each including a leg into which the carcass of quadrupeds is divided." Or, "The four parts, each containing a limb of a human body similarly [as above] divided, as was commonly done for those executed of treason." To quarter is to cut into quarters such as the "body of a person, especially of a traitor or criminal." Thus there are two important meanings of "quartering:" the quartering of animals and then the quartering of humans on the model of the former.

The first is the standard way in which animals, domestic or wild, are cut up after slaughtering; it is thus they are hung up in European butchers' stalls. Animal quartering has had a long history in Europe; it existed in early Greece as is evident in the Homeric verses of my epigraph. The *Oxford English Dictionary* also gives some wonderful examples from English history of the display of human quarters. From a chronicle of circa 1330: "His hede tei of symtem [smitten] . . . the quarters wer[e] sent to henge [hang] at four cites." From 1387: "His body was i-quartered and i-sent into dyvers places of Engelonde." And a 1440 account of hanging and quartering meted to traitors: "The said hongman [hangman] smot of there [their] hedes and there quartered hem [them]." And if in case you think this is only a medieval custom, here is Samuel Pepys confiding to his diary in 1660: "Mr. Carew was hanged and quartered . . . but his quarters . . . are not to be hanged up," which means that in Mr. Carew's case there was no public display of the quarters after the formal hanging. And a 1773 account says: "The quarters of a number of robbers were hung up upon hooks," the model for many cannibal engravings in European texts.

We can now get back to Mendana's gruesome display. Neither hanging nor quartering were formalized as rule-governed native custom. By contrast sticking heads on poles, the savage custom popularized in *Heart of Darkness*, was, like the discourse on cannibalism itself, something shared by both warlike savages and civilized males, both obsessed with the killing and the symbolic castration of the enemy whose heads were being cut off. If so the natives performed a strange scenario in offering a quarter of a youth to the Spanish officers. Having adopted the European custom of quartering, they then offered a quarter to the Spanish whom they believed were cannibals. But the question is: How did the savages know or learn of this civilized custom? My answer would be that Mendana's spectacle would not be the first they witnessed during this situation of "first contact." If they had earlier seen one or more instances of quartering, then it would prove that the Spanish were cannibals (or confirm a preexisting prejudice about aliens and outsiders).

There is unfortunately no explicit evidence for this assumption, but I am going to read between the lines of the Spanish texts to suggest one possible instance. In Catoira's narrative he says that the quarter was meant for the master of the camp who had killed a native. The master of the camp did not say how and when it was done, and no one else mentions it either. Killing a native in itself is not something to hide; in fact it is recorded everywhere. My guess is that it was not mentioned because the native was in fact the very boy whose quarter was presented to the master. But who was this boy? Two hypotheses are in order. My first conjecture is that it was a boy from Baso's group who was deliberately or accidentally killed because the Spanish were having a hard time fighting the Baso natives. If so, then Ortega ordered the boy to be quartered and hung in the conventional European manner to strike terror among hostile Indians. But this must contend with the enormous public spectacle where two sets of canoes, numbering eight total, came up in full panoply of war, in procession as it were, before Mendana and his crew on shore. It is possible that this was a ceremonial offering of a quarter by one group of cannibals to another. However, if the procession concerned the death of a young person of renown, then we are forced to make another possible interpretation. We know from the pioneer work of Robert Hertz that the rituals of death vary with the social status of a person such that when a social minor dies the funeral ceremony is not pronounced; when it is a stranger there might be no ceremony at all; and only minimal ceremonial mourning for a child, even if the grief is acute.[35] Thus it seems reasonable to suppose that in the present case the personage who was killed, though a youth, was someone especially significant. Hence the second conjecture that the quarter was from the body of the pretty son of the chief mentioned in Catoira's account; he too was a youth of about fifteen years. Unfortunately, not even Catoira identifies the dead person because all these accounts were written on the basis of evidence from Ortega himself or others in the same expedition. And even if it was the chief's son who was killed, there is no reason that the journalists were aware of it and that they knew that the quarter gifted to them was this very youth.[36] It is impossible to resolve the issue of the identity of the dead person, but I think it is certain that the youth whose quarter was presented to Mendana in the absence of the master of the camp was someone killed and quartered by the latter during the fighting at Baso.

If however such a horrendous act did take place, then one should inquire into the role of the ubiquitous priests that accompanied the Spanish expeditions, four Franciscans in this case. Prior to any exploration of the interior Mendana himself had decided to seek priestly advice on February 15 or thereabouts. It was inevitable that the crew needed food and would have to have it from the native population. The vicar, Fray Francisco de Galvez, praised Mendana on his diplomacy and behavior thus far and advised him about proper and morally responsible conduct toward natives. Mendana then summoned the master of the camp, Pedro Sarmiento, and others and publicly announced norms of proper behavior for the first expedition of Sarmiento's. Sarmiento should discover native food resources, bargain with them in a proper way, "take nothing against their will, and to do them no harm," but if they refused he could take "some provision by force."[37] It should not surprise us that the master of the camp, Ortega, who had accompanied Captain Sarmiento and witnessed the violence unleashed on the native population on the first expedition, would want a priest to accompany him on his own expedition to the interior "to enlighten him as to what he ought to do for the unburdening of his conscience."[38] Thus the Vicar assigned him Fray Juan de Torres "whom he charged strongly, that in all which should happen there with the natives he should have regard for their welfare, and for all that was in accordance with Christianity and our consciences."[39] When Ortega's expedition returned the priest affirmed that he "was much edified with the good Christian purpose and order which the Master of the Camp had shown in all that occurred."[40] Surely a priest would not condone the killing of a youth and his quartering? Remember that this was the period of the Inquisition and acts of violence against unbelievers were justifiable. Hence it should not surprise us if the priest absolved the master of this particular act. The priests even found nothing objectionable in Mendana himself quartering and hanging natives, one of whom was still alive.

The episode of quartering further complicates our discussion of cannibalism. The Spanish already had a preconception that the Solomon Islanders, like "Indians" everywhere, were cannibals, and this was confirmed by their bringing in a quarter of a youth for the master of the camp to consume. "To eat, to eat," they told the Spanish. From the native point of view why on earth would anyone quarter a human being, if not to eat him? The *native* dread of cannibalism, the cannibal as Other, was now foisted on the European, and this was confirmed by the Spanish act of quartering, occurring in the troubled context of deadly first contact. It seems then that both were bound together by the dark fantasy that united the savage and the civilized, the idea that the Other will eat us. This fantasy does not help us to understand whatever form of anthropophagy that the Solomon Islanders practiced, if any. In fact it inhibits any such understanding because the Spanish assumed, as did later ethnographers and historians, that because the natives brought a gift of a quarter they must surely be cannibals. Nor does it help us to understand the sacrificial form of Spanish anthropophagy, the Eucharist, which in my thinking could hardly be called "cannibalism." It has been thoroughly ritualized and refigured and symbolically removed from actual anthropophagy through "the work of culture," a process described at length in my book, *The Work of Culture*. Otherwise, one would have to say that if the Eucharist is a form of cannibalism, then Catholics are cannibals just like their savage counterparts![41] Nevertheless, I think that the Spanish dread of cannibalism was exacerbated by the Christian practice of the Eucharist, on the unconscious level. The quarter of the youth was brought while the Spanish were performing Mass, and it is not unlikely the idea of cannibalism and the idea of the Mass were conjoined in the unconscious imaginings of the crew.

Beyond the European dread of the Other there is another form of life that binds both quartering and cannibalism. In quartering the head is severed from the body, which in general is disemboweled, hence the expression "drawn and quartered." The body is cut into four quarters that are separated and then hung up, sometimes in different sites, even different cities, as an example to others. An extreme and debasing form of punishment, it is typically meted out for treason. For us contemporary intellectuals the most famous example comes from Michel Foucault who begins his *Discipline and Punish* with the dramatic case of the attempted regicide Damien whose extremities were ordered to be torn apart by four horses. When this failed Damien was drawn and quartered in the most brutal fashion (see figure 9).[42] Take another famous case from British history of the Scottish resistance fighter Sir William Wallace: "After being dragged to the usual place of execution, at the tails of horses, he was there hanged on a high gallows, on the 23rd of August 1305; after which his bowels having been taken out while he yet breathed, and burned before his face, his head was struck off, and his body hacked into quarters. His right arm was set up at Newcastle,—his left at Berwick."[43]

The humiliation practiced on the dead is only part retribution. In Wallace's case, as in others, it did not permit kinfolk to engage in normal mourning, another familiar debasement of the Other. Further, a more ghastly retribution awaited those quartered. The traitor is treated on the analogy of an animal because only animals are routinely quartered. The traitor's soul is also lost like that of an animal (who does not possess one). Finally, his chances of bodily resurrection are impeded because he has been cut up and his body parts separated whereas the resurrection must entail the integrity of the whole physical person, the ideal case being that of Christ himself, who though wounded had his body intact. Hence some medieval theologians' anger at the worship of Christ's tooth and foreskin: such actions would imply that "Christ had not risen in total bodily perfection."[44] Thus the idea of maintaining the wholeness of the body at the resurrection may have had little theological sanction, but it was a popular episteme in Christian nations. The traditional Christian hostility to dissection of corpses, cremation of the dead, and of imagined necrophagia is based on the same dread.[45] As Peter Hulme has rightly mentioned, the unconscious European dread of cannibalism must also be seen in relation to the dismemberment and scattering of the body, the loss of bodily wholeness that in turn might affect the resurrection of the body.[46] Beyond this one could further argue that the dread of cannibalism tapped the latent European dread of quartering and all its associations. This dread then can also be used in colonial power in grim ways, as in the case of Mendana. Or when the first governor of New South Wales suggested that any new convict who committed murder or sodomy (the two seem to be equivalent) in the colony should be confined until "an opportunity offered of delivering him as a prisoner to the natives of New Zealand, and let them eat him. The dread of this will operate much stronger than the fear of death."[47]

CANNIBALISM AS QUARTERING: A MAORI EXAMPLE

In the preceding discussion I have made the point that quartering and cannibalism are fused in the European imagination, though outside of conscious awareness. In

PORTRAIS DES · SOUFRANCE·DE·R·F·DAMIEN·ATTANTATEUR·DE·LAS
PERSONNES·SACRE'DUROY·LOUIS·XV·LE·5·JEANVIER ···· 1757

FIGURE 9
The quartering of Robert-François Damien. From Anne Salmond, *Between Worlds: Early Exchanges Between Maori and Europeans, 1773–1815* (Auckland: Penguin Viking, 1997). Photograph by Leo Hsu.

a psychological sense the two forms of imagining are isomorphic such that the one can take the place of the other. Hence it is not surprising that the cannibal of the European imagination is depicted in literary and pictorial representations as quartering his victims. In the French case that I discuss later I show that even European peasants given to quartering and dismembering are imagined to be cannibals. This was also the fate of the Tupinamba cannibals made famous by André Thevet, Jean de Léry, and Hans Staden, whose ventures into Brazilian cannibalism are well known. In engravings the Tupinamba are depicted cutting and quartering the bodies of their victims; in some representations the victims' body parts are hung up just as animals are quartered and hung up in European butchers' shops and in the imagined cannibal land in the Congo.

The text I now examine appeared in five installments in the *Sydney Monitor* during April and May 1833 and dealt with the defense of the pa of Nga-Motu by Maori villagers aided by some European settlers in 1832. This account was written by "the historian of the siege," Daniel Sheridan, who was one of eight European defenders and a "Negro" cook.[48] It is a piece of virulent and unmitigated racism grafted on to what might have been a historical event, a kind of grafting with which we are now familiar. The relevant background is provided by a historian of the Taranaki coast, W. H. Skinner.

According to Skinner the letters describe the closing scenes of a "bitter blood feud" between the Waikato-Maniapoto and allied tribes and the Ngati Awa-Ngati Tama-Taranaki combination. "For generations, these tribes had been warring against each other, and in a general summing up, as long as the old Maori weapons were in use, honours may be said to have remained even" (DN, 38). But the musket changed all this and those who possessed them—the Bay of Islands tribes—started to move down south in the early nineteenth century. Those living south of the Bay of Islands tribes facing the prospect of extermination soon began to get guns themselves and in turn began to move still further south in a series of migrations, or heke. Among them was the great and ferocious leader Te Rauparaha of Kawhia, who, fearing the power of the tribes of the north and east, decided in turn to push south (in the famous migration mentioned in chapter 5) joining forces with some of the Ngati-Awa and Taranaki people. This left the remaining Taranaki people weakened and "an easy prey to the Waikato combination, that, besides greatly outnumbering the Taranaki people were armed almost to a man with firearms" (DN, 39). Their opponents mostly possessed traditional Maori weapons (DN, 39–40). The Sheridan letters describe the Waikato siege of Pukerangiora on the Waitara River "and the accompanying horrors of lust and cannibalism." "Flushed with success and overburdened with human flesh, upon which they fed unstintedly, the great *taua,* or war party, moved on the Nga-Motu . . . with the avowed object of capturing and devouring the remnant of the tribe sheltering at that settlement, and also of the Europeans who were working a whaling and trading station at that place," established in 1828 or early 1829. According to Skinner, Sheridan describes a three-week siege "with a vividness and reality that could only be infused by one taking an actual part in it" (DN, 40). Although the defenders were successful, the remainder of the Ngati-Awa was afraid of the enemy coming in larger numbers to extract utu (reprisal) that they migrated further south to join Rauparaha and other noted leaders in the region of Kapiti and Port Nicholson.

Let us now hear Sheridan's account of the siege. I have italicized those statements in his account that I think come from European rather than native discourse or from native discourse reformulated in European terms. In December the Waikato tribes proceeded toward Pukerangiora, and the Taranaki tribes went down to meet them but "perceiving the multitude" decided to fall back on Pukerangiora where about three thousand men, women, and children enclosed themselves within a "slight fence," about six miles from the white trading post. Sheridan does not tell us why the Ngati Awa did such a foolish thing. "On their approaching near the place, they took two men and one woman, slaves, which they killed, but did not eat, as it is their custom to feed their gods with the first slain in battle" (DN, 42). This is a bit strange because it is Maori custom to offer the "first fish" as a sacrifice, but the offering of a slave would violate that norm. Sheridan does not tell us how he got the above information or why the Waikato pointlessly killed slaves, a valuable commodity, unless it was for fun.

Now for the realism that Skinner talks about. "January 2, 1832, they surrounded Bucharangcoala (Pukerangiora), and on the 3rd at daybreak, they attempted to take it by storm, in which they were defeated, with the loss of four chiefs and ten men killed; on our side two killed. On the 9th the enemy had one man killed; on the 10th four killed; on the 11th one chief killed; on the 13th six killed; on the 14th ten killed; on the 19th twelve killed." On January 21 "the besieged wretches" being utterly exhausted and starving tried to escape in open daylight by breaking the fence instead of facing the enemy boldly, "so ignorant are these wretches." "Those who had plenty of provisions would not divide with the starving, and not even with the distant tribes who voluntarily went into their part to their assistance." Naturally, the enemy wrought great havoc "not sparing man, woman, or child" while those "at the opposite end of the par [pa] not being aware of the intention of breaking down the fence, at this critical moment, took their children in their arms and threw themselves over cliffs of a tremendous height, so great is the dread of these savages of being eat by one another" (DN, 43). This did not help much because "a party of the enemy were employed in despatching *[sic]* as many as would be sufficient for the evening's meal" while their slaves were getting the ovens ready (DN, 44).

We now come to the critical passage.

> On the 23rd they commenced the slaughter of the prisoners that were taken alive. They were all crammed into huts, well guarded, the principal chief, executioner, with a sharp tomahawk in his hand, ready to receive them. They were then called out, one by one. Those that had well carved or tatooed hands, hand *[sic]* their hands cut off on a block, *the body quartered and hung on fences, which were erected for that purpose;* those with indifferent heads received one blow, and then dragged to a hole to bleed. The chief (Te Wherowhero), com-

> plaining of his arm being tired, after dispatching about three hundred, *very mercifully* [author's italics] respited the remainder until next morning, when this monstrous cannibal commenced business with as much cheerful gaiety as if he was going to some grand entertainment. *The young children, and grown up lads, were cut down the belly, then roasted on sticks before the fire* [a somewhat unusual style of cooking for Maoris and Polynesians in general].

Our historian visited this spot somewhat later to "view the remains of this horrid carnage." Within several miles of the pā he saw pieces of wood painted red and left as memorials by relations or friends of the slain. He also saw a "heap of bones" of about three hundred persons; further away were skeletons and "the ovens still remaining where they had been cooked," this time suggesting that the flesh had been removed from some of the bodies but leaving the skeletons (DN, 44). The ovens, however, were empty; there were no bones in them which then warranted Sheridan's conclusion that the people did not eat the meat here but took it elsewhere. However, the "*block they struck the fatal blow on,* was still remaining, the blood and the notches from the axe were still quite fresh" (DN, 44–45). The branches of trees in the surrounding area were denuded of leaves that had been used for cleaning the corpses. "On taking a general view of the place, I observed that the enemy had formed three different settlements, and in each of them was a heap of bones similar to the first spot I had seen, *and also to each, a rack, placed along the spot where they eat their victual; on it they put the head of their unfortunate victims*" and this included children roasted on sticks. This "disgraceful race" engages in a "constant study," which is "meditating the death of their fellow countrymen."

Meanwhile the victors proceeded to Moturoa where there were, along with a handful of natives, also a group of Europeans who "had firmly resolved to die rather than be taken alive" (DN, 45). The next few pages contain an account of the defense of the pā by both natives and Europeans. To briefly sum this part of the text: the superior discipline and weapons of the white defenders helped trounce the enemy, consisting of the Waikato and their allies. The conclusion expectably brings us back to cannibalism and quartering. The enemy soon disappeared but "so rapid was their flight, that they did not take time to burn all their dead, but placed them on the top of their huts, and then set fire to them; *others who had relations wounded so that they could not walk, they would quarter and divide amongst them to carry, in preference to letting them remain for the enemy to eat;* in twenty minutes there was not one of them to be seen"—thus providing ethnographic evidence, I am sure, for the savage custom of endo-cannibalism. While this activity was going on, Mr. Sheridan's native friends indulged in their own kind of man-eating "of which I was thus compelled to be an eye-witness." "I have not sufficient words to express my weak *[sic]* opinion of a race of the most depraved wretches that nature ever formed." They dragged one of those slightly wounded, put a tomahawk between his teeth "*while another pierced his throat for a chief to drink his blood, others at the same time were cutting his arms and legs off . . . ; they then cut off his head, quartered him and sent his heart to a chief, it being a delicious morsel, they being favoured with such rarities after an engagement*" (DN, 56). A traitor who had come to see his wife and children in their camp got the same treatment. "Oh, what a scene for a man of Christian feeling, to behold strewed about the settlements in every direction, and hung up at every native's door; *their entrails taken out and thrown aside*, and the women preparing ovens to cook them." Sheridan and his comrades persuaded the savages not to cook inside the white settlement or come to their houses while "*they were regaling themselves, on what they termed their sumptuous food, far sweeter than pork*."

Sheridan now regales us with more exact information: the enemy lost three hundred men and a great number of chiefs. For each chief lost "they would put to death, in the most cruel manner, ten slaves as a satisfaction for his death." Unhappily, the enemy did not have many dead bodies to eat (Sheridan seems to have forgotten the many slaves who have been killed earlier). Yet, the enemy did manage to get sixteen bodies "besides a great number that were half roasted, and *dug several up out of the grave, half decayed which they also eat*." "Another instance of the most brutal depravity of the Wicatto [Waitako] wretches; a woman slave endeavouring to make her escape from her master, Howhogeia, was pursued and *unfortunately taken by the monster, who, after a short time after ordered her to prepare a large oven, which she very innocently complied with, not expecting her miserable doom; when she was ready, she went to her master and told him she had nothing to put into it—he very carelessly told her to get into it—the poor woman looked rather surprised at the command, scruple a little, expecting mercy; the infidel was not possessed of any. Come, come, says he, I am in a great hurry, and immediately tied her, hands and feet, and put her in alive. When cooked he made a sumptuous meal along with his friends*" (DN, 57). Sheridan could have given us more information about this historic event but unhappily "being very scanty of paper, for which reasons, columes *[sic]* of the disgraceful conduct of these cannibals remains unpenned by DANIEL HENRY SHERIDAN" (DN, 58).

What makes "The Defence of Nga-Motu" especially interesting is that it is not just about "quartering"; virtually everything attributed to the Maori comes from

European discourse. In addition to quartering, there is the drawing of the intestines, which are cast aside; there is the grilling of human meat in skewers over an open fire; necrophagia and the desecration of graves; and putting the victim in an oven reminding one of children in European fairy tales, and this includes the familiar language of fairy tales, such as "delicious morsel" and "sumptuous meal" normally associated with man-eating ogres.[49] The latter is also part of the larger discourse of savagism wherein the victim is cut up while he is alive or made to eat his own quivering flesh, as I have shown in the invented stories that Cannibal Jack and Peter Dillon have previously narrated for Fiji. Vampirism where a chief sucks the blood of the enemy reappears in other Maori discourses indicating yet a much wider attribution of savagery of the sort found among the Iroquois, summed up by Pierre François-Xavier de Charlevoix in his *Histoire ET description générale* (1756) in a wonderful phrase, "the hydropic thirst they had for human blood" (*C*, 221, n. 27; *C*, 135). Some of these themes may be shared by the Maoris' own discourses on cannibalism and anthropophagy, but it is doubtful whether Sheridan is reacting to that. More likely, Sheridan's account was based on the fact that a battle did take place and maybe even some kind of anthropophagy did as well, but it is impossible to disentangle any reality from this racist fantasy of "Indian hating."

Beyond that several questions arise. This horrendous account easily becomes truth to contemporary settlers and even for serious scholars not just in the early twentieth century but up until 1960, the date of Vayda's *Maori Warfare*.[50] Sheridan gives an aura of verisimilitude that deceived the later historians, who wanted to be deceived, a deception easily fulfilled because the defense of Nga-Motu might well have taken place. Yet the cannibal discourse is an invented one and inserted into an actual historical event that then makes it believable. Further, in almost every instance Sheridan writes as if he has seen what he describes or has strong evidence for his assertions when in fact he was in the white settlement and could possibly have seen only one instance of "quartering." Verisimilitude resurfaces again to deceive us when he gives exact numbers of enemies killed in the first battle (which occurred in a different area to his); exact numbers of the invading force, and in one instance the exact number of those eaten (sixteen) and the exact number of the enemy killed (three hundred) during the attack on Nga-Motu. Sheridan's highly disturbing narrative injects so much racial hatred that one must see it, as similar discourses do, as a theodicy for colonization on the basis of a crude metaphysics of savagism because it is in the nature of the Indian to commit these horrors. But there is a more immediate context also: the previous year the brig *Elizabeth* event occurred in which Europeans and Te Rauparaha's men jointly engaged in killing and anthropophagy and provoked considerable outrage in England (though little in Sydney). Sheridan's history might have been an attempt to annul or reverse that event and show that villainy is exclusively on the other side by inventing a bizarre superstructure on the actuality of the defense of Nga-Motu.

REVISITING EUROPEAN QUARTERING IN THE FRENCH "VILLAGE OF CANNIBALS"

The European preoccupation with quartering and cannibalism, one might imagine, would not be operative in Europe of the late nineteenth century, but it seems that when the formalized procedures associated with quartering have lost their force, the old ideas nevertheless continue to exist in the popular consciousness. Alain Corbin illustrates this in his case study of the murder of a young aristocrat by an infuriated mob on August 16, 1870, in Hautefaye, a commune in the Nontron *arrondissement* of the Dordogne *département*.[51] I refer the reader to Corbin's account of the roots of the conflict between the nobles and peasants of the region and the belief that the former were agents of the neighboring Prussians trying to dismantle the monarchy of Napoleon III. These animosities based on the earlier antinobility feeling of the French Revolution were, according to Corbin, fomented by the wealthy bourgeoisie who had "an interest in disguising or concealing its avarice, usury, lack of charity, sharp dealing, and mistreatment of tenant farmers" (*VC*, 3). What interests me here is the manner in which Alain de Monéys, a perfectly ordinary and decent member of the local landowning aristocracy and deputy mayor of the commune was killed by an infuriated mob estimated between three and eight hundred peasants, all male, including a few adolescents and children, almost all of whom were gainfully employed without a prior history of criminality or violence. The fear that the Prussians were coming and would rape their women, pillage their villages, and burn their homes constituted a kind of "collective psychoses" that lead to several riots and attacks on persons erroneously suspected of being Prussian agents. We should not be surprised, living in our troubled times, if the term Prussian "was applied not to actual foreigners but to those suspected of being enemy agents or merely accused of being enemy supporters" and that violence against the Other was viewed as a species of patriotism (*VC*, 45).

The tragedy itself coincided with the traditional fair of August 14–16 and also with the national holiday in honor of the emperor on August 15. The fair drew people from a radius of more than fifteen miles, and many of those who participated in the murder came from outside the commune where the incident took place, including the ring leader, Chambert, a blacksmith living in a nearby hamlet. The murderers apparently did not know each other; neither did they know the victim. Hence, all the attempts made by a few local people to protect de Monéys were to no avail. "Most of them thought they were attacking not a noble, a great landowner, but a 'Prussian' who had shouted 'Vive la République'"—an accusation that had no basis in reality (*VC*, 63). Alain de Monéys was at the fair on business, but he was in the wrong place at the wrong time.

What is fascinating about Corbin's account is that though the public and the legal system defined the mob as "monstrous brutes," they were simply acting according to the current definition of the situation, however unrealistic that was. In killing an enemy of the nation "the Hautefaye murder [expressed] a cry of love to an imperiled emperor" (*VC*, 84). It is therefore not surprising that after de Monéys was killed (or partially killed) the leader, Chambord, packed the wood around the stake and danced around it, shouting "Vive l'Empereur!" (*VC*, 77). When the verdict gave death sentences to four and prison sentences to many participants, ordinary peasants were appalled and could not grasp this patriotic act being treated "as a crime of common law" (*VC*, 78). This we noted was the case when Captain Dudley and the survivors of the *Mignonette* were convicted of shipboard anthropophagy for the first time under the common law of England. Yet unlike Captain Dudley these people expected monetary rewards from the government because, as one person put it, "We did it to save France. Our Emperor will surely save us" (*VC*, 80).

The public reaction would have been quite different a few decades previously, Corbin argues, because such acts were not only common but condoned and rarely treated as serious crimes. Why so? "As the nineteenth century progressed, people sought to distance themselves from the violence of the past, to affirm the alien nature of barbarous acts whose strange proximity made a powerful impression, to forget that the sight of bloodshed and torture had only recently inspired no revulsion in ordinary people" (*VC*, 96). Corbin adds:

> In its own way, the Hautefaye mob shared the humanitarian sentiments that had been on the rise in Europe since the beginning of the eighteenth century. It did not indulge in the 'ceremonious mutilations' that had still delighted revolutionary crowds from July 1789 to September 1792. . . . Dismembering ones enemies had become, since the Revolution, a mere figure of speech. Organs were no longer plucked from bodies. Alain de Money's head was not chopped off and paraded through the hamlet in public mockery. Of the old ritual all

that remained was the attempt to cut up and desecrate the corpse, which was dragged like dead meat to what looked like a garbage dump. (*VC*, 76–77)

Corbin insists that the nineteenth century witnessed continued acts of mass violence, though historians influenced by the developing liberal and humanitarian ethics have sanitized them. As a corollary those who indulged in collective violence were given pejorative labels: rabble, monsters, cannibals, savages, and so forth (*VC*, 101). They were given to mass delusions and to an atavistic return to savagery or primitivism. This is not to deny, says Corbin, that mass delusion did not play a part, but more significantly the attackers ignored the real status of the victim and were not willing to listen to those who importuned them to desist; they acted according to their own "perceived identity" of the victim. Further, because many were outsiders there was no local authority to effectively check the development of the action before it reached its crescendo.

Corbin describes in graphic detail the horrifying tortures inflicted on the victim and the attendant Nietzschean spectacle reminding us that Mendana's world was alive and well in nineteenth-century Europe, especially the dismemberment and desecration of the body, though less so than in prior centuries. Formerly, "ritual violence was directed mainly against corpses. Bodies were frequently stripped and castrated; faces were mutilated; eyes plucked out, limbs chopped off, heads severed. Angry mobs dragged corpses face downwards towards rivers or sewers. Burial was not allowed. Severed heads, limbs and genitals were paraded about in noisy processions and exhibited as trophies" (*VC*, 89–90). These experiences are the stuff of cannibal stories I have narrated but there projected unto the Other. Yet it must be stated that such actions need not necessarily be exclusively European. I know of similar ritualized torturing and mutilation of corpses in the late 1980s during the "times of dread" in Sri Lanka described in the previous chapter. And who is to say that the savage was exempt from savagery?

To come back to the present case: to start with, the victim was beaten and lead in a bloody procession through town. One person had a stake in his hand and another had a hook. Both were used on the victim while people in the café nearby watched the events from their tables (*VC*, 65–66). De Monéy's defenders tried to pacify the mob with bottles of wine and later tried to deflect them by saying they should go home, get their guns, and shoot the victim. The vacillating mayor tried to protect the victim by hiding him in his sheepfold. But the mob snatched the victim. "Clearly their intention was to reduce the 'criminal' to the status of an animal:

the ritual of slaughter proceeded from the blacksmith's bench to sheepfold to fairground market-place" (*VC*, 75). Two people tried to "quarter the cadaver" of the man who had only lapsed into a coma, though soon the body began to twitch. When the murderers stopped in front of the inn and shouted, "We want to kill him, burn him, and eat him," the mayor allegedly replied, "Eat him if you like" (*VC*, 74). Corbin says that though this statement was not founded on fact, it later formed the core of the allegations of cannibalism.

Animal metaphors continued as some yelled, "Roast him." Because the mob intended, says Corbin, not just to kill the victim but to inflict pain, the gruesome spectacle continued. Clubs were preferred to fists; some "armed with prods poked at his lower abdomen as they might tickle an animal on the market block," very much in the spirit of the women in some of the Fijian narratives (*VC*, 75). "Bludgeoning, reminiscent of the stunning of the animal prior to slaughter, was the preferred method of attack." The brutal torturing of the victim went on for two hours because the "killers collectively wanted their victim, the epitome of all they felt threatening, to suffer while they enjoyed the spectacle" (*VC*, 76).

The culminating spectacle was the burning of the victim, which, says Corbin, was reminiscent not only of the bonfires of St. John but also continued the dominant image equating the victim with the animal, in this case resembling "the sow-burnings that were part of the usual hog-slaughter ritual." A more "direct connection" with "roasting choice parts of the pig at the time of slaughter" can be established when several of the perpetrators said, "We roasted a fine pig in Hautefaye." In court a thirty-year-old man said, "[J]ust as the fire blazed up, Monsieur de Moneys flailed his arms and legs and made sounds like the noises a hog makes when you stick a knife into its neck" (*VC*, 79). Later in the night when bravado was being eroded by anxiety people began to boast of the violence committed on the body of the victim. Corbin notes that European "[m]assacres were literally a theatricalization of damnation. The disfigurement of the dead, the mutilation of the corpses by ravenous dogs, anticipated the tortures of the damned" (*VC*, 89).

But were the peasants aware that they were enacting such a drama? Leaving this question aside for the moment, Corbin shows how other myths were woven on the basis of these realities during the trial and afterward. Especially significant is the public's reversal of the peasant view of their action. In committing these acts, the peasants are the damned and the doomed. They "were drunk on blood," "a brutish mob," "creatures with human faces" (*VC*, 101). They were the savages, they were the animals. A later newspaper account developing a single incident stated that, in a sequence familiar to us now, the cannibals "danced round the body, while the mayor, symbol of subverted authority, watched helplessly" (*VC*, 102). This trope of savagism was fully developed during the trial indicating its back-and-forth movement.

The accusation of anthropophagy had no basis in reality in the Hautefaye incident; perhaps equally false were some of the previous cases of the same propensity in Europe. Yet, let us hear the voice of L. M. Prudhomme, who "documented" cases of cannibalism in Europe that were, I am sure, mostly attributed anthropophagy, just as it was with the savage anthropophagy that I presented in earlier chapters. Consider the murder of one Belzunce in Caen on August 11, 1789, which resonates with earlier ones like the St. Bartholomew massacres of August 14, 1572: "His body was dismembered. His head was placed atop a stick and carried about, as had been done in Paris" (*VC*, 94). This account is probably true to the reality of the times. Then fantasy takes over, perhaps interspersed with pieces of reality: "But," says Prudhomme, "something happened in Caen that had not been seen in the capital: many citizens wanted a shred of his flesh. Some took pieces home in their pockets. Others saw to it that the head was preceded by a pike beribboned with the victim's entrails. One man, or rather, savage, sent a chunk of the flesh off to a bakery to be baked for a family meal. One midwife went even further: she did not rest until she had obtained a piece of the victim's genitals, which she kept in a jar filled with wine spirits."[52]

FLOATING MYTHEMES IN A FIELD OF ANXIETIES

In my discussion of quartering among Europeans in this chapter I referred to its formalized nature, very much like the sacrificial anthropophagy of Polynesians and that of the Aztecs earlier in history. Human quartering is a juridical act that entails proper, even ritualized, procedures, but not surely mob violence: one cannot say that the killing of de Monéys was a formal juridical procedure. The acts performed by the mob were "ritualized" only in the sense that they had precedence in ritualized crowd behavior in the past and in European mythology. De Monéys was picked as the victim or scapegoat (if you want to employ René Girard's sense of that term);[53] the mob acted with fury but against a backdrop of a cultural definition of the situation in which fears of "Prussian spying" and the threat to the monarchy were involved. The fear of spies comes in a field of anxiety (or anxieties) that in turn spurs the initial mobilization of crowd action. Consider the following acts: the equation of the victim with an animal; attempt at quartering the body; the use of a stake for impaling the victim; scapegoatism; dancing around the grisly pyre; degradation of the corpse; dismemberment; body parts as trophies.

These acts unfolded situationally as part of the larger spectacle. They were not rational, calculated acts analogous to judicial quartering but rather sporadic ones. The spectacle produced by the mob did not have a cast of characters performing preassigned roles. Rather, later audiences, listeners, or writers of the event put together the acts of violence into systemic wholes—as "theatre" by Corbin and as differing narratives by the prosecution, the defense, judges, and the media. From these venues they begin to circulate and recirculate to various publics. Thus these acts are systematized only in retrospect: in their emergence they can be better analogized as improvised spectacle put together in bricoleur fashion, but outside the level of conscious awareness by the crowd that gathered on that fateful day.

If I am right that the sporadic yet meaningful acts are put together systemically only later, could it not be that it is from such acts that the more formalized enactments of the criminal code, in this case the law pertaining to treason and quartering, were put together into a coherent, rational order? Consider the murder scenario: one man wanted to quarter the victim, but his act had little or no connection with the juridical act of quartering. As the animal tropes indicate, it arose from the very life of the peasantry, from animal quartering, which in turn has moved away from the heroic cultural model represented in the Homer of my epigraph. The act of treating the victim as an animal and then torturing him is again based on the experience of the farm with pigs that are pretty much treated in the same way. And demeaning the dead body and refusing it decent (Christian) burial are based on familiar mythemes (that is, mythic themes or bits and pieces of cultural representations) independent of the animal-human homology.[54] But while the peasants did not in all likelihood make the connection between dismembering and the wholeness of the body on Judgment Day and the denial of salvation that criminal quartering is said to ensure, I think it is out of such collective acts on the level of the village and the farm that the idea of quartering itself as a punishment for criminal conduct would have arisen. With the development of that latter form of life a more powerful set of sacred symbols comes to be associated with the enactment.

I now pose a further question: How do formal acts that had salience in past ritualized scenarios reappear sporadically in the present of the late nineteenth century, not systemically, but in public spectacle in the context of the fury and passion that has been unleashed in Hautefaye? Can one do better than posit the idea of mass delusion or collective psychoses that Corbin and others, including the court, speak of? Such terms, as I see it, refer to phenomena to be explained, not an explanation. Let me look at these acts of violence through another set of lenses beginning with the title of this section: floating mythemes in a field of anxieties.

The idea of "floating mythemes" suggests my indebtedness to the now-popular notion of floating signifiers. But long before this Freud postulated the idea of anxiety that has "indefiniteness and lack of object."[55] Freud made a distinction between known danger or "fear" that provokes anxiety, and neurotic anxiety in which there is no clear known danger. He also showed that in reality the distinction can be blurred such that in some situations (as the one in Hautefaye) the "external and internal dangers, real dangers and instinctual demands converge" producing a "surplus of anxiety" and a kind of "psychical helplessness."[56] Moreover, anxiety does not remain "free-floating" but can attach itself to ideational forms of various sorts ranging from purely personal fantasies, to such things as childhood castration phobias and in adult life in differing ways to "obsessive acts and religious practices"—to use the title of one of Freud's papers.[57] But just as Freud gave priority to free-floating anxiety one can also make the reverse case that ideational forms, whether cultural or idiosyncratically personal, may get attached to anxiety such that the one cannot exist without the other. Further, anxiety or anxieties themselves can be generated out of social and political conditions of the sort that animated the French incident. The public actions performed there can in turn get attached to the kind of psychic anxieties that Freud talks about. Thus, in my thinking, floating mythemes (and bits and pieces of cultural memory) and free-floating anxieties are intrinsically interconnected and emerge into the field of awareness during specific contexts, such as in mob action and other ethoses of collective dread.

Mythemes of the sort I have isolated are part of cultural memory. They are embodied in public consciousness through stories and as gossip, folklore, and newspaper representations. These various representations feed into each other to form new representations. The context of collective fury determines what acts get resurrected and by whom. But how is it possible for members of the French mob to decide which acts of violence to choose from a traditional repertoire? It should seem obvious that cultural memory is not only a thing in itself manifest in multiple texts but also existing in the memories of people, some of it outside of their conscious awareness. I am not talking of a Freudian unconscious but something analogous to everyday context-specific or context-dependent recall. As one can speak of unconscious motivation, one should also be able of speak of being "unaware, yet aware." In the de Monéys case the context—both the immediate social context of the fair and the larger political context of Prussian spying—permits enactments of mythemes and other bits and pieces of ideation enshrined in cultural memory to emerge from unawareness into the awareness of individual members of the crowd. And these mythemes when translated into action in turn reproduce in others mimetic or imitative reactions that then build up quickly, coalescing to form the spectacle or scenario being displayed to the public gathered at the fair. An audience or public is a necessary component of spectacle as it is of any collective performance, even if some of the audience lazed around in a pub drinking beer, watching the scene through untinted glasses. But as I already noted, these fragments of memory floating into the field of awareness can coexist with deeper motivations of the Freudian sort. For example, male castration anxieties are activated in such contexts and overdetermine the motivational picture, as Corbin himself recognizes. And beyond that, one might add, are even earlier infantile motivations that I have discussed previously, especially what Jacques Lacan has labeled as the *corps morcelé*, the images of the fragmented body that are a by-product of the child's pre-mirror stage of psychosexual development before the development of self-consciousness in ego (moi) formation. And these images are mobilized in the dread of castration that is further enacted and expressed in a wrathful talion reaction as the dead body is cut up and, often enough in European riots, the head severed from the body and paraded along with other body parts.

I would like to link the murder scenario in our French village of the late nineteenth century (and similar scenarios from earlier European history) with the events in Mendana's expedition and the Maori narrative I have depicted in this chapter. Mendana's actions are easy to explain: he simply transferred a European model of quartering criminals and traitors to the new context of discovery and exploration that had already produced its own horrors. But the European fantasies associated with the Maori narrative are more consonant with the peasant situation in France. Given the context of combined anxiety and fear that beset white settlers living among the Maori (predefined as dreaded cannibals), unorganized mythemes contained in European cultural memory float into their passive awareness. These bits and pieces of memory are woven, sometimes systemically, sometimes not, into the narratives of war or of life that settlers have constructed, not however without some anchorage in the real life of the native. Many of the mythemes that form Sheridan's narrative and the ones I have presented in earlier chapters are from the antecedent culture of Europe such as those of the French incident in the Hautefaye commune and inherited by the settler culture and then imputed to the savage. But some of these memory pieces are not just European; they belong to a common, mostly male, humanity—the "psychic monstrosity" within us, in both the savage and the civilized that then accounts for the Maori and others to impute cannibalism to the European and the European to the Maori.

As we move backward into history when much of our contemporary dread of the Other was first formulated, that is, in the discovery of the New World, we find similar though perhaps more stable mythemes that overdetermine and complicate the Spanish representation of the Aztec. In their human sacrifice Aztec priests surgically open up the heart of the victim whose body then is ritually consumed by their priests and select others. I am suggesting that these actions would evoke in the Spanish a "surplus of anxiety" not only because Aztec sacrifice seemed a desecration of the Eucharist, but also because it brought out into the "awareness" of the conquistadors the well-known medieval idea of the sacred heart of Christ now represented in parodic horror, as it were. Horror and parody: because the conquistadors inherited a medieval Christian worldview in which mystics, especially female ones, had visions of the sacred heart of Christ, visions that continued into modern Catholicism on the popular level. Thus Margaret Ebner (1291–1351), a mystic belonging to a Dominican convent, writing in her book, *Revelations*, mentions that when she was in prayer before a crucifix, the image of Christ bent down "and let me kiss his open heart and gave me to drink of the blood flowing from his heart."[58] Take another mystic, Lutgard of Aywières (b. 1182), a Beguin and a Cistercian who, like many others then and now, was shown the bleeding body of Christ.[59] While she was still an adolescent and a "beginner" at St. Catherine's, the crucified Christ appeared to her on her way to Matins and allowed her "to drink from the wound at his side."[60] These images of the wounded body of Christ and his sacred heart must surely have been in the minds and hearts of believers in the fifteenth century, such that their visual confrontation of the Aztec sacrifice would necessarily have evoked an unbelievable horror that then has to be displaced or dealt with in other ways.[61] In my view the Spanish "paranoid imagination" that converted the Aztec sacrifice into cannibalism must be seen against this psychic backdrop.

CANNIBALISM AND THE PARANOID IMAGINATION

How does this paranoid imagination arise? In the first essay I wrote on Peter Dillon I suggested that men and groups who feel threatened by real or imagined dangers might well begin to see the world through "paranoid lenses," that is, as a threatening and fearful place.[62] I deal with situations where the threatening outside reality, imagined or compounded of imagination and reality, impels a person to see that world through a lens of suspiciousness. My usage does not pertain either to clinical paranoia or even to the "paranoid position" made famous by Melanie Klein and dealing with the persecutory fears among children during the first few months (the oral stage) of childhood. As with Hautefaye, many ordinary people felt threatened by Prussians and by spies within their own society. In such situations a "paranoid imagination" develops and the distinction between imagined and real dangers becomes blurred, the latter often swallowed up by the former. Those who see the world through paranoid lenses fail to make the distinction between imagined and real dangers because for them imagined dangers are real. We are dealing here with the power of "psychic reality" in fostering the paranoid imagination. This imagination is at work in Sheridan and his bizarre vision of Maori cannibalism, a vision that gets accepted as truth by the rest of the settler community living in isolation in hostile territory. A paranoid imagination such as Sheridan's fantastic has political relevance because it is intrinsically connected with "Indian hating."

The paranoid imagination appears and reappears all the time in the isolated worlds of the early European missionaries in New Zealand and Fiji, and it appears in Hans Staden and others like him living in lonely forts and townships surrounded by cannibals and in Staden's case exacerbated by his capture and his dread of being eaten. Those creatures outside begin to live inside one's mind and are nurtured there. Consider the psychic fate of sexually repressed, even politically repressive and misogynist Christians like Jean de Léry or Hans Staden without access to women who might help mitigate the bleakness of their existences in alien Brazil. They become prisoners of their fantasies; no wonder "women with sagging breasts" and greedy appetites take the place of real-life Tupinamba women.

What makes an individual see the world through paranoid lenses is overdetermined. Its roots lie in childhood fears now objectified in the cannibal, the Other who is going "to roast and eat us." Hans Staden, for example, refers to his friend Hieronymus captured and killed by the Tupinamba as the "roasted Christian."[63] The childhood fantasy now becomes an imagined reality. It is this psychic reality and the subjective "definition of the situation" in which one is located that matters in the closed or partially closed communities mentioned in this work. As prisoners of their own thoughts settlers become obsessed with the dread that they might be captured or killed and eaten by fearful cannibals. Thus stories circulating about the Other get magnified in their telling and retelling, and the cannibal-Other becomes an obsessive component of one's Being. The story one narrates to cope with such fears is, when seen as a totality, an invented one. A few bits and pieces might have an empirical truth-value that one might, through astute detective work, be able to disinter, as I did in the Fijian cases.

Cannibal stories then are both expressions of the fear of the Other and a means of dealing with that fear by talking about it with one's friends and neighbors. A friend and neighbor in responding to my story might, through *his* paranoid lenses, embellish it further with bits and pieces of the fantastic. Putting down such stories in writing can be an imaginative act as are the invention of ghost stories, nursery rhymes, and other tales of terror that humans love to hear and write about. A ghost, like a monster of the nursery, "elides the distance between the actual and the imagined" irrespective of whether one knows they are imagined or real, because "the fictional *takes place* in the everyday."[64] It occupies our everyday space with the fantastic, just as is the case with settler stories of the cannibal-Other. In most societies and in premodern Europe, one believed in the existence of ghosts as one did in witches, cannibals, and other monstrous creatures. Thus these creatures have a physical and psychic reality, such that even when one hears or reads patently fictional stories about them, they tend to have a frightening quality. Nevertheless, in modern socialization the physical-cum-psychic reality of ghosts, witches, and cannibals have diminished because one can shut the book or turn off the TV and banish the creature from one's living room. This is the key difference between traditional ghost stories or children's cannibal stories, in contrast with modern books and modern films about ghosts, vampires, the walking dead, and cannibals. In these latter examples the creature does not walk out of the book or the cinema to invade our everyday spaces, though he might come to haunt us in our dreams and imaginations.

The return of the dead and the return of the cannibal have another feature in common: they often are conjoined with the return of the repressed of the European imagination. One cannot ask the question of Hans Staden if his story is true or not in an empirical or historical or factual sense without asking similar questions for other kinds of invented genres. Stories circulating in ships and settler communities and other claustrophobic arenas are believed to be true even though they may be compounded by what one might inappositely call a combination of fact and fiction. Even when the physical spaces of a community might remain open, psychic arenas can get narrowed down so that one can speak of a psychic community in a larger nation living in claustrophobic closure, as in times of dread such as the ones I mention from my Sri Lankan experience or everywhere else in situations of modern political terror or the political invention or magnification of terror. Even when the story is a deliberately constructed yarn or fabrication the intention of the author might be otherwise. He wants us to believe in the truth of his story. This was the case with Hans Staden, Cannibal Jack, Peter Dillon, and even the cunning Endicott. When I was a child I believed that the ghost stories told by my peers and socializing agents were true. But when I became a man, did I entirely get rid of such childish things? At some deep level, it is the child in each of us who, having banished the cannibal from our living rooms, can yet take for granted the literal truth-value of cannibal stories of the raconteurs who inhabit this book and who inhabited the savage worlds in which they lived for short or long periods.

CONCLUSION

As I hinted in my preface, the several chapters in this book can either be read as a continuous narrative or as separate essays held together by the theme of "cannibal talk." I now want to discuss a few of the issues that might not have been clear in the preceding chapters. This will provide an opportunity for my critics to disagree with me, because it must be remembered that falsification, let alone disproof, is difficult to realize in respect of the open narratives that I have constructed here. *Disagreement* by positing alternative narratives, contrary evidence, and their interpretation is both possible and welcome. What holds the book together are not only the discourses on "cannibalism," in the sense I have defined that term, but also a kind of broad ethnographic unity with my primary emphasis being the British and European relations with Polynesia. Even when I discuss the Solomon Islands of Mendana's time I am not departing too far from that concern. All the chapters in this book are also held together in terms of the "deconstructive-restorative" strategy that I have adopted.

I begin with the well-known assumption that Polynesia constitutes a large culture area showing remarkable similarities in language and culture. So far as anthropophagy is concerned, most contemporary ethnographers would not deny that it is related to human sacrifice or to something they label "ritual cannibalism." But the paradox is that like the lay public, scholars from the very beginning have come to believe that the Maori, Fijians, and Marquesans belonged to an elite group of man-eaters living in the "cannibal islands" and consuming inordinate amounts of human flesh. This is nothing new because it has been said of a multitude of non-Western societies. It therefore should not surprise us that in colonial representations sacrificial anthropophagy tends to get absorbed into the man-eating myth. Proof comes from travelers and missionaries who suggest that, alongside conspicuous anthropophagy, there occurs an expanded "consubstantial community" to include common folk, women, and children. The problem with these societies is that one does not have any reliable empirical information regarding pre-European and precolonial forms of sacrificial anthropophagy, except the obvious fact of its practice. Such information comes from another Polynesian society, Tahiti, in Cook's wonderful description of a human sacrifice that I have already presented in chapter 3. There is no conspicuous anthropophagy in this account, nor are there any large-scale sacrifices of the sort that consumed the scholarly mythopoeic imagination especially in the later eighteenth to the early twentieth centuries with respect to the cannibal islands already mentioned. Banana trees as symbolic substitutes for human beings, yes, but not real corpses. So is it for the most part in Hawai'i, where, as with Tahiti, there is a symbolic eating of the sacrificial victim bringing Hawaiian sacrifice in line with many sacrificial forms the world over, including the Christian Eucharist which, as "theophagia," was denounced by Catholicism's opponents as a form of anthropophagy.[1] I then mention that, owing to complex historical conditions eluding us, there might well occur a "slippage" into an actual consumption of the sacrificial victim, and this was true of the Maori and Fijians. But those examples are still within the sacramental frame of a consubstantial community. This form of sacrificial anthropophagy could in the colonial situation lead to what I have called its later "pejoration."

What about the many human skulls hanging in shrines in both Hawai'i and Tahiti that could have been the heads of sacrificial victims, as indeed Cook himself seems to postulate? I suggest that if the death-head skulls in European churches were put in restricted spaces one would have a similar impressive picture, though it is much easier to peek into catacombs and witness the enormity of the European religious obsession with skulls and bones (see figure 10). And so would it be if the heads of those guillotined in the French revolution were piled up in a Parisian location, as was the case when skulls and skeletons from the killing fields of Cambodia or Rwanda were showcased for haunting the public conscience (see figure 11). Just as one cannot construct a single picture of human violence from these real or imagined sites, so with Polynesia. The heads in Hawaiian marae might have come from several sacrifices or from the enemies slain in battle, for I must reiterate that decapitation is a widespread male custom in warfare, having its psychic

FIGURE 10
View in the Catacombs. Photograph by Gaspard Nadar, 1861.©The J. Paul Getty Museum, Los Angeles.

roots in both male violence and castration anxieties. The elaboration of these psychic attributes through the work of culture into forms of headhunting should not blind us to this core reality of decapitation in warfare prior to the development of modern technologies of violence. In other words the existence of human heads stuck in various Polynesian shrines must not lead us to assume that they were all sacrificial victims, and if they were, that they proved the existence of mass sacrifices of humans. Nevertheless, I think that when a society perceived itself threatened, a large but indeterminate number of people would have been sacrificed, but

FIGURE 11
Skull exhibits from Cambodia killing fields. Photograph by Per-Anders Pettersson. ©Getty Images, Inc.

even here the type case is not Polynesia but the Aztecs. The presence of the conquistadors and their threat to the very existence of Aztec society would have resulted in the multiplication of sacrificial victims. It is an error to make the inference that such was the case in more normal times.

There are, however, two possible disagreements with the above argument. First, Cook's description of a human sacrifice was preparatory to war, but what about persons captured in war? And would there not occur multiple sacrifices in that situation? This is difficult to answer, but at least Valerio Valeri's study of Hawaiian sacrifice does not suggest it. By contrast among the Maori, it is possible that more than one chief was ritually sacrificed during warfare. In my thinking traditional Maori warfare simply did not permit large-scale capture of chiefs or large-scale killings because retaliatory action would in the long run have denuded a group of people considered essential for the well-being of society. Even where the "first fish" or the "fish of Tu" was concerned, it was carefully regulated with women, children, and commoners being excluded and chiefs not even permitted in the environment where human flesh was being cooked. Europeans and foreigners were also excluded from the sacrificial scene, which then permitted these outsiders to replace the sacrifice with the cannibal scene and its fantastic elaborations. The Maori sacrificial scene is not located in the ceremonial centers or marae familiar to us from Tahiti and Hawai'i. But I do not find this a serious issue because sacred and bounded spaces can be temporarily created by priests within larger profane environments. I have described such demarcations for Sri Lanka, and it is easy to demonstrate it for many other societies.[2]

For me the eating of human flesh is a highly charged sacramental act, once again bringing Maori anthropophagy in line with both Aztec and Christian sacrifice. The discourses and discursive practices of the cannibalism of my usage was built on this edifice, though I show in chapter 5 and elsewhere that colonialism and European intervention produced a complex self-fulfilling prophecy that resulted in conspicuous anthropophagy, thereby confounding the interpretation of Polynesian sacrifice.

Another possible area of disagreement is myth. Maori myths describe cannibalistic acts of large- and small-scale man-eating divorced from a sacrificial context. But can one extrapolate a reality from the myth? I have suggested that myths, like other cultural phenomena, must be placed in their historic contexts though this is not to deny that some cosmogonic myths, even where written texts do not exist, are remarkably resilient and persist as structures of the long run.[3] My proviso compounds the issue but does not exonerate us from seeing myth as a changing cultural form responding to events such as colonialism. Moreover, myths are of different kinds, some being more significant than others, and one cannot extrapolate a particular Polynesian man-eating myth as an indicator of anthropophagy without assessing its cultural significance for the group rather than for the ethnographer or historian. If myth, in its broadest sense, is significant for understanding anthropophagy, then Europeans, whose cultures I pointed out are permeated from times long past with man-eating myths, should be classified as notorious cannibals.

Cannibal myths can exist independently of the sacrifice (or of any other form of anthropophagy) as much as the sacrifice exists for the most part independently of cannibal myths. I do not doubt that there are myths, such as those pertaining to origins, closely tied to the sacrifice, the Vedic-Indian and Greek cases being good examples. But even in such cases the sacrificial ritual is not a direct refraction of the myth. This makes interpretation of the sacrificial anthropophagy more complex and more interesting for those who want to venture into that realm. I am suggesting however that a comparative strategy of the sort sketched for Polynesia might well work for the classic Brazilian material. Rather than being bogged down by the dubious ethnographies of Thevet and others, especially of the unreliable Hans Staden, one ought to work on the Aztec material in combination with the archaeological information from such sources as ancient Peru and elsewhere and then develop a comparative and transformative framework for the Brazilian material using the sixteenth-century "ethnographies" advisedly.

Although I think that the key institution for comprehending forms of "ritual anthropophagy" is human sacrifice, I do not deal with that phenomenon explicitly. This is too vast a topic for me to handle, but I want to make clear that I do not regard human sacrifice as "a thing in itself." It shows variability even in a fairly well-defined culture area. Nevertheless, I think it fair that the reader should know my own take on human sacrifice, because my "prejudices" stem from my South Asian perspectivism. Here is my wish list of the minimal elements of human sacrifice that can be elaborated in many ways through the work of culture.

Human sacrifice has an act of oblation as its most obvious feature. There is a positive or negative component to it: the positive is where the victim is offered to a god who will then bring favor to the community or person offering the sacrifice, for example, in war or for the general welfare of the group. This is true of Polynesia and the Aztecs and perhaps true of ancient Vedic sacrifice. But later Vedic sacrifice used animals for the most part, and this tradition went into popular Hinduism. But the animal can be a substitute for the human being as indeed the human being might be a substitute for the animal. Human sacrifice when it is eaten is the more awesome one because it violates a normal taboo against eating fellow humans and more generally against violence. As Georges Bataille put it, "Man is never looked upon as butchers' meat, but he is frequently eaten ritually. The man who eats human flesh knows full well that this is a forbidden act; knowing this taboo to be fundamental he will religiously violate it sometimes."[4]

The negative cult of human sacrifice is where an oblation of a man or child is used for black magic or for obtaining treasure, as in South Asia. In the South Asian case the offering is to a demonic figure or a divine figure that has demonic attributes, such as the goddess Kali or Bhairava, the god of the underworld. Polynesian human sacrifice for the inauguration of new canoes fall, I think, into that category. It is analogous to the act of offering a human victim for the inauguration of a dam or irrigation project in other parts of the world.[5] In this negative sacrificial cult, it is the deity who consumes the sacrifice enhancing his power and thereby his capacity to fulfill the dark wishes of the supplicant.

Where the positive form of human sacrifice exists there is, generally, an actual or symbolic eating of the sacrificial victim. Why so? The god to whom the sacrifice is offered is made to be present in the sacrificial victim such that, in consuming the victim, I am consuming the essence, or mana, of the deity and I am spiritually enriched and empowered by the experience. I think this is what for the most part occurs in Polynesian sacrifice, especially when an ordinary victim is clubbed and killed and offered to the god, as in Hawai'i and Tahiti. When a chief is killed in the battlefield and offered to the god in a temporarily consecrated sacrificial arena as among the Maori and more formally among the Fijians, a powerful variation occurs. The chief is one who already possesses the power or mana of the god. In consuming his body, I am in effect consuming the mana of the chief, which ultimately is the mana of the god. Hence its enormous power as a sacramental act. The *mysterium tremendum* of this act requires only eating small amounts of the body consecrated in special ways. In this sense anthropophagy is essentially theophagy. Mass anthropophagy has no place in this scheme of things.

The work of culture can produce all sorts of symbolic variations around this positive form of the sacrifice, the most obvious being the multiple forms of the Christian Eucharist. Hence my reason for rejecting the simplistic view that one could classify the Eucharist as a form of "cannibalism" though it certainly could be brought within the comparative frame of the human sacrifice. God had to become human before he could be sacrificed and eaten in an act of symbolic remove from actual anthropophagy.

The more symbolically removed from actual sacrificial anthropophagy, the more the cases multiply until it reaches a point where it makes no sense to call such symbolic consumption sacrificial anthropophagy.[6] For example, Hindus often break a coconut before the image of the deity in an act of abnegation and then eat the white kernel of the coconut. Although the interpretation of this act might vary, some Hindus believe that eating the coconut is eating the god whose essence has infused the fruit. But then this act is not all that different from what the Hindus call *prasad*, that is, food offered to the god and later consumed By contrast, it is unthinkable to eat of the food given to demons, as it is unthinkable to consume the victim of the negative sacrificial cult. Yet, even this norm can be transgressed in some rare instances. In some personal Tantric rites, one might eat a piece of human flesh but in performing this terrifying act one is identified with the demonic form of the god or goddess, such as Kali, who is an eater of corpses, or performing a deliberate act of transgression of mainline Brahmanic values or both.

Human and animal sacrifices are separate, but it is hard to believe that the one does not influence the other. Animal sacrifices are the more common even in those societies that have human sacrifices. Which came first is a futile chicken-and-egg question, and I won't deal with it. But what adds to the awesomeness of human sacrifice is that the sacrificial victim, the person or persons making the sacrifice, and the god for whom the sacrifice is made belong to the same class, they look alike, the one being modeled on the other. Human beings were created in the image of god and god was created in the image of the human being. Even Indian gods with multiple hands and heads have basically human features though elaborated from the normal model. Therefore, in the positive cult of the sacrifice, the sacrificial victim can be a substitute for the person or persons making the sacrifice. I am offering myself to the god.

How does cannibal talk intersect with human sacrifice? Obviously, there are the discourses pertaining to the sacrifice itself, in Polynesia as well as everywhere else, including the Aztec, Christian, and Vedic forms. Further, wherever you have a discourse on the sacrifice you also have coexistent indigenous stories and discourses of cannibalism that, in the context of the European incursions, can be projected in different ways onto the intruder. The commonest expression is the threat to eat the Other, to humiliate the enemy by verbal and gestural actions, as when a Maori will hold up a bone and descant on it. Almost always this is intended as a threat against the European or an attempt to frighten him. Sometimes it is the native who is frightened by his misunderstanding of the European discourse, as with Cook and crew imitating the dreaded cannibal. On the European side the threats of cannibalism, I pointed out, have terrifying unconscious reactions activating fears of dismemberment and quartering. To complicate matters, in all these societies there is a pronounced development of cannibal humor, something poorly developed or undeveloped, according to my limited knowledge, in respect of societies that have no such tradition. Cannibal humor in the West is well known; I have tried to speculatively understand its prevalence in Polynesia. Finally, I think while many societies have cannibal myths, they proliferate in those with an antecedent tradition of human sacrifice, and this is especially so in Europe owing to its history of a profoundly ambivalent and complicated relation between anthropophagy, theophagy, quartering, and dismemberment that I have already discussed. These conditions will account for Europe's fascination with anthropophagy-cannibalism, a fascination that embraces professional ethnographers out to prove the most trivial hypotheses pertaining to the historical omniprevalence of anthropophagy the world over. I do not believe that it is possible to interpret human sacrifice through a society's cannibal myths unless these myths are also proved to be myths of human sacrifice.

Let me now deal with further problems that arise in respect of cannibal talk and the attribution of uncanny anthropophagous appetites to the native. I deal with basically two forms of cannibal talk: the first are simply dialogues of varying levels of complexity between people talking about cannibalism and generally misunderstanding the Other's discourse. The second are cannibal narratives that I deconstruct in order to show that, once we trace their genealogy, these discourses prove "empty."

These narratives can provide fuel for disagreement. A prospective critic can make a reasonable argument for saying that there are *other* narratives that might prove the reality of conspicuous anthropophagy and not just the cannibalism fantasy. Given my work it seems to me that my critic has no longer any choice but to show, through sustained and critical analyses, that a particular narrator's account is a "true" one, or even a partially true account that helps us understand genuine Fijian or Maori man-eating propensities. In other words I am suggesting that to refute my argument it is necessary to adopt the same genealogical strategy that nullifies or qualifies my hypotheses about cannibalism. My work indicates that one can no longer view cannibal narratives as innocent statements of truth, nor can we take missionary and settler accounts of natives eating loads of human flesh as empirically true. Equally fallacious is to argue that because bits and pieces of cannibal narratives might have empirical truth-value, the narrative as a whole is also true. I wonder how one can read Western historical fiction with this assumption.

A more serious area of disagreement remains. I have shown how the colonial presence not only changed the tenor and directions of native life and warfare but also produced the occasional practice of conspicuous anthropophagy (that is, the empirical realization of cannibalism). This, I have suggested did not exist prior to the European presence. Can such a hypothesis be seriously maintained? If conspicuous anthropophagy existed in the context of colonialism, could it not have occurred in the precolonial era? Although this is entirely possible, I would counter that such occurrences do not happen in a sociopolitical vacuum. My strategy could in fact be helpful in isolating the conditions that led or would have led to other forms of conspicuous anthropophagy, for example, conditions of passionate rage against felt injustice or against a prior outrage. But, as with contemporary communal violence and Europe's religious riots in the past, I cannot imagine *occasional* anthropophagy of this sort being normalized into a "tradition" of conspicuous anthropophagy. The ethnographic tendency to adopt that position illustrates that "symbolic traditionalization" is not something that occurs in the other culture. Rather, it is something that occurs in the contemporary professional ethnography of these societies wherein information collected during the colonial period in a context of violence and rapid social change is assumed to be valid for the precolonial one.

The preceding discussion indicates that the primary sources of information I have used are so opaque that interpretation is not an easy task. This comes out clearly in my incidental discussion of circulating mythemes, that is, clusters of ideas that keep moving in ships and on islands and get grafted onto a multiplicity of discourses on savagism and civilization, including texts and discourses on cannibalism. Some of them I think are European in origin: necrophagy, vampirism, and fattening and eating of children—mythemes attributed to natives in different parts of the world in European cannibal texts. I believe that similar fantasies exist in other cultures, but the European construction of the cannibalism of the Other must surely come from their own traditions, or by the incorporation of native beliefs within the frame of European ones.

Other instances of circulating mythemes are not so clear. Let me give one example. Bernal Díaz reports for the Aztecs about talk (that is, cannibal talk in my usage) whereby they insisted that they will eat the Spanish in a special dish presumably used in ordinary life. Thus the Aztecs "were planning to kill and eat our flesh, and had already prepared pots with salt and peppers and tomatoes."[7] Juxtapose this with a record in the early nineteenth century for the Bataks of Indonesia by William Marsden, an employee of the East India Company who mentions that the Bataks "with savage enthusiasm" eat the flesh of humans with "a dish of salt, lemon juice and red pepper" all ground together as a *sambal*, an indigenous dish.[8] And Sir Stamford Raffles, utilizing the same authority, says that the scrumptious parts were the palms of the hand and adds that "formerly it was usual for people to eat their parents when too old for work."[9] Because Marsden and those who followed him interviewed real-life informants, this ought to caution ethnographers naively interviewing older informants on the truth of the past practice of cannibalism.

Mythemes such as the consumption of the Other with sambal went with the development of trade and the movement of chili peppers from South America to everywhere in Asia. In a few years they were carried by sailors, travelers, missionaries, and storytellers as truth. But there is no way that evidence of this sort can be proved or disproved; the pile up of similar examples must suffice. Nevertheless, there remains a problem: Because cannibal talk is part of our dark humanity, is it not possible for these mythemes to be independently invented elsewhere? This certainly is possible, but one cannot get away from the fact that one is dealing with Western narratives that attribute these propensities to the native, and one can only show their thematic persistence in the history of Western cannibal talk.

Although these cannibal discourses on the Other have had a long ancestry in the West, I suggested that, after the voyages of discovery, they were implicated in a larger dialectic of Savagism and Civilization. Each had its "metaphysics," though I have focused primarily on the metaphysics of savagism and its consequences that I think anticipated the metaphysics of Orientalism, that is, the West's essentialized fantasy of the Orient, which, as with savagism, contains a positive and a negative component, sometimes real, sometimes surreal. Cannibalism is easily grafted onto savagism and becomes a defining component. The discourse on savagism is almost impossible to eradicate and continues to our very day. It is certainly the case that the major anthropologists of the late nineteenth century could not get rid of the essential features of savagism and civilization in its doctrine of human evolution from a stage of savagery to that of civilization. I am not sure how much of these ideas went into the liberal ethnography of the next century. When I was in graduate school the term "savagery" was nearly out, but not the term "primitive," which we used without too much discrimination until the advent of poststructuralist thought. Hence Michel-Rolph Trouillot could rightly say that now "the time is right for substantive propositions that aim explicitly at the destabilization and eventual destruction of the savage slot."[10]

CANNIBAL TALK: A RESTORATIVE UNDERSTANDING

I have said that my analysis of cannibal talk is "deconstructive-restorative." Let me begin with what I mean by "restorative" focusing on the Maori where my analysis is restorative in several senses. I speculatively restore the historical and discursive continuities between Cook's time and the beginnings of white settlements and trade in New Zealand up to 1840 when that country was declared a colony. I restore the continuities and breaks between traditional (precolonial) Maori culture and the arrival of whites insofar as it pertains to cannibalism, anthropophagy, and human sacrifice. Above all, my sense of restoration is ethical: I hesitantly restore the self-worth and integrity of a people defined as "savage" by the attribution to them, as part of their very being, the lust and relish for indiscriminate man-eating. Colonial power sometimes brought about a realization of that view of the savage among the very people it subjugated ("self-primitivization") as it did in many other areas of social life, both for good and for ill. But the genealogical method, in the Nietzschean sense, can restore the historicity of native anthropophagy without sentimentalizing the native's point of view or reifying it as truth. Anthropology is a human science; I try to restore the humane face of that science.

What about the term "deconstruction," the other term in the set? I am indebted to Jacques Derrida and other postmodernists, but I try to avoid their abstract terminology and the intellectual baggage that comes with their deconstruction theories. My usage is intrinsically tied to "restoration" such that one cannot have deconstruction without the restoration of meaning. Although this might not sound quite kosher to some of my colleagues, let me spell out this idea by going back to Nietzsche.

Nietzsche has been considered the avatar of our modernity by those poststructuralists who have appropriated and refurbished his ideas. There is nothing wrong with this approach, although in my reading Nietzsche rejected the modernity of his time and in fact despised it. He constantly tried through his genealogical method to restore an ethical understanding to the dilemmas of late nineteenth century modernity through such movements as Dionysianism, an idea that he retained to the very end of his life; through the upholding of (imagined) aristocratic values and the condemnation of the herd instinct; or through the upholding of an ideal prophet of the future, Zarathustra, without whom Bertolt Brecht could not have created Adzak, one of my favorite madmen. It seems to me that Nietzschean genealogy is inextricably tied to the restoration of values, alongside an attempt to formulate a transvaluation of all values that cannot be divorced from Nietzsche's critique of modernity.

Adopting Nietzsche's example, though not some his own unappetizing moralities, I have a special take on "deconstruction." That take is based on our knowledge that cultural meanings are *constructed* by human beings. One has therefore to deconstruct (or better still "un-construct") these texts to demonstrate how they came to be constructed in the first place. Further, and here I depart from some contemporary thinkers, I refuse to take texts at face value, especially those charged with emotional meaning. Thus, deconstruction or un-construction in this double sense leads us to the hermeneutics of suspicion formulated by Paul Ricoeur based on the thinking of the great "masters of suspicion," Marx, Nietzsche, and Freud. Marx was a great deconstructionist of capitalism, and he tried to restore an ideal of a classless society. Unrealistic though it was, one cannot understand Marx of the one without understanding Marx of the other. Michel Foucault is the poststructuralist thinker who has most influenced modern ethnography, critically probing the genealogies of texts and questioning the premises of the human sciences. It seems to me that his thought ought to be reconciled with that of Paul Ricoeur from whom I have borrowed the notion of "restoration" even though the two thinkers are viewed by themselves and others as antagonists.

This is the strategy I follow in my examination of cannibal talk: the unconstruction of a text to reveal its genealogy followed by the restoration of its multiple meanings and its ethical implications. But one must admit that, however rigorously we formulate our thinking, interpretation remains a vulnerable exercise, not only because of the difficulty of verification, but also because some texts are simply *impossible* to interpret. Freud mentioned that there is a point where "the tangle of dream-thoughts" cannot be unraveled, which is the "dream's navel, the spot where it reaches down into the unknown."[11] In the case of cannibal talk, unlike in psychoanalytic talk, this is due to the relative lack of historical, cultural, and archival material to make a reasonable genealogical exhumation of a text—what I have called "historical ignorance," prompting I am sure some of my critics to complain that historical ignorance is a mask for plain ignorance. Alternatively, one can be bold and attempt a partial interpretation as I do with some of the cannibal texts, or simply practice intelligent guesswork as I do with Lockerby and Smith in chapter 6. Either way one will always be open to charges of ignoring relevant texts or incompleteness in interpretation. I will admit this and then unashamedly steal another thinker's aphorism: "One must be very humane to say, 'I don't know that,' to afford ignorance."[12]

NOTES

PREFACE

1. I wish to acknowledge permission to reproduce in whole or in part from the following academic publishers. "'British Cannibals': Contemplation of an Event in the Death and Resurrection of James Cook, Explorer," published in *Critical Inquiry*, special issue on *Identities*, ed. Anthony Appiah and Henry Louis Gates, 630–54 (Chicago: University of Chicago Press, 1992), all rights reserved. "Cannibal Feasts in Nineteenth-Century Fiji: Seamen's Yarns and the Ethnographic Imagination," in *Cannibalism and the Colonial World*, ed. Francis Barker, Peter Hulme, and Margaret Iversen, 65–86 (Cambridge: Cambridge University Press, 1998). "Narratives of the Self: Chevalier Peter Dillon's Fijian Cannibal Adventures," in *Body Trade: Captivity, Cannibalism and Colonialism in the Pacific*, 69–111 (Melbourne, Australia: Pluto Press and New York: Routledge, 2001). Chapter 1 has a section entitled "The Savage Cannibal and the Divinized Civilizer: The Sun Myth in Melville's *Mardi*." This work originally appeared as "Response to Victor Li" in *CR: The New Centennial Review* 1, no. 3 (2001), published by Michigan State University Press.

CHAPTER ONE: ANTHROPOLOGY AND THE MAN-EATING MYTH

1. Peter Hulme, "Introduction: The Cannibal Scene," in *Cannibalism and the Colonial World*, ed. Francis Barker, Peter Hulme, and Margaret Iverson (Cambridge: Cambridge University Press, 1998), 1–38; and William Arens, "Rethinking Anthropophagy," in *Cannibalism and the Colonial World*, 39–62.

2. Marshall Sahlins, "Cannibalism: An Exchange," *New York Review of Books* 26, no. 4 (March 22, 1979): 45–53.

3. Frank Lestringant, *Cannibals: The Discovery and Representation of the Cannibal from Columbus to Jules Verne*, trans., Rosemary Morris (Berkeley: University of California Press, 1997), 6, my italics. Subsequent references to this work are cited with the abbreviation *C*.

4. Anthony Padgen, *The Fall of Natural Man: The American Indian and the Origins of Comparative Ethnology* (Cambridge: Cambridge University Press, 1986).

5. Jean de Léry, *History of a Voyage to the Land of Brazil*, 1580, trans. and intro. by Janet Whatley (Berkeley: University of California Press, 1992), lx.

6. Hans Staden, *Hans Staden: The True History of His Captivity*, 1557, trans. Malcolm Letts (New York: Robert M. McBride and Company, 1929), 23.

7. Michel de Montaigne, "Of Cannibals," in *Essays of Michel de Montaigne*, trans. Charles Cotton (New York: Doubleday, 1947), 63–77.

8. Whatley, "Introduction," to Lery, *History*, xx.

9. Bernadette Bucher, *Icon and Conquest: A Structural Analysis of De Bry's Great Voyages* (Chicago: University of Chicago Press, 1981), esp. 43–118.. See also *C*, 77.

10. Philip P. Boucher, *Cannibal Encounters: Europeans and Island Caribs, 1492–1763* (Baltimore, Md.: Johns Hopkins University Press, 1992), 18.

11. The major work on this subject is by J.-D. Penel, *Homo Cadautus* (Paris: Laboratoire de langues et civilizations, 1982).

12. Hulme, "Introduction," 16.

13. Ibid., 17.

14. Ibid., 18.

15. Cited in Hulme, "Introduction," 18–19.

16. See Marina Warner, *No Go the Bogeyman: Scaring, Lulling and Making Mock* (London: Chatto and Windus, 1998). Shakespeare's *Titus Andronicus* is well known for both the cannibal feast and the woman whose hands have been dismembered. The latter, Warner points out, "is a recurring, even stock topos in medieval romance and thence fairy tales, as is the ogre's cannibal feast" (60).

For a psychoanalytically oriented discussion of cannibalistic ogres in nurseries and stories, see Maria Tatar, *Off with Their Heads: Fairy Tales and the Culture of Childhood* (Princeton, N.J.: Princeton University Press, 1992), esp. ch. 9, "Table Matters: Cannibalism and Oral Greed," 190–211.

17. Roy Harvey Pearce, *Savagism and Civilization: A Study of the Indian and the American Mind* (Berkeley: University of California Press, 1988), revised version of his 1953 work, *The Savages of America*.

18. Ibid., 22.

19. Ibid., 31.

20. Ibid., 10–11; the phrase is from Richard Slotkin, *Regeneration through Violence:*

The Mythology of the American Frontier, 1600–1860 (Middletown, Conn.: Wesleyan University Press, 1973).

21. This literature has been recently reviewed in two important essays by Hayden White: "The forms of wildness: archaeology of an idea" and "The noble savage theme as fetish," in his *Tropics of Discourse: Essays in Cultural Criticism* (Baltimore, Md.: Johns Hopkins University Press, 1978), 156–82, 183–96. See also Richard Bernheimer, *Wild Men in the Middle Ages* (Cambridge, Mass.: Harvard University Press, 1952); Mary Campbell, *The Witness and the Other World* (Ithaca, N.Y.: Cornell University Press, 1988); Roger Batra, in his *Wild Men in the Looking Glass* (Ann Arbor: University of Michigan Press, 1994), reexamines this topic, though I am not persuaded by his thesis that the European experiences in the Americas lead to the erosion of the idea of the "wild man." Bernheimer has a neat summary of the wild man on the basis of depictions in art, literature, and sculpture:

> It is a hairy man curiously compounded of human and animal traits, without however sinking to the level of an ape. It exhibits upon its naked anatomy a growth of fur, leaving bare only its face, feet, and hands, at times its knees and elbows, or the breasts of the female of the species. Frequently the creature is shown wielding a heavy club or mace, or the trunk of a tree; and, since its body is usually naked except for a shaggy covering, it may hide its nudity under a strand of twisted foliage worn around the loins. (*Wild Men*, 1)

22. Margaret Hodgen, *Early Anthropology in the Sixteenth and Seventeenth Centuries* (Philadelphia, Pa.: University of Philadelphia Press, 1964), 409. The reference is to "The first English book on America," in Edward Arber, *The First Three English Books on America, 1511–1555 A.D.* (New York: Kraus Reprint, 1971), xxvii.

23. Hodgen, *Early Anthropology*, 366.

24. Cited in ibid., 367.

25. Campbell, *Witness*, 180.

26. Helen Wallis, "The Patagonian Giants," in *Byron's Journal and His Circumnavigation 1744–66*, ed. R. E. Gallagher (Cambridge: Cambridge University Press for the Hakluyt Society, 1964), Appendix iii, 185–96, 185. This fantasy, as Marina Warner points out, was widespread and goes into the Yeti, Abominable Snowman, Bigfoot, Sasquatch, and others. (Warner, *No Go the Bogeyman*, 97.) The fantasy of special beings with big feet is found even in religions like Buddhism where the Buddha's big foot is portrayed in grand style in pictorial, iconic, and literary representations.

27. Wallis, "Patagonian Giants," 186.

28. Ibid., 191.

29. This is P. Gleisberg a follower of Carl Vogt writing in 1864 and cited in Gus-

tav Jahoda, *Images of Savages: Ancient Roots of Modern Prejudice in Western Culture* (London: Routledge, 1999), 86, brackets in original. Examples of humans or part-humans with tails abound in Penel's work, and this includes Voltaire who took it seriously in his *The Singularities of Nature* (1766) and, as one would expect, rationally defended his views with evidence (Penel, *Homo Cadautus*, 54). In the late nineteenth century while much of this myth was being exploded a famous Norwegian explorer, Carl Bock went in search of them in Borneo. These were the Organg Buntut, and he urged the sultan of Pasir to find him a supply. The sultan's reply was that the tailed people were part of his retinue and anyone who wanted them would have to take them by force. This playful reply was in the spirit of much of cannibal responses as was the dead seriousness of the scholar. See, Kiki Bunder, "In Search of the Orang Buntut," *IIAS Newsletter* 8 (spring 1966): 33.

30. Bernard Smith, *European Vision and the North Pacific*, 2nd ed. (New Haven, Conn., and London: Yale University Press, 1985), 34–35.

31. Boucher, *Cannibal Encounters*, 1.

32. Peter Hulme, *Colonial Encounters: Europe and the Native Caribbean, 1492–1797* (London: Routledge, 1986), 86.

33. Francisco López de Gómara, *Cortés, the life of the conqueror by his secretary Francisco López de Gómara*, 1552, trans. Lesley Byrd Simpson (Berkeley: University of California Press, 1964), 293. For an indirect confirmation of Gomara from the man on the spot, see Bernal Diaz, *The Conquest of New Spain* (Harmondsworth, Eng.: Penguin, 1963), 406–7.

34. This field is outside of my area of competence but for a sensible review, see John Kantner, "Anazasi Mutilation and Cannibalism in the American Southwest," in *The Anthropology of Cannibalism*, ed. Laurence R. Goldman (Westport, Conn.: Bergin and Harvey, 1999), 75–104. For recent studies of Fijian cannibalism, see David DeGusta, "Fijian Cannibalism and Mortuary Ritual: Bioarchaeological Evidence from Vunda," *International Journal of Osteoarchaeology* 10 (2000): 76–92; and "Fijian Cannibalism: Osteological Evidence from Navatu," *American Journal of Physical Anthropology* 110, no. 2 (1999): 215–41. Although I have some criticisms of de Gusta's work, I believe it is on the right track and does not contradict my own stance on Fijian anthropophagy. I especially appreciate the distinction he makes between Vunda, which has no indication of "cannibalism," and Navatu, which does. For me the most responsible account of pre-contact Maori cannibalism is Ian Barber, "Archaeology, Ethnography, and the Record of Maori Cannibalism before 1815: A Critical Review," *Journal of the Polynesian Society* 101, no. 3 (September 1992): 241–92. While he does not deny Maori anthropophagy, he admits that "the general assumption of cannibalism on the basis of the site evidence is generally unconvincing and/or unnecessary" (279). I have two problems with archaeological studies, however, and these include those of the American Southwest.

The first is that of motivation or meaning I have already mentioned. Second, is the distinction between midden and human burial sites because it is in the middens, alongside of other junk, that broken bones indicative of cannibalism have been found and not in the formal burial sites. But, the fact is the enemies killed in battle are rarely if ever formally buried; hence it is not surprising that their broken body parts (either as a result of war or consumption or both) are found in middens and not in formal burial grounds. I do not know the implications of this critique for the archaeology of cannibalism.

35. A recent outstanding study is Beth A. Conklin, *Consuming Grief: Compassionate Cannibalism in an Amazonian Society* (Austin: University of Texas Press, 2002). Conklin relies on living informants commenting on a dead practice; hence, one has to view the data with some skepticism, especially the idea that the living ate "roasted" flesh of dead kinfolk. It may well be that the meat is both physically and symbolically transformed in the compassionate cannibalism of the Wari'. The Wari' do not themselves think of their practice as "cannibalism." More persuasive to me is the idea of roasted and ground bones found elsewhere in both Melanesia and South America. Conklin also cannot explain how the Wari' gave up their practice within a very few years without much protest.

36. Georges Bataille, *Erotism: Death and Sensuality*, trans. Mary Dalwood (San Francisco: City Lights Books, 1986), 63.

37. John Rickman, *Journal of Captain Cook's Last Voyage to the Pacific Ocean* (London: Newberry, 1781; Readex Microprint, 1966), 332.

38. Rickman, John. Log, Adm 51/4529/46 Public Records Office, London, 1779, entry for 1 March; Gananath Obeyesekere, *The Apotheosis of Captain Cook: European Mythmaking in the Pacific*, 2nd ed. (Princeton, N.J.: Princeton University Press, 1997), 72, 208.

39. "Mr. Broughton's narrative," in George Vancouver, *A Voyage of Discovery to the North Pacific Ocean and Round the World, 1791–1795*, ed. W. Kaye Lamb (London: The Hakluyt Society, 1984), vol. 1, 387 [379–92].

40. For a demythologization of the "innocent" Moriori of nineteenth-century scholars, see K. R. Howe, *The Quest for Origins: Who First Discovered and Settled the Pacific Islands* (Honolulu: University of Hawai'i Press, 2003), 164, 167, 181–82.

41. James Kenneth Munford, ed., *John Ledyard's Journal of Captain Cook's Last Voyage* (Corvallis: Oregon State University Press, 1963), 112–13.

42. William Hamlin, "Attributions of Divinity in Renaissance Ethnography and Romance, or, Making a Religion of Wonder," *Journal of Medieval and Renaissance Studies* 24 (1992): 415–47; see also his "Imagined Apotheoses: Drake, Herriot, and Raleigh in the Americas," *Journal of the History of Ideas* 57 (1996): 405–26; and my comments in the second edition of *The Apotheosis of Captain Cook*, 197–210.

43. López de Gómara, *Cortés*, 289.

44. Herman Melville, *Mardi: And A Voyage Thither, 1849* (New York: Signet Classics, 1964).

45. Ibid., see esp. chs. 41–58 and 128–30.

46. Melville, *Mardi,* 142. Subsequent references to *Mardi* will be cited with the abbreviation *M.*

47. For the Maori itself there is a great deal of "imaginary apotheoses" during first contact and later. Here is Ann Salmond on Tasman's visit. "It is possible that they [Maori] had decided that these [the Dutch] were spirits of some sort, since in early times when people were afraid of ghosts at night, they commonly blew trumpets and shouted to frighten them away" (Anne Salmond, *Between Worlds: Early Exchanges Between Maori and Europeans, 1773–1815* [Auckland: Penguin Viking, 1997], 78. This work is hereafter abbreviated as *BW*). Again: "Nor would Ngaati Tumatakokiri yet have been able to decide whether the Dutch were human, or perhaps white-skinned patupaiarehe (fairy folk) or some other kind of fabulous being." When Cook arrived, according to texts collected by later antiquarians, he and his crew were also viewed by Maori as "goblins." Presumably, Marion and his crew were also goblins, but then the question arises about their newly acquired taste: How did the Maori eat goblins? I am not dismissing the discourse on goblins because its genealogy could be understood in terms of other Maori myths, irrespective of whether they were foundational ones.

CHAPTER TWO: "BRITISH CANNIBALS"

1. James King, *A Voyage to the Pacific Ocean undertaken by the command of His Majesty, for making discoveries in the Northern Hemisphere,* 1784, 2nd ed. (London and Dublin: G. Nichol, 1785), 66.

The first two volumes of this work were by Captain Cook (edited somewhat drastically by Canon Douglas) and the third volume by James King (Cook having being killed in Hawai'i). These are the volumes that the British public was familiar with until the recent scholarly editions by J. C. Beaglehole, with the general title *The Journals of Captain Cook* in five volumes dealing with all three voyages with the following identifying subtitles: vol. 1, *The Voyage of the Endeavour, 1768–1771* (1968); vol. 2, *The Voyage of the Resolution and Adventure, 1772–1775*; vol. 3, part 1, *The Voyage of the Resolution and Discovery, 1776–1780* (1967); vol. 3, part 2, *The Voyage of the Resolution and Discovery, 1776–1780* (1967); and Vol. 4, *The Life of Captain James Cook* (1974) (Beaglehole's biography of Cook). All these volumes were published by the Hakluyt Society, London, by Cambridge University Press. In this book I will use the following abbreviations: the three 1785 editions will be referred to as *Cook D, 1, 2* and *3;* the later Beaglehole editions will be *Cook B 1* for the voyage of the *Endeavour; Cook B 2* for the *Resolution* and *Adventure; Cook B 3a* and *3b* for the two volumes dealing with the last voyage of the *Resolution* and *Discovery;* Beaglehole's biography of Cook is *Cook B 4*.

2. There is a slightly different version in *Cook B 3b*, 661, where King makes pretty much the same utterance but adds, "All our enquirys before convinced us pretty well that they were not cannibals." This must refer to King himself because Cook and Anderson both thought the Hawaiians were cannibals.

3. The crew was instructed by the admiralty to inform native chiefs who they were and why they were in a particular place. Thus, in Hawai'i and everywhere else Polynesians knew that the foreigners came from "Brittanee," contrary to ethnographic myth that imputes to the Hawaiians the idea that the British came from a mythic land known as Kahiki. In Hawai'i, the priest Koah changed his name to "Brittanee" in honor of the new arrivals.

4. I have dealt with this issue in detail in two places, first in *The Apotheosis of Captain Cook;* and more recently in *Imagining Karma: Ethical Transformation in Amerindian, Buddhist and Greek Rebirth* (Berkeley: University of California Press, 2002), 285–86.

5. Reported by William Anderson, "A Journal of a Voyage Made in His Majesty's Sloop Resolution," in *Cook B 3b* [723–986], 827.

6. Ibid., 837.

7. See Max Horkheimer and Theodor W. Adorno, *Dialectic of Enlightenment*, trans. John Cumming (New York: Continuum, 1989), 71.

8. Arthur Bryant, *Years of Victory 1802–1812* (London: The Reprint Society, 1945), 68–69. See also Iona Opie and Peter Opie, eds., *The Oxford Dictionary of Nursery Rhymes* (Oxford: Oxford University Press, 1951), 59, for minor variations and the inclusion of two extra stanzas.

9. Joseph Jacobs, *Little St. Hugh of Lincoln* (London: The Jewish Historical Society of England, 1893–94), 95. See also Thackeray's own cannibal poem, "Little Billy" in William Makepeace Thackeray, *Ballads and Critical Reviews*, vol. 1 (New York and London: Harper and Brothers, 1903), 103–4.

10. This mytheme appears in virtually so many well-known European fairy tales and nursery tales that one can only refer the reader to the work of the Opies, *Oxford Dictionary of Nursery Rhymes*, and also their edition of *The Classic Fairy Tales* (Oxford: Oxford University Press, 1974). For the movement of this and similar folklore mythemes into the contemporary Western world, see the work of Marina Warner, especially "Fee fie fo fum: The Child in the Jaws of the Story," in *Cannibalism and the Colonial World*, ed. Francis Barker, Peter Hulme, and Margaret Iverson (Cambridge: Cambridge University Press, 1998), 158–82; and developed fully in Marina Warner, *No Go the Bogeyman: Scaring, Lulling and Making Mock* (London: Chatto and Windus, 1998).

11. I use the term *paranoid lenses* to depict the mutual suspiciousness that exists

between groups or individuals during tense times. For details, see the concluding section of chapter 8, entitled "Cannibalism and the Paranoid Imagination."

12. "Draught of Instructions to Mr. Menzies, (Banks Papers)," in *Historical Records of New Zealand*, vol. 1, ed. Robert McNab (Wellington: Government Printer, 1908), 117 [115–18], hereafter volumes 1 and 2 of this work is abbreviated as *HR 1* and *HR 2*.

13. Reinhold Forster, *The Resolution Journal of Reinhold Forster*, 3:427; the four volumes were edited by Michael E. Hoare (London: The Hakluyt Society, 1982). It should be remembered that Banks himself started collecting heads in the very first voyage. See *The Endeavour Journal of Joseph Banks*, 1768–1771, 2 vols., ed. J. C. Beaglehold (Sydney: Angus and Robertson Ltd., 1962), 1:31 and 1:457.

14. Anne Salmond, *Between Worlds: Early Exchanges Between Maori and Europeans, 1773–1815* (Auckland: Penguin [Viking] [NZ], 1997), 94; hereafter abbreviated as *BW*.

15. George Forster, *A Voyage Round the World*, 1777, 2 vols. ed. Nicholas Thomas and Oliver Berghof (Honolulu: University of Hawai'i Press, 1999), 1:279. For a statement by a contemporary anthropologist who literally agrees with Forster, see Marshall Sahlins, "Cannibalism: An Exchange," *New York Review of Books*, 26, no. 4 (March 22, 1979): 47.

16. William Bayly's log entry is for December 18, the same date as Burney's log and one day after the massacre. However, the date of the log is not necessarily the date in which the entry was made. Journalists often insert into the appropriate place in the log accounts written much later. Bayly's reference to entrails is probably general shipboard consensus because Captain Furneaux also mentions "the entrails of five men lying on the beach," though how this could be figured out is dubious. Furneaux however reiterates Burney in saying there was only one head found, that of his servant (*Cook B 2*, 744). I think the only reliable account is Burney's.

17. John Marra, *Journal of the Resolution's Voyage in 1771–1775* (New York: De Capo Press, 1967 [1775]), 95.

18. The best evaluation of the events in Grass Cove are the two papers by Ian Barber, "Archaeology, Ethnography"; and the recent "Early Contact Ethnography and Understanding: An Evaluation of the Cook Expeditionary Accounts of the Grass Cove Conflict," in *Voyages and Beaches: Pacific Encounters, 1769–1840*, ed. Alex Calder, Jonathan Lamb, and Bridget Orr (Honolulu: University of Hawai'i Press, 1991), 156–79. Unfortunately, Barber tends to take texts at face value. However, Barber is right that the Grass Cove incident was not a premeditated conflict, but rather one that arose as a result of the tense situational interaction between Maori's of Wharehunga Bay and Rowe and his people.

19. Cited in *BW*, 84.

20. William Wales in *Cook B 2*, 790, Wales's italics.

21. Cited in *Cook B 2*, 790. This mimetic action so impressed the British that several mentioned it, including Furneaux in "Furneaux's Narrative," in Appendix 4 [729–45], *Cook B 2*, 740.

22. Ibid. All of Wales's citations are from the "Journal of William Wales," Appendix 5, in *Cook B 2*, 776–869.

23. See *BW* 322–24.

24. A. W. Brian Simpson, *Cannibalism and the Common Law* (Chicago: University of Chicago Press, 1984); and hereafter abbreviated as *CCL*.

25. Lord Byron, "Don Juan," Canto the second, stanzas LXXV, LXXVI, LXVII, and LXXXI, 1819, *Byron: Poetical Works* (London: Oxford University Press, 1967), 669–70.

26. Joseph Conrad, "Falk: A Reminiscence," in *Stories and Tales of Joseph Conrad* (New York: Funk and Wagnalls, 1968), 198–271.

27. Nathaniel Philbrick, *In the Heart of the Sea: The Tragedy of the Whaleship Essex* (London: Viking Penguin, 2000), 193.

28. Ibid., 102; see also 147.

29. Owen Chase, *Wreck of the Whaleship Essex: A Narrative Account by Owen Chase, First Mate*, edited by Iola Haverstuk and Betty Shepard (New York: Harcourt, Brace and World, 1965), 105. The whalers tend to be racially segregated. The blacks were confined to the forecastle, "the cramped, poorly lit quarters in the extreme forward part of the vessel, separated from steerage by the blubber room," while the Nantuckers and boatsteerers were in the steerage section forward of the officers quarters. "Reflecting the prejudices typical of a Nantucket whaleman, Thomas Nickerson considered himself 'fortunate indeed to escape being so closely penned up with so large a number of blacks' in the forecastle." Philbrick, *Heart of the Sea*, 34.

30. Philbrick, *Heart of the Sea*, 192.

31. I do not know how far this scenario is overdetermined by the idea that both blood and human flesh might have medicinal value. Marina Warner says that the drinking of human blood as an elixir had been advocated by an Italian scholar in the fifteenth century. She adds, "Medical literature continued to explore the theme; chemists mixed human blood, oil and flesh for invigorating powders and poultices in the seventeenth century," and the cadavers of criminals were also used for these purposes (*No Go the Bogeyman*, 132–33).

32. These phrases are scattered all over in the journals of Cook and his officers. The phrase "banquet of human flesh" goes back to at least Homer, *The Odyssey*, book 9, line 389. See translation by Robert Fagles (Harmondsworth, Eng.: Penguin, 1996), 222.

33. Michel de Certeau, *The Writing of History*, trans. Tom Conley (New York: Columbia University Press, 1988), 231. For more details, see de Certeau's essay,

"Ethno-Graphy. Speech, or the Space of the Other: Jean de Lery," 209–43, in *Writing of History*.

34. Reinhold Forster, *Observations Made During a Voyage Round the World* (London: G. Robinson, 1778), 77. For Hitihiti-Mahine's interest in curiosities, see George Forster, *Voyage Round the World*, 1:334, 1:339.

35. W. Ellis, *An Authentic Narrative of a Voyage Performed by Captain Cook and Captain Clerke in His Majesty's Ships "Resolution" and "Discovery" during the Years 1776, 1777, 1778, 1779, and 1780* (New York: Da Capo Press, 1969 [1782]), 1:192. Ellis was unaware or simply forgot to mention that these curiosities were bought during the first voyage itself.

36. Ellis, *Authentic Narrative*, 192.

37. Ibid., 202.

38. Banks, *Endeavour Journal*, 1:458.

39. Ibid., 457.

40. Banks, *Endeavour Journal*, 2:31.

41. R. Forster, *Resolution Journal*, 4:679.

42. Sydney Parkinson, *Journal of a Voyage to the South Seas in HMS Endeavour*, 1784 (London: Caliban Books, 1984), 20–21. Apparently Maori did eat native rats, but the Tahitians did not; in any case, Parkinson had no knowledge of rats as part of a native diet. Apparently rat hunting, if not rat eating, was a well-established British custom, as is evident from Jane Austen's *Persuasion* (London: Penguin Books, 1965), 224, where Mr. Musgrove says, "He [Mr. Benwick] is a brave fellow. I got more acquainted with him last Monday than ever I did before. We had a famous set-to at rat-hunting all the morning, in my father's great barns; and he played his part so well, that I have liked him better ever since." Chief Finau of Tonga, who also enjoyed rat hunting, seemed to have learned this art from his British colleagues.

43. John Rickman, *Journal of Captain Cook's Last Voyage to the Pacific Ocean* (London: Newberry, 1781; Readex Microprint, 1966), 232. Although new to these British officers, "fricasseed rats" seems to have been a French dish and consumed owing to starvation during the massacre of Sancerre. Jean de Lery invented recipes to render them palatable. It must surely have often occurred under conditions of starvation on ships and islands. See Jean de Lery, *History of a Voyage to the Land of Brazil*, 1580, trans. and intro. by Janet Whatley (Berkeley: University of California Press, 1992), "Introduction," xviii.

44. Banks, *Endeavour Journal*, 1:337.

45. R. Forster, *Resolution Journal*, 2:302.

46. Banks, *Endeavour Journal*, 1:322.

47. Ibid., 1:393; all italics are Banks's.

48. Ibid., 1:457.

49. Ibid., 1:292.

50. Ibid., 1:292–93.

51. Parkinson, *Endeavour Journal*, 20.

52. Ibid., 81.

53. Ibid., 122.

54. R. Forster, *Resolution Journal*, 2:303.

55. Ibid., 2:304.

56. Ibid., 2:318–19.

57. G. Forster, *Voyage Round the World*, 1:138; see also 1:135, where he says that "New Zealand dogs are fed on the remains of their masters' meals; they eat the bones of other dogs, and the puppies become true cannibals from their birth."

58. R. Forster, *Resolution Journal*, 2:304.

59. Ibid., 2:357. See also 2:349.

60. J. C. Beaglehole, in *Cook B 3a*, xcviii–xcix, citing George Home, *Memoirs of an Aristocrat* (London: Whittaker, 1838), 271–73. My italics indicate that it was desire for fresh meat that impelled Home and friends to eat dog.

Anne Salmond has a very interesting interpretation of the Rhio episode. Citing Robert Darnton she suggests that during this period "mock trial of animals was one way for subordinates (apprentices, sailors and so on) to express themselves on matters of justice, and the message of this one was clear. Cannibals, especially ones that chewed Europeans, should be 'doomed to death', but Cook was not of a mind to do it" (*BW*, 127). The reference is to Kahura who boldly claimed in Cook's presence that he was the one who killed Sergeant Rowe and his comrades in Grass Cove and perhaps ate them. But Salmond's hypothesis, though plausible, meets with a serious objection because the evidence of the journals suggest that it was not so much the sailors who demanded justice but Mai, Cook's Tahitian interpreter, and many of Kahura's envious fellow Maori, those belonging to other tribes. Indeed, Cook said, "[I]f I had followed the advice of all our pretended friends, I might have extirpated the whole race" of Maori (*Cook B 3a*, 62). Moreover, the mock trial was held by junior officers, not ordinary sailors, and it resulted not so much in a parody of justice but, insofar as the officers ate the dog, in a parody of cannibalism. Salmond graciously gave me a typescript of her early paper, "Tute: The Impact of Polynesia on Captain Cook," which I have used. As my book was going into press I was able to read the relevant parts of her new book, *The Trial of the Cannibal Dog: Captain Cook in the South Seas* (London: Penguin, 2003), 1–9.

61. Robert Darnton, "Workers Revolt: The Great Cat Massacre of the Rue Saint-Séverin," in his, *The Great Cat Massacre and other episodes in French Cultural History* (New York: Basic Books, 1984), 75–104.

62. Salmond quotes James Burney to substantiate her hypothesis of resentment by the young officers. "It seemed that many of them held us in great contempt and I believe chiefly on account of our not revenging the affair at Grass Cove, so contrary

to the principals by which they would have been actuated in the like case" *(Trial of the Cannibal Dog,* 4; *HR 2,* 199). Actually, the context of utterance here is more complicated. Here is the full text: "They [the Maori] often appeared to have a great deal of friendship for us, speaking sometimes in the most tender, compassionate tone of voice imaginable; but it not a little disgusted one to find all this show of fondness interested and that it constantly ended in begging. If gratified with their first demand, they would immediately fancy something else, their expectations and importunities increasing in proportion as they had been indulged. We had instances of them quarrelling after having begged 3 things, because a fourth was denied to them." Burney then adds that the Maori held them in contempt for not seeking revenge for the incident at Grass Cove but qualifies by saying that that their contempt might be due to another reason. Because they got so many valuable things from the ships they "regarded us dupes to their superior cunning" (*HR 2,* 198–99). Burney is qualifiedly giving two reasons for why the Maori held the British in contempt; he is not saying that he or the other officers believed that Kahura should be punished. One must also remember that no one on board knew for certain whether Kahura was the man responsible for the crime.

63. Byron, *Don Juan,* Canto the second, stanza LXX, *Poetical Works,* 669. Dog eating did occur in the Spanish traditions and perhaps elsewhere. Here is Bernal Díaz after one of their engagements with the Tlascans on their way to Mexico reporting in his *The Conquest of New Spain* (Harmondsworth, Eng.: Penguin, 1975): "We slept near a stream, and we dressed our wounds with the fat of a stout Indian whom we had killed and cut open, for we had no oil. We supped very well on some small dogs, which the Indians breed for food" (143; see also 160).

64. R. Forster, *Resolution Journal,* 4:599.

65. Reinhold Forster, *Observations Made During a Voyage Round the World,* eds., Nicholas Thomas, Harriet Guest, and Michael Dettelbach (Honolulu: University of Hawai'i Press, 1966), 211. George Forster makes the same point when he, with others, went to shoot some birds and reached a native plantation: "Here the natives began to make their threats, and, if possible, made it more plain to us than before, that we would be killed and eaten if we went on" (G. Forster, *Voyage Round the World,* 2:301).

66. Robert McNab, *From Tasman to Marsden: A History of Northern New Zealand from 1642 to 1818* (Denedin: J. Wilkes, 1914), 158; see also John Rawson Elder, *Letters and Journals of Samuel Marsden 1765–1838* (Dunedin: Otago University Council, 1932), 214–15; hereafter referred to as *LJS.* Governor Macquarie was initially reluctant to send Marsden to New Zealand, fearing that Maori might harm him (McNab, *From Tasman,* 163–64).

67. Tom Dutton, "'Successful Intercourse Was Had with the Natives': Aspects of European Contact Methods in the Pacific," in *A World of Language: Papers Presented*

to *Professor S. A. Wurm on His 65th Birthday*, ed. Donald C. Laycock and Werner Winter (Canberra: Dept. of Linguistics, Research School of Pacific Studies, Australian National University, 1987), 153–71.

68. George Robertson, *The Discovery of Tahiti: A Journal of the Second Voyage of H.M.S. "Dolphin" Round the World, under the Command of Captain Wallis, R.N., in the Years 1766, 1767, and 1768* (London: The Hakluyt Society, 1948), 137; cited in Dutton, "'Successful Intercourse,'" 158.

69. R. Forster, *Resolution Journal*, 4:595.

70. Ibid., 4:676.

71. Ibid.

72. W. Arens, *Man-Eating Myth: Anthropology and Anthropophagy* (New York: Oxford University Press, 1980), 21.

CHAPTER THREE: CONCERNING VIOLENCE

1. For an alternative view of the Grass Cove incident, see Ian Barber, "Early Contact Ethnography and Understanding: An Evaluation of the Cook Expeditionary Accounts of the Grass Cove Conflict," in *Voyages and Beaches: Pacific Encounters, 1769–1840*, ed. A. Calder, J. Lamb, and B. Orr (Honolulu: University of Hawai'i Press, 1999), 155–79.

2. John White, *The Ancient History of the Maori: His Mythology and Traditions*, vol. 1 (London: Sampson Low, Marston, Searle, and Rivington, 1889), 24.

3. Joseph Banks. *The Endeavour Journal of Joseph Banks*, 1768–1771, ed. J. C. Beaglehold (Sydney: Angus and Robertson Ltd., 1962), 1:401.

4. Ibid.

5. Ibid., 1:402.

6. Ibid.

7. This practice of understanding the other culture was an accepted convention in voyages of discovery; it was practiced by de Surville (*HR 2*, 257) and prior to that in Spanish voyages. It was continued in the British naval tradition when two Maori were brutally captured by Lieutenant Hanson under orders from Vancouver (who served under Cook) in 1792 and taken to Port Jackson and thence to Norfolk Island in order to instruct new settlers the art of weaving cloths from flax. "Vancouver's Instructions to Lieutenant Hanson," in *HR 1*, 160 [158–60]. Unhappily, these two young people knew little about flax!

8. Actually Banks has detailed and graphic descriptions of the violence in New Zealand during first contact. See Banks, *Endeavour Journal*, 1:399–443. His own conscience as he records in his journal on p. 403 is worth noting: "Thus ended the most disagreeable day My life has yet seen, black be the mark for it and heaven send that such may never return to embitter future recollection." And the very next sentence

which concludes the paragraph: "I forgot to mention in its proper place that we pickd up a large pumice stone floating in the bay in returning to the ship today, a sure sign that there either is or has been a Volcano in this neighbourhood." Conscience is a peculiar thing, and so is science.

9. Pickersgill in *Cook B 1* recollects the same event indicating the surreal nature of British fears, their demand for bones and the ghastly Maori supply of them:

> [W]e saw one of the Bodys and two arms with flesh upon them which we saw them eat this is the first proof positive we have had of the Inhabitants being CANNIBALS . . . who kill their fellow creatures purely for the meat . . . by their laying in wait one for another as a sportsman would for his game and they carry this detestable crime so far as to glory in carrying in their ears the thumbs of those unhappy sufferers who fell in their way. . . . [T]heir *[sic]* was a young girl seized upon by some people in the same bay and eat one morning whilst we were here and about two hours afterwards they brought the bones to sell to some of our people. (236, n. 1)

10. In addition to McNab's translation I use here a newer but less accessible translation by Isabel Olliver, in a series on the "Early Eyewitness Accounts of Maori Life." The Marion expedition is volume 2 of the series and is entitled *Extracts from Journals relating to the visit to New Zealand in May-July 1772 of the French ships Mascarin and Marquis de Castries under the command of M.-J. Marion du Fresne* (Wellington: Alexander Turnbull Library Endowment Trust, 1985). I find both translations close enough for me to retain McNab; in respect of important passages I shall also refer to Olliver's page references following my citation of McNab and with the abbreviation *EE*, so that the reader can refer to the newer translation. In one instance I use Olliver's translation because it made more sense than McNab's.

11. George Forster noted a similar propensity in 1773 in Tahiti in *Voyage Round the World*, 1:161. However, Forster might simply have mistaken admiration for simple curiosity. Yet, during the Vietnam War with the first influx of Americans to Thailand, young Thai women used to touch the white skin and then touch their own, magically transferring the color from one source to another.

12. Lawrence M. Rogers, *Te Wiremu: A Biography of Henry Williams* (Christchurch: Pegasus, 1973), 57, n. 14.

13. Barber, "Early Contact Ethnography," 172–73.

14. Brad Shore, "Mana and Tapu," in *Developments in Polynesian Ethnology*, ed. Alan Howard and Robert Borofsky (Honolulu: University of Hawai'i Press, 1989), 164 [137–73].

15. Alan Howard and John Kirkpatrick, "Social Organization," in *Developments in Polynesian Ethnography* (Honolulu: University of Hawai'i Press, 1989), 64, [47–94].

16. See Ranjini Obeyesekere, *Portraits of Buddhist Women: Stories from the Saddharmaratnavaliya* (Albany: State University of New York Press, 2001), 74. Cannibal stories abound in popular demon rituals in Sri Lanka.

17. Cook's interest is expressed in his second voyage during his visit to Tahiti in September 1773. Bougainville, he says, mentions human sacrifices in Tahiti, and in order to check him out he visited a marae in Matavai and his preliminary inquiries convinced him of its reality. See *Cook B 2*, 233–34.

18. For an identification of these places and names, see Cook B 3a, 198, nn. 1–6.

19. Beaglehole says that Cook was wrong in stating that the spirit of the *atua* entered the sacrificial victim; instead "the sacrifice formed a sort of spiritual food for the god." (*Cook B 3a*, 201, n. 2). But both interpretations have certain plausibility and they can also be reconciled.

20. Valerio Valeri, *Kingship and Sacrifice: Ritual and Society in Ancient Hawai'i*, trans. Paula Wissing (Chicago: University of Chicago Press, 1985), 228–30, 252.

21. Teuira Henry, *Ancient Tahiti* (Honolulu: Bernice P. Bishop Museum, 1828), 189. Teuira Henry's book is based on material collected by her grandfather, J. M. Orsmond in the early- and mid-nineteenth century.

22. Ian Barber, "Archaeology, Ethnography, and the Record of Maori Cannibalism before 1815: A Critical Review," *Journal of the Polynesian Society* 101, no. 3 (September 1992): 241–92.

23. R. W. Williamson, *Essays in Polynesian Ethnology* (New York: Cooper Square Publishers, 1975 [1939]), 13

24. Ibid., 14.

25. For an excellent discussion of the varieties of sacrifice in Tahiti and Tonga in the early years of the European incursions, see Meredith Filihia, "Rituals of Sacrifice in Early Post-European Contact Tonga and Tahiti," *Journal of the Polynesian Society* 34, no. 1 (1999): 5–22; see also Henry, *Ancient Tahiti*, 197–98.

26. Williamson, *Polynesian Ethnology*, 14–16.

27. William Mariner, *An Account of the Natives of Tonga Island . . . Communications of Mr. William Mariner*, compiled by John Martin (London: J. Martin, 1817), 1, 52. The relevant quote reads: "At this time a boy, who had just come into the canoe, pointed to a fire at a little distance, and addressing himself to Mr. Mariner, pronounced the word mate (meaning to kill), and made such signs that could give him to understand nothing less than the idea that he was to be killed and roasted."

28. Cook says, "These people [Tongans] stand in much fear of those of Fidgee, and no wonder sence the one is [a] Humane and peaceable Nation, whereas the other is said to be Canibals, brave, Savage and Cruel" (*Cook B 3a*, 163).

29. Mariner, *Tonga*, 1:345–46.

30. Ibid., 115.

31. Ibid., 116.

32. Ibid., 117.

33. Ibid., 203.

34. Ibid., 204.

35. Ibid.

36. Ibid., 104.

37. The first few chapters of Mariner's account are full of exact details and dates. This is because when the ship was captured by Finau he ordered all the papers and books aboard the ship to be burned. But Mariner smuggled the ship's journal under some matting so it wouldn't get burned and later gave it to his adopted mother, one of Finau's wives, for safe-keeping. Later on he hid it in, of all places, in the middle of a barrel of gunpowder! This accounts for the details of the voyage, though the vicissitudes of the journal sound too good to be true.

CHAPTER FOUR: SAVAGE INDIGNATION

1. This chapter's title is from W. B. Yeats's poem, "Swift's Epitaph."

2. Reinhold Forster, *Observations Made During a Voyage Round the World*, ed. Nicholas Thomas, Harriet Guest, and Michael Dettelbach (Honolulu: University of Hawai'i Press, 1996 [1778]), 287.

3. James Burney, *With Captain James Cook in the Antarctic and Pacific*, ed. Beverley Hooper (Canberra: National Library of Australia, 1975), 76–77.

4. Forster, *Observations*, 289.

5. "Wales's Journal," cited in *Cook B 2*, 842–43.

6. Cook pretty much admits it himself when in Nomuka, on the return trip home, an old lady gave him a girl "who did not want beauty," and roundly abused him "sneering in my face and saying what sort of man are you thus to refuse the embraces of so fine a young Woman" (*Cook B 2*, 444).

7. Mary Kawena Pukui, "Hawaiian Beliefs and Customs During Birth, Infancy, and Childhood," *Occasional Papers of the Bernice P. Bishop Museum* 16, no. 17 (1942): 371.

8. Douglas Oliver, *Ancient Tahitian Society*, 3 vols. (Honolulu: University of Hawai'i, 1975), 1:410–11.

9. Ibid., 410; the citation is from Edward Edwards and George Hamilton, *Voyage of the H.M.S. Pandora*, ed. Basil Thomson (London: Francis Edwards, 1915), 110.

10. S. Percy Smith, *Maori Wars of the Nineteenth Century*, 2nd ed. (Christchurch: Whitcombe and Tombs, 1910), 96–120; hereafter abbreviated as *MW*.

11. The phrase is from C. J. Rawson, *Gulliver and the Gentle Reader: Studies in Swift and Our Time* (London: Routledge, 1973), 1.

12. Ethnographic knowledge has it that Maori and Fijians used bones of cannibal victims as flutes and other musical instruments. None of the earliest sources mentions them; and I am not sure whether these were later inventions, especially fakes for European markets. The problem is that the Tupinamba and other Brazilian cannibals also used these for similar purposes. I am not sure whether the Polynesian's (and Caribs) invented this independently or whether this is a custom foisted on them by sailors, based on Europe's own antecedent history of using enemy bones as flutes. It is however possible that cannibal flutes were independently invented by the Caribs and Brazilians, or perhaps adopted after the European imputation to them of this custom.

13. Julia Blackburn, *The White Men: The First Response of Aboriginal Peoples to the White Man* (London: Orbis Publishing, 1979).

14. Only very recently, after I had read the paper by Kendrick Smithyman, did I realize that the original version of this text has not been found (Kendrick Smithyman, "Making History: John White and S. Percy Smith at Work," *Journal of the Polynesian Society* 88, no. 4 [1979]: 375–413). Smithyman has a beautiful genealogical analysis of this text, showing the emendations and fabrications in the several versions of Smith's text, itself borrowed from equally unreliable accounts in John White. However, Smithyman thinks there must have been an original text that White used or misused. The upshot of Smithyman's argument is that whatever this account might be, "it is not history" (411). Of course he is right; it is surely not history but a deliberate antihistory by a native informant, and it possesses a logic of its own. I suspect that the spoof part of this text did come from a native informant originally and that Smith's retelling preserves the spirit of the original and perhaps much of the contents also.

15. Thomas Love Peacock, *The Misfortunes of Elphin and Rhododaphne* (London: Macmillan, 1897), 82.

16. Edward Tregear, *The Maori Race* (Manganni, New Zealand: A. D. Willis, 1926).

17. Ibid., 358.

18. Ibid.

19. Bowden, "Maori Cannibalism: An Interpretation," *Oceania* 55 (1984): 82 [81–99].

20. A. P. Vayda, *Maori Warfare* (Wellington, NZ: The Polynesian Society, 1960), 94.

21. Ibid., 97.

22. Theodore de Bry was one of the most famous and well known of travel writers, and this volume was published in Frankfurt in 1593.

23. Elsdon Best, "Notes on the Art of War as Conducted by the Maori of New Zealand," *Journal of the Polynesian Society* 12 (1903): 16.

24. Tregear, *Maori Race*, 357.

25. Ibid.

26. Bowden, "Maori Cannibalism," 87.

27. Cited in Vayda, *Maori Warfare,* 95.

28. The italicization in the last few sentences is all mine.

29. Best, "Notes on the Art of War," 3.

30. Elsdon Best, *The Maori,* 2 vols. (Wellington: Harry H. Tombs, 1924), 2:299.

31. Ibid., 555.

32. Ibid., 338.

33. Ibid., 251.

34. Raymond Firth, *The Economics of the New Zealand Maori* (Wellington: Government Printer, 1959), 148.

35. Vayda, *Maori Warfare,* 68.

36. Jules Verne, *Among the Cannibals* (London: Arco Publications, 1964). This is the second part of a larger adventure story, entitled *Captain Grant's Children.* For the horrendous discourses on Maori cannibalism, see Verne, *Among the Cannibals,* 91, 120–33.

37. Bowden, "Maori Cannibalism," 82.

38. Ibid.

39. Peggy Reeves Sanday, *Divine Hunger: Cannibalism as a Cultural System* (Cambridge: Cambridge University Press, 1986), 9–10.

40. Extract from "Evangelical Magazine" for 1821, in *HR 1,* 573–74.

41. J. M. R. Owens, *Prophets in the Wilderness: The Wesleyan Mission to New Zealand 1819–27* (Auckland: Auckland University Press, 1974), 19.

42. Ibid.

43. Ibid.

44. Ibid., 28.

45. Ibid., 16.

46. Ibid., 17.

47. Ibid., 29–30.

48. Ibid., 27.

49. Ibid., 26.

50. For the heroization of Leigh, see Alexander Strachan, *Remarkable incidents in the Life of Rev. Samuel Leigh, missionary to the settlers and savages of Australia and New Zealand* (London: Hamilton and Co., 1853).

51. Vayda, *Maori Warfare,* 70.

52. Sigmund Freud, "Leonardo da Vinci and a Memory of his Childhood," in *Standard Edition,* vol. 11 (London: The Hogarth Press, 1981 [1910]), 63–137.

53. Vayda, *Maori Warfare,* 70.

54. George Clarke, *Notes on Early Life in New Zealand* (Hobart, NZ: Walch, 1903), 15–16.

CHAPTER FIVE: THE LATER FATE OF HEADS

1. Herman Melville, *Moby Dick* (London: Penguin Books, 1994 [1850]), 37, 36.

2. For a sympathetic account of Marsden, see A. T. Yarwood, *Samuel Marsden, the Great Survivor* (Melbourne: Melbourne University Press, 1996).

3. Paul Turnbull, "'Rare Work among the Professors': The Capture of Indigenous Skulls within Phrenological Knowledge in Early Colonial Australia," in *Body Trade: Captivity, Cannibalism and Colonialism in the Pacific*, ed. Jeannette Hoorn and Barbara Creed (New York: Routledge, 2001), 5–23.

4. Judith Binney, *The Legacy of Guilt: A Life of Thomas Kendall* (Oxford: Published for the University of Auckland, 1968), 63.

5. Ibid.

6. Ibid., 64.

7. Ibid.

8. Robert McNab, *From Tasman to Marsden: A History of Northern New Zealand from 1642 to 1818* (Dunedin: J. Wilkie, 1914), 112.

9. Ibid., 115.

10. Ibid., 130.

11. Ibid., 201–2.

12. John Savage, *Some Account of New Zealand; particularly The Bay of Islands and Surrounding Country* (London: John Murray, 1807), 35.

13. Ibid.

14. Ibid.

15. Savage's short book is one of the most sympathetic, indeed empathic, early accounts of New Zealand I have read. His book gives a vivid account of young Mohanga's reaction to the world outside his home, never fazed by it, but maintaining a great sense of dignity and self-worth. It is to Savage's credit that he sent his friend home before he got overwhelmed by English culture and prejudice.

16. Ibid., 56.

17. Ibid., 27.

18. Song composed by Tamarah of Ngati-Whatua on the death of Hongi Hika, lamenting the destruction caused by guns (*MW*, 400).

19. Angela Ballara, *Taua: 'Musket Wars,' 'Land Wars,' or Tikanga? Warfare in Maori Society in the Early Nineteenth Century* (Auckland: Penguin, 2003), 411; hereafter abbreviated as *T.* Ballara's book is the latest in a continuing debate on whether muskets caused the destruction that colonial scholars and missionaries had claimed. The most recent work on supporting such a claim is R. D. Crosby, *The Musket Wars: A History of Inter-Iwi Conflict, 1806–45* (Auckland: Reed Publishing, 1999). Although Crosby is a mine of information, his work is devoid of bibliographical references, which makes it almost useless for scholarly research. New Zealand historians have written serious

articles on this issue: K. R. Howe's detailed case history from the Loyalty Islands in New Caledonia suggests strongly that the number of deaths from firearms have been exaggerated but notes the cultural significance of the new weaponry. However, as Howe recognizes, a single case history in New Caledonia does not make the case for similar results elsewhere. See "Firearms and Indigenous Warfare: A Case History," *Journal of Pacific History* 9 (1974): 38. An early and important paper is by D. U. Urlich, "The Introduction and Diffusion of Firearms in New Zealand 1800–1840," *Journal of the Polynesian Society* 79, no. 4 (1970): 399–410, where he deals with the spread of guns from "innovation centers" to other areas until they reached saturation when virtually everyone owned guns, a thesis that Howe, above, has criticized. Finally, a balanced article by Paul D'Arcy gives a larger Polynesian perspective to muskets and their significance, in his "Maori and Muskets from a Pan-Polynesian Perspective," *New Zealand Journal of History* 34, no. 1 (2000): 117–32. Equally balanced is James Belich's account of "the musket wars" in *Making Peoples: A History of the New Zealanders: From Polynesian Settlement to the End of the Nineteenth Century* (Auckland: Penguin, 1996), 156–64.

20. In Judith Binney, *The Legacy of Guilt: A Life of Thomas Kendall* (Oxford: Published for the University of Auckland, 1968).

21. For details, see Ranguini Walker, *Ka Whawhai Tonu Matou, Struggle Without End* (Auckland: Penguin, 1990), 82–84.

22. Harrison M. Wright, *New Zealand, 1769–1840: Early Years of Western Contact* (Cambridge, Mass.: Harvard University Press, 1959), 91.

23. Elsdon Best, "Notes on the Art of War as Conducted by the Maori of New Zealand," *Journal of the Polynesian Society* 12 (1903): 12 [1–19].

24. Elsdon Best, *The Maori* (Wellington, NZ: Harry H. Tombs, 1924), 2:285.

25. A. P. Vayda, *Maori Warfare* (Wellington, NZ: The Polynesian Society, 1960), 22–24.

26. Ranguini Walker is probably right when he estimates a decline of about 40 percent by 1840, but all such estimates remain guesswork (Ranguini Walker, *Ka Whawhai Tonu Matou,* 80). For further details, see Ballara, *Taua,* 45–46.

27. Walker, *Ka Whawhai Tonu Matou,* 83.

28. Best, *Maori,* 2:234.

29. Howe, "Firearms," 25.

30. D'Arcy, "Maori and Muskets," 129.

31. Ibid., 121. As with Polynesia, guns in Sri Lanka formed part of the panoply of the retinue of the king, and on the more practical side, kings began to have their own regiments of gunners. Initially, kings captured or enticed Europeans to serve them as gunners; soon expert indigenous marksmen emerged.

32. Belich, *Making Peoples,* 206.

33. I am deeply indebted to Ballara's book, which helped me to reformulate my

own thinking in this section. *Taua* is enviable in its scrupulous regard for empirical detail and, especially for a nonspecialist like me, for its fine discussions of traditional warfare and especially Maori "peace-making techniques." However, there are serious weaknesses that I hope she, or some younger scholar, would eventually address. The subtitle of her work is "*'Musket Wars,' 'Land Wars,' or Tikanga? Warfare in Maori Society in the Early Nineteenth Century.*" The problem lies right there: surely the war parties, or *taua*, in the nineteenth century were all of this; any "either this or that" phrasing of the issue is a mistake. Ballara says that muskets had an accelerating effect on warfare but did not play a causal role. However, muskets do not "cause" wars anywhere; in practical, though not in symbolic terms, they are a technology of warfare implicated in larger discursive actions. Ballara says that wars provided "a significant check on population growth, though not as great as some accounts would have us believe" (12). But the question still has to be answered: How significant? Again, the "cultural determinants of Maori warfare were ancient, continuing and still largely unchanged by 1840 despite the creeping infiltrating and internalization of exotic ideas" (14). Here anthropologists must share the blame for reifying "culture" and perhaps even contributing to the idea of a static unchanging culture in the face of such events as the impact of colonialism and the world system. Ballara also believes that bloody wars were an ancient phenomenon: "[S]ome of the bloodiest battles involving large numbers of fighting men moving over long distances took place in the late eighteenth century or in the first decade of the nineteenth, a generation before muskets had been introduced" (23). She mentions two wars, one in 1807 and another around 1793. But surely these wars occurred long *after* the arrival of Europeans and the beginnings of trade. In the former war about sixteen thousand men participated and "so many chiefs died that it was called the 'Fall of Parrots', a name which compared the many chiefly casualties alone to the results of a pre-contact hunt for parrots for a feast, in which hundreds of birds might be killed in a single drive." In the later 1793 war "so many Bay of Islanders were killed by a combined taua of Ngati Paoa and Ngati Maru that their bodies could be used to build a causeway across a swamp in order to attack a *pā*" (23). But if she is right, and if one considers the numbers of the dead in the wars that appear in her work, and if all of these were "traditional," then I doubt many Maori would be left to fight wars.

There is a further problem in Ballara, the idea that while Western colonial historians have misunderstood the nature of warfare, not so with "traditional" historians whose voices come mostly from late colonial land records. But one can make an argument that the will to acquire land, an increasingly scarce resource owing to new crops and plantations and the usurpation or buying of land by whites, must be seen in terms of the Maori movement into capitalism. (See Belich, *Making Peoples*, 225–27, for details of land grabbing.) Therefore one must confront the reliability of these records for constructing the past. If colonial historians invented Maori tradition, then one must recognize that Maori historians could also, and with good reason, invent or reinvent their traditions. The literature on the invention of traditions must be an embarrassment to Ballara. The Maori of Ballara live in a kind of ethnographic time capsule; colonialism has made little or no difference to their warfare, their thinking, or their lives. Her work also exists in a theoretical time capsule; not a single older or contemporary writer in the human sciences or of historiography appears in her work.

34. Best, *Maori*, 2:21–22, 2:60, 2:386–387, 2:555. See also Elsdon Best, *Maori Religion and Mythology* (Wellington, NZ: Government Printer, 1924, Dominion Museum Bulletin, #10), 140–90, which has detailed accounts of human sacrifices for the following: new canoes, new pā, on the death of a chief, during war, and for the dubious case of agriculture.

35. Ross Bowden, "Maori Cannibalism: An Interpretation," *Oceania* 55, no. 2 (Dec. 1984): 96.

36. The fear of colonization began quite early. Several chiefs of the east coast visited Port Jackson (New South Wales); they knew of colonization there firsthand; Norfolk Island to the north and west of New Zealand was also a white penal colony they knew about. Even more germane: several important chiefs, among them Ruatara, Korokoro, and Hongi of the Bay of Islands area, were with Marsden just before he sailed with them to New Zealand in 1814. Here some people (we do not know who) told these chiefs that the British would colonize New Zealand and the Maori would lose their lands and become slaves of the whites. This put Ruatara into a deep depression (McNab, *From Tasman*, 159). Marsden, somewhat disingenuously, told the chiefs that this would never happen, but even if Ruatara believed in him, it is not likely that Hongi did (*LJS*, 171–72).

37. Gavan Daws, *A Dream of Islands: Voyages of Self-Discovery in the South Seas* (New York: W. W. Norton and Company, 1980), 109–10. The quotation marks are from Melville's *Moby Dick*.

38. The references to lances, javelins, knights, and squires are found in several places but see especially, 124–28 in a chapter entitled "Knights and Squires"; demigorgons on 172; and Perseus, St. George, and dragons on 348–50. The two main chapters used by Gavin Daws are chapter 95, "The Cassock" and the wonderful chapter 96, "The Try-Works." All page references are to the Penguin Popular Classics, 1994.

39. Melville, *Moby Dick*, 212.

40. Ibid.

41. Nathaniel Philbrick, *In the Heart of the Sea: The Tragedy of the Whaleship Essex* (London: Viking Penguin, 2000), 13.

42. Ibid.

43. Ibid.

44. Cited in Philbrick, *Heart of the Sea*, 65.

45. For details, see Harrison M. Wright, "Whalers and Traders," in *New Zealand, 1769–1840: Early Years of Western Contact* (Cambridge, Mass.: Harvard University Press, 1959), 19–37; *BW*, 314–30.

46. Robert McNab, *The Old Whaling Days: A History of Southern New Zealand from 1830 to 1840* (Auckland: Golden Press, 1975 [1913]), 1; hereafter abbreviated as *OWD*. For a comprehensive bibliography, see Honore Forster, *The South Sea Whaler: An Annotated Bibliography* (Sharon, MA: Kendall Whaling Museum, 1985).

47. Ibid., 22. My guess is that Kapiti Island had come into prominence in Cook's own time when a brisk interchange of goods and services took place there because it was the "entry" to Cook's favorite landing place, Queen Charlotte Sound. For further details on Kapiti Island, see the uneven history by W. Carkeek, *The Kapiti Coast: Maori History and Place Names* (Wellington, NZ: A. H. and A. W. Reed, 1966).

48. Ballara, *Taua*, 338; and Urlich, "Introduction and Diffusion," 407. For details of this remarkable migration, see Patricia Burns, *Te Rauparaha: A New Perspective* (Auckland, NZ: A. W. Reed, 1980), esp. 81–102; Ballara, *Taua*, 315–54; and W. T. L. Travers, *The Stirring Times of Te Rauparaha* (Christchurch: Whitcombe and Tombs, 1926), 80–128.

49. Urlich, "Introduction and Diffusion," 407. Wright says, "The number of tons leaving Sydney for London jumped from 60 in 1828, to 841 in 1830, and 1062 in 1831" (*New Zealand, 1769–1840*, 28). It steadily declined thereafter.

50. Salmond's explorers were from the Bay of Islands area, and contrary to Salmond, their fates were grim indeed. Salmond gives a detailed picture of Teina at Port Jackson whose governor was Philip Gidley King, a friend of the Maoris. Teina stayed at Government House from early June to mid-September 1803, then he went to Norfolk Island. Along with another Maori named Maki, he visited Tahiti and from there went to Brazil, then to St. Helena, until their ship, the *Alexander*, arrived in London in June 1806. Neither Teina nor Maki were paid for their work. They had little food and clothing, so that Teina soon fell ill and died. And Maki? "Shortly after, however, Maki was kidnapped by a notorious crimp (an agent who supplied labour to the ships) and sold to work for the captain of another British vessel" (*BW*, 325). I have no information on the eventual fate of poor Maki.

Te Pahi, one of the most famous of Maori chiefs, was a friend of both Governor King and of Samuel Marsden. He sent one of his sons, Maa-Taara, first to Port Jackson and on a second voyage to London to see the king and seek foreign aid for development of New Zealand (*BW*, 360). Maa-Taara did not see the king but managed to see Banks before he got back to Sydney. He was not destined to live long as he had contracted a lung disease in London (on account of the London fog or because of a lack of one) and died soon after.

George Bruce and his wife Atahoe were another set of explorers mentioned by

Salmond. George Bruce was a white who nursed Te Pahi during a long voyage from Norfolk Island to New Zealand but was flogged for theft, disobedience, and embezzlement and ran ashore and soon married Te Pahi's youngest daughter, Atahoe (*BW*, 356–57). In October 1807 *General Wellesley* commanded by one of the most brutal captains, Dalrymple, with chief officer James Ceroni arrived in the Bay of Islands. I refer to Salmond's account for details, but eventually Atahoe was brutally treated by sea captains and in one voyage simply became a servant for a woman passenger from Sydney (*BW*, 364). Later Dalrymple sailed with his wife to Penang, where he sold Atahoe to a Captain Ross as a slave for his own wife (*BW*, 365). Bruce did manage to get back to Penang; eventually the loving couple went to Bengal seeking passage to New Zealand; during the voyage Atahoe went into labor where she delivered a daughter. But the Captain instead of delivering them to New Zealand took them to Dervent; Atahoe died in Port Jackson a few weeks later on February 27, 1810, at age eighteen. I do not want to go into the details of Bruce's own saga except to say that he did go to London and begged for a living, an object of scorn because of his facial tattoos. How this couple could be labeled "explorers" is difficult to imagine.

Te Ruatara was a close relative of Te Pahi and the warrior Hongi Hika and a member of the local aristocracy. Marsden, who wanted to start a mission in New Zealand, found Ruatara and made friends with him. With the commencement of the whaling season of 1805, Ruatara joined the *Argo* with two other Maori whose captain discharged him at Port Jackson without pay. But the lure of travel no doubt enticed him to join other whalers. In one trip he was dumped in one of the Bounty Islands along with other unwanted natives including ten Europeans. Without clothing and proper food they lived for a year by eating seals and sea birds and drinking rainwater until provisions were provided by another whaler, *King George*. Finally the *Santa Anna* collected the survivors with their harvest of 8,000 seal skins. There "he was forced to work without pay and was beaten and abused by the captain," but he did manage to get to London hopefully to see the king (*BW*, 410). To his dismay, this was not possible; he was without adequate clothes either but managed to be shipped back in the *Ann* where Marsden found him "wrapped in his great-coat and spitting up blood" (*BW*, 410). Marsden and some missionaries nursed him back to health which, says Salmond, resulted in "their hau and Ruatara's [being] brought together" (*BW*, 411). I don't know how Salmond figured the hau of this affair. Owing to complicated political reasons, Ruatara worked in Marsden's extensive estates along with some English artisans being trained for future hard work as missionaries. Ruatara's wife was anxious to have him back, and Ruatara persuaded Marsden to send him home on the *Frederick*. It just happened that the captain refused to drop him off at the Bay of Islands where they had stopped for provisions! Instead the ship went to Norfolk

Island; Ruatara nearly drowned there, but the ship sailed to England without paying Ruatara anything (*BW*, 423). He was given a ride to Port Jackson and after five months at sea came back home to be joyously welcomed by his people. There he planted wheat from the seeds given to him by Marsden. Not a bad ending, but surely he was no explorer.

The only explorer who managed to come back with some dignity is Te Mohanga or Te Mahanga, who went with John Savage to London in 1806 and who appears elsewhere in this chapter. He did manage to see the now decrepit king and queen. Consequently, he was later called King Charley. He often acted as an interpreter to Marsden and others. Later he traveled with another famed "explorer" Peter Dillon. Not exactly the life of an explorer, but not a bad one either.

51. Such violence was not exclusively directed to savage monsters. McNab has an ugly example of a sea captain treating his own crew as if they were savages (see *OWD*, 14–17).

52. The term *synchronicity* was developed by Jung to designate the manner in which physical and psychical events are interconnected not through causality but by a spiritual affinity. His example was divination where coincidence is not a matter of chance but an interdependence of events that can also connect with the subjective or psychic state of the observer. I use it in a much narrower sense to designate the psychic interdependence of people interacting with each other.

53. McNab, *From Tasman*, 579.

54. See depositions of Pery and Brown, *HR 2*, 582–83, 584–86.

55. The other instance I know where fingers are collected as mementos is that of Jean-Jacques Dessalines, the first president of Haiti and its emperor who was murdered in October 17, 1806, and mutilated and whose fingers were collected for sale by American merchants. See Joan Dayan, "Haiti, History, and the Gods," in *After Colonialism: Imperial Histories and Postcolonial Displacements*, ed. Gyan Prakash (Princeton, N.J.: Princeton University Press, 1994), 74. A Reuter's report for October 19, 2003, in the *Island*, a Sri Lankan newspaper, informs us that a U.S. unit in Vietnam not only tortured and killed civilians but also severed ears and scalps for souvenirs. More recently *The New York Times* of Sunday, December 24, 2003, mentions American soldiers in Vietnam who "gunned down men, women and children, sometimes mutilating bodies—cutting off ears to wear on necklaces" ("National" sect., 24).

56. My interpretation here differs from most New Zealand scholars who have seen Te Rauparaha's heke, or migration, down to Kapiti in traditional terms as utu and take, though in reality Patricia Burns's book *Te Rauparaha: A New Perspective* suggests much more complex economic motivations at work. Most New Zealand scholars would strongly object to my characterization of Te Rauparaha as the "new man." The detailed accounts of this complex and commanding personality are found in Burns, *Te*

Rauparaha, but this and an earlier study, Travers, *Stirring Times of Te Rauparaha*, tend to heroize Te Rauparaha. A balanced study of this national icon is long overdue.

57. For Rauparaha's alcoholism, see Carkeek, *The Kapiti Coast*, 99, and ch. 8, 75–91, for his role in the resistance. James Belich does not mention him in his authoritative *The New Zealand Wars* (Harmondsworth, Eng.: Penguin, 1988), though he does refer to him in his recent *Making Peoples*.

58. Bowden says that "food and all things associated with its preparation were profane (and thus potentially polluting and degrading of tapu)" ("Maori Cannibalism," 91). Further, "high ranking men . . . never went near cooking huts and steam ovens" And domestic cooking was by women and slaves (ibid., 92). In some instances even the act of ordinary eating became problematic for chiefs, and they had to use a "primitive fork" to put food into the mouth.

59. Carkeek, *Kapiti Coast*, 49.

60. Belich, *Making Peoples*, 171.

CHAPTER SIX: CANNIBAL FEASTS IN NINETEENTH-CENTURY FIJI

1. This is chapter 26, in Herman Melville, *The Confidence Man: His Masquerade* (New York: Signet, 1964), 151–59. Melville's Colonel Moredock who hates Indians "like snakes" is an isolated figure carrying out his lonely destructive fate. Whereas in my work Indian hating is communal like black hating or Jew hating or Arab hating. Among settlers in strange lands "Indian hating" in a nonliteral sense is everywhere based on the metaphysics of savagism.

2. Anthony Padgen, *The Fall of Natural Man: The American Indian and the Origins of Comparative Ethnology* (Cambridge: Cambridge University Press, 1986), 73–74, 134–35. Padgen does not use the term "metaphysics of savagism," though, in my view, his thinking nicely highlights that idea.

3. Ibid., 174–76; the major works of Vitoria was 1526–37; of Las Casas around 1552, and of Acosta, whose work heralded what Padgen calls "comparative ethnology," between 1573–77.

4. Ibid., 164.

5. Judith Binney, *The Legacy of Guilt: A Life of Thomas Kendall* (Oxford: Published for the University of Auckland, 1968), 72.

6. Thomas Williams, *Fiji and the Fijians* (London: Alexander Heylin, 1858; reprint, Suva: Fiji Museum, 1982, with a new introduction by Fergus Clunie), 53.

7. Ibid., 213.

8. Walter Lawry, *Friendly and Feejee Islands: a missionary visit to various stations in the south seas in the year MDCCCXLVII* (London: Charles Gilpin, 1850), 88–93.

9. Ibid., 92.

10. Ibid., 96.

11. Marshall Sahlins, "Cannibalism: An Exchange," *New York Review of Books* 26, no. 4 (March 22, 1979): 47.

12. Ibid., 46–47.

13. John Jackson, "Jackson's Narrative," Appendix A in John Elphinstone Erskine, *Journal of a Cruise Among the Islands of the Western Pacific . . .*, 1853 (London: Dawson, 1967), 426–27.

14. Basil Thomson, in *The Fijians: A Study in the Decay of Custom* (London: William Heinemann, 1908), 104–9, mentions the use of these forks and that during his time there was an industry in fakes because "genuine forks" were not available. I do not know whether cannibal forks was a European invention as Arens suggests, or whether it was modeled on the European by Fijians, or whether it was a precontact practice. In Europe of Homer's time five pronged forks were used in their animal sacrifices, and it might well be that a similar function obtained in Fiji. The sacred (tapu) chiefs had to be fed by others, but because even this action might entail touching the chief, forks might have become a useful culinary implement. The use of forks does not imply they were cannibal forks, though they could have been put to this purpose in the context of human sacrifice also. This whole question merits serious archaeological and curatorial investigation, as with the bone flutes of cannibal victims.

15. Fergus Clunie, *Fiji Weapons and Warfare* (Suva, Fiji: Bulletin of the Fiji Museum, 1977).

16. Peggy Reeves Sanday, *Divine Hunger: Cannibalism as a Cultural System* (Cambridge: Cambridge University Press, 1986), 151.

17. William Endicott, *Wrecked Among the Cannibals in the Fijis: A Narrative of Shipwreck and Adventure in the South Seas* (Salem, Mass.: Marine Research Society, 1923), 55; hereafter this work will be abbreviated as *WC*.

18. Clunie, *Fiji Weapons*, 37.

19. According to Albert J. Schutz, this phrase is probably a corruption of "a bokola boi ca," which means "stinking corpse to be eaten."

20. See also Clunie, *Fiji Weapons*, 38.

21. Oliver wrote two books: the title of the first book is called *Wreck of the Glide with an account of Life and Manners at the Fiji Islands* (Boston: William D Ticknor and Co., 1846). It has up to chapter xi, whereas the 1848 addition has up to chapter xxv, which is mostly about Wallis Island and Hawai'i. The second is James Oliver and William G. Dix, *Wreck of the Glide with Recollections of the Fijis and of Wallis Island* (New York: Wiley and Putnam, 1848). Both have the Fijian cannibal feast. The 1846 edition tells us very little about the author; only the 1848 edition does. I use the latter, abbreviated as *WG*.

22. Marshall Sahlins, "Artificially Maintained Controversies: Global Warming and Fijian Cannibalism," *Anthropology Today* 19, no. 3 (June, 2003): 3, n. 3 [3–5].

23. William S. Cary, *Wrecked on the Feejees* (Fairfield, Wa.: Ye Galleon Press, n.d.); hereafter referred to as *WF.*

24. Oliver's 1848 edition has a brief unpaginated preface by James Oliver in which he says that though the events occurred in 1832 it was written during a three-month residence in Oahu and that "the narrative is for the most part the production of my memory." However, he says that Messrs. E [Endicott], P[Poole], and F[Fowler], his shipmates in the Glide "favored me with a perusal of their manuscripts." He used E's logbook from which he has taken his dates, but Endicott's log has no reference to a cannibal feast. The preface is dated November 11, 1844, and the author died in January 1845, according to the extension of the preface written by his brother William G. Dix. William Dix helped his brother to write the original account but also adds, "Some extracts from the manuscripts of my brother's shipmates, who kindly submitted them for the purpose, have been interwoven with the original narrative, being transformed into its general style, for resemblance of expression."

25. Sahlins, "Artificially Maintained Controversies," 3–4, n. 3.

26. Owing to the bad state of the Fowler manuscripts I regret I will not be able to use page references.

27. Erskine, *Journal,* 173.

28. Herman Melville, *Typee* 1846 (Hammondsworth, Eng.: Penguin, 1972), 193.

29. William Diapea (alias John Jackson), *Cannibal Jack: The True Autobiography of a White Man in the South Seas,* ed. James Hadfield (London: Faber and Faber, 1928), xvi; hereafter abbreviated as *CJ.*

30. Melville, *Typee,* 33.

31. Greg Dening, *Islands and Beaches: Discourse on a Silent Land* (Honolulu: University of Hawai'i Press, 1980), 129–56.

32. The title of the book as conceived by its author reads as follows: "A Few Extracts From The Autobiography of William Diapea Alias 'Cannibal Jack.' These Extracts Embrace The Long Gone-by Years of 1843 Up To 1847—The Last Inclusive." For details on Jack's "sobriquet" and references to him by those who met him, see my earlier paper with the same title in *Cannibalism and the Colonial World,* 265–66, nn. 6, 8, 9. For a truly entertaining account of Cannibal Jack, see W. Wyatt Gill, *Jottings from the Pacific* (London: The Religious Tract Society, 1885), in a section entitled "White Cannibals," 242.

33. Cannibal Jack refers to the "reader" several times pointing clearly a literate audience given to reading books. "The reader may be tempted to think . . ." (*CJ,* 79); "the difficulty with the reader of these extracts . . ." (90).

34. "Jackson's Narrative" has clear reference to dates: the adventures start in Samoa in 1840 and continue into 1841 and 1842, both dates being mentioned. The adventures in *Cannibal Jack* start in 1843 with the Bonaveidogo episode, which, accord-

ing to the previous text, started in 1841. It seems that John Jackson is treating *Cannibal Jack* as quite distinct from the other work, even though the crucial Bonaveidogo adventure overlaps both. If one is to pick actual dates, "Jackson's Narrative" sounds more plausible to me as the period when Cannibal Jack was in Fiji (whether he was ever there during this period we will never know for sure). He was probably in and out of the Fijian islands right through his life.

35. Jackson, "Jackson's Narrative," 436.

36. Ibid., 437.

37. Ibid., 437–38.

38. Ibid., 438; see also Clunie, *Fiji Weapons*, 36.

39. This is one of two excerpts that the publisher omitted.

40. The futility of searching for history or ethnography from fictional narratives has been nicely highlighted by Eagleton. Eagleton makes the point that "the literary text does not *take* history as the object, even when (as with 'historical' fiction) it believes itself to do so; but it does, nevertheless, *have* history as its object in the last instance, in ways apparent not to the text iself but to criticism. In this *distantiation* of history, this absence of any particular historical 'real', which confers on literature its air of freedom; unlike the historiographical work, it seems to be liberated from the need to conform its meanings to the exigencies of the actual" (Terry Eagleton, *Criticism and Ideology: A Study in Marxist Literary Theory* [London: Verso, 1978], 74). For insightful comments on the relation between history and literature, see Eagleton's chapter, "Towards the Science of the Text," 64–101.

41. The author translates *vasu* as someone dependant on a powerful lord, whereas it generally refers to the relationship between a man and his sister's son. "Vasu i taukei," according to *Capell's Dictionary* means, "when he is born in his mother's village." The missionary Thomas Williams writes in *Fiji and the Fijians*, 34: "The word means a nephew or niece, but becomes the title of office in the case of the male, who, in some localities, has the extraordinary privilege of appropriating whatever he chooses belonging to his uncle, or those under his uncle's power."

42. Peter Hulme, *Colonial Encounters: Europe and the Native Carribean 1492–1797* (London: Methuen, 1986), 141.

43. Cannibal Jack makes much of the fact that he collected books from ships and had a small library (*CJ*, 233). This might well have been the case: he also refers to Byron's poetry (*CJ*, 199), to Locke (*CJ*, 173), to phrases like the "yellow and sere," and to Bligh's account of the mutiny.

44. Greg Dening writes, "John Coulter, a supernumery on board the *Stratford* . . . stayed some months at Fatuiva and Hiva Oa in 1833 and wrote of his experience in *Adventures in the Pacific* [1845]. William Torrey, sparked no doubt by the success of Melville, published in 1848 the *Life and Adventures of William Torrey Who for a Space of Twenty-five Months within the Years 1835, 1836, 1837 Was Held Captive by the Can-*

nibals of the Marquesas." Dening adds that Torrey's capture was "more in his mind, or perhaps in the mind of his publisher, than in reality" (Dening, *Islands and Beaches*, 132). See also Neil Rennie, *Far-Fetched Facts: The Literature of Travel and the Idea of the South Seas* (Oxford: Clarendon Press, 1995), ch. 7, 181–95.

45. Stuart Hannabuss, "Ballantyne's Message of Empire," in *Imperialism and Juvenile Literature*, ed. Jeffrey Richards (Manchester: Manchester University Press, 1989).

46. Salman Rushdie, *Midnight's Children* (New York: Avon Books, 1992), 325.

47. Erskine, *Journal*, 411.

48. Harold Beaver, "Introduction" to Edgar Allan Poe, *The Narrative of Arthur Gordon Pym of Nantucket*, ed. Harold Beaver (London: Penguin, 1986), 8.

49. Poe, *Arthur Gordon Pym*, 146; my italics. For more explicit use of shipboard log style, see 182–87.

50. Ibid., 193. Whether Poe's account of Arthur Gordon Pym's adventures should be taken as a hoax, a spoof, a straightforward romantic novel, or a complexly interwoven symbolic narrative has been the subject of considerable recent debate. See David Ketterer, "Tracing Shadows: *Pym* Criticism, 1980–1990," in *Poe's Pym: Critical Explorations*, ed. Richard Kopley (Durham, N.C.: Duke University Press, 1992), 233–74.

51. Walter Benjamin, *Illuminations*, trans. Harry Zohn (London: Fontana, 1992), 90; Melville, *Typee*, 70.

52. Benjamin, *Illuminations*, 90.

53. Rennie, *Far-Fetched Facts*, 183.

54. Melville, *Typee*, 316. Paul Lyons tells me that irrespective of Melville's anti-imperialism he might have been guilty of inventing Typee cannibalism. His wife, Elizabeth Melville, wrote in response to a 1901 article by Mary Ferris: "Mr. Melville would not have been willing to call his old Typee entertainers 'man-devouring', as he has stated that whatever might have been his suspicions, he never had evidence that it was the custom of the tribe." See Jay Leyda, *The Melville Log: A Documentary Life of Herman Melville, 1819–1891* (New York: Gordian Press, 1969), 137; Paul Lyons, "From Man-Eaters to Spam-Eaters: Literary Tourism and the Discourse of Cannibalism from Herman Melville to Paul Theroux," in *Multiculturalism and Representation: Selected Essays*, ed. John Rieder and Larry E. Smith (Honolulu: University of Hawai'i Press, 1996), 72. For a more benign view of Melville's cannibalism as a fictional device, see T. Walter Herbert, *Marquesan Encounters: Melville and the Meaning of Civilization* (Cambridge, Mass.: Harvard University Press, 1980), 160 *passim*.

55. Jackson, "Jackson's Narrative," 435.

56. Forms of widow immolation existed in Fiji (and elsewhere), but we will never learn about these practices from texts like Cannibal Jack's or the missions. As with cannibalism and infanticide, the numbers are grossly exaggerated.

57. Roger Milliss, *Waterloo Creek: The Australia Day Massacre of 1838: George Gipps and the British conquest of New South Wales* (Ringwood, Australia: McPhee Gribble, 1992), 198. Millis is quoting the colonial missionary Lancelot Threlkeld writing in 1838: "A war of extirpation would be found to have long existed, in which the ripping open of the bellies of the Blacks alive—the roasting them in that state in triangularly made log fires, made for the very purpose;—the dashing of infants upon the stones; the confining of a party in a hut and letting them out singly through the door-way, to be butchered as they endeavoured to escape, together with many other acts of atrocious cruelty, which are but the sports of monsters boasting of superior intellect to that possessed by the wretched Blacks!" The Litia episode where people of the opposing party were tomahawked as they tried to escape through the doorway seems also to be derived from this or a related source.

The captivity narrative I mention comes from Ann Eliza Bleecker's 1783 novel *History of Maria Kittle* and deals not only with gruesome Indian killing of whites but also of taking an infant to "dash his little forehead against the stones" (cited in Roy Harvey Pearce, *Savagism and Civilization: A Study of the Indian and the American Mind* [Berkeley: University of California Press, 1988], revised version of his 1953 work, *The Savages of America*, 198). However, I am not sure whether this is not a "circulating mytheme" traveling across continents and seas because a similar event in recorded in 1640 where a Carib dashed the head of a white child against a rock. See Philip P. Boucher, *Cannibal Encounters: Europeans and Island Caribs, 1492–1763* (Baltimore, Md.: Johns Hopkins University Press, 1992), 42.

58. Jackson, "Jackson's Narrative," 472.

59. Clunie, *Fijian Weapons*, 39.

60. Cited in Erskine, *Journal*, 294.

61. *Anderson's Journal*, in *Cook B 3b*, 815.

62. Jacques Lacan, "The Mirror Stage," in his *Ecrits: A Selection*, trans. Alan Sheridan (New York: W. W. Norton, 1977), 4.

63. Jackson, "Jackson's Journal,"473; Clunie, *Fiji Weapons*, 39.

64. Peter Brooks, *Psychoanalysis and Storytelling* (Oxford: Blackwell, 1994), 51.

65. Jackson, "Jackson's Narrative," 434. The god Degei has a serpent form in Fijian mythology, and it is likely that Jackson incorporated some of this mythology into his text. The infant-eating eel is, I suspect, Jackson's own invention but based on the Fijian fantastic.

66. William Lockerby, *The Journal of William Lockerby: Sandalwood Trader in Fiji 1808–1809*, ed. Everard Im Thurm (London: The Haklyut Society, 1925), 42; hereafter abbreviated as *WL*.

67. I originally used the term *learned ignorance*, punning on Nicholas de Cusa's idea that absolute truth is not comprehensible, but this term was so loaded with theological implications that it was hard to give the phrase the secular signification I wanted.

68. Thomson, *Fijians*, 103.

69. Lawrie, *Friendly and Feejee Islands*, 72.

CHAPTER SEVEN: NARRATIVES OF THE SELF

1. J. W. Davidson, *Peter Dillon of Vanikoro, Chevalier of the South Seas*, ed. O. H. A. Spate (Melbourne: Oxford University Press, 1975); hereafter abbreviated as *PD*. Without Davidson's pioneering biography of Dillon my own work on Dillon would have been much poorer.

2. La Perouse's expedition was meant to be a French response to Cook's exploration of the Pacific; its loss meant a great deal to French pride. Several attempts were made to find the wrecks of the two ships, including a famous expedition led by D'Entrecasteaux during 1792. For an account of this voyage see, Frank Horner, *Looking for La Perouse: D'Entrecasteaux in Australia and the Pacific 1792–1793* (Carlton South, Australia: Melbourne University Press, 1995).

3. Peter Dillon, *Narrative and Successful Result of a Voyage in the South Seas Performed by Order of the Government of British India to Ascertain the Actual Fate of La Perouse's Expedition, interspersed with accounts of the Religion, Manners, Customs, and Cannibal Practices of the South Sea Islands*, vols. 1 and 2 (London: Hurst, Chance and Co., 1829). Hereafter I refer to this in the text as La Perouse Expedition, abbreviated as *LPE*. Unless otherwise specified all references are to volume 1.

4. For references to "the immortal Cook" see his preface in *LPE*, xx and xxxi.

5. Here and elsewhere I am only using Davidson's account. Davidson is trying to reconcile several versions of Dillon's adventures: his shipboard version, the version in the *Sydney Gazette* of October 23, 1813, and his sworn deposition of November 6, 1813. All three accounts refer to the same load of sandalwood but give different versions of it.

6. *PD*, 35–36. These are Davidson's words, not Dillon's. As Davidson recognizes there is no way one can clearly identify the place from Dillon's own vague description; "Korolevu" simply means "high mountain," not a specific place.

7. "Narratives of the Self: Chevalier Peter Dillon's Fijian Cannibal Adventures," in *Body Trade: Captivity, Cannibalism and Colonialism in the Pacific*, ed. Jeanette Hoorn and Barbara Creed (Routledge: New York, 2001), 69–125.

8. I am, however, not sure whether the title was invented by Davidson or by his editor, O. H. K. Spate.

9. Dillon's rock poses all sorts of problems. There was rock with that name, as Mrs. Mary D. Wallis notes in 1851 in *Life in Feejee, or Five Years Among the Cannibals* (Boston: William Heath, 1851), 331. Davidson thought "that Dillon's Rock lay towards the seaward end of the low but uneven peninsula of Koro-i-vita . . . lying to the north of Naviqiri-Wailea track." But others have disputed it, and the details are found in

Davidson's Appendix 2, which was written by Davidson's editor, O. H. K. Spate. As Spate himself says, "It cannot be identified with absolute certainty" (312). It is possible that there was no such rock in the first place, but this cannot be proved either. Most commentators have been fooled by the engraving in Dillon's book, which, given Dillon's overfertile imagination, cannot be taken seriously. See Appendix 2 by O. H. K. Spate in Davidson, *Peter Dillon*, 312–15.

10. Davidson, *Peter Dillon*, 17.

11. Peter Dillon, "Extract of three Letters addressed to the Right Honorable LORD JOHN RUSSELL, Secretary of State for the Colonies, by the Chevalier Dillon, on the subject of Colonizing New Zealand, A.D. 1840." Copy in Davidson collection, NLA (National Library of Australia).

12. *Sydney Gazette*, October 23, 1813 (n.p.); and "The Deposition of Peter Dillon," *Historical Records of Australia*, series 1, vol. 8 (Sydney: Government Printer, 1916), 103–7.

13. *Sydney Gazette*, October 23, 1813.

14. Ibid.

15. Ibid.; my italics.

16. Ibid.

17. Ibid.

18. Peter Dillon, "Deposition," *Historical Records of Australia* 1, 106.

19. Ibid.

20. *Calcutta Government Gazette*, May 8, 1828, reprinted as an appendix in *LPE*, 433 [428–34].

21. Dillon has a further addendum not found in the *Calcutta Gazette*, though the unsuspecting reader would not have noticed it. Once again this addendum brings the *Calcutta Gazette* of May 8, 1828, in line with the La Perouse account: "All the persons whom we have already mentioned as living among the natives of Bough [Bau] lost their lives in the melancholy contest, as did also Mr. Norman and Mr. Cox, officers; Hugh Evans seaman; and a Lascar named Jonno, belonging to the vessel; in all fourteen persons. The same day (the 7th) they left the dreadful place, and kept company as far as the New Hebrides, where they (the Hunter and Elizabeth) parted, the 22d ult" (*LPE*, 433).

22. Dillon's character—his propensity to violent rage, emotion, and loss of self-control—was noted by Davidson and further documented in detail in my earlier account of him. Bayly says he was "the most passionate man I ever saw." He frequently thrashed his wife and once "broke his telescope to pieces about her head" (*Journal of Voyages To Various Parts Of The World Written by Geo Bayly For The Amusement Of Such Of His Friends As Feel Themselves Disposed To Read It*, 12, typescript in two volumes at the NLA). Unless otherwise noted my references are to volume 1, hereafter abbreviated as *JV*. Dillon was also given to alcoholic hallucinations

that lasted for weeks. Davidson's own research assistant, Honore Forster, scribbled a note to him about Dillon from her own perspective: "He seems to me to have been a ruthless, mean-spirited, selfish, arrogant, double dealing [man] and a snob—and what's more he beat his wife. Maybe he treated Pacific Islanders well (by his standards) but on the other hand he beat his Bengalee steward with a cat o'nine tails. . . . A thoroughly nasty man, if you ask me." This note was on a scrap of paper found among Davidson's notes, and I quote it with permission from Honore Forster.

23. He was born November 6, 1821, and named Napoleon according to the birth certificate, a copy of which is available among Davidson's documents. Interestingly he was also known as Joseph Napoleon.

24. Obviously Dillon has been proclaiming his pseudotitle because Bayly meeting Dillon in 1836 in *JV,* 2:331 says that Dillon had been appointed French consul for the South Sea Islands.

25. Letter to the Duke of Bedford, August 4, 1841, Colonial Office 209/13, copy in the Davidson Manuscripts in NLA, 5105, box 10.

26. For the power of this fantasy, see Otto Rank, *Myth of the Birth of the Hero,* ed. Philip Freund (New York: Random House, 1959), 65.

27. The date is probably a typographical error and not a lapse of memory on Dillon's part.

28. Dillon to the Duke of Bedford, Davidson Manuscripts, NLA, 5105, box 10.

29. Tzvetan Todorov, *The Fantastic: A Structural Approach to a Literary Genre,* trans, Richard Howard (Ithaca, N.Y.: Cornell University Press, 1975); Gananath Obeyesekere, *The Work of Culture: Symbolic Transformation in Psychoanalysis and Anthropology* (Chicago: University of Chicago Press, 1990).

30. Natalie Zemon Davis, *The Return of Martin Guerre* (Cambridge, Mass.: Harvard University Press, 1993).

31. *The New York Times,* March 4, 1996, 20.

32. George Bayly says that the "marvellous escape of Dillon and Buchert was described to me circumstantially by both of them independently, and their accounts agree in every particular" (George Bayly, *Sea Life Sixty Years Ago* [London: Kegan, Paul and Tench, 1885], viii; hereafter abbreviated as *SL*). Davidson takes this statement to show that the events that Dillon describes in the *LPE* account did take place. This is a mistaken inference. First, the Bayly and *LPE* versions are quite different in thrust and detail. Second, it is unlikely that Buchert confirms Dillon. Buchert could hardly speak English (and Tikopian only imperfectly), according to Dillon in *LPE,* 156. It is hard to believe that this native Prussian could retain the little English he knew as a sailor during his fifteen or so years in Tikopean self-exile.

33. My argument in this section is that the Bayly account was based on Dillon's own narration and it could only have been during the trip from Valparaiso to Calcutta after picking up Buchert in Tikopia. Dillon employed Buchert both as a butler and an

aide to find the French relics. Buchert's presence probably triggered Dillon's narrative imagination. Buchert would not contradict any of this owing to his poor knowledge of English and also because he, like any subordinate, dared not contradict Dillon and face his explosive anger. Bayly met Dillon twice in "after years," but neither visit constituted a proper context for storytelling. The first visit was on April 7, 1828, when Bayly's vessel passed Dillon's as he was returning from the discovery of the French wrecks. He and Mrs. Dillon invited Bayly on board, but it was a very brief visit. The other was between October 12 and December 2, 1836, in Sydney, according to Davidson's notation on a copy of Bayly's manuscript. Bayly says playfully that his motivation for regaling Dillon with food was because Dillon kept him half starved on the voyage from South America to Calcutta. This too does not strike me as the proper context for storytelling. In any case Bayly tells us that Dillon used to regale them with stories on board ship, not during a dinner on land.

34. *Asiatic Journal* xxiv (1827): section on Polynesia, 778–79.

35. Ibid. The Sydney paper says that the massacre occurred in 1826 when this is not the case because it occurred in 1813. Although I have not been able to track down this particular Sydney paper, the problem is easily resolved. Very likely Dillon gave an interview to the Sydney paper in 1826 and simply narrated the story. The newspaper reported it as if it were a recent event.

The *Asiatic Journal* says that according to this same Sydney paper "the Elizabeth cutter, commanded by Capt. Dillon (whose name is familiar to our readers, as the discoverer of the traces of La Perouse, in the New Hebrides) visited the Feejees, in company with the Hunter" when it is clear that Dillon was an officer of the *Hunter* (not in command of the cutter, *Elizabeth*.) Dillon was first mate or commander of the cutter after the Fijian adventure and when he was instructed by Robson to take Buchert and the lascar with him. However, it appears that Dillon is now inventing himself as the commander or first mate of the cutter from the very start, which is how Bayly also reports about him.

36. *Asiatic Journal*, 779.

37. I am being partly facetious: needless to say, Dillon may simply have got the numbers of the dead all wrong; in any case, it is possible that the defenders of the rock were those from the ship who did not die.

38. Dillon's La Perouse narrative also retains the number fourteen and lists their names of fourteen dead but, like the deposition, cannot account for their deaths. However, there are six from the ship who died (not four) and eight (not ten) of the Bau residents. The two lascars in the Bau list are omitted and instead two seamen with Muslim names (Hassen and Mosdean) substituted.

39. For more information on Buchert, see Basil Thomson, *The Fijians: A Study in the Decay of Custom* (London: William Heinemann, 1908), 29.

40. Bayly has two versions of this meeting. The first version is from *JV*, 40; it is

close to Dillon's own and refers to their landing in Tikopia on May 13, 1826: "He [Buchert] was tattooed all over the body and several marks on his face. He did not recognize Captain D. at first but after being reminded of some of the circumstances of the flight to the Feejees, he was overjoyed to see Captain D." Bayly has another story in his later reminiscences in *SL,* 150. Apparently Buchert recognized him but not immediately. Yet, "when Dillon held out his hand, and said, 'Well, Buchert, my old comrade, how are you?' he started. That voice brought back the long past to his mind in an instant. He seized Peter's hand in a transport of joy, struggling to pour forth his delight in a mixture of German, French, English, Fijian and Tucopean." I do not find this a reliable account and much prefer Dillon's own version and Bayly's first account.

41. Friedrich Nietzsche, *On the Genealogy of Morals,* trans. Douglas Smith (Oxford: Oxford University Press, 1996), 42, where Nietzsche says that "there is, perhaps, nothing more frightening and sinister in the whole prehistory of man than his *technique for remembering things* [mnemotechnics]. 'Something is branded in, so that it stays in the memory'" (translator's italics).

42. Dillon, "Deposition," 106.

CHAPTER EIGHT: ON QUARTERING AND CANNIBALISM AND THE DISCOURSES OF SAVAGISM

1. There are many references to quartering in *The Odyssey* also, for example, book 19, lines 75–79. See translation by Robert Fagles (Harmondsworth, Eng.: Penguin, 1996), 404.

2. This chapter was delivered with some modification as the Huxley Memorial lecture mentioned in the preface. This explains the references to Huxley and African cannibalism.

3. Thomas H. Huxley, *Man's Place in Nature,* ed. Stephen Jay Gould (New York: The Modern Library, 2001), x.

4. Ibid., 57–58.

5. Ibid., 57.

6. Ibid., 58.

7. Ibid.

8. Ibid.

9. Ibid., 57.

10. Lord Amherst of Hackney and Basil Thomson, eds. and trans., *The Discovery of The Solomon Islands by Alvaro de Mendana in 1568,* vols. 1 and 2 (London: The Hakluyt Society, 1901). Mendana was the discoverer of the Marquesas Islands twenty-seven years later. I was unaware of a paper originally written in Italian in 1971 by Valerio Valeri and recently translated and published as "The Solomon Islands Discovered by

the Europeans: From the Social Contract to Utilitarianism," in *Fragments from Forests and Libraries: A Collection of Essays by Valerio Valeri* (Durham, N.C.: Carolina Academic Press, 2001), 57–92. This paper deals with Mendana's voyage and that of later explorers, but Valeri does not touch on the themes of this chapter and accepts the conventional wisdom of Mendana's humanity and goodness.

11. Amherst and Thomson, *Discovery of The Solomon Islands,* 1:x–xi.

12. Ibid., 1:1.

13. Ibid., 1:6, n. 1. This is from the "The Journal of Hernando Gallego," in Amherst and Thomson, *Discovery of The Solomon Islands,* 1:5–80. The other journals employed in this essay are, "The Narrative of Pedro Sarmiento," 1:83–94; "The Narrative of Mendana," 1:97–158; "The Second Narrative of Mendana," 1:161–91; "An Anonymous Narrative," 2:197–214; "Narrative of Catoira," 2:217–462.

14. Ibid., 1:1, and "Journal of Hernando Gallego," 1:19–20.

15. Ibid., "Second Narrative of Mendana," 1:167–69; and for details "Narrative of Pedro Sarmiento," 1:83–94.

16. For example, Catoira records for July 9 during the third voyage of the brigantine exploring San Christoval in hostile conditions. "Upon this it seemed to the captain that it would be well to take two or three boys as interpreters, because of a lack there was of them, and therefore he seized a boy and a shield-bearer seized another, and they put them on board the brigantine, and then the others fell into confusion and fled, and were seen no more" ("Narrative of Catoira," 2:396).

17. Amherst and Thomson, *Discovery of The Solomon Islands,* 1:xxvi.

18. Ibid., "Narrative of Gallego," 1:20.

19. Ibid., "Narrative of Catoira," 2:255.

20. Ibid., "An Anonymous Narrative," 2:198.

21. Paul van der Grijp, "Travelling Gods and Nasty Spirits: Ancient Religious Representations in Tonga (Polynesia)," *Paideuma* 48, no. 252 (2002): 243–60.

22. Ibid.

23. Mendana's first narrative written by him is incomplete. The missing information is found in the second narrative written by another person but using Mendana's name.

24. Ibid., "Narrative of Catoira," 2:255. Valerio Valeri in "The Solomon Islands Discovered" (74–75) is puzzled by the Polynesian term *Te Ariki* found on this Melanesian island and speculates that perhaps at one time there were political relations between Santa Isabel and Ontong Java and that the title must come from that source. My guess is that the relations between so-called Melanesian and Polynesian groups in this region were very widespread at one time; hence the pan-Polynesian worship of "serpent spirits" in Santa Isabel mentioned earlier.

25. Ibid., "Narrative of Mendana," 1:169.

26. Ibid., "Narrative of Catoira," 2:248–49.

27. Ibid., "Narrative of Mendana," 1:169.

28. Ibid.

29. Ibid., "Narrative of Gallego," 1:21.

30. Ibid., "Narrative of Mendana," 1:115.

31. Ibid., "Narrative of Catoira," 2:258. For Mendana's version, see "Narrative of Mendana," 1:170.

32. Ibid., "Narrative of Catoira," 2:258, n. 1.

33. Ibid., "An Anonymous Narrative," 2:198–99.

34. Ibid., "Narrative of Catoira," 2: 377–78.

35. Robert Hertz, *Death and the Right Hand,* trans. R. Needham and C. Needham (Glencoe, Ill.: Free Press, 1960).

36. My two conjectures however must confront the fact that two journalists mention that the chief of the native expedition was "Bene," and there is no indication that he was from Baso. But this is a bit of confusion on the part of the journalists because "Bene" in these accounts is not Chief Bene, known to them earlier but another "Bene" further west (xxvii). Because we know that Ortega fought with the people of Baso, Bene must surely be a Baso person or at the very most an ally of the Baso chief and acting on his behalf. Gallego says he comes from the western and northern part of the Island, which seems to be the area of Baso.

37. Ibid., "Narrative of Mendana," 1:119.

38. Ibid., "Narrative of Catoira," 2:255.

39. Ibid.

40. Ibid., "Narrative of Catoira," 2:255–56.

41. This point of course has been made by the critics, both religious and secular, of Catholicism for a long time.

42. Michel Foucault, *Discipline and Punish: The Birth of the Prison,* trans. Alan Sheridan (New York: Random House, 1979), 3.

43. Henry Marshall, *Ceylon: A General Description of the Island and its Inhabitants,* (London: William H. Allen, 1846), 220. Marshall has a moving account of the execution of Kappitipola, one the great resistance fighters in Sri Lanka, on November 25, 1818. Marshall himself took Kappitipola's cranium for depositing in the museum of the Phrenological Society of Edinburgh. As a Scotsman he admired Kappitipola and compared him to Wallace. Consequently, he was one of the few British officials who could write sympathetically about the Sri Lankan rebellion of 1818.

44. Carolyn Walker Bynum, *Fragmentation and Redemption: Essays on Gender and the Human Body in Medieval Religion* (New York: Zone Books, 1991), 243. The orthodox position seems to be fairly clear: even fragmented body parts like fingernails, the tortured and severed genitals of martyrs, and every particle of the body will be recovered and resurrected in the wholeness of the body. But the many debates on the subject indicated popular anxiety concerning dismemberment and even cannibalism,

such that, says Bynum, the effect of cannibalism on bodily resurrection was debated from the second to the thirteenth centuries: "If human remains were eaten by other human beings, in which person would the common matter arise?" (Bynum, *Fragmentation*, 244). And Bynum adds that while "debates about the resurrection of foreskins or eaten embryos have baffled modern historians and theologians" (Bynum, *Fragmentation*, 244), they continue in some form or another in such modern surgical interventions as transplants.

45. According to Marina Warner the first public dissection of a human body was in Bologna in 1302, and it brought about considerable outcry. Often wax images of human cadavers were used instead, or the bodies of criminals. Marina Warner, *No Go The Bogeyman: Scaring, Lulling and Making Mock* (London: Chatto and Windus, 1998), 132.

46. Peter Hulme made this point at the Essex Symposium "Consuming Others: 'Cannibalism' in the 1990s" held at the University of Essex in July 1995; see also Anthony Padgen, *The Fall of Natural Man: The American Indian and the Origins of Comparative Ethnology* (Cambridge: Cambridge University Press, 1986), 85, for a related view of the scattering of the body.

47. This marvelous quote is from *BW*, 180.

48. This text is entitled, "The Defence of Nga-Motu, 1832" and appears in Robert McNab, *The Old Whaling Days: A History of Southern New Zealand from 1830 to 1840*, 1913 (Auckland: Golden Press, 1975), 38–59; hereafter abbreviated as DN.

49. Maria Tatar calls this "oral greed" in her chapter "Cannibalism and Oral Greed" in *Off with Their Heads: Fairy Tales and the Culture of Childhood* (Princeton, N.J.: Princeton University Press, 1992), 190–211.

50. A. P. Vayda, *Maori Warfare* (Wellington, NZ: The Polynesian Society, 1960), 78–79; I have not checked later references to this horrendous narrative.

51. Alain Corbin, *The Village of Cannibals. Rage and Murder in France, 1870*, trans. Arthur Goldhammer (Cambridge, Mass.: Harvard University Press, 1992); hereafter abbreviated as *VC*.

52. Cited in *VC*, 94, from L. M. Prudhomme, *Histoire générale et impartiale des erreurs, des fautes et des crimes commis pendant la Révolution française* (1797), 3:149.

53. René Girard, *Violence and the Sacred*, trans. Patrick Gregory (Baltimore, Md.: Johns Hopkins Press, 1977).

54. Levi Strauss uses "mythemes" to designate minimum definable units of myth much as phonemes are minimum definable units of sound. I use that term in its more literal and looser sense as "themes that appear in myth."

55. Sigmund Freud, "Inhibitions, Symptoms and Anxiety," in *Standard Edition*, vol. 20 (London: Hogarth Press, 1981), 165 [77–172].

56. Ibid., 168. The term *surplus of anxiety* is on p. 166, and this for Freud indicates the neurotic element in anxiety.

57. See Sigmund Freud, "Obsessive Acts and Religious Practices," *Standard Edition*, vol. 9 (London: Hogarth Press, 1982), 117–27. For Freud, obsessional acts and religious practices are isomorphic if not identical. The relation between the two can only be saved by the notion of "symbolic remove" that I developed in Gananath Obeyesekere, *The Work of Culture: Symbolic Transformation in Psychoanalysis and Anthropology* (Chicago: University of Chicago Press, 1990).

58. Bernard McGinn, *The Flowering of Mysticism: Men and Women in the New Mysticism*, vol. 3 of *Presence of God: A History of Western Christian Mysticism* (New York: Crossroad Publishing Company, 1998), 312. For graphic accounts of recent Spanish visions of the sacred heart, read, William A. Christian Jr., *Visionaries: The Spanish Republic and the Reign of Christ* (Berkeley: University of California Press, 1996), *passim*.

59. She also had an erotic relation with Christ with their two hearts merging. See McGinn, *Mysticism*, 165.

60. Ibid.

61. For the continuity of the bleeding heart of Christ into modern times in Mexico, see Olivier Debroise, "Heart Attacks: On a Culture of Missed Encounters and Misunderstandings," in *El Corazón Sangrante, The Bleeding Heart*, ed. Olivier Debroise, Elisabeth Sussman, and Matthew Teitelbaum (Boston: Institute of Contemporary Art, 1991), 12–61.

62. Obeyesekere, "Narratives of the Self," in *Body Trade: Captivity and Colonialism in the Pacific*, ed. Jeanette Hoorn and Barbara Creed (New York: Routledge, 2001), especially the section entitled "The Ethos of Mutual Suspicion: The Dillon-Tytler relationship," 84–92, which was omitted from chapter 7 above.

63. Hans Staden, *Hans Staden: The True History of His Captivity*, 1557, trans. Malcolm Letts, (New York: Robert M. McBride and Company, 1929), 115.

64. Gillian Beer, "Ghosts (Review of Julia Briggs, *Night Visitors*)," *Essays in Criticism* 28, no. 3 (1978): 260 [259–64].

CONCLUSION

1. For example, see J. T. Lloyd, *God-Eating: A Study in Christianity and Cannibalism* (London: Pioneer Press, 1921), which argues a development from anthropophagy to theophagy; and for a general account, see Preserved Smith, *A Short History of Christian Theophagy* (Chicago: Open Court, 1922).

2. See Gananath Obeyesekere, *Cult of the Goddess Pattini* (Chicago: University of Chicago Press, 1964), 73.

3. For a good discussion of this issue for the Maori, see Margaret Orbell, *Hawaiki: A New Approach to Maori Tradition* (Christchurch, NZ: University of Canterbury Press, 1985).

4. Georges Bataille, *Erotism: Death and Sensuality* (San Francisco: City Lights Books, 1986), 71. I do not know what Bataille means by "frequently" unless he means the Eucharist. I find Bataille's work on taboo, transgression, and sacrifice full of insights and more useful for the study of human sacrifice than the systematization of his work by René Girard, *Violence and the Sacred*, trans. Patrick Gregory (Baltimore, Md.: Johns Hopkins University Press, 1977).

5. Gananath Obeyesekere, "The Myth of the Human Sacrifice: History, Story and Debate in a Buddhist Chronicle," in *Identity, Consciousness and the Past: Forging of Caste and Community in India and Sri Lanka*, ed. H. L. Seneviratne (Delhi: Oxford University Press, 1997), 70–93.

6. For the idea of *symbolic remove*, see Gananath Obeyesekere, *The Work of Culture: Symbolic Transformation in Psychoanalysis and Anthropology* (Chicago: University of Chicago Press, 1990), esp. 56–62.

7. Bernal Díaz, *The Conquest of New Spain* (Harmondsworth, Eng.: Penguin, 1963), 199.

8. William Marsden, *The History of Sumatra*, 3rd ed. (London: Longman, Hurst, Rees, Orme and Brown, 1811), 391.

9. Ibid. The historical persistence of Batak cannibalism is dealt with in an unpublished paper by Andrew Causey, "A Tenacious Rumor: Western Reports of Cannibalism among the Toba Bataks from 1790 to 1990."

10. Michel-Rolph Trouillot, *Global Transformations: Anthropology and the Modern World* (New York: Macmillan, 2003), 28.

11. Sigmund Freud, *The Interpretation of Dreams*, in *Standard Edition*, vol. 2 (London: Hogarth Press, 1981), 525.

12. Friedrich Nietzsche, *The Will to Power*, trans. Walter Kaufmann and R. J. Hollingdale (New York: Vintage Books, 1968), aphorism 229, p. 132.

INDEX

Compositor:	BookMatters, Berkeley
Indexer:	Andrew Christenson
Cartographer:	Bill Nelson
Text:	10.25/14 Fournier
Display:	Fournier
Printer and Binder:	Sheridan Books, Inc.